"God is the strength of my heart, and my portion for ever."

Psalm 73:26

The Lord as Their Portion

*The Story of the Religious Orders
and How They Shaped Our World*

⸻ ◦⚬⧓⚬◦ ⸻

Elizabeth Rapley

WILLIAM B. EERDMANS PUBLISHING COMPANY
GRAND RAPIDS, MICHIGAN / CAMBRIDGE, U.K.

Published 2011 by

Wm. B. Eerdmans Publishing Co.

2140 Oak Industrial Drive N.E., Grand Rapids, Michigan 49505 /

P.O. Box 163, Cambridge CB3 9PU U.K.

Printed in the United States of America

16 15 14 13 12 11   7 6 5 4 3 2 1

Library of Congress Cataloging-in-Publication Data

Rapley, Elizabeth.

The Lord as their portion: the story of the religious orders and how they shaped our world /
Elizabeth Rapley.

p.   cm.

ISBN 978-0-8028-6588-5 (pbk.: alk. paper)

1. Monasticism and religious orders — History.   I. Title.

BX2461.3.R37   2011

271.009 — dc22

2010045309

www.eerdmans.com

For Bob
Gentle critic, constant support

Contents

Acknowledgments

I am deeply grateful to Norman A. Hjelm, without whose encouragement and advice I would never have written this book. I want to thank Pierre Hurtubise, O.M.I., for sharing with me his passion for history, and giving me some useful suggestions. Thanks also to Linda Hayes, who helped me to make the text more readable. And finally, to my husband, who knows this work almost as intimately as I do, thanks and thanks again.

Introduction

"Lord, what about us? We have left everything and followed you."

This book is for those people for whom monks and nuns are only a distant memory, or who have never known them at all. This means not only Protestants, non-Christians, and agnostics, but also many, many Catholics. The times have changed at lightning speed, and the recent past seems terribly long ago. The generations born since Vatican II in the 1960s may never have so much as laid eyes on a nun, or a monk, or a friar. Their parents and grandparents harbor memories that may vary, depending on whether Sister Martha strapped a mean strap, or hugged you when you hurt yourself, or taught you to love Shakespeare; whether Brother Philip was the gaunt, scary person who appeared once a year to preach hellfire, or the young red-headed guy who hitched up his robes and played football with you in the school yard. Our memories are all over the place. But whatever the case, those people belong in the past; they appear to us as anachronisms in our twenty-first-century world. In an era that is called post-Christian, many religious orders appear to be passing into oblivion.

This is all the more reason to spend a little time calling them to mind. Their diminished visibility here and now may lead us to underestimate the vital part they played in the building of the world we live in. That would be a mistake. After the collapse of the Roman Empire and throughout the violent centuries that followed, it was monks who kept the memory of Christianity alive. When, inch by inch, western Europe emerged from its Dark Ages, much of its developing dynamism came from them. There was nothing they did not turn their hand to. The building and adornment of churches and cathedrals, the copying and illumination of the written word, the development of new techniques in agriculture and animal husbandry: all these achievements bore their imprint. Then, as society matured and settled down, their services expanded and became more complex. They preached, taught, nursed the sick, championed the poor. Above all they explored, and advanced, the faith. Later, as the world beyond Europe came into view, they went out to win it in the name of the Lord. Western civilization without them would have been a very different thing.

There is another reason why the orders should interest us. To look at them is to see into their times. They may have been elite, but they were not apart. They shared the outlooks, virtues, faults, and limitations of their contemporaries. They were a living part of the societies that gave them birth, drawing their strength from these societies and responding to their needs. On this depended their vitality. If the needs were no longer there, they were in trouble. Their ups and downs depended closely on the circumstances surrounding them.

What was (and is) a religious order, and where did it start?

Actually there was no such thing in early Christianity. There was only monasticism. Many men, and some women, sought to save their souls by taking up a life of prayer, either alone or in communities of like-minded people. First around the Mediterranean, then across the vast face of Europe, they built their houses and expanded their holdings. But to begin with, there was no link between one community and another. Each monastery was a kingdom unto itself, governed by its own abbot or abbess, pursuing its own salvation within the compass of its own walls. It was close to a millennium after the birth of Jesus Christ before the germ of a religious order — a collection of monasteries that owed allegiance, in feudal fashion, to one supreme abbot — appeared. This was Cluny. After that things moved faster. Within two hundred years, a sort of federal system was worked out, in which participating monasteries remained independent but accepted correction from each other, and oversight by a central abbot in concert with a general chapter. With that, a true religious *order* came into being. This was the Cistercian order, the model many subsequent orders would come to imitate.

But whether in autonomous monasteries or in houses belonging to an order, the parameters of monasticism did not soon change. The avowed purpose of monks and nuns remained the same: *contemptus mundi*, contempt for the world, the service of God through an inward-turning daily round of liturgy and private prayer. Then, in the thirteenth century, there appeared a new tribe of religious persons, the friars. Consciously, audaciously, these men took their religious life into the world, contending that God is served best when prayer is combined with the saving of souls, in what they called "the mixed life." "Leave God for God" was their rallying cry; this opened a door through which hundreds of future orders, male and female, would pass. From that point on, there were two main forms of religious life, the contemplative and the active.

Along the way, the active orders abandoned another of the fundamentals of medieval monasticism, lifelong stability. Their members were no longer vowed to one community; instead, like soldiers in an army, they were committed to going wherever they were sent and doing whatever they were told. Obviously this could not work without sophisticated organization and central direction — all of which they set about providing. During the centuries that the peoples of Europe were hammering out their political systems of control and consensus and representation, the religious orders were doing much the same thing, and, often, doing it first.

During the early ages of our civilization, the orders were home to many of the brightest and best. Eventually, after hundreds of years of growth, secular society caught up with them and became their equal in learning and inventiveness. But they continued to be a strong, dynamic presence. They gave their members training, they motivated them, and they sent them out to convert the world. If the Catholic Church became a global institution, it was largely thanks to them.

However, the respect that the religious population enjoyed, and the wealth that flowed from it, was a mixed blessing. The day came when sclerosis set in, and they were forced to cede their place of privilege to thinkers more attuned to the times than they. As the Enlightenment dawned, they ceased to be the outrunners of progress and became its footdraggers. The orders entered a dark time, when morale and reputation sank exceedingly low. But they rebounded, to become the doers par excellence of Catholicism, and they retained that distinction until the twentieth century.

There were, over the years, countless more religious orders than exist today. Many communities have come and gone. Sometimes they were large and powerful in their day, as, for example, the Templars, who, with the Holy Land lost, had no further reason to continue, and within a short time fell prey to the designs of avaricious princes. Sometimes they collapsed from internal rot, as did the Celestins in the eighteenth century. Many of them never even climbed out of the cradle. Hundreds, perhaps thousands, of small religious groupings had a brief day in the sun and then disappeared, leaving little or nothing to mark their passing. This does not mean that they had no impact on their own times. It is simply that having left no records, they are beyond our reach. We cannot do them justice. It has been said that history is written by the victors; certainly for the religious orders it is written by the survivors, the groups that have stood the test of time. But impressive as these are in number, they are still only a fraction of the huge army of men and women who, in age after age, have taken the Lord as their portion.

So it is a massive subject, and no work such as this can do anything more than simply touch its edges. For every order or congregation described here, many more go unmentioned. While some of them are defunct, others are very much alive. Their members are still hard at work, in evangelization, in education, in work with the poor and marginalized, in the promotion of social justice. And they still pray for us and our world.

Their numbers have dwindled and their future becomes more and more problematical: it lies in the hands of the God they chose to serve. But their past — that is a different matter. It is there for anyone to see. It deserves to be recognized.

CHAPTER I

The Beginnings of Christian Monasticism

"If You Wish to Be Perfect . . ."

The Greek word *monos* signifies "alone." At the very foundation of early Christian monasticism lay the imperative of aloneness, flight from the world, submersion in deep and holy silence. And the traditional setting for this was the desert.

Christian monasticism took root in the Egyptian desert in the fourth century. This is not to say that the monks of that time and place had no precursors. From the second century, and possibly earlier, groups of men and women had sought separation from the world through practices of chastity and self-denial. These Christians, and those others, less radical, who lived ascetic lives without renouncing their ties to society, were not wholly out of step with the mood of the times. Asceticism was prized in Judaic tradition, and even more strongly promoted in the Christian sacred books. "To set the mind on the flesh is death, but to set the mind on the Spirit is life and peace," wrote Saint Paul. What is more, asceticism appealed, to some degree, to the spirit of contemporary paganism. Self-control and sexual continence were held in high esteem, at least among the elites. While the pagan world did not noticeably practice asceticism, it gave it a wary respect. So all in all, there was an openness in public opinion to the notion of self-control.

However, the men we know as "the Desert Fathers" took things to a new level. They laid the ground rules for Christian monasticism. What is more, by their example they "sold" the idea of monasticism to their contemporaries, so that within a short time the desert became home to thousands of monks. The literature that developed around them — personal writings, biographies, collections of sayings, and collections of anecdotes — spread with remarkable speed across the empire, and, arguably, did for monasticism what the histories of the martyrs had done for martyrdom. Throughout the Christian centuries, Egyptian monasticism, mediated through this literature, was a model for the greater part of European monasticism.

The movement to the desert began at about the same time that the status of the church changed under Constantine. This was no coincidence. In A.D. 313 the great emperor decreed an end to the persecution of his subjects on religious grounds. Suddenly Christians, who had lived for generations under the threat of martyrdom, and who had identified themselves in that light, found their faith comfortably tolerated, even privileged. They no longer risked anything by believing. The fading of the threat left them in a spiritual void. Monasticism came to fill that void. The grace and high esteem once awarded to the martyr's death were transferred to the death of the flesh represented by virginity and the asceticism that accompanied it.

But why the desert? According to a tradition originating with Saint Jerome, they went there to find solitude and serenity. However, ancient tradition also saw the desert as the place where demons lived, and in time hagiography, and historiography, represented the monks as self-appointed shock troops advancing against these enemies of God. And they may have had another motivation. They may have gone into the desert in the first place to find God, by placing themselves in a situation where they were physically free from all distraction and entanglement. Once there, loneliness and hardship made them subject to forces that they may well not have anticipated.

This sequence of events is traced in the life of Saint Anthony (250-356). Anthony, still a young man, was left by his parents' death in charge of house, property, and a younger sister. His call came suddenly, in the words of the Savior: "If thou wilt be perfect, go sell all that thou hast, and give it to the poor; and come, follow me and thou shalt have treasure in Heaven." He immediately gave away his property, as his early biographer wrote, not wishing "to encumber himself or his sister in any way whatever." Within a short time, again upon hearing the word of the Lord, he gave away even the small sum that he had reserved for his sister. Without leaving his village, he took up a life of self-denial and search for spiritual direction. And yet this was not enough; thoughts of his home and his attachments continued to plague him, and he gradually moved farther away, first to another town, then to the tombs that lay some distance away (where he made his first acquaintance of the demons), then across the river and into the desert, and then, finally, to an inaccessible mountain near the Red Sea. Here he fought the epic battles against the demons that have been memorialized so often in literature and in art. He prevailed, and lived to a peaceable old age, with the devil still keeping a close eye on him, but no longer able to disturb his calm.

In a sense, Anthony's journey into the desert can be compared to that of an explorer. He did not know, when he started, what he would find. As a young man he had asked for nothing more than to follow Christ, to carry his cross. The desert provided the pedagogy, so to speak, of asceticism: the loneliness, the dangers, the harsh and sterile environment. His body was subjected to the constant need for food, which could be won only by unremitting labor. His thoughts constantly went astray, back to the home he had left, and thence into images of impurity. What Anthony experienced first, other hermits experienced after him. Gradually a collective self-knowledge built up, to be passed on by the "old men" to the neophytes. This marked a new stage, a "professionalization" of asceticism, and the beginning of a long drawn-out war of attrition waged in the desert, by Anthony and by the others who followed him, against unchastity in all its forms.

The principal weapon was the fast. The old men were soon teaching what they themselves had learned, that "the drier the body, the more flourishing is the soul." If the monk wished to approach God with an "undivided heart," he had to eliminate all other demands upon himself. For the hermits of the desert, fasting and other self-denials such as sleeplessness were necessary if the flesh was to be subdued. Greed and fornication were twin vices with shared roots in the flesh; "the defeat of the first weakens the one that depends on it." The eradication of the two together could be achieved only by "mortifying the flesh, by vigils, fasts and back-breaking labor." These practices were not seen as self-destructive; indeed, in Saint Anthony's view, they brought the body back to the uncorrupted state that it had enjoyed before the Fall, free from anger, physical appetite, and sexual urge. Thus clarified, the body would one day pass with the soul into glory. But it was not an undertaking for the faint of heart. In the stillness of the desert, inner struggle was intensified; sexual urge and the desire for food became a torment. Some of the greatest monks confessed that they had carried these agonies with them into their old age.

But at the end of the day, the ascetics of the desert knew that physical mortification had to have a purpose; it had to prepare man for virtue. Without the proper dispositions it was worthless. This was a lesson not always

easily learned. The hermit could very easily fall into a sort of spiritual ath-
leticism and become more concerned with breaking records of self-
abnegation than with being humble of heart. A whole lifetime of penance
could be washed away by a moment of pride. The "old men" had a warning:
"Drinking wine within reason is better by far than drinking water in arro-
gance." Very early on, it became the general practice of solitaries to moderate their aloneness by submitting to the spiritual direction of others.

Another solution to the problem was quickly arrived at: a sort of lower-
ing of the bar, in the form of cenobitism. The great architect of this form of
monasticism was Pachomius. A contemporary of Saint Anthony (he died in
346, ten years before Anthony), he first attempted life as a hermit, before
being inspired in prayer to gather his followers into a community. The form
of life he established was so successful that by the end of the fourth century
there were some seven thousand Pachomian monks and nuns in Egypt.

Instead of living alone, these men and women joined together in communities, retaining the privacy of their cells but otherwise working and
praying together under the direction of an abbot. This removed one of the
most oppressive burdens of monasticism, the burden of solitude. In positive
terms, it offered individuals the opportunity of regular spiritual direction.
It also tended to moderation in daily life. A monastery was not a cave in the
hills. Food was adequate and predictable, work was hard but not overwhelming, clothing was sufficient though simple. There was even provision
made for the occasional snack, and a fire when the weather was cold. As for
private practices of mortification, they were allowed but not promoted.
Space was made, in this system, for the brothers "who do not give themselves up to great practices and to an excessive ascesis, but walk simply in the
purity of their bodies and according to the established rules with obedience
and obligingness." Not for these monks the austerities and the struggles of
the desert.

It was a natural progression. A community cannot tolerate too many
rugged individuals; it has to maintain a certain level of humility, sociability,
and obedience. It was this last, destined to become one of the three great
monastic virtues, that Pachomian monks and nuns had to practice, as compensation, so to speak, for the alleviation of their ascetical load. Their obedience was to be total, unhesitating, uncomplaining. It involved an assault
on nature as ruthless as any physical self-mortification. Or at least, so its
practitioners would claim. For others, both at the time and in the long centuries ahead, it was a lower form of monasticism or, at best, a stepping stone
toward the more perfect eremitic life. The competition between "obedi-

ence" and "sacrifice" would resurface many times in the monasticism of the future.

The circumstances of the fourth century, and the conditions of the Egyptian desert, set the scene for an extraordinarily rich period of development in monasticism. The literature, ancient and modern, emphasizes over and over again the need for the monk to "know himself." It may be argued that during Saint Anthony's lifetime monasticism as an institution came to "know itself": to recognize the heroic efforts required to reach its goal of an "undivided heart," the importance of asceticism as a means of clearing the mind for prayer, the importance of the Scriptures, of spiritual direction; the value, even for hermits, of charity toward neighbor, the great profit, for cenobites, to be gained from mutual support and edification and the practice of obedience and humility.

Many of these elements were as old as Christianity; some were even older. But in a crowded period of time they were practiced, experimented with, added to, all in the most demanding and uncompromising of physical conditions. Within a few short years there emerged a living institution capable of filling the spiritual void that had appeared when the age of the martyrs drew to its close, and of setting the basic patterns of monasticism for centuries to come.

*   *   *

Within a few years of Anthony's death, monasticism appeared in Europe, not through any conscious policy of church or civil rulers, but more or less by accident. In the words of one of its best-known historians, Dom David Knowles, "it spread gradually and sporadically as a plant spreads from seeds that are blown abroad." In the Roman Empire of the fourth and fifth centuries, people traveled for all sorts of reasons, and with them traveled their ideas and concepts. Among the concepts that traveled from Egypt to Europe was the concept of monasticism. Here and there along the Mediterranean coast and in Italy, small communities of men and women began practicing one form or other of eastern monasticism. From there the practices spread inland, into Gaul and Spain, carrying with them — perhaps in a shadowy and attenuated form — the imprint of Egypt, of Anthony and Pachomius. But they were not long-lived, because the environment was too unstable. For this was the start of the age of the great *Völkerwanderung,* the inrush of tribes from the east — Visigoths, Ostrogoths, Lombards, Slavs.

The first European monastery to achieve permanence was Lérins, founded in 410 on a little island off the southern coast of France. To the men who joined it, it offered rigorous discipline along with a serious course of studies in Scripture and religion. In time a number of them became bishops in various parts of Gaul, and established monasteries in their dioceses; here we see a foreshadowing of the role monasticism was to play in the future, as a moving force in the development of the Western Church.

One of the great men of the age (and some of us would surely say the greatest!) who carried the influence of Lérins with him was Patrick. His story is often told: how he was snatched by pirates from his own home in Britain and kept for some time in Ireland; how around 440 he escaped and made his way to Gaul, to return some years later to Ireland, a bishop now, and charged with the task of evangelizing the country. What is perhaps less well known is that while in Gaul he had some sort of contact with Lérins, enough to assimilate some of its monastic spirit. Certainly, when he came back to Ireland the seed of monasticism came with him, and the Christianity he brought to the country bore, from the very start, a monastic imprint. In time it had a remarkable flowering. Irish monasticism developed its own spirituality, rigorous in the extreme: a "white martyrdom" of self-denial to replace the "red martyrdom" of the heroic past. More than that: the sixth and seventh centuries would see Irish monks going out as missionaries to the world, building communities not only in the homeland but also in Scotland and England and the Continent from Brittany to the Rhine to the Alps. Some of their foundations made their mark in history: we think of Bangor in Ireland, another Bangor in Wales, Iona in Scotland, Lindisfarne in England, Luxeuil in Burgundy, Saint-Gall in Switzerland, Bobbio in Italy. But these are only a few of the many monasteries they established across Europe, each of them a force for the evangelization of the neighboring peoples. For whereas in established monastic practice stability (staying put within one's walls) was one of the principal obligations of a monk, the Irish monks saw "wandering" and evangelization as central to their vocation. And consequently, for many years northern Europe, from west to east, bore the imprint of Celtic monasticism.

*   *   *

These were all promising beginnings. But they were engulfed, in their time, by the huge tidal wave already coming out of the east: wandering tribes who poured across Europe, down through Gaul and into Spain and North Africa, obliterating old landmarks and old ways of life as they went. In 476 the

Roman Empire officially died, along with its last emperor. But its decline had begun much earlier, with a steady shrinking of population, trade, wealth, culture and learning, the rule of law — of virtually everything that, to the ancient Romans, constituted civilization. Whole cities with their stately homes, their paved streets and public baths and massive public buildings, turned into deserts; opulent country villas crumbled and fell apart. The newcomers had little use for these luxuries; they lived simply and close to the land; their law was the law of the tribe. And in any case, no sooner did they begin to settle than another wave of invaders came to push them on. For many lifetimes to come, Europeans were too busy struggling to survive, or to prevail, to care for the niceties of "civilization."

The nascent Christianity of the West suffered the shocks of the barbarian invasions, but it survived. In one way, it benefited. The collapse of the old structures of civil power left many areas with no viable authority except that of the Christian bishops. They stepped into the void, taking control of their cities and the surrounding areas. We have here the birth of the prince-bishop, very much a figure of the early Middle Ages: by unshakable custom an aristocrat, an autocrat, sometimes even a warrior for the protection of his interests and those of his people. It should be noted that those people were city people; the church of the Roman Empire was very much an urban institution, with little outreach as yet into the countryside.

Compared to the episcopal system, which was the linchpin of the church's structure, monasticism was a strange, amorphous entity. It did not fit in anywhere; it had no official part to play, either in the church's governance or in its apostolate. Monks, after all, had no special status; they were, as often as not, only laymen (and occasionally laywomen) who chose to pursue holiness in their own peculiar way. But from early days, by the practice of that holiness, they gained a place of honor among Christians, and their influence grew accordingly. Their relationship with the episcopate remained ambiguous, however: for every bishop who encouraged and endorsed them, there was another who worried about keeping them in their place. If truth be told, monks could be hard to control. As collectivities they were often highly independent, answering to no higher authority, practicing their own rules, going sometimes to extremes that the bishops considered dangerous. As long as they were few in number, it did not matter too much, but as monasticism found its place in the sun, the episcopate had to take note. A relationship developed that was sometimes warm, sometimes fractious.

On the other hand, the value of monks soon became obvious: they could go where the secular clergy could not. From very early days they became the church's advance guard, forging out into new territories, ready to freelance for the faith in societies where there were as yet no supporting ecclesiastical structures. The question was whether, once a region was converted, they were ready to turn it over to the episcopate and withdraw into their cloisters, into a more settled way of life. Sometimes they did, sometimes they did not. There were grounds here for future conflicts, and they happened aplenty. But the fact remained: the monks were the church's great missionaries. Without them, how would much of Europe have been introduced to Christianity?

"Hearken, My Son, to the Precepts of Thy Master"

So the Christendom that finally emerged from the long period of disorder that we call "the Dark Ages" owed a great deal of its spiritual and cultural formation to its monasteries. With the passage of time these monasteries became, overwhelmingly, Benedictine. After a period of experimentation, when there were almost as many monastic rules as there were monasteries, one rule came to prevail, partly thanks to the patronage of powerful men but partly also because of its intrinsic quality. That was the Rule of Saint Benedict.

Benedict of Nursia was born to wealthy parents sometime around 480 and educated in Rome. Then, against all sensible advice, he went off and found a cave in which to live as a hermit. After a while he was petitioned by a group of monks to come and be their abbot. However, his rigorous ways soon put them off; they parted company, and Benedict went back to being a hermit. Later, however, as his reputation for sanctity grew and he found himself surrounded by would-be followers, he gave up his solitude and accepted an alternative way of life, that of community. In 529 he moved with his disciples to Cassino, a mountain some distance south of Rome, where together they threw down a pagan temple and built a monastery. Some years later, he drew up his rule there.

Though it would one day become the charter, so to speak, of European monasticism, the Rule of Saint Benedict was originally written with only one community in mind: Monte Cassino, a monastery of some twenty men, sheltered by its mountainous terrain from the dangers of an increasingly unstable society. This community, according to Benedict, was to be freestanding, electing its own abbot and then living in total obedience to him, taking nothing from the outside world and giving nothing back to it. Its connection to the hierarchy was very slight. In a worst-case scenario, if the abbot was flagrantly deficient, he could be removed by the local bishop. Other than that, there needed to be no contact, no oversight.

Ideally, the community should produce for itself all that it required, in food and clothing. The text of the rule allowed for one exception to this: a suggestion that the work of the fields might be done by outside laborers, with the brothers helping to bring in the harvest only "if the circumstances of the place or their poverty require them." But the many tasks within the monastery and its gardens were the responsibility of the monks themselves, without the help of domestic servants (Benedict did not even imagine lay brothers). Everybody was to participate. It was a simple form of society, which recognized no ranking. All members of the community, from the old men down to the novices and the "oblates" (children given to the monastery at an early age), were subject to the single authority of the abbot, and their seniority was decided by the time they had spent in the community. They might be learned or unlettered, they might be of noble or commoner origin; it made no difference. Significantly, there was little room in the community for priests, apart from the one or two required to celebrate Sunday Mass and administer the sacraments. Those few priests who were admitted were warned not to think themselves superior to their brothers.

Given the future history of Christian monasticism, it is important to note that Benedict's monks were not expected to be useful to society, either by teaching or by preaching or even by intercessory prayer. Their only aim was to serve God and to save their own souls, always within the closed circle of their community. For about four hours a day they performed "the work of God," the *Opus Dei,* singing together the psalms and antiphons that made up the divine office. The service was simple, and performed in a simple, unadorned oratory. For four more hours they read, or prayed, or perhaps worked at copying manuscripts or educating the oblates. Six more hours were given over to manual, or domestic, labor. The timetable breathed moderation; so did the prescriptions for food, fasting, and dress.

This all served Benedict's purpose, to create "a school in the Lord's service, in founding which we hope to ordain nothing that is harsh or burdensome." It was a far cry from the fierce asceticism of the hermit life, and it was, even in Benedict's own mind, a less ambitious calling. But the rule, by teaching how to love God and live in harmony with the brothers, was the perfect guide for the times to come. Benedict could not have known it, living as he did in the lengthening shadows of the ancient civilization. But the way of life that he mapped out would in the future be a humanizing and civilizing force among people emerging from barbarism.

What is remarkable is that, amidst so much ruin and destruction, it even had a future. It is an extraordinary tale of survival. A half-century after its foundation, in 581, Benedict's monastery of Monte Cassino was destroyed by Lombard invaders, the first of several destructions (the latest one being in 1944, under Allied bombardment). Its monks were scattered; Benedict himself, dead since 547, was little more than a memory; the rule more or less went underground, at least as far as historians can see. But by some unknown trajectory it found its champion. Gregory the Great (590-604), while still a monk in Rome, learned of it and, once he was pope, championed its use. Most memorably, the missionary monks he sent to England in 597 brought with them, if not a copy of the rule, at least a grounding in its spirit. They themselves built only one monastery (in Canterbury), but from there, as house after house was provided by pious benefactors, Roman-style monasticism spread throughout the island, eventually overwhelming the Celtic monasticism of the north. With time, and more exposure to the mainland, the monks of England drew closer to the rule of Monte Cassino. Then, in the eighth century, they made repayment for the gift they had received from the Continent. In 716 a young monk whose baptismal name was Winfrid but who would be known to history as Boniface, "the doer of good works," left his monastery near Southampton to become a missionary. By the time he died a martyr in 754, he and his followers had pushed the frontiers of Christianity deep into Germany. Wherever they went they established monasteries — scores of them, large and small. The early evangelization of Germany was, above all, an enterprise mounted and carried through by Benedictine monks.

An all-important feature of Boniface's brand of monasticism was his commitment to the Holy See. He had visited Rome, and he felt himself tied to the papacy. All his conquests (if we may call them that) were fed back into the church's system: dioceses were set up, Roman rituals were established. This need not have happened, for Europe was still physically fractured: Rome was a long way off, and monasticism in the north — especially northern Gaul — was more or less removed from its influence. What is more, decades of warfare had left the monasteries vulnerable to the eighth-century version of robber barons, who seized their lands and buildings and left their communities in a poor way. Gradually, however, the English variation of monasticism, both Roman and Benedictine in inspiration, filtered back into Gaul. When the Holy Roman Empire came into being, with the coronation of Charlemagne by the pope in 800, Benedict's rule was observed, more or less, by most of the monasteries in the empire. But the operative words are "more or less." A great miscellany of rules and customs, some borrowed from the ancients, others of more recent invention, still cluttered up its original simplicity.

Now, however, the Benedictine version of monasticism enjoyed the full benefit of imperial support. "Is there any Rule other than that of Benedict?" the emperor is supposed to have said, and he decreed that all monks should observe this one rule. He did not manage to impose the uniformity that he so desired, and in his later life it appears that he lost interest in it. But his son, Louis the Pious, gave it his best effort. By nature much more attuned to monasticism than had been his father, Louis brought his protégé, a saintly monk from Aquitaine whom we know as Benedict of Aniane, to his capital at Aachen to develop a universal, purified monastic way of life. Benedict, who had given up his baptismal name of Vitiza when he adopted his namesake's rule, was an eloquent spokesman for it — and a potent one, since he had the authority of the emperor behind him. At a council held in Aachen in 817, the abbots of the empire agreed, under his prodding, to adopt the Rule of Benedict of Nursia, to which were added the customs and adaptations of Benedict of Aniane.

In certain ways, Benedict II modified the Rule of Benedict I. For one thing, he played down the obligation of daily work. Many monks were now aristocrats by birth, and the very thought of manual labor was repugnant to them. In any case, most monastic lands were already being worked by laborers. But if the time allotted to work declined, the time allotted to the liturgy increased. The original Saint Benedict had seen the singing of divine office as the most important work of the monk, but by no means his only work. It was to be accomplished in a simple way, within a simple space. And it was to share the day with the other occupations of physical or mental labor and private prayer. But in these opening years of the ninth century, the liturgical element began to play a larger part, to the detriment of the others. The number of antiphons to be sung, and prayers to be said, and ceremonies to be observed, increased by leaps and bounds. This, the ritualization of Benedictine life, would later be carried to extremes, as we shall see.

Contributing to this was another profound alteration in the nature of monasticism: the introduction (thanks to the English missionaries) of the idea of intercessory prayer. In other words, monks were in the future to have a distinctive function in society, which was to pray for other Christians, living and dead. It had not been a requirement at Monte Cassino, but then, Monte Cassino was by its founder's intention detached from the world. The monks of the Middle Ages were not detached from the world, far from it; they owed their continuation to its support, both moral and material. More and more, the aristocratic patrons who endowed the monasteries demanded something in return: prayers for themselves and their families. And of all possible prayers, the prayers intoned in monasteries were the most certain to ascend to the throne of God.

There was a further logic to this way of thinking. The prayers of monks were good; masses said by monks were better still. Imperceptibly, the first Benedict's ideal of a community of laymen-monks shifted into a new ideal in which most of the monks were priests, and much of the work of those priests was to say mass. In monastery churches the number of altars multiplied, the number of masses said at them multiplied even more, and the donations and bequests came flowing in.

All this is pointing the way toward the time to come, the tenth and eleventh centuries that we call the central Middle Ages. But between the early ninth century and those later years there was a terrible hiatus. Charlemagne's empire would break up under his descendants, with the usual accompaniment of internal violence. At the same time, external scourges were gathering force. The Germanic peoples of Scandinavia whom we know as Vikings or Norsemen first appeared off the British coasts around 800, the year Charlemagne was crowned. By mid- and late ninth century they were terrorizing the island and sweeping on to the Continent, plundering the seacoasts all the way to Italy, traveling the rivers deep into the heart of Gaul and Germany. Everywhere they went, monasteries were their favored targets, because the invaders knew they were both vulnerable and rich in gold and silver. The result was deep dislocation. In England, for instance, the destruction was so thorough that monastic life ceased for the greater part of a century, until it was more or less rediscovered by Saint Dunstan around 940. In Normandy, where the Vikings settled and took control and turned into Normans, there were ruin and desolation until the early tenth century, when the new rulers "got religion" and became the fervent patrons of monasteries, male and female.

At the same time, Moslem corsairs, firmly established in North Africa and Spain, began raiding along the coasts of Italy. In time they penetrated the interior, as far as the Alps. They surrounded Rome and devastated the hinterland so thoroughly that the city, with its monasteries and churches, shriveled up for lack of sustenance. They succeeded in occupying Sicily and many of the Mediterranean islands, from which they were able to bring the

Europeans' sea traffic to a dead halt. Finally, in the late ninth and early tenth centuries, Hungarian freebooters came in from the east, ranging across Germany and deep into France, carrying home wagonloads of loot along the Roman roads. For all these invaders western Europe was a rich target, all the more tempting because, since the collapse of imperial power, it was more or less defenseless.

There was a lesson to be learned here, and Europeans learned it. They must arm themselves. From the ninth century onward cities that had hitherto been open to trade and travel began to surround themselves with defensive walls. Castles complete with moats and donjons appeared in ever-greater numbers. The surge in building was the physical sign of a deeper transformation taking place in the power relationships of Europe. When the central rulers could no longer protect all their principalities, they surrendered the duty, and the rights of kingship that went with it, piece by piece to local strongmen. Thus were born the great feudal dynasties: noble families who ruled their own territories and raised their own armies, while only owing fealty to the monarchy. And when they, in turn, were unable to maintain full control over all their territories, they allowed the work to be parceled out to their retainers, on the same terms: loyalty and military service in return for the benefits of ruling their own smaller domains.

This was the process that brought feudalism into being. It was a response to the danger of invasion and a way of reestablishing some sort of order across an unstable continent. It created a chain of authority that reached, theoretically at least, from the king down to the lowliest peasant. But it also consecrated a culture of warfare and, at local levels, the acknowledgment that might makes right. The many, many castles that came to dot the landscape were not just defensive; they also served as bases from which to repress, and extort, and raid.

The monks of Europe were deeply affected by the changing climate. Just as their treasures had attracted the avarice of the pagan predators, so did their property now attract the avarice of their new Christian "protectors." In a society that still had little access to money, land (and the laborers that went with it) was the chief source of wealth and power. And already, thanks to many pious benefactors, the monasteries owned a great deal of the Continent's workable land. Without any central control, there was very little to stop the new masters from laying hands on it. One by one, religious houses fell under the sway of powerful families, and their wealth and independence were drained away. In many cases they were "secularized"; that is, the office of abbot, on which everything depended, passed to laymen who might then, if they wished, bring their wives and dependents, horses, hunting dogs, and falcons into the monastery, with predictable consequences for community life. In other cases the office was simply handed to a hastily tonsured younger son, or sold to the highest bidder (as often, in the same years, was the episcopal office). Under these conditions, much of Europe's monastic life languished. Then, in the early tenth century, a corner was turned.

Cluny

In 909 William, duke of Aquitaine, donated one of his domains for the founding of a new Benedictine monastery. "I thought that it was wise," his charter went, "to put to the profit of my soul a small part of the temporal goods which have been accorded to me." It was the traditional bargain: the monks were to repay his liberality with prayers for his salvation and that of his family. But William went further. "For the love of God and our Savior Jesus Christ, I cede the property of the domain of Cluny with everything that depends on it to the apostles Peter and Paul." In other words, no power on earth — "no secular prince, no count, no bishop, not even the pontiff of the Roman see" — could encroach upon the property and privileges of the house without offending the apostles themselves. The monastery was to be free from all meddling, either ecclesiastical or secular, even his own. The monks were to have the power, which Saint Benedict had stipulated but which was long defunct, to elect their own abbot, thus defending themselves from outside interference.

William's donation was not unique; a few other founders had used the "Peter and Paul" formula to keep their monasteries from being grabbed. But he gave Cluny a second gift that guaranteed the first. He chose as its first abbot a monk already well known for his reforming activity, a Burgundian of noble birth named Bernon. With Bernon, an extraordinary succession of great abbots commenced at Cluny that lasted uninterrupted for two centuries (909-1109), during which the monastery became the powerhouse of monasticism in Europe.

They wielded three weapons, these remarkable abbots: their authentic dedication to reform; their close identification with the society of their time; and their remarkable flair for organization. By the time Cluny came on the scene, the evil days of the ninth century were past, more or less, and a religious revival was under way. The men and women of the age were ever aware of the supernatural, and anxious to placate it; as a result, paradoxically, the very same people who despoiled one church or monastery were ready to give generously to another, for the good of their souls. Where better to be generous than to a fine community of observant monks? And of course, the people who had the wherewithal to support the monasteries were the seigneurs and chevaliers, the lesser aristocracy of that feudal society into which the monks themselves had been born. They were comfortable giving not only their worldly goods but also their sons, and this tied them even more closely to the monasteries. Early medieval monasticism was something that belonged more or less exclusively to the powerful.

But what marked the Cluniac out from the other reform movements, and the reason why it flourished so spectacularly, was its organization. Without initially intending to, Cluny developed into something like a religious order — the first in Christendom — in which it exercised a quasi-feudal power over a web of dependent houses.

It happened like this. By custom, the abbots of observant houses were ready, when asked, to move to other monasteries, reform them, and then return home. There would be no further bond between the two communities except, perhaps, the bond of charity. In 929 the queen of Burgundy offered the second abbot of Cluny one of "her" monasteries, on the understanding that once reformed, it would remain under his control. In other words, the new community would henceforth be subject to its motherhouse. It would no longer have its own abbot, and the prior (the second-in-command in the community) would take an oath of fealty to the abbot of Cluny, much as a feudal tenant swore fealty to his liege lord. From that point on, the community would submit to the authority of a supreme abbot who lived somewhere else. In 931 the pope authorized the action, and several years later Cluny began to collect monasteries. By the end of the tenth century, thirty-seven Benedictine priories owed obedience to the abbot of Cluny.

This was only the start. A hundred years later Cluny was the supreme head of more than a thousand priories large and small, in France, Italy, Spain, Germany, and England. In addition to these priories, numerous prestigious abbeys were affiliated more or less closely with the great monastery, and numerous more, though independent, felt its influence. Among its alumni it boasted bishops, cardinals, and popes. And from the popes it had secured an enormous privilege: total exemption from episcopal authority. No bishop could enter the precincts of a Cluniac monastery unless he was invited. No Cluniac monk could be corrected or sanctioned by a bishop. If a dispute arose, Cluny could go straight to Rome.

The word "huge" is not often applicable to the medieval scene. Yet in its day Cluny was huge. Before it ceased to grow, its network numbered 10,000-12,000 monks and novices, all of them owing obedience directly to the abbot of Cluny. As for the abbey itself, some 300 monks lived within its walls, as well as who knows how many domestics, toiling to serve their needs. Its domains were vast and far-flung. Its church, dedicated by the pope in 1130, was larger than any other in Europe until the building of Saint Peter's in the sixteenth century, and in its time was considered the marvel of Christendom. We can see in this gigantism a metaphor for the influence that it wielded. By 1100, though many independent monasteries still dotted the landscape, Cluny *was* Benedictinism for most of the Western world.

But if Cluny became, and for many years remained, great, it was not so much because of its wealth and organization as because it fitted so perfectly into the mind of its times. It has been said that early medieval men and women "lived in the plural," as a collectivity. They saw themselves not as individual beings, but as members belonging to a vast human body. Within that body, they believed, God had created three distinct roles. There were those who prayed, and those who fought, and those who labored: that was the way it was meant to be, and no one was entitled to transgress the boundaries of his own station. Therefore, for prayer that really worked, laypeople could not rely on their own efforts; they had to go to the specialists in prayer, the intercessors who could effectively petition the Almighty on their behalf. What Cluny came to offer was the most elaborate, the most sumptuous, form of liturgical prayer. Over the years its ritual was perfected and the time given to it increased, until some eight hours of every day were dedicated to the *Opus Dei,* to the singing of masses, and to a great body of additional prayers, antiphons, and psalms. This was a broad departure from the Benedictine Rule. For example, it is recorded that the monks of Cluniac monasteries were required to sing 215 psalms per day, where Saint Benedict had prescribed 40. On occasion they sang three versions of the office of lauds where originally they would have sung one. On high feasts their office extended almost nonstop from nightfall to dawn of the following day. All in all, the time available for private prayer and meditation was cut short so that the sounds of praise could rise endlessly to heaven. The labor, manual or otherwise, that Benedict had recommended disappeared altogether. The quiet self-sufficiency of the sixth-century monastery was replaced by a constant round of intercession on behalf of the countless souls that needed saving.

It was not an unworthy way of life, nor an easy one. To a saintly critic who complained that the old rules of fasting were being loosened in Cluny, a saintly abbot replied that he should try a week following all the monastery's observances, and then see how he felt. And in its purpose it was perfectly attuned to the needs and fears of feudal society. For this was an age obsessed with the four last things: death, judgment, heaven, and hell. The wrath of God awaited sinful man. No one could be confident of salvation. What Cluny's contemporaries asked of it, and what it gave them, was prayer, prayer, and more prayer, for the souls in purgatory.

The observance of All Souls' Day on November 2, a ceremony which it instituted, is about all that is left to us of Cluny. The abbey itself was destroyed at the time of the French Revolution, and its massive stone walls were used as a quarry during the following decades, so that only a few tall arches remain to commemorate its greatness. But in fact, the decline of Cluny had begun many centuries earlier. Too powerful and too rich, it had become the object of hostility for both princes and secular clergy. By the end of the eleventh century their criticisms were open and insistent. Most damaging of all was that which developed within monasticism itself. Deep in the soul of Christendom there still remained a hankering after the desert, the silence, the aloneness in God's presence. In different places and at different times, this was making itself felt.

"The Poor Men of Christ"

Without knowing it, Europeans were living in changing times. The change was slow enough to be imperceptible, but it was real. And like the receding of the glaciers that opened new Alpine passes to traffic, or the calming of the oceans that opened new possibilities to seafarers, or the few extra days of warmth that allowed farmers more time to bring in their crops, it had a pronounced effect on the living conditions of the people of Europe. The rise of a few degrees, together with the drying trend that accompanied it, was not such good news for Italy or Greece, but it worked wonders across the great northern plains. At a time when 95 percent of Europeans lived directly off the land, an improvement in the harvest meant, first, better nutrition for everybody, and second, a small surplus that worked to the benefit of those who could take advantage of it. By the year 1000 population was rising steadily, and both wetlands and forests were giving way before it. New towns were appearing, old towns were filling up, and merchants were moving in greater numbers along the ancient tracks. They had more to work with: precious metal was trickling in from the east and from Africa, which put more coin in circulation. Consequently, where two centuries earlier most of the Continent's treasure had fitted into the coffers of a handful of princes, bishops, and monasteries, it was now beginning to circulate, to be visible on a larger scale. People — some people — were getting rich. And for the first time medieval society faced the fact that while a few were rich, others were poor. Some asked themselves if this was what the gospel taught.

Until that time no one had criticized the wealth of the greats. For temporal rulers, descended as they were from chieftains of wandering tribes, wealth was seen as an absolute necessity; how else could they follow the proper lifestyle, consuming conspicuously while showering largesse upon their followers? For bishops, too, wealth represented power and legitimacy; they owed it to their people to provide impressive religious services in impressive surroundings, and to care for those in need. So it made sense for them to be fiercely protective of their sources of income. As for rich monasteries like Cluny, the magnificence of their buildings and the splendor of their sanctuaries were things for Christians to be proud of, for they demonstrated how well the people of this world were ready to treat their God. But with rising prosperity, a great sea change began to wash through the European psyche. Poverty was on the way to being a moral issue, and wealth was on the way to being a moral problem.

In response to this awakening consciousness, people desirous of spiritual renewal reached back to an old institution, eremitism. They saw the hermit's life as a rejection of everything that Benedictine monasticism had come to represent. It was a call to poverty, and asceticism, and contempt for the world — in other words, purity of purpose in a society that had become corrupt and complicated. Before the eleventh century was many years old, hermits, either alone or in groups, began to appear across Europe, in Italy first, and then in France and Germany, and later in Britain. More often than not, they followed a similar pattern. Involved in some fashion with the ecclesiastical establishment, either as monks or as cathedral canons, some men became disillusioned with what they saw as its infidelity to the gospel and managed, sometimes with difficulty, to break free of their commitment. Then, alone or with a few like-minded companions, they began wandering from one place to another, subsisting on next to nothing while searching for a more perfect form of life. After a few years, those who wearied of wandering found a place to settle down, somewhere set apart, yet close enough to friendly neighbors that they might hope for the occasional alms. Over time, others decided to join them. The group needed to agree on a modus vivendi, which in their case meant a rule, which they might compose for themselves out of whole cloth or by borrowing from established rules. And most certainly, they needed to choose a leader. On these conditions — the strength of their vocation, the suitability of their environment, the viability of their rule, and the character of their leader — depended their survival. It was a tenuous existence. For every pocket of hermits that lasted more than a few years, there is evidence that many went down to early extinction.

Of the communities that did succeed, the most famous is that of the Grande Chartreuse, founded by Bruno of Cologne. Originally the chancellor of the cathedral school of Reims, and therefore a person of consequence, Bruno left his career behind in 1080 and lived for a while with a group of hermits in Calabria. Then, in 1084, he moved with a few companions to a remote mountain valley near Grenoble, and there set up his community of hermits. The way of life that he and his successors established was essentially eremitical, though maintained within the physical framework of a community. The monastery was an enclosed compound made up of small individual dwellings grouped around a central church. The brothers gathered in the church for part of the daily office, but otherwise they prayed and studied and worked within their own space. Apart from the occasional communal meal and conversation, theirs was a life of deep silence and solitude. Their physical needs were seen to by a parallel community of lay brothers, or *conversi,* who lived in a separate building farther down the hill.

The words "community" and "hermit" might seem to us irreconcilable. This is because in our mind hermits are characterized more by physical separateness, complete with uncombed hair and ragged clothes, than by anything else. For the Carthusians (their name taken from the Latin for the Grande Chartreuse, where they first gathered) what mattered was that their environment should leave them free to pursue that goal for which the Egyptian monks, too, had longed: an "undivided heart," undistracted by the background noises of the world and open to God's presence. To reach that state, aloneness was a necessary precondition, and one that the standard community life, with all its interactions, disrupted. On the other hand, the infrastructure that a community provided, by offering spiritual support and eliminating concern for the daily necessities, was a liberation. By fusing the eremitical and cenobitic forms, the Carthusians managed to keep the advantages of both. Thus in the later eleventh century an alternative form of monasticism developed in western Europe. Whereas the raison d'être of contemporary Benedictine monks was prayer and intercession, that of

Carthusian monks was contemplation, practiced within a life of asceticism and penance.

The Carthusians were not the only hermit-monks to appear in the twelfth century and to achieve permanence; similar groups sprang up, especially in Italy, and at least two of them (the Camaldules and the Vallombrosians) lasted until modern times. But the order that grew out of the Grande Chartreuse was by far the most successful. Because of the uncompromising severity of its way of life, it never achieved large numbers, but what it lacked in size it made up for in reputation. "Never reformed because never deformed" — that was its claim; and through the centuries, as other orders came to struggle with problems of compromise and mediocrity, it held fast to its standards. One example of its unshakability stands out. English history records that when the Reformation came and all the king's subjects were ordered to recognize him as head of the church, the Carthusians of London, almost alone among churchmen, defied the law — and paid for their defiance with a gruesome death.

*   *   *

The monasteries of Grande Chartreuse and Camaldoli and Vallombrosa do not tell the whole story of the medieval hermit movement. The men who entered those communities chose to reject the world by removing themselves entirely from it, in the tradition of the Egyptian monks. But there was another way to reject the world, or at least its values: by embracing the "desert" yet leaving it from time to time to preach repentance and conversion. Saint Anthony himself had done this, as, with even greater authority, had the ancient prophets and John the Baptist. With population increase and the growth of towns, such preaching had an audience. So eleventh-century society found itself under siege by a host of itinerant preachers, whose targets included not only the usual slate of personal vices but also institutional sins, especially those that involved the church. Simony (the buying and selling of benefices), clerical marriage, and the inordinate wealth of some churchmen were all subjects for their tongue-lashings. Of course, they made enemies aplenty (one preacher was nearly lynched by a band of priests' wives), but they also made friends. Reforming bishops and, above all, the papacy itself gave them support. For these were the years when Rome, under Pope Gregory VII (1073-1085), was initiating far-reaching church reform; for Rome the preaching of the hermits was altogether helpful.

Nevertheless, the authorities came to treat the hermit-preachers as a mixed blessing. They offered a message that people were ready to hear, of return to a simpler, purer form of religion. But they were also given to high rhetoric, too high perhaps for the stability of contemporary society. And because they were outside the "system," not easily restrained by church discipline, they could stray into dangerous territory. Their hearers, unsophisticated and for the most part unlettered, were likely to respond with overexuberance to their preaching. Sometimes the consequences were disastrous. The extraordinary career of Peter the Hermit, a strange little prophet out of Picardy, is a case in point. Even though he was ragged and filthy and allegedly had a face that resembled that of his donkey, he exercised an extraordinary power over people. "Whatever he said or did," wrote an acquaintance, "it seemed like something half-divine." In 1095, after the pope had proclaimed what was to become the First Crusade, Peter took up the call and left France for the east, preaching and gathering disciples as he went. By the time he reached Cologne he had a following of some fifteen thousand men, women, and children, all ready and willing to go and fight for Jerusalem. They traveled across the Continent at the speed of about twenty-five miles a day, wreaking havoc and destruction as they went. It was a true "people's crusade," and it met the fate that such popular movements always encountered. In Asia Minor, in late 1096, all but a few of the thousands were massacred. It was not the last time in European history that simple people following a charismatic leader would suffer a terrible end. Peter himself survived, to return to France and become the founder of a highly reputable monastery.

In his time Peter was unique, as was the magnitude of the catastrophe that his preaching provoked. But lesser men could also be destabilizing. Their criticisms of the church's failings helped to fuel a new mood among their hearers — outright anticlericalism. Naturally, the clergy reacted negatively; a rift opened up between them and the people. In several places in both Italy and France there was open conflict between townsmen and their bishops. It was an awakening of the laity, to be sure, but one that was extremely dangerous to authority. Over the course of the following century (the twelfth), religious ferment ballooned, here and there, into out-and-out heresy. And only too often, hermits, or men who claimed to be hermits, were at the heart of it.

So much for the negative side of the mixed blessing. The hermits' preaching also bore much that was positive. First of all, they spoke truth to power, at a blessed moment in time when power (the papacy) was ready to listen. Secondly, they opened an important argument that would resonate within Christendom for a long time: that poverty was Christlike. Finally, because as free spirits they were able to go where the wind blew them, they reached marginal people, in places where the church's infrastructure was still far from perfect.

One of the most famous of eleventh-century preachers was Robert of Arbrissel. He was the quintessential hermit. After some time in an influential position in the diocese of Rennes, he found he could not stand it, and in 1095 made for the "desert," which for him was a forest on the border of Anjou and Brittany. But if what he wanted was solitude, he failed to get it, because he was too good a preacher. Crowds gathered around him, crowds not only of men, but also of women of every type and description — as his biographer put it, "widows and virgins, elderly and youthful, whores and spurners of men." Together he and his followers wandered the roads, in a sort of holy footlooseness that inspired the faithful but alarmed the hierarchy. In a church council at Poitiers in 1100, Robert was taxed with complaints about his behavior, which included the accusation that he actually slept among women as a test of his continence, and that in his following were wives who had left their husbands, and whom he refused to send back. Under pressure, he agreed to become respectable. He settled his followers in a religious house, at a place in Anjou called Fontevrault.

The community that Robert set up was certainly unusual for its time. Though it was to hold both men and women, it was centered on the women. The men were to act as chaplains if they were qualified, and otherwise as property managers or laborers; the women who were illiterate were to act as servants. The central monastic work of the house, the service of the choir, was reserved for the women of higher class and/or learning. The charge of the entire community was entrusted to a woman of aristocratic birth. That it should be an aristocrat was a given; all the world expected that. But that a woman should rule over men — that was certainly original, though in keeping with the mind of this original man.

Having organized everybody, Robert left again, to continue his life as an itinerant preacher. In his absence, things changed quickly. The nuns began to receive donations and to buy land, mills, vineyards, taxation rights, serfs, and other forms of property. Even before his death in 1116, the community had begun its transformation. By mid–twelfth century it was the head of an order of fifty houses, all of them mixed, headed by women, and selective in their choice of novices. Through the following centuries until the French Revolution, Fontevrault remained the head of one of the most exclusive religious orders in all of France.

Though less successful economically and socially, this was in fact the way many hermit communities ended. They became Benedictine monasteries, either within or outside of Cluny. Or they adopted the rule and lifestyle of a new religious order, which rose to prominence just as they were beginning to fade.

Cîteaux

In 1098, twenty-one men walked away from their monastery — an up-and-coming community perched strategically close to the main Paris-Lyon road — and made for a clearing in the Burgundian forests, a wilderness of ponds and wetlands thick with a marshy covering of the *cistelli* (reeds) that gave it its name. In this unpromising place, once they had built their huts and begun clearing away the undergrowth, a new religious entity came into being: the Cistercian order, destined to be a hugely dynamic force in monasticism, in the church, and in the Western world.

The men did not intend to found an order. It was all they could do to keep themselves alive and their community afloat in these unfriendly surroundings. Nor in their own minds were they starting something new. What they desired was to live without all the impedimenta with which the existing Benedictine monasteries had been loaded, in a community that was true to the rule as Benedict had written it, "down to the last punctuation mark." To do this they were resolved to distance themselves from the world and its corrosive wealth: to keep at arm's length all donors, patrons, and well-wishers, whether ecclesiastics or laymen. Equally, they planned to reject the sorts of riches that traditional monasteries took for granted: possession of tithes and benefices and of feudal properties and rights and — most importantly of all — the ownership of serfs. They were to be their own workforce, tilling the land by themselves with little or no help from outsiders, living on the fruit of their labors. They were to give up all amenities not specified in the rule, whether in clothing or in food. All liturgical ornaments, and all vestments, were to be of commonplace materials: iron and wood rather than silver and gold, linen rather than silk. In every aspect of their daily life, extreme simplicity was to be the byword.

In the same spirit, they resolved to shed all the encumbrances that over the years had been loaded onto the monastic liturgy. The *Opus Dei* was to be stripped of its elaborate accretions; the extra offices and litanies and processions were to be abolished, along with all elaborations of chant and ceremonial. In doing this, the monks of Cîteaux reestablished what the monks of Cluny had lost: time for private prayer and contemplation. The monastery became a place of recollection, rather than something akin to a giant prayer wheel turning out intercessions. As David Knowles puts it, a comparison of Cluniac and Cistercian practices "gives the reader something of the sensation of passing from a stale and heavy atmosphere into the fresh air. Once more there is space to move about in."

However, for several years the future of the community looked bleak. The hardship of their existence was almost too much for the monks. Several of them left, and there were few new recruits. Then, in 1112, Cîteaux experienced a providential rescue. A young man of chevalier background, Bernard of Fontaine, entered the novitiate, along with thirty friends and relations. The benefits of this infusion, and above all, of Bernard's huge energy and talent, were almost instantaneous. By 1113 the community was so full that it had to create its first subsidiary, at La Ferté. By 1115 there were four such "daughter" monasteries, and in one of them, Clairvaux, Bernard was abbot. With each of these abbeys propagating its own offspring, the Cistercian population continued to grow exponentially. When Bernard died in 1153, the order numbered some 350 houses, to be found as far east as Poland, as far north as Scandinavia, south into Italy and Christian Spain, and across the water in Britain and Ireland. Wherever the Church of Rome held sway, there were Cistercians.

Two chief reasons are given for this rapid expansion. One is that the people of the age were ready for a renewal of monastic idealism, and Cîteaux gave it to them. A would-be cenobite now had a choice: to enter one of the traditional Benedictine communities (now known as "black monks" by the color of their habits) or to join the Cistercians (or "white monks," who wore coarse undyed wool). The differences were radical. On the one hand, the older monasteries, the beneficiaries over the years of extensive feudal properties and privileges, offered their members a lifestyle not unlike that of their secular neighbors, with serfs to work their lands and servants to care for their households; with open-house traditions that welcomed guests of all stripes into their precincts; with access, almost always, to towns and cities nearby — in other words, with full and comfortable participation in contemporary society. On the other hand, Cistercian monasteries were built in removed and often inhospitable places, which the monks cleared and cultivated by their own labor, and where they lived, as far as possible, in silence and simplicity. To serious searchers after perfection, there was no contest. As Bernard of Clairvaux put it: "Enter here: live as we do: this do, and thou shalt live."

The second reason is Bernard himself, the most influential, most magnetic personality of the twelfth-century church. From the start, through his reputation as a spiritual director, theologian, and writer, he made himself felt. But as well as all these qualities he had another: he loved a good fight. He did not take long to start criticizing the lifestyle of various highly placed prelates. Having made his mark, he was drawn into church politics as an adjudicator in several contested episcopal elections. Then, in 1130, when a disputed election in Rome pitted two papal claimants against each other, Bernard decided which was the genuine pope, and persuaded other decision-makers in the church to agree with him. The ultimate success of that pope, Innocent II, cemented the Cistercian order's bond with Rome. From then on, Bernard was listened to with respect. And he made good use of that respect. For close to forty years he towered over everyone who came within his orbit, fighting the good fight as he saw it with a vigor and persuasiveness that nobody could resist. He took aim at churchmen whose behavior was below standard — and this, in his mind, included the monks of Cluny, whose wealth and ostentation he criticized in the strongest terms. Thanks to his intervention, Peter Abelard was condemned for heresy; through his good services, Louis VII of France was reconciled to the count of Champagne; when the papal legate traveled south to deal with a major heretical movement (that of the Cathars), Bernard was persuaded to go with him, commencing a Cistercian involvement in what was to become the tragic Albigensian crusade. Finally, in 1146, he was invited to preach the Second Crusade. Enflamed by his oratory, the king himself, as well as nobles and lesser men of every condition, joined the ill-fated venture. And throughout all these momentous years, Bernard continued to extend the reach of his order. To onlookers, it seemed that all the world was becoming Cistercian.

If Bernard stood so tall among his contemporaries, it was not just because of his personality and oratorical abilities. He was a mystic, a true holy man, who by his writings and his preaching pointed the way to a new spirituality. In this age of change, Christian men and women were ready for more inner direction, for a personal closeness with the divine that the old ritual forms had not encouraged. Bernard invited them to turn to the suffering, human Christ with love and reverence. Furthermore, in these very years when chivalric ideals were coming into fashion, he taught respect for the greatest of all ladies, the Virgin Mary. The timeliness of his thinking can be judged by its successful reception. From this time on, and increasingly throughout the Middle Ages, these two images, that of the suffering Christ, that of the gentle Virgin, became the central objects of devotion and artistic inspiration.

So by reason of both his leadership qualities and his genuine holiness, Bernard was the magnet that brought men flocking into Cistercian monasteries. (Women came too, as we shall see.) With the crowds of entrants, however, came problems. In a sense, the great man's extraordinary success altered the nature of the order. From a poor and isolated community depending on no one but God, Cîteaux became a great monastery and the head of a great order, powerful in the eyes of the world and open, too, to the issues that preoccupied that world. It has been argued that the order grew too rapidly, and that this contributed to its later decay.

That it held together as well as it did is a tribute not only to the clarity of its original purpose but also to its efficient organization. Whereas Cluny held all its dependencies in a quasi-feudal relationship, with one man ruling hundreds of houses, Cîteaux was the head of a federation of abbeys, in which each abbot was responsible for the good order of his own house but subject to visitation by the abbot whose monastery had founded his; where the decisions that needed to be made for the whole order were made not by the chief abbot alone but by an annual general chapter of abbots. The abbot of Cîteaux held a position of eminence, but other than that, he was but an abbot, like all the rest. We should add that — again unlike the Cluniac system — every abbot was elected by his own community, and was expected to remain with it, as its father and guide. In this respect Cîteaux was a model for later religious orders.

Cîteaux was responsible for another great innovation in monasticism. Having rejected the practice of holding serfs, the monks realized, very early on, that they had a problem. Even with a pared-down liturgy, they could not do all the work that the fields required. So they decided to do what other small communities were already attempting, but to do it on a larger scale. They recruited *conversi,* or lay brothers: men whose chief duty would be, not the choir, but the care of the farms and flocks. They would receive spiritual direction and have their own limited liturgy; they would eat the same food and wear the same habit and, when they died, be buried in the same cemetery. In other words, they would be full members of the community. This, too, was an idea that fitted perfectly into the age. For the first time the monastic life was opened up to men of peasant origins, men who could not read but knew how to farm. In the early twelfth century, thanks to population growth, such men were in abundance. And they flocked in the thousands to join the order. The result: under their hands the "desert places" — forest, scrub, and wetlands — that the Cistercians chose to inhabit soon became fertile and productive.

But the Cistercian regimen, because it placed labor along with prayer as a daily obligation, would, over time, have unintended consequences. Whereas the black monks, for all their property holdings, were often the victims of their tenants' apathy and their own fecklessness, the white monks reaped the benefits of a strong work ethic. And these benefits were, in a way, a poison pill. In less than a century the company of "poor men of Christ" became a company of rich producers, fully integrated into a burgeoning market, buying and selling with the best of them. There are no better examples of this transition than the Cistercians of Yorkshire.

The first Cistercians, a group of fewer than thirty monks, came from Clairvaux to Yorkshire in 1132, to a tract of wasteland chosen not by them but by their benefactor. They took up residence in a scattering of wooden huts that, within a very few years, became the great abbey of Rievaulx. By midcentury the population of the abbey had already reached three hundred, many of them distinguished men, but two-thirds of them *conversi,* ready to give their working lives for the privilege and blessing of belonging to the order. In the same short span of time Rievaulx's overflow filled twelve new monasteries. The remarkable rise continued. Before long, fifty-one Cistercian monasteries had taken root in England and Wales, and a significant agricultural revolution was under way.

One of the Cistercians' attractions, for their benefactors, was their value for money. Their prayers were as good as any — perhaps better — but their initial requirements were less. Unlike the black monks, they did not need finished buildings, or ground rents, or serfs, or good arable fields. All they wanted were a few rudimentary buildings and some land; the land could be stony, or inaccessible, or covered with scrub. Of this kind of land there was plenty in the north of England. Within a short time they did wonders with it. They brought more and more of it under cultivation; the land they could not cultivate, they turned over to sheep.

They were not only good farmers, they were good farmers who did not consume all they produced. As long as the Cistercians kept to their austere way of life, they found themselves with surpluses. It did not take long for these surpluses to make their way into the market, first of grain, and then of wool. Wool was in great demand; someone has said that it was the "oil of the twelfth century." The infertile wolds and moors turned out to be a gold mine, supporting great flocks of sheep whose wool attracted foreign merchants every year to the monasteries' collection points. With their profits, the monks bought more land, sowed more fields, brought in more sheep, and developed more markets. Within a surprisingly short time — before the end of the twelfth century — the "poor men of Christ" had become protocapitalists, and, in the eyes of some contemporaries, men who, collectively if not individually, were guilty of the sin of avarice.

The English Cistercians may have outstripped their Continental brothers in the pace with which they declined from their early ideals. The conditions they faced — the empty landscape waiting for cultivation, the growing value of their chief product — may have allowed their wealth to build up with unusual speed. But in general, what applies to the English applies to the rest. The rise of Cîteaux was rapid to the point of being demoralizing. Its heyday as a spiritual force was as brief as it was brilliant. In 1200 the order was still powerful, even though its growth had slowed markedly. But it was rich now because along the way it had started acquiring the kinds of feudal revenues and ecclesiastical benefices that the early fathers had renounced. Some of its monasteries even held serfs. And it was beginning to relax its discipline, ever so gently. It no longer held the monopoly of virtue of which Saint Bernard had been so certain. Other orders were making their appearance, and with them, new forms of religious life were being developed.

The "Mixed Life"

In fact, one of these "new" forms was an adaptation of one of the oldest institutions of Western Christianity, the canonicate. The early church had operated as a composite of smaller church communities, each based in a city, each ruled by a bishop. The physical center of the city-church community was the cathedral. Attached to the cathedral was a group of priests whose duty it was to assist the bishop in tending to the needs, both spiritual and material, of the faithful. These priests came to be called canons.

In the fourth century bishops here and there began to collect their assistant priests into religious communities. Saint Augustine of Hippo was one such bishop: he spent forty years living with his priests and following what might be called a semimonastic way of life. His community, along with his city, was destroyed by the Vandals in 430. Such was Augustine's reputation that the concept endured, and was adopted by bishops far and wide. But through the hundreds of years that followed, while Europe went through its dark ages, there was no possibility of uniformity in church discipline. Every bishop constructed his own set of rules, and applied them as he saw fit. Most of them, however, did one thing in common: they adopted elements that were strictly monastic, like the daily singing of divine office. For the purists, this blending of two ways of life — that of monk with that of canon — was not altogether comfortable. In the tradition of medieval Christians (except for the Irish), a monk's life was supposed to be one of prayer and penance, aloof from society, whereas a canon's calling was to action within that society. What was more, the monk could well be a layman while the canon, by the very nature of his profession, was a priest. Charlemagne, who seems to have been of a tidy mind, objected to the blending, and in 805 ordered the clergy of the empire to separate into one form of life or the other. In 817, at the council of Aachen, Benedict of Aniane made it even clearer: monks were to live in their monasteries under the Benedictine Rule; canons were to live in their compounds, dress like ordinary clerics, and perform the public duties that their bishops assigned them.

Fatefully, nothing was said at Aachen about personal property. This was to be the Achilles' heel of the canonicate: its members were allowed to be rich. In time, as donations flowed into their churches, many of them became excessively rich. With wealth came decadence. Canons ate well, drank well, dressed well, hunted, carried weapons (and sometimes used them), and often married. What was more, they began to build and live in their own houses. In every way they excused themselves from the basic obligation of community living. Naturally, a life as sweet as this, with prebends guaranteed and workload not too onerous, was a magnet for the more influential members of society. During the centuries when the church was at a low ebb and the canonicate was subordinate in almost every respect to the laity, the canonicate became the preserve of the aristocracy, and the criterion for admission was family influence. The standard to which its members were held was none too high.

In the eleventh century, as desire for religious reform began to permeate the European psyche, a critical eye was turned upon the canons. Their case was discussed in Rome in 1059, and a papal decree was issued urging them to return to "the apostolic life" — life as the first Christians lived it, in common and sharing all things. Easier said than done, though. If the common life meant living as Benedictine monks, many canons wanted no part of it, arguing that the demands of community would clash with their duties to the faithful. Besides, there was no authoritative rule, no great founder, to guide them into this new way of life. The change that Rome mandated received only a grudging assent, until the difficulty was solved by a timely resurrection. Churchmen rediscovered the "Rule" of Saint Augustine, a rule buried for some six centuries.

This rule, so-called, was in fact only the outlines of a rule. It started with a letter that Augustine had written to his sister, a nun, giving her advice on how to run her community, concentrating largely on charity and forbearance and equality among the sisters. The letter was later expanded — perhaps by Augustine, perhaps by someone else — into a rule for men. Compared to the Rule of Saint Benedict, it was short on detail, and this was its great advantage. The very sparseness of the text allowed for adaptation to changing circumstances. Subsequent founders and reformers were able to spin their own rules and customs around it, while still claiming the authority of the great man. With its rediscovery a new form of religious life became possible, monastic yet not wholly monastic in character.

One after another, communities of canons began to adopt the Rule of Saint Augustine: to live in community under obedience to a prior, to wear a distinctive habit, to follow a set routine of religious practices. They came to be known as regular canons, to distinguish them from their fellows who remained secular. However, because the rule was so loosely woven, they were not constrained to a single pattern of life. Some gravitated to a regimen almost indistinguishable from that of the monastery. Others continued their pastoral work around the city churches; still others became scholars, or hospitallers, or mission preachers, or crusaders. In all these roles they expanded mightily, so that by the start of the thirteenth century their houses numbered some two thousand, mostly in Germany and eastern France, Spain and Portugal, and the Holy Land. Much of their success must be attributed to the fact that they gave the religious life a broader, more inclusive meaning. Until then, the ideal of perfection had been tied to the concept of contempt for the world — in other words, to monasticism, as Saint Benedict had patterned it. But as the Rule of Saint Augustine took hold, another kind of perfection was proposed: that of life as Christ had lived it, the "mixed" life in which prayer and contemplation were joined to action and compassion. It is hard for us to imagine this as a novel idea, but novel it was, and in an age that distrusted innovation, it was not easily received. For many years there was a running argument between monks and canons as to whose life was the more perfect. Despite the objections of the traditionalists, the "mixed" life was there to stay. Perhaps its most extraordinary application was that which came into being together with the Crusades.

"Soldiers of Christ"

"In our time God has instituted holy wars, so that the equestrian order and the erring people, who like ancient pagans were commonly engaged in mutual slaughter, might find a new way of meriting salvation. They are no longer obliged, as used to be the case, to leave the world and to choose the monastic life and a religious rule; they can gain God's grace to no mean extent by pursuing their own profession, unconfined and in secular garb."

This revealing comment on the why and wherefore of the Crusades comes from someone who was actually around at the time, Guibert de Nogent. In the last years of the eleventh century the deliverance of Jerusalem from the hands of Muslims may have been in the forefront of men's minds, but the deliverance of Europe from the slaughter of Christians by Christians came in a close second.

Throughout the Middle Ages, Western Christianity had had to reconcile its gospel of nonviolence with the ingrained bellicosity of its people. It had never been easy. For the aristocracy, the bearing of arms was their badge of honor. Not only did they live by it and define themselves by it, but they also had the blessing of that universal custom that anointed them, the *bellatores,* or fighters, as the second of the three "estates" of society. Furthermore, not only prestige but also practicality were at stake. Military service was the glue of feudalism; it was the foremost obligation that the tenant owed his lord, in return for the land and privileges he received from him. It would have been as difficult to tell the knights of old to stop fighting as it would be to tell the capitalists of today to stop lending money at interest.

But if the Church could not stop the fighting altogether, it might at least contain it. In the years immediately before and after the turn of the millennium, the bishops of France made a valiant effort to do just that. In 989, and again in the following year, they urged all men to seek peace. Their appeal struck a chord, and over the following years nobility and clergy discussed various ways to reduce the damage caused by warfare. The practical solution, decided in 1027, was a half-measure: to declare all Sundays, as well as Good Friday, Easter Monday, and Ascension Day, off-limits for fighting. Gradually the truce was extended to cover the winter months, as well as the Church's major feast days. What was more, they agreed that the goods of the Church and of the poor should at all times be protected. The exhortation to seek peace was given teeth when, in 1054, the Church was emboldened to rule that anyone defying the truce of God would be excommunicated, "for he who slays a Christian sheds the blood of Christ."

The scandal continued, however; Christians continued to kill Christians. And in the meantime, thinking Christians were looking at greater dangers, further afield.

Since 711, when the Muslims invaded Spain, a long-term threat to Christendom had been building. At the millennium almost all the Iberian Peninsula was in Muslim hands, with only the Pyrenees standing between them and the rest of Europe. To the northeast, Barcelona had been taken; to the northwest the city of Santiago, a pilgrimage site of major importance, had been attacked and burnt. This affront to a holy place had its consequences. When, in 1014, the king of Navarre appealed to his fellow Christian princes to join him in a counterattack, he got more of a response than he could have hoped for. The order of Cluny, then at the height of its influence, mobilized its political forces and pushed for a holy war. Gradually other powers took up the challenge. Throughout the rest of the century, Christian knights streamed into Spain, and the Muslim tide began to recede.

The example of Spain was on the mind of Urban II, distinguished pope and Cluniac monk, when in 1095 he received an appeal from the Byzantine emperor for military assistance. What was being asked for was the loan of some mercenaries. The Byzantine empire had long frontiers, from the Danube to Armenia, and many enemies and restive subjects, but not sufficient manpower to control them all. This was what bothered the emperor. But to Westerners, what mattered were the Turks in Asia Minor, and their banditry. The road to Jerusalem lay through their territory. Until that time, even though it was under Muslim control, Christian pilgrims had been able to travel to the Holy City. Now their route was barred, or at least dangerous.

In Urban's mind, the emperor's call for western soldiers triggered a much more momentous idea. Why were the holy places in Muslim hands anyway? If Christian knights could do battle for Spain, why could they not do battle for Jerusalem? There were plenty of warriors in Europe. How meritorious it would be for them to kill infidels, rather than other Christians! And with these arguments, at the Council of Clermont in 1095, he launched the First Crusade. His appeal was received rapturously. Within a short time great hordes of people of all descriptions, from noble captains to foot soldiers to beggars and camp followers, began to move eastward. In 1099, in an orgy of death and destruction, Jerusalem was taken and a new Christian kingdom was founded.

The First Crusade was an extraordinary feat of arms. The whole world was shown the ferocity and fighting spirit of the Western peoples. But there was one problem: once the battles had been won, many of the soldiers who won them decided to go home. Within a short time there were barely enough left to hold on to the territory they had taken — or even to protect the pilgrims traveling to Jerusalem.

It was to protect the pilgrims that the Order of the Temple came into existence. It appeared out of nowhere when, sometime around 1118, two knights started patrolling a narrow and particularly dangerous defile on the pilgrim route. After they were joined by a few more men, the king of Jerusalem recognized their service by giving them quarters in his palace, close by the great building that is today the al-Aqsa mosque but was then the Temple of Solomon. From that time on they were known as the Templars.

This, the firstborn of the great military orders, was to have a spectacular rise and a spectacular fall, with less than two hundred years separating the one from the other. Known at first as the Poor Soldiers of the Temple (so poor that their first official seal shows them riding two on a horse), the Templars became an international power, with riches that far exceeded those of any individual prince. Their rise to greatness came after 1128, when during a fund-raising campaign in France they asked for, and received, a religious rule. From that time on they had an official status that everyone recognized. They were canons, but canons of a special kind who, in addition to the three vows of poverty, chastity, and obedience, took a fourth: never to give way in battle, never to ask for mercy. It was a perfect fusion of religious idealism with the military qualities that the century held dear, and to the elite young men of the times, schooled in the art of fighting, it proved irresistible. By 1200 the order boasted 1,500 knights plus innumerable chaplains, sergeants at arms, and common brothers.

The Temple was the greatest but by no means the only military order to appear in the Holy Land. Of the others, the two best known to history are the Order of Saint John of Jerusalem and the Teutonic Order. Both originated in Jerusalem as simple hospital communities whose task was to care for sick pilgrims. Only later did they follow the example of the Templars, to become fighters living under a religious rule.

What the military orders gave to the crusader kingdoms was a solid core of experienced warriors. By its very nature, the feudal fighting force was a sometime thing. Vassals did not expect, nor were they asked by their lords, to stay in the field indefinitely. The campaigns in the east stretched them. If they had families and possessions and interests back home, they needed to get back to them. What was more, even their comings and goings were disruptive. Many of them arrived full of hubris but short of local experience, undisciplined greenhorns who might easily be mown down in their first encounters with the native warriors. All too soon they left again, sometimes abruptly and without regard to the situation on the ground. The military orders, on the other hand, were professionals. They stayed. In battle they were disciplined, strong, and highly motivated. They earned the respect of both Christians and Muslims, as the fiercest of fighters. The great Saladin was said to order the immediate execution of any of them who fell into his hands, "because of the violent hatred which they bore against the Muslims, and because of their bravery." They built great strongholds, and manned them. In battle after battle, they fought to the very end. Their exploits adorned the pages of medieval literature.

But their glory was transitory. More than any other religious order, perhaps, the military orders were linked to an event, or a series of events. Once the Crusades ended, they found themselves severely diminished. This did not happen overnight: even after the surrender of Jerusalem to Saladin in 1187, a century of serious fighting remained. But with the fall of their last stronghold, Acre, in 1291, the Western presence in the Holy Land came to an end — and so did the original raison d'être of the military orders.

In less than twenty years, between 1307 and 1312, the Order of the Temple would be dragged down into a nightmare of torture and judicial murder. There were several reasons for its destruction, but one of them must have been its great wealth and influence. The other two military orders survived, because both found a purpose to continue, even after the Holy Land was lost. The knights of Saint John of Jerusalem were forced to withdraw to the island of Rhodes, from which, after many years, they withdrew again to Malta, and turned that small but strategic island into an armed camp in the Mediterranean. The order became a naval power to be reckoned with. Throughout the sixteenth and seventeenth centuries its corsairs harassed the sea traffic and terrorized the coastal towns of Islam, all in the name of the Catholic faith. But it also continued in its hospitaller vocation, setting up hospitals in Malta and on the European mainland. In this one of its several personae it has survived to this day. The Teutonic Knights withdrew to central Europe and there took up a war against the pagan peoples to the east, across the great swath of territory that stretched from Pomerania northward to Estonia. In the end, and with much brutality, the order established its own state, which it Christianized as much by force as by persuasion, and proceeded to rule with a heavy hand. The Teutonic state lasted until 1525, in which year the grand master, Albrecht von Brandenburg, having converted to Lutheranism, transformed it into a secular state, Prussia, with himself as its hereditary duke.

"The Killer of Moors"

For the rulers of the various countries in Spain, all deeply involved in their own holy wars, the military orders of the Holy Land presented an opportunity too good to miss. As early as 1128, when the Templars were first appealing for help in Europe, certain Spanish sovereigns appealed right back, offering them territory in generous amounts if they would first come and liberate it. By midcentury both Templars and Hospitallers were fighting the Moors.

After a while, however, it became clear to the Spanish rulers that the Templars and Hospitallers did not perfectly serve their purpose. For one thing, the great orders demanded that some of the wealth and manpower they collected in Spain be transferred to the Holy Land. For another, they had a clear mandate, to fight the Muslims. The princes wanted to keep their fighters at home, and under their own direction. And they wanted to have them available, if needed, to fight their own wars against each other. So it was only a matter of time before new military orders were set up, composed exclusively of Spaniards and dedicated to the wars in Spain.

Whatever the rulers had in mind, the first strictly Spanish military order, Calatrava, was not their brainchild. It came into being almost by accident. In 1147 the king of Castile gave Kalaat Rawa, a stronghold newly taken from the Moors, to the Templars. Ten years later, under renewed threat from the Moors, the Templars warned the king that they could not hold the fortress and were going to withdraw. On learning this the abbot of a local Cistercian monastery, Raymond Serrat, supported by a single lay brother, offered to take their place. Inspired by the courage of the two monks, other men joined them, in sufficient numbers and with so much zeal that the Muslims retired. In the breathing space that followed Abbot Raymond brought in monks from his monastery and formed them into a fighting force. Without modifying their monastic life much, he gave them arms and horses and permission to fight. Thus was created the first Cistercian militia. In 1164 the community approached Cîteaux, asking to be incorporated into the order.

There was at first some perturbation in Cistercian ranks over the formation of this unusual body of monks. Much as the order approved of holy war, it had not envisaged fighting it itself. The monks of Calatrava were true fighting men, killers if necessary; this stuck in many Cistercian throats. But the needs of the times spoke louder than words; the battling along the frontiers drowned out all objections. In 1187 Calatrava became a full member of the order of Cîteaux, and each of its castles became a Cistercian monastery. Unlike most other monk-knights, the brothers continued to bear the full weight of their monastic obligations, fasting and abstaining, praying and chanting like their more peaceable fellows — until it was time to go to war. "Wolves at the sound of the trumpets, lambs at the sound of the bells": thus were they described by someone who knew them. And so they continued, until, three centuries later, the reconquest of Spain was complete.

The greatest of Spanish military orders was the Order of Santiago. In 1170 a group of knights joined with a local community of regular canons to create a fighting order, with a rule that drew upon the Augustinian rule, but with one notable difference. The order accepted married men, substituting a vow of conjugal fidelity for the usual vow of chastity, and thus allowing them to keep their wives, an unusual concession that may explain the attraction of the order. Matrimony did not dampen their fighting spirit, however. Under the banner of Saint James *Matamoros* (the killer of Moors), the knights of Santiago plunged into war and took part in all the great campaigns until the fall of Granada in the late fifteenth century.

The appearance of these and several other military orders in twelfth-century Spain was most certainly a response to the "clear and present danger" posed by the Moors. They were there, as were the orders in the Holy Land, because they were needed. But the long war against Islam created another kind of need, and Europeans addressed it in the same way, by creating religious orders expressly to meet that need.

It was the practice after a battle for the victors, whether Christian or Muslim, to send all lowborn captives into slavery. Thus in 1187, after his decisive victory at the Horns of Hattin, Saladin sent the vanquished Christians in several directions: the barons to honorable captivity, the Templars and Hospitallers to death, and the rest to the slave market. This was perhaps the greatest Muslim victory of the wars, but it was by no means the only one. Countless numbers of Christians followed the same route, becoming slaves and living out the rest of their time among infidel peoples.

In 1198 and in 1238, two orders, the Order of the Holy Trinity and the Order of Mercy, were founded specifically for ransoming Christian slaves. Both adopted the Rule of Saint Augustine, modifying it to meet the demands of their vocation by adding a fourth vow: to be ready to offer themselves in place of any captives whose souls appeared to be in mortal danger. Because they were poor to begin with, they had to raise the money through begging, either directly or through the agency of charitable confraternities.

Then, money in hand, they went to prisons in North Africa and Constantinople and bargained for the captives' lives. Their work did not end with the Crusades, because for many years — indeed, for centuries — Barbary pirates continued to scour the Mediterranean and its coastlines, and the Atlantic as far as Iceland, in search of human merchandise. Before their work ended in the nineteenth century, the two orders were responsible for the ransoming of thousands upon thousands of captives. The story is told that in 1830, when French troops captured Algiers, they found two thousand slaves in its prisons, and, among them, an Italian Trinitarian who had chosen to remain with them.

"Spouses of Christ"

The centuries 900 to 1200 were a golden age for Benedictine monasticism. Until close to the end of the period, what intellectual and literary life there was in western Europe was more or less in monastic hands. Monks frequently occupied high positions in the church, as bishops and archbishops, sometimes even as popes. The cooperation of the great abbots was important to kings and princes and to the papacy. Monastic values permeated society. In increasing numbers as the eleventh century gave way to the twelfth, new monasteries appeared. "It was as if the world, shaking itself and throwing off its great age, were clothing itself everywhere in a white mantle of churches," wrote a contemporary not long after the millennium. Many of the churches he saw about him were monasteries. And men, by the thousands, were entering those monasteries.

Where were the women?

As long as there had been monks in the Christian church, there had been nuns. That is to say, as long as men had sought out a life apart from "the world" for the sake of God, women had done so, too. In 280, when Anthony went into the desert, his sister was already living in a community of virgins. Pachomius (286-346) created female as well as male communities. In 385, when Jerome (one of the church's original misogynists) went to the Holy Land to take up a life of asceticism, prayer, and learning, he did so in the company of a pair of distinguished Roman ladies, Paula and Melania. These are only a few examples among many; they point to a broader, though for us shadowy, reality. Wherever there was Christian monasticism there was a female element, slight but persistent. By the mid–fifth century it had appeared in the West. There was certainly a nunnery in France, and possibly others in Ireland and in Spain. From this time on there were always women in Europe leading a monastic life.

Their circumstances changed, however. As long as the Roman Empire lasted and the Church retained command of its structures, most religious activity centered on the diocese. Bishops were the movers and shakers; it was normally under their wing that ecclesiastical institutions were established and maintained. After the barbarian invasions, however, another power overshadowed that of the hierarchy. The Germanic nobility, new to the West and not far removed in time and tradition from tribal chieftains, had different ideas about who should be in charge of church affairs — themselves. Thus began the age of "proprietary churches." Bishopric, parish, or monastery: no matter what its standing in the eyes of God, it had to belong to someone here on earth. And that someone, and after him his descendants, was the arbiter of its purpose and its personnel.

This question of power was to cause a centuries-long struggle for the Church, rising to a crescendo in the Gregorian reforms of the eleventh century. But during the early Middle Ages there was no argument: he who pays the piper calls the tune.

Before the invasions of the fifth and sixth centuries, women's communities had been the work of bishops, usually within their episcopal cities. Afterward, when a certain level of stability was restored, the world was a different place. Society had been tossed about and power redistributed. Since the new nobility regarded bishoprics as their property, they made sure that the incumbents came from their own ranks. So the bishops now wore two hats, so to speak: as church leaders on the one hand, and as members of influential dynasties on the other. They were partnered by the lay members of their clans, strong men and women with ideas of their own. In other words, it was families that founded monasteries, both male and female. In female houses they often had a second motive: fully aware of the dangers of the world around them, they wanted to provide sanctuaries for mothers, daughters, sisters, wives. For five hundred years — from about 500 until after the millennium — the pattern of foundation remained the same: aristocrats taking care of aristocrats. Thus the Saxon king Alfred had a nunnery built at Shaftesbury for his daughter Aethelgifu, who became its first abbess. The dukes of Normandy showered endowments on the nunnery at Montivilliers, while stocking it with their female relatives. In Lorraine, after the bishop, a member of a noble house, established a nunnery at Bouxières, other family members followed with a string of donations, while at the same time placing a number of their womenfolk in the house as nuns. And the list goes on. Inevitably, this aristocratic input affected the nunneries' character. The families continued to control the communities. None but the blue-blooded were invited to apply, because, as a contemporary nun put it, "those who are well-born are unlikely to degenerate." As long as female monasticism was an affair for the highborn, it would be exclusive, and limited. It is estimated that in 1000, when monasteries for men were appearing at a rapid rate, there were only some seventy nunneries in all of England and France.

There is another reason why, at a time that male monasticism was so robust, female monasticism was so limited. The Viking invasions had done great damage to the nunneries of Europe, and they had been slow to recover. Some were destroyed outright, along with the women in them; others passed into the hands of predators, lay or clerical, and lost their monastic character. It was the late eleventh century before the number of houses available to religious women surpassed that of the seventh century.

The slow pace of rebuilding is attributable to the fact that benefactors were always less generous to religious women than to men. This bias may be blamed in part on ambiguity in the female vocation. From very early days, nuns had been seen as "spouses of Christ," whose chief attribute was the purity of their bodies. In the words of Caesarius of Arles, a sixth-century founder, they were "consecrated virgins, souls vowed to God, who await the coming of the Lord with lighted lamps and a tranquil conscience." Throughout the coming centuries this image would not dim. By their own intention, perhaps, but also by the walls and locked doors that surrounded them, chastity was what gave meaning to the life of nuns. And there was always that rider: they needed those protections to keep their bodies pure and their consciences tranquil. It was hardly a heroic vocation. In the heavenly Jerusalem, early medieval nuns were second-class citizens.

So what was their value to the world? Why would those all-important benefactors, whose support could make or break monasteries, give to them rather than to monks? For the reason outlined above, certainly: nunneries provided a decent and virtuous place of retirement for the female relatives of the affluent. But also because nuns were intercessors who prayed for the souls of the living and the dead. The charters of foundation make it plain that this was how they were expected to pay back the generosity of their patrons. Like monks of the same era, nuns prayed hard and long for the souls in purgatory. However, a society that counted on its monastics' prayers was not slow to note that the prayers of priests counted for more than those of mere women, no matter how holy. As more and more monks became priests, capable of interceding for their patrons through the sacrifice of the Mass, benefactions flowed more and more toward their institutions. Through the centuries to come, men's foundations would always be more generously endowed than women's.

At the millennium there were probably fewer than three thousand nuns in the convents of France and England, a tiny fraction of the male monastic population. But commitment to holiness is never measured by institutional capacity alone. Without the benefit of monastic institutions, many women still pursued a quasi-monastic life, either in their own homes or in a more public way, as recluses or anchorites. We know little about these latter; they are mere shadows that flit across the face of history. In the tenth century there was Aethelfleda, a recluse who lived in a small cell next to the church at Glastonbury and counseled the young Dunstan on things spiritual. In the eleventh there was Walburge, who lived in a cell by a church in Verdun until she was called to become abbess of a Benedictine nunnery. Here and there the records speak of women living alone or in groups, usually close to churches or monasteries. But we have to go to the twelfth century for a clear picture of what their life entailed.

Aelred, the abbot of Rievaulx (d. 1145), wrote a letter to his sister on the subject. It is a letter full of warning. "Ah, the recluses of our day!" he sighs (a lamentation with a familiar ring). Too many people think that by enclosing themselves within four walls, they are also enclosing their minds. Instead, their thoughts fly away "in a thousand wanderings" and their tongues wag endlessly to the visitors who happen by their window. "From time to time they slip into more piquant talk, on the looseness of young girls, on the freedom of widows who think that anything goes, on the malice of wives who are capable of deceiving their husbands and slaking their lusts." Or, he adds, they mull over their investments, their sales and purchases of land and flocks, and take pleasure in the accumulation of wealth. "This is not for you, my sister: you ought rather to receive alms yourself, poor among the poor, than seek to obtain the goods of others."

So we learn from the letter that recluses could own property, could communicate with the outside world, could manage business affairs with the help of a servant, could get rich without leaving their cells. It was a life full of pitfalls for those without a solid grounding, and it is no wonder that spiritual advisers, including Saint Bernard, warned people against it. But for a chosen few it was a vocation that worked. A woman known only as Eve traveled from England to France to find a place of solitude in the company of other hermits. After twenty years she moved again, seeking greater solitude. She died "in the odor of sanctity" in 1125. Another woman, Liutbirga, lived as a recluse for thirty years, and her reputation was such that people came from all around to seek her counsel. Christina of Markyate made a vow of virginity at the age of seven; then, at seventeen, she had to resist the sexual advances of her bishop, followed by her parents' determined efforts to force her into an unwanted marriage. She fled and for six years lived away from home, first with an anchoress, then with a hermit. When the hermit died she made her way back to Markyate, to live with a group of women under the protection of the abbot of Saint Albans. In time, with the abbot's help, the group became a Benedictine community.

In Germany, at a place called Disibodenburg in the diocese of Mainz, and during the same early years of the twelfth century, the local Benedictine monks found themselves in a similar situation, with a small cell of female recluses tucked up against the walls of their monastery, dependent on it for both spiritual and material support. To begin with, the community consisted only of Jutta, a young noblewoman with a reputation for holiness, her disciple (her only disciple), an eight-year-old girl called Hildegard, and a servant. But so good was its reputation that it soon drew in other aspirants, and by the time Hildegard was old enough to make her profession as a nun, it had outgrown its cell and become a little Benedictine nunnery, still sheltered, directed, and managed by its big brother.

Jutta died in 1136, and Hildegard took her place at the head of the community. Five years later, Hildegard had an experience that changed her life, a vision of "blinding light" that opened her mind, as though in an instant, to all the truths of the faith. With the vision came a command: "O fragile one, ash of ash and corruption of corruption, say and write what you see and hear." And so this nun, whom we know as Hildegard of Bingen, began to speak and write. Before her long life ended in 1179, she authored several major works on subjects ranging from theology to natural history to medicine, composed seventy songs and a musical play, corresponded with hundreds of advice seekers, and undertook four public preaching tours throughout the region. All this while performing her duties as abbess and making her community into a sizable abbey in a new location, largely separate from Disibodenburg.

It would have been an impressive achievement for anyone; for a woman, it was absolutely astounding. Putting it mildly, the twelfth-century religious environment was hardly favorable to teaching, preaching women. Yet this woman gained the approval of kings and bishops and popes, and even the great Saint Bernard himself. One could start by simply saying that there are exceptions to every rule. It can also be pointed out that canon law would not take on the question of women's place in the church until the 1230s, so there was still some latitude for someone as unusual as Hildegard. She certainly received invaluable support from male members of the church. But most important, from the earliest days of Christianity it had been accepted that women were capable of prophesying. Everything Hildegard said and did she attributed not to learning or human wisdom, but to divine revelation. It was as a visionary that she gained the respect of her world.

Both Christina of Markyate and Hildegard of Bingen began their religious life as recluses and ended it as nuns, and we may assume that their experience was not unusual. During the twelfth century the number of recluses appears to have dropped, probably because women were finding more conventional outlets for their religious fervor. Quite suddenly, women's monasteries began to appear at an unprecedented rate. In England, at the time of William the Conqueror's famous Domesday Survey of 1086, only eight nunneries were large enough to attract the notice of the surveyors. A century later, there were at least a hundred. Northwestern Europe offers the same story: between 1070 and 1170 the number of nunneries quadrupled. Some of these nunneries housed more than a hundred women.

Various forces were at work in their creation. The old mixture of motivations still persisted: people of substance who were also devout looked for a way of gaining merit before God while simultaneously providing for their womenfolk. There was a difference, however: these people of substance now often came from the lesser ranks of the nobility. Fewer houses were established by dukes and counts, more by local lords and knights. As a consequence, their endowment might be more modest. But women joined them anyway. And here is the second novelty: it was often they who initiated the projects. What makes the twelfth century striking is the pressure brought by more and more women for inclusion in the monastic way of life. The surge in women's monasticism, for all that it was encouraged by bishops and priests and a pious laity, came from the grass roots.

The process could be disarmingly straightforward. A cluster of women might follow a hermit until, impressed by their devotion and their perseverance, he worked out a way for them to live together with some degree of security. For this was still an era of disorder and social violence, and it was not safe for women to be alone. Needless to say, he would provide them with a rule, either one already established or one of his own making. Or the women might gather spontaneously in a house close by a monastery, and there adopt a lifestyle that imitated that of the community within. Without necessarily being invited to, they would look for direction and support from the monks. This happened frequently to the Cistercians, and they were not too pleased. But since the women were often relatives — even, sometimes, the wives of men who had decided to become monks — they felt a certain obligation toward them. They accepted them in a loose kind of way, and then stood by as the women's communities increased and prospered. "Virgins came in numbers, widows hastened in, and married women, with their husbands' agreement, abandoned carnal marriage for a spiritual wedding." So wrote a monastic historian. By the late twelfth century some forty-five nunneries in England and France claimed the name "Cistercian," without however being formally affiliated with the order. If the sisters were enthusiastic, the brothers were less so. Without the full discipline of the order constraining them, they feared that these self-styled nuns might stray from the beaten path and bring discredit to the name of Cîteaux. They first tried to discourage women from entering these new convents, but it did not work; the women kept coming anyway. So they took the alternative route: if they could not deter them, they must control them. In 1213 a general chapter ruled that henceforth all nunneries practicing the Cistercian rule must be tightly cloistered; later legislation placed every house under the close supervision of an abbot. It was a heavy price to pay, but the women paid it. From then on they were legally, indisputably, Cistercian nuns.

"In the Name and Profession of Continence You Are One with Us"

So wrote Peter Abelard to the nuns of the Paraclete, the monastery he himself had established, whose abbess, Heloïse, had once been his lover. But was it really true? Were the nuns of the twelfth century really "one" with the monks?

There is little argument among historians: the church of the Middle Ages was never altogether comfortable with women who entered religion. During the years that saw Abelard and Heloïse working through their conflicted lives, it was perhaps more uncomfortable than ever before. The movement that had started a century earlier, which goes under the name of the Gregorian reform, had put clerical celibacy high on the agenda, with the inevitable consequence that women, and the temptation they presented to men, had become a popular target for moralists and preachers. And because so many more women than ever before were becoming nuns, they presented a more visible target. Yet at the same time, there was the uncomfortable fact that women *did* have souls, *could* become holy; and who was the man who had the right to deny them that grace?

The clash of approaches is illustrated to perfection in the story of Prémontré, an order of canons founded by Norbert of Xanten in 1120. Norbert's earlier career followed a familiar pattern. Native of a small town in the Rhineland, endowed with good looks and a pleasing personality, destined for a comfortable career as a canon in the local church, he was nevertheless discontented with his prospects and resisted ordination to the priesthood. Then, while on a journey in 1115 (and in a strange foreshadowing of another event four hundred years later), he was caught in a terrible thunderstorm and thrown off his horse by a nearby lightning strike. In his terror he heard words from the Scriptures: "Turn away from evil and do good." He turned around, literally, and went back to Xanten, where he became a priest and an ardent champion of church reform.

Before long, however, his fervor began to grate on his fellow canons, and Norbert decided to look elsewhere. He sold all his possessions and set off on pilgrimage. By 1119 he was wandering through the countryside and preaching repentance and poverty, and gathering, as he went, a following of men and women. Before long, under the urging of the hierarchy, he settled his people into a monastery at Prémontré in northeastern France. To serve his disciples, he planned for a double community, the men to be canons and the women to be cloistered nuns. Unlike Fontevrault, however, Prémontré was from the start centered on its men. The main purpose of its nuns, apart from prayer, was making, washing, and repairing the clothes of the brothers. It was a subordinate role, to be sure; but there was no shortage of women ready to undertake it, and as Prémontré branched out and founded other communities, it attracted at first more female members than male. But after Norbert died in 1134 there was a course change. The general chapter began moving the sisters away to separate locations. Not many years later, it declared that no more women would be received into the order. After that it was only a matter of time until the women's communities disappeared. The renunciation of Norbert's original purpose was justified in trenchant terms a century later, by a Premonstratensian abbot: "we have decreed with common consent . . . that we should under no conditions receive, to the increase of our perdition, any more sisters, but avoid their reception as if they were poisonous animals."

But an idea had taken hold in women's minds that could not easily be exorcised: that there was nothing in the *vita apostolica* that women of all walks of life — not only the richly endowed — could not achieve, if only it was allowed to them. Out of the transitory experience of Prémontré, it has been argued, something was started that within a few years became a "women's movement": a massive grassroots reaching-out by thousands of women for the monastic life, or something close to it. It took much longer for the Church to work out how to accommodate them.

Other women had happier experiences than the sisters of Prémontré, and other double monasteries had longer, more successful lifetimes. A famous example is the Gilbertines, an English order that flourished for many years. Like quite a few other founders, Gilbert of Sempringham was an inspiring preacher, and his preaching brought him a harvest of female followers. In 1131 he built a small convent for some of them, with lay sisters to do the housework and lay brothers to manage the property. Later he added another component, regular canons, to give the community spiritual direction. Before the end of the century the single house had grown into an order, with ten monasteries holding hundreds of women and men. The Gilbertines had to bear their burden of scandal (the premier scandal of its time, no doubt) in the famous case of the nun of Watton, whose pregnancy led to the castration of her lover by the other nuns, and the miraculous spiriting away of her unborn child by two otherworldly women who appeared to her in a dream. The imputation of sexual misconduct affected the whole order. Gilbert himself had to answer to Rome, and in time the segregation of the nuns from the canons was tightened up. But the double monasteries survived.

Obviously, the nun of Watton with her unfortunate Romeo proves the point: nuns could behave scandalously, even while living within their cloisters. But did they? And how often? The answers are yes, and we don't know. A number of cases appear in the episcopal records, but whether the list was exhaustive or just the tip of the iceberg, we cannot tell. The general consensus, however, both of contemporaries and of later commentators, is that they did so, and prodigiously. Without much evidence to confirm it, the image persisted of convents full of wayward nuns. The image may always have been as much about a prurient wish fulfillment on the part of the critics as about any reality. "Désir de fille est un feu qui dévore / Désir de nonne est cent fois pis encore" (a girl's desire is a devouring fire / a nun's desire is a hundred times worse); so ran a medieval ditty. Through centuries to come, people would take salacious pleasure in tales of sex-starved nuns.

One kind of community gave some credence to the stories. In the Holy Roman Empire, during the unsettled years of the early Middle Ages, some nunneries evolved into houses of "secular canonesses." One of these was the abbey of Remiremont in Lorraine, founded as a double monastery in the early seventh century. In time the monks disappeared and only women remained. Sometime during the following centuries the house fell under the full control of the aristocracy, and the community became a "chapter of noble ladies," with the relaxed mores that went along with such chapters. Just as the secular canons continued to own property and to enjoy a fairly open lifestyle, secular canonesses lived independently within their abbeys, with their own circles of friends, relations, and servants. They were given, as prebends, share of the abbey's considerable income, which they were entitled to use as they wished and on their deaths to direct to whomever, within the community, they chose — usually, of course, family members. In the meantime they enjoyed the good life. "They dress in purple and fine linen, in furs and other rich garments, their heads ringed with dressed hair, enveloped in precious ornaments," wrote a disapproving monastic chronicler. Their performance in choir, according to him, was something to behold, with canonesses on one side, canons on the other, trying to outdo each other in elegant psalmody. They were allowed to visit their families, sometimes for months at a time. Most significantly, they were free to leave the abbey if and when their parents found them a suitable bridegroom.

It is not difficult to make the further logical step: entry into these houses was limited to the rich and powerful. "These secular canonesses . . . wish to receive only the daughters of knights and nobles, because they rate the nobility of sin above the goodness and nobility of behavior," wrote the same chronicler. Even he admitted that some canonesses lived austere and prayerful lives. But his point was a valid one: they did not have to, as long as they were noble enough. In years to come the requirement of blue blood would become an imperative, to the point where every entrant had to provide legal proof, going back for hundreds of years, of the nobility of her ancestors. Six centuries later the rules still applied; Louis XV of France joked that his own escutcheon would not have been aristocratic enough to allow him into Remiremont.

These communities were relatively few in number, and confined to the Holy Roman Empire. What distinguished them from their sisters in other parts of Christendom was the limit placed upon their commitment; they were free, if they and their families so wished, to exchange one life for another. But as far as wealth goes, they were not unique: by the end of the twelfth century many women's monasteries across Europe were sitting on vast holdings. We should remember, though, that many more were poor, and some were struggling to survive.

So what did the religious women of the early Middle Ages have in common with each other? By a large majority, those who succeeded in entering established houses were "gentlewomen" in the ancient sense of the word. They were few in number, compared to their male counterparts. Whereas in the nineteenth century the ratio of religious women to religious men was about ten to one, in the twelfth century it would have been the opposite. Their impact on the official church was accordingly slight, if we can judge by (a) the brevity of attention paid to them in papal and episcopal documents and (b) their poor showing among the church's canonized saints. Exactly what they meant to the ordinary people around them we cannot say, because neither those people nor the nuns themselves left much in the way of records. What is certain is that there were learned women among them, like Heloïse, brilliant visionaries like Hildegard of Bingen, saintly women like Christina of Markyate, and efficient women like the first abbesses of Fontevrault. But of the great masses of them, the hidden souls "who await the coming of the Lord with lighted lamps," we know next to nothing.

Conclusion: "How Do You Ask to See Me in My Brightness, You Who Do Not Know Yourself?"

With the collapse of the Roman Empire, the greater part of Western Christianity was torn from its moorings. Much of its contact with its birthplace was broken off; much of its foundational literature was lost. A whole civilization was more or less submerged by a great wave of barbarism. It was, as one historian has put it, a case of "prehistory bursting into history."

Fortunately for the survival of the Church, the newcomers had no great quarrel with the institutions they had overrun. They were willing to use them, if they only knew how. It did not take long (historically speaking) for them to begin adopting the Christian faith in its most basic forms — they were baptized by tribe, in some instances. But they were certainly not ready for its depths and its complexities. As a result, Christianity in western Europe reverted to infancy, and only with the passage of centuries and the maturing of its people did it rise again toward adolescence and adulthood.

The institution that aided and nourished its growth was monasticism. It occupied a lonely position. For centuries virtually all Europeans, including most of its potentates, were illiterate. Educated churchmen were few and far between; the noble and knightly classes positively despised book learning. Only a small nucleus of men could read; they were, in large part, monks. The body of learning that the monks inherited was only a meager fragment of what had once been, but they guarded it fiercely, transcribed it — and interpreted it. Consequently, for lack of input from other sources, Christian thought and practice as it evolved in the centuries before the millennium bore a heavy monastic imprint. "Contempt for the world" combined with an intense preoccupation with the afterlife led the faithful to see the monasteries as the focus of all that was holy, and the monks as the mediators par excellence between heaven and earth. In an unstable age, when violence and death were always close at hand, such mediation seemed achingly necessary. And it suited a population that in any case had little capability for personal prayer. Hence the "professionalization," if one may call it so, of prayer: the great mobilization of intercessors to plead for the souls of the dead. The liturgy, with its set forms of worship performed by its own cadre of specialists, became the principal channel of communication between Christians and their God. And the rest of the world was content to leave it that way.

But once the millennium had turned (leaving the world still standing), other things began to happen. The level of violence began to subside. The climate improved, and with it, the living conditions of many Europeans. Population increased, cities appeared, trade picked up, a comfortable class of "burghers" began to make themselves felt: people who had more, and wanted more. Their children, and the children of the petty nobility, were learning to read. For all such people, the simplicity — and indeed the flatness — of past religious practice no longer sufficed.

What is more, there was a new consciousness of society's sinfulness — its violence, corruption, sexual immorality, rampant avarice — and a sense that the Church, far from combating the problem, was a part of it. There were two possible ways to respond to this: by establishing a purified form of life, away from all worldly entanglement, or by attacking the evils head-on with preaching and personal example. In increasing numbers, monks and hermits and canons did both things. They received powerful support from a reforming hierarchy; then, in the heat of the battle, they drew in the laity. For the first time in many centuries, the "people of God" became active in his cause.

Perhaps no event in the history of Western Christianity has been as heartily condemned as the Crusades. And indeed, the thought of Christian soldiers wading ankle-deep in blood through the Church of the Holy Sepulcher, crying out "God wills it" as they go, offends our every sensibility. But it has been pointed out that the Crusades were the first of the great devotional movements of the Middle Ages; that they signaled the readiness of ordinary Christians to participate in their Savior's cause as they saw it, and by a means they understood. The willingness to kill or be killed was still part of the ethos of medieval men, and would be for a long time to come. A few monastic thinkers questioned it, but only a few, and Saint Bernard was not among them. With the Crusades, and the development of the military orders, ordinary men were able to gain the great man's approval as "soldiers of Christ."

The First Crusade (1096-1099) heralded the opening of a truly remarkable century, an era of ebullience and creativity that seemed to come out of nowhere and involve every field of human activity. It has been called "the great thaw," and likened to the sort of sudden spring that the snowbound countries of the north know only too well. In art and architecture, in technology, in agriculture, in philosophy and other intellectual fields, Europeans made sudden and significant advances. And nowhere was the thaw more dramatic than in religious thought and practice. Twelfth-century men and women began to exhibit, by their words and their actions, a collective aspiration to holiness that had seldom been evident before. They crowded the pilgrimage routes, they gathered around the preachers, they joined ascetic movements, they built beautiful churches, often with their own hands. And above all, those lettered few who were capable of it began to turn inward, to a more spiritual, more personal relationship with God.

Since time out of mind, monasticism had held a monopoly on holiness. That monopoly was now broken, much to the consternation of the old order. But no one was more responsible for the breaking of it than the monks themselves, if under the term "monks" we may include lay brothers, hermits, canons, religious women, and everyone who went out in search of a holy life. It was their example that eventually infected society, and sent it in new directions. The times ahead were marked by holiness and heresy, soaring mysticism and harsh repression. And always, at the center of things, were "monks."

For centuries, religious practice, like the society responsible for it, had been one-dimensional and monotonous. Certainly nobody can say that about the religious practice of the coming centuries. The Christianity of the Western world was no longer an infant; for better or for worse, it was in the full flush of adolescence.

Suggested Reading for Chapter 1

For an introduction to the monasticism of medieval Europe, there is nothing better than the chapters contributed by Dom David Knowles to the multiauthor, multivolume work *The Christian Centuries* (1964-). He is the author of a number of other books, of which *Christian Monasticism* (1972) is a good overview, while if you want more depth on a narrower subject, *The Monastic Order in England* (1948) is very helpful. Knowles, himself a Benedictine monk, felt a strong empathy with his subjects, an empathy he has shared with his readers. He was also able to tell his readers what worked and what didn't. If you are interested in the way the orders developed, and the way they dealt with their structural problems, read his book *From Pachomius to Ignatius: A Study in the Constitutional History of the Religious Orders* (1966).

Major religious orders also have their own histories, often in large numbers. As a rule, for lack of space, I shall not mention these. But they can easily be found in any academic library, specially if it is Catholic.

For a look into the more distant past, M. Dunn's *Emergence of Monasticism* (2003) is a good start. For the central Middle Ages, read Peter King, *Western Monasticism* (1999), Brenda Bolton, *The Medieval Reformation* (1983), H. Leyser, *Hermits and the New Monasticism* (1984).

The history of religious women in the Middle Ages, once neglected, has now come into its own. There are numerous studies of famous individuals, but perhaps the best place to start is the more general work by Joy McNamara, *Sisters in Arms: Catholic Nuns through Two Millennia* (1996). For a look at female monastic life, see Bruce Venarde, *Women's Monasticism and Medieval Society* (1997), and Penelope Johnson, *Equal in Monastic Profession: Religious Women in Medieval France* (1991).

CHAPTER 2

1200-1500: The Middle Ages

"Thou Art Peter . . ."

In 313, the year the emperor Constantine decreed an end to religious persecution, the Church found itself, for the first time, in a situation fraught with ambiguity. Formerly, no matter how deadly and dangerous the circumstances, its soul had been its own. For Christians the situation had been clear-cut. Caesar was a secular ruler to whom they owed a certain kind of obedience and a certain number of duties, and he had the power to do them great harm; apart from that, between ruler and ruled there stood a sort of spiritual safety barrier. They were dwellers in the house of God; he was an outsider. Now Caesar had stepped inside their sacred precincts. What was more, he was offering the Church a compact: protections and privileges that could make its life immeasurably easier, in return for its acknowledgment of him as guardian of the faith. It was an offer the Church could not refuse, but it meant the end of the previous clarity. From then on, the successor of Saint Peter shared his authority with a king-priest in the Old Testament tradition.

Before many centuries had passed, guardianship had become control. So far as they had the strength, emperors treated the Church as the spiritual wing of the imperium. In reaction to that attitude, but only gradually, the popes began to find their voice, to claim their inheritance. They had one strong argument: their power to bind and to loose, given to them by the Lord himself, and never wholly discounted throughout the length and breadth of the Christian centuries. But by any measure of realpolitik their position was weak. Rome was little more than a petty Italian principality that owed much of what it had to the emperors, and depended on them for its protection.

With Charlemagne (742-814), imperial control reached its apex. Benevolently but firmly, he managed the Church, taking for himself the title of "lord and father, king and priest, governor of all Christians." The breakup of his empire under his sons put an end to such claims, and gave the papacy a chance to reassert itself. In the middle years of the ninth century a strong pope, Nicolas I, proclaimed supremacy over the faithful, both lay and clerical — and managed, for a while, to make it stick. But evil times were at hand, with the irruptions into Europe of the Vikings, the Muslims, and the Magyars. In the turmoil that followed, both empire and papacy more or less fell apart. What eventually emerged was the fragmentation of civil power that we call feudalism, and the regime of the *Eigenkirchentum,* when the Church became property and every ecclesiastical office, from the papacy itself to the lowliest parish church, fell under lay control.

Monasticism began to extricate itself at the beginning of the tenth century, with the foundation of Cluny. It took the papacy longer. For some two hundred years a crowded succession of popes, some good, some mediocre, some frankly awful, battled, in turn, with a new dynasty of emperors, men whose power base was Germany and whose main concern was the consolidation and extension of their own authority, then with the influential families of Rome, and then with each other, for the degraded privilege of wearing the papal crown. Finally, in 1048, with the election of Leo IX, the papacy climbed back into the saddle and began the long journey toward reform.

The first objective of reform was the elimination of clerical vice: the simony, the concubinage, and the general laxity that had come to characterize many churchmen. To get there the Church had first to shake itself free of lay control. As long as powerful members of society "owned" bishoprics and abbacies, and were able and often willing to sell them to the highest bidder, and as long as the papal office itself was for sale, there could be no serious cracking of the whip. Reform would take a long time, given the strength of the vested interests. The papacy struck a blow for its own independence in 1059, decreeing that henceforth papal elections would be the prerogative of the cardinals, and the cardinals alone; neither the emperor nor the princes of Europe nor the Roman mob would be allowed to dictate terms. This was no mean feat, but it was child's play compared to the next step, the liberation of the rest of the hierarchy, wherever in Europe it might be, from lay control. In this Rome faced massive resistance. The principal stakeholder in the status quo was the emperor himself. From time immemorial his fore-bears had chosen the bishops of Germany and invested them with their powers, and he saw no reason to give up the right. The emperor had tradition on his side (unless one can argue that three hundred years of practice do not constitute tradition). He could claim, with justification, that it was the pope who was breaking new ground.

In 1073 the monk Hildebrand, a known reformer, was elected pope, taking the name of Gregory VII. Within a short time he was putting all the weight of his office behind what history knows as the Gregorian reform. Not content with taking action on the usual issues of simony and unchastity, he moved to rearrange the basic order of things. He had a document drawn up claiming broad, even supreme, papal power vis-à-vis the princes of Christendom. According to this document, entitled the *Dictatus Papae,* the pope, by virtue of his office, was above all earthly judges; because his powers were given to him by God, he had the authority to depose emperors and release subjects from their allegiance to unworthy rulers. The words did not remain mere words for long. In 1075 the German king (later emperor) Henry IV had a bishop of his own choosing installed in Milan, exercising what he considered his inalienable right, in spite of the pope's protests. Then, to show Gregory who was master, he summoned an assembly of "his" bishops and declared "the false monk Hildebrand" deposed. The pope promptly excommunicated Henry and deprived him of his kingship. Thus began a power struggle that was to rumble on for more than thirty years. Gregory himself did not last that long. In 1085 he was chased out of his city, and died in exile. But the genie (if one may dare to call it that) was out of the bottle. Church reform was in the air, and it had behind it not only elite public opinion but also a growing body of canon law.

Since we are concerned not with popes but with religious orders, it is enough here to point to the growth of papal power over 150 years, without going into detail. A succession of mostly able popes (many of them canon lawyers) gradually expanded Hildebrand's claim to universal overlordship. The climate was favorable. Across Europe the clerical establishment was struggling with its disarray while, thanks to the thundering of reforming monks and hermits, the laity was becoming ever more critical, more demanding. The emperors, their office much diminished since the days of Charlemagne, were deeply embroiled in their own internal struggles, and the maintenance of their sprawling empire. The princes of Europe, too, were busy with their own agendas, which involved swallowing other people's territory and smacking down rebellious feudatories. There was a vacuum of power at the center. And from 1095, when Urban II went north to Clermont and preached the crusade, Rome could fairly claim to fill that vacuum. The public response to his preaching was as massive as it was unexpected. As never before, Europeans experienced a sense of common purpose. Throughout the twelfth and thirteenth centuries, the papacy was the closest thing then in existence to a pan-European power.

Then it all came crashing down. In 1302 Pope Boniface VIII issued the bull *Unam sanctam,* which claimed universal dominion over every power both spiritual and temporal, and stated that no human could be saved except by submission to the Roman pontiff. It was a logical extension of the pronouncements and actions of previous popes. But Boniface overreached badly, and furthermore, he did so while failing to know his enemy. The papacy's antagonist du jour, King Philip IV of France, was not fazed by excommunication, nor bothered by undue respect for the see of Peter. Within months Boniface was snatched by French forces and carried off into custody. The shock killed him. Not long after, when a more pliant pope had been elected, the papacy itself went into what has been called "the Babylonian captivity." To be fair, Avignon was not Babylon, but it was not the city of Peter either; while the papacy continue to function efficiently enough, its standing as the guardian and arbiter of Christendom was sadly diminished. After sixty years, a further disaster befell it, as it stumbled into the Great Schism.

But this is the story of the fourteenth century. The thirteenth century comes first, and it was, in many respects, a golden age for the church, a time of reform and expansion and profound spiritual growth. And for this, Christians had above all to thank the papacy and its most devoted servants and facilitators, the friars.

"Naked, Following the Naked Christ"

It is a commonplace among great religious teachers that for the spirit to be genuinely free it must shed its attachment to earthly things. To be truly undivided, the heart must have no truck with material possession, whether it be land, or house, or fine clothing, or rich food, or, above all, money. "The love of money is the root of all evil," Saint Paul said. From it sprang pride, and avarice, and envy, and all the debilitating habits of self-indulgence. However, Paul did not condemn money altogether. Rather, as he suggested to the Corinthians, it should be handled in a balanced way, so that "the one who had much did not have too much, and the one who had little did not have too little." This prescription fitted the times in which he lived. The fact is that every generation that has enjoyed the benefits of money has had to face the question of its morality, and every generation has answered in its own way.

Where the people of the twelfth and thirteenth centuries were concerned, it was a matter for considerable angst. For them the possession of money was a relatively new experience. Not so long before, most of their forebears had lived at subsistence level, without much in the way of creature comfort. As long as everybody was poor together — apart from a tiny coterie of nobles and ecclesiastics in their separate world — there was no great virtue in doing without.

But now the old world was being turned upside down. Europe was growing richer. Trade with the Levant and, through it, the huge, mysterious world of Asia was flourishing. Textiles, metals, furs, and leathers traveled eastward; luxury goods and spices came west. The two streams of trade converged in Italy. From its ports and cities merchants moved northward across the Alps to meet with their counterparts and make their deals at great international fairs, such as those held annually in Champagne. Needless to say, their transactions depended on the exchange of money — money that was sometimes lent at interest. And this was another problem. In defiance of countless ecclesiastical fulminations and under the very nose of Rome, a banking industry was being born. For that huge section of society that had, as yet, no experience of commerce, this seemed like a step toward the abyss.

In the face of all this material development the Church could find no clear answer. In the age-old tripartite division of society into those who prayed, those who fought, and those who tilled the earth, commerce had had no place. Yet here, now, were Christians growing wealthy through trade and — yes! — through borrowing and lending. It was an affront to traditional values. "Only with difficulty and in very few cases can a merchant be pleasing to God," said Gratian's decretals, drawn up around 1140. But were such a merchant and others like him not also enriching the Church? One way and another, a good proportion of the Continent's property was passing into the hands of churchmen; while some were scandalized, others were delighted. Saint Bernard scolded the latter, putting these words into the mouths of the poor: "Our livelihood goes to make up your superfluity. Whatever is added to your vanity is stolen from our needs." But the enrichment continued, and the anxiety grew deeper.

Because, of course, not everybody was growing rich. Even as the general standard of living rose, broken men wandered the roads, begged at monastery gates; cripples and lepers clustered around town walls. The men and women of the Middle Ages were generous in their almsgiving. They handed out food and money; they built hostels and leper houses. But it was never enough. The poverty that had once been a simple fact of life now became, for them, an indictment. With wealth came a new kind of guilty conscience: one that dwelt on the rich man of the Bible, thrust down into hell while the beggar who had lain at his door was carried up to heaven. For the more committed among the laity, the matter was taken even further, with wealth itself becoming an offense, and the lack of it a positive virtue. They gathered together under the standard of poverty, giving themselves such names as "the Poor of Lyons," "the Poor of Christ," "the Humiliati." They stripped themselves of their possessions and, thereafter, preached poverty to their neighbors. They caused the clergy considerable unease, which found its justification when some of them veered into outright heresy. Only the perceptiveness of a brilliant pope, Innocent III, saved many of them from alienation and kept them and their idealism within the Church. That, and the living witness of one small, frail, sickly man.

By the thirteenth century a sea change was already under way in the way Westerners lived their religion. Serious restructuring was taking place within the Church. From the days of Gregory VII, the papacy had been criticizing the clergy for its laxity and ignorance; its criticisms had been relayed to the people by a chorus of wandering preachers. For the first time, ordinary Christians began to evaluate their priests and bishops. What was perhaps even more significant was that as the world grew richer and more sophisticated, universities and cathedral schools appeared in ever-greater numbers, and the tiny segment of society that was literate began to expand. It was, above all, this small nucleus of clerics and laymen, and sometimes laywomen, who demanded more out of life, and out of their faith. No longer content to leave praying to the professionals, they looked for their own personal relationship with God. And they found it in a piety of which Christ was the center, not the divine Christ enthroned above the angels, but the human Jesus, who was born of the Virgin Mary, suffered under Pontius Pilate, was crucified, died, and was buried.

This Jesus was poor. He began life in a stable; during his preaching years he had, as he said himself, nowhere to lay his head; he died a death reserved for criminals. His humanity was brought home to Christians in ways they had never experienced before, in preaching, in art, in the statues and wall paintings and stained glass windows of the many churches and cathedrals that were now taking shape. The message was clear: as Jesus had suffered, so must his followers suffer, by adopting a penitential lifestyle and accepting both pain and poverty.

Today, throughout the Western democracies, the supreme desideratum is freedom. We praise it, we idealize it in symbols and words and song, we insist that it is the foundation on which all good things are built. Committed Christians of the early thirteenth century considered poverty in the same light, seeing it as the foundation for the other virtues: humility, simplicity, selflessness, a spirit of brotherhood, and, above all, love of God. What had once been a state to be despised now became, for them, a badge of honor. For this new approach they had, above all, to thank Francis of Assisi.

Francis the *Poverello*

He was born around 1182 in Assisi, a town of some five thousand souls, one of many such towns in central Italy. His father, Pietro Bernardone, was a successful cloth merchant who traveled regularly to the Champagne fairs. When Francesco (Francis) was old enough, he was taken along to learn the tricks of the trade. Unfortunately for Pietro, his son turned out to be a spendthrift, more given to throwing money away than to making it. Having proved a dead loss as a merchant, Francesco turned to soldiering, but with no greater success. On the occasion of his first fight, when Assisi went to war with its neighbor Perugia, he was captured and spent some time in a Perugian prison. After his release came several years of riotous living. "Francis wasted his time miserably, encouraging wickedness until he was nearly twenty-four years old," his biographer Thomas of Celano would later write. But the revels were now giving way to periods of depression and acts of impulsive generosity. It was the latter that caused the final rupture with his father. Pietro discovered that Francis was handing out his goods, right, left, and center. Furious and determined to recoup his losses, he had his son summoned before the city consuls. It was in their presence, in a public square on a cold, wintry day, that Francis renounced the world with a gesture that illustrated his extraordinary personality. He stripped himself naked and laid his clothes and everything that he had at his father's feet. From now on, he said, he had but one Father, and that Father was in heaven.

Francis was twenty-four. He had only twenty years left to live, but they were extraordinary years. His first thought was to become a hermit, and throughout his life he retained an attraction to lonely, peaceful places. But he soon knew that his work was elsewhere. Without any training and without any authorization, he went out into the towns and villages of Italy and began to preach the gospel. When others joined him, he simply asked them to do as he did: to love God first, and then to use the overflow of that love in the service of God's people; to live as much like Christ as possible; to spurn even the touch of money; to avoid all temptations to pride such as honors in the church or the satisfactions of higher learning. In an age that set great store by status and outward appearance, these were severe demands, but they did not discourage others from following him. When he died, the order he had inspired already numbered five thousand men, in Italy, France, Germany, England, Spain, and the Holy Land.

But it soon became apparent that Francis's religious genius, while it appealed to the idealism of the people, was extremely hard to follow in its entirety. Innocent III himself, and other influential men in the church, loved the *Poverello* and everything he stood for, and gave him every encouragement, but they did not believe that his way could work for everyone. They saw the power of his message and his example, but they questioned its practicality. Even many of the friars who followed him argued that, as good as the life was, it needed more direction and more codification on the one hand and a less radical interpretation of the gospel message on the other. Was it reasonable to own nothing but a tunic and a pair of breeches, with a rope for a belt? Was it really necessary to "give no thought to the morrow" if that meant refusing to soak the beans overnight for the next day's meal? What should friars do, sworn as they were to avoid the touch of money, when well-meaning donors thrust money into their hands? Must they renounce all privileges, and all ownership, even that of books? Just because Francis himself never became a priest, and never desired higher learning, did that mean his followers should be neither priests nor scholars? Did they really have to take the lowest place at the church's table, as their title of "Friars Minor" implied?

And so, when friars from across Europe gathered in a general chapter in 1219, and the hierarchy came along to give advice, the adjustments began, the process that within a few years would turn Francis's little brotherhood into a religious order of a more conventional mold. Francis was so grieved that he fled the scene and went off to Egypt to preach to the sultan. In his absence the adjustments multiplied. When he returned it was to a changed environment, one more regulated on the one hand but more internally divided on the other. Alongside his loyalists, the men determined to follow him in everything, there was now a party of pragmatists who looked for some relaxation in the rule, and yet another group, formed of the many high-powered men who had joined the order, who loved the austere life up to a point but were convinced that the future lay in learning, and in the universities.

With his health declining and his mystical spirit expanding, Francis withdrew more and more from the company of men and into the company of God. When he died in 1226, the brothers found the wounds of the cross imprinted on his hands, feet, and side. One of his last acts was to dictate a final testament for those brothers, enjoining them to continue in obedience, prayer, humility — *and poverty,* the radical poverty that he himself had practiced. But this was something that even he could not command. Only four years later the new pope, though an admirer of Francis, issued the bull *Quo elongati,* dispensing the friars from the literal observance of his testament. While the brothers were to be poor personally, they were to be allowed the use of books and other equipment, and their institutions might have the use of property as long as it was held by surrogates. Thus was Francis's ideal gently but effectively undermined.

The good news, for the papacy, was that the Order of Friars Minor was fast becoming a powerful army for the Church at a time when it was badly needed. The thousand Franciscans working in Italy at the time of Francis's death may well have been the reason why Italy did not join southern France in long-term heresy. Similar success followed them wherever they went. Skilled as they were in the art of preaching and greatly respected for a way of life that was still admirably austere, they were able to draw the sting out of the old argument that the Roman Church was fat, corrupt, and out of touch with the gospel of Jesus Christ. Their successes as preachers, confessors, and scholars would be repeated many times over, in different parts of Europe and North Africa and in mission territories as distant as China. The medieval church had to thank them, if not for its survival, at least for the recharging of its energy and the reclaiming of its soul.

But still, the simple life that Francis had given his followers was lost. The poverty he had loved so much that he had called it his mistress, his beautiful "Lady Poverty," was officially declared to be out of reach. The friars who clung to his example were harassed and eventually declared to be heretics. The Order of Friars Minor grew rich in property and privilege; its scholars shone in the universities of Europe; its members became bishops and popes. As if to illustrate the paradox, one of the most magnificent monuments to thirteenth-century Christianity that we have today is the great basilica that was built above the town of Assisi to house the *Poverello's* bones.

Dominic

When western Europe opened up to the east, a process that began in a major way with the First Crusade, it acquired more than new consumer products, new trading patterns, and new disparities in wealth. It acquired new ways of thinking. Among other things, it came to grips, for the first time in centuries, with heresy.

Heresy had been a major preoccupation of the early church, but in recent times cases of unorthodoxy had been few and far between. During the twelfth century there were enough of them to cause concern. But they were rooted in the homegrown problem that so greatly exercised reformers: the inordinate wealth of churchmen and the avarice that went along with it. There was nothing subversive about attacking the sins of the clergy; many monks, hermits, and other people in good standing did that. The difficulty arose when some took the attack one step further, claiming that sacraments dispensed by unworthy priests were valueless, and, by extension, that true religious authority depended less on clerical standing and more on blamelessness of life. The authorities had heard this one before, and the movement received some harsh treatment from their hands. But it was based in solid religious values, and what eventually neutralized it was the advent of the friars.

Much more lethal was the heresy that came in from the east. This was a latter-day version of Manichaeism, an ancient dualist religion that held all creation to be the work of two opposing eternal principles, one of good and of the spirit, the other of evil and of the flesh. According to its believers, the human condition was that of spirit trapped within flesh: the spirit could be saved only by freeing itself from that flesh, through renunciation of everything material. Procreation was to be avoided; death of the body was to be welcomed. The sect was sophisticated in its doctrine and organization, and missionary in its spirit; in spite of the cold severity of its ethical demands, it had great appeal, even among the more affluent, educated classes. By the mid–twelfth century its network of secret cells, each with its own ordained leader, had spread from the Balkans to northern Italy, and thence across the Alps. The name by which its members were known — the Cathari, or "the Pure" — establishes without need for further explanation where its attraction lay. The contemporary Catholic clergy, rich and corrupt, and not yet freed from the shackles of feudal patronage, were no match for its missionaries, who were revered by its adherents as "the perfect." In some regions of Europe their converts came close to outnumbering Catholics.

Their greatest successes were in the Midi, the south of France. Here, by the start of the thirteenth century, orthodox Catholicism was in danger of falling apart altogether. "The priests themselves give in to the contagion. The churches are deserted and fall into ruin": warnings such as these came loud and clear to Rome. Pope Innocent had no doubt that the rot started at the top: "That is where the insolence of the heretics comes from, and the scorn of the lords and people for God and His Church. In this region the prelates are a byword for the laity." It was plain to him that since he could hope for nothing from the local clergy, his only possible course was to send in preachers from elsewhere. He summoned Cistercians to do the job, and they arrived, twelve abbots in all, along with a papal legate and a retinue of servants, surrounded by a pomp and splendor that surely must have made Saint Bernard turn in his grave. But after several years of fruitless effort, they had to admit that their mission was a failure.

It was then, in 1206, that some of them chanced to meet a pair of clerics from Castile, Diego de Azevedo and Dominic de Guzman. The two were canons regular, members of a chapter recently reformed under the Rule of Saint Augustine. Diego, a bishop, had been sent by his king on a diplomatic mission to Denmark and had taken Dominic along as his companion. Traveling through southern France, they were shocked by the situation of the churches there, and they made no bones about what had caused it and how it should be remedied. When the Cistercians asked for their advice, they gave it with brutal frankness. The people would not be converted until the preachers of orthodoxy were ready to go among them with the same humility and austerity as the Cathari "perfect." The Cistercians agreed to try this approach, but only if the Spaniards would join them. Thereupon the party sent away their horses and servants and together set out on foot to preach the gospel across the Midi.

Diego was soon forced to retire. In time the Cistercians, too, went home. But Dominic had found his purpose in life. He was well educated, he was forceful, he was eloquent. He knew how to move the common people; he was capable intellectually of taking on their leaders in debate. And he was a man of deep faith. So he remained in the Midi, alone at first, and later with six or seven companions. Unprotected, barefoot, they walked and preached their way through the hostile countryside.

But before their work had time to bear fruit, they were overtaken by events. In 1208 the papal legate, Pierre de Castelnau, was assassinated by an official of the count of Toulouse. Innocent III, reacting swiftly to this turn of events, called on the king of France to mount a crusade against the heretics. This was red meat to the French barons. Seeing an opportunity to enrich themselves while at the same time gaining papal indulgences, they brought their armies south into Languedoc. Thus began the Albigensian crusade (so-called because the city of Albi was in the heart of Cathari country) and two decades of bloodshed in the name of religion. And in the longer term, a papal policy of repression, which we know as the Inquisition.

In the war itself Dominic had no part. Indeed, the fighting proved an impediment to the work he had undertaken. The future involvement of his followers in the Inquisition is another story, which must wait until later. What comes first is the creation of his order and the reasons behind it.

By 1215 Dominic and his companions had made so good a name for themselves that Fulk, the bishop of Toulouse, invited them to settle in his city and become his official diocesan preachers. This gave Dominic a certain degree of stability, which he used to increase the professionalism of his group by giving them further formation. He found a theologian to instruct them; then he went off with Fulk to Rome, to show the pope his plan for an order dedicated entirely to preaching. Innocent III welcomed the idea, but with one major caveat. The great Lateran Council that he himself had summoned had recently called for an end to the creation of new religious orders. Any future such body must be subject to one of the existing rules, which meant, in essence, a choice between the Benedictine and the Augustinian.

This was no problem for Dominic, because he was already an Augustinian canon, and he knew that the Rule of Saint Augustine was flexible enough to allow for adaptation. After a year in Toulouse spent discussing and planning with the brothers, he returned to Rome with his own version of the rule — a revolutionary one, as it turned out. While paying due respect to Augustine and traditional monasticism, Dominic added a new dimension. The entire life of the projected order was to be built around a single purpose — preaching. Not just the traditional kind of preaching, the sort of call to penance and conversion that even an unlettered preacher could make, but a preaching informed by serious study. The brothers were to be students first, in order that they could be preachers afterward. In a society still deeply ignorant of the Christian faith, they were to raise the general level of understanding. In a region where heresy was rampant, they were to marshal superior knowledge and argument, and prevail. To do this they must have time to study, and if that meant trimming down the traditional monastic activities, or even on occasion giving them up altogether, then so be it. Their primary purpose was not self-perfection within the walls of their community, but the defense and expansion of the faith in the wider world.

In early 1217 the new order was given official recognition. The brothers were awarded the title of "Preachers," a title they carry to this day.

Fulk had got what he wanted: an order capable of dealing with the very real problem of heresy in his diocese. But his contentment was short-lived. Almost at once, Dominic decided to disperse the brothers, some to Paris, some to Madrid and other places. What had been a purely diocesan initiative was suddenly globalized. The bishop, along with other local notables, expressed unhappiness, but to no avail. "Don't contradict me," Dominic told them. "I know perfectly well what I am doing." And he was right. Further moves were not long in coming. Within five years there were communities of Preachers in dozens of cities, from England to Hungary.

In the meantime, another great change had taken place. While he was in Rome, Dominic had met Francis, and had been greatly impressed by the way of life that the Friars Minor had undertaken. In 1220, at the meeting of their first general chapter, the Preachers decided, also, to give up their sources of revenue and become mendicants. And with that, the second great order of friars was born.

It is said that each of the orders borrowed something from the other. The Preachers gave up title to corporate wealth and exchanged their status of canons for that of mendicants. The Minors, over time, adopted elements of the Preachers' organization. Francis, for all his inspirational leadership, had no idea how to manage the hordes of followers who were gathering around him. He gave them an example and a vision, but very little structure. The Franciscans would pay dearly for that in the following centuries, as different understandings of the rule collided with one another. Dominic, on the other hand, was a born organizer, and the constitution he drew up for his order gave clear directions for its future development. Whereas traditional monasticism was built around the autonomous community and the perfecting of those who vowed to live within it, the Order of Preachers was designed, from the beginning, to be a transnational body of men ready to go wherever they were sent, to preach the gospel. The inward-turning ethos of monasticism was exchanged for an ethos of mission. And whereas all monasticism was built on the patriarchal principle, with the abbot as a father to his "sons," Dominic saw his friars as soldiers in an army that depended as much on competency in its leaders as on obedience in its troops. To ensure this, he designed an elective system in which every local chapter elected its own prior, representatives from the priories gathered to elect the officers of the provinces, and representatives from the provinces gathered to elect the master general. Dominic brought a different understanding to the concept of obedience. He believed in obedience to the rule and to superiors, but he wanted those superiors to be the very best possible, to bring the very best talents to the task in hand: the full reestablishment of the faith. Some historians have remarked on an incipient democracy at work here. But efficiency, rather than democracy, seems to have been the underlying principle.

*   *   *

How perfectly the new orders of friars fitted into their times! Three centuries before, when the world had lain enmeshed in a feudalism that was at the same time violent and static, it was Cluny that provided a responsive form of religious life. The demons against which the human race had then to contend were supernatural ones, and Cluny offered relief in the form of prayer and intercession. Now the world was on the move, and while the old demons still roamed free, there were also new evils: social disharmony and doctrinal deviance. Traditional monasticism had no capacity to deal with these problems. But the friars had. They moved easily into the new world, because they were a part of it. Drawn largely from the urban middle classes, they were comfortable with city living. It provided them with the support they needed, and it offered them a perfect venue for their work of conversion. Where else, as an early Dominican general observed, was so much sinfulness to be found in so compressed a space? (And we can add, where else was so much support to be had, both in money and in talent?) Before many years had passed, there would hardly be a European town of any size that did not have at least one convent of friars.

Inevitably, as their numbers increased, the two orders began to compete with each other. The Franciscans always held the numerical lead, but this may have been because the Dominicans were more cautious with their foundations. Every new Dominican community had to number at least twelve friars, one of whom was a trained lecturer in theology. Every man entering the order had to undertake intensive study as a necessary means to the end, which was the salvation of souls. The study was graduated: following a carefully thought-out program, students who showed unusual promise were moved on from their priories to provincial houses where they could receive higher instruction; from there exceptional students could step up again, to even more rarefied institutions of learning. And this brings us to an outstanding characteristic of early Dominican develop-

64

ment: its focus on university communities and on the intellectual elites who inhabited them.

When the first Dominicans arrived in England in 1221, they were welcomed both in Canterbury and in London. But they pushed straight on to Oxford. This was their modus operandi: to target the centers of learning, and start recruiting there as soon as possible. "The Lord has given us hopes of a good catch," Jordan of Saxony, the Preachers' second master general, wrote home. Before long they made that catch: a regent in theology, who entered the order and brought with him a following of students. Jordan reported even greater success in Paris: "In the space of four weeks, I have received twenty-one novices, six of them masters of arts, the others bachelors, well instructed, suitable for their mission." It was the same story elsewhere, in Bologna, in Montpellier, in Cologne, and in other academic communities now forming up. Wherever the friars went, they creamed off many of the elites, both professors and students. As can be imagined, the universities' secular faculties were not much pleased, and the future was heavy with confrontation. Still, the friars' triumphal march continued, and before long they were a dominant force in the schools.

It must be said that in this invasion of the centers of higher learning, the Minors were as much in evidence as the Preachers. The intellectual history of the thirteenth century is thick with the names of distinguished Franciscan scholars. But the difference is that for them it was a long step away from the wishes of Saint Francis — "O Paris, thou hast destroyed Assisi!" one brother lamented — whereas for the Dominicans it was the fulfillment of the founder's design. He had aimed for an elite force of preachers to lift Christianity out of the massive ignorance into which it had fallen, and even before his death in 1221, that force was in place.

In fact, Dominic built better than he knew. Despite the originality of his organization, his own objectives were conventional: his men were to take on the dual threats of ignorance among the common people and heresy among "the pure," and they were to do this through the power of superior knowledge and more effective preaching. There was nothing new in this. But even as he was building his order, another crisis was threatening the orthodoxy of the Church. It formed in the universities, or more accurately, in the groups of scholars that were at this very time, in several European cities, coalescing into universities. For some decades ancient works of philosophy and science, lost to the Western world with the breakdown of Roman civilization, had been entering the Continent again through Spain and Sicily. With them came works of Arabic learning in medicine and mathematics.

The impact they made on the laggardly, hidebound scholarship of Europe cannot be overstated. They were welcomed enthusiastically by the universities, and treated with alarm by the local hierarchies. Because buried within the wonderful fund of knowledge were concepts that were frankly pagan, and therefore deemed irreconcilable with Christian doctrine.

Foremost among these were the works of Aristotle, translated into Latin along with their Arabic commentaries. Certain of them seemed to contradict Christian teaching on the nature and immortality of the soul. The official church's first reaction was to condemn the works, and to forbid any further public lectures on them. But the lectures went on anyway, proving that Aristotle could not be ignored. The academic community had four choices: to embrace him at the expense of received teaching, to reject him out of hand, to let him stand alongside orthodox teaching in a sort of "doublethink," or to work out some sort of a synthesis between Christian doctrine and Greek philosophy. Under the leadership of the Dominicans they chose the last. It was a herculean struggle but a necessary one, if Western Christian learning was to be given room to grow and mature.

The great protagonist in this struggle, Thomas Aquinas, was born in 1224/1225, the youngest of eleven children of an Italian knight. While still a boy he was placed in the monastery of Monte Cassino, but at the age of twenty he threw his lot in with the Dominicans. With them he found scope for his brilliant intellect. By 1256 he was a regent master of theology in Paris, and shortly afterward he began writing the first of his many great works of theology. By 1269 he was deep in the controversy over Aristotle.

Aquinas believed with all his heart and all his intellect that reason and faith could not conflict. In some way or another, the thinking of Aristotle must be reconciled with the biblical truths. He undertook a series of commentaries to make his case. When he died in 1274, the project was still incomplete and fierce controversies were still to come, but finally, as the century drew to an end, he was accorded a posthumous triumph. His work became his order's official teaching, and he himself would one day be awarded the title of "Doctor of the Church." And if his name was made great for Christian generations to come, so was another's. Aristotle was, in a manner of speaking, received into the church and baptized into orthodoxy. As it has been said, "his conversion was largely the work of the friars."

Dominic could have foreseen none of this. The burning question of what to do with Aristotle does not seem to have impacted on his particular world of action. But it was he who envisaged, and built, the framework that enabled intelligent men to underpin their faith with learning, and take that learning to higher levels. This was what brought his order to prominence. Whereas, sooner or later, most secular scholars left the universities to become church functionaries or the servants of princes, the friars were free to pursue their studies forever, or at least as long as their superiors allowed them. Learning, especially in the realm of theology, became their profession. Once their reputation was established, they were more and more called upon to solve serious matters of faith and discipline. For the simple reason that its members were so well prepared, the Order of Preachers came to be regarded as an authority in questions of doctrine, and the guardian of orthodoxy in the Catholic Church. And, for better or for worse, the papacy's strong right arm.

Domini Canes — the Hounds of the Lord

The new orders owed their meteoric rise to the power of their message, and to the enthusiasm with which Western society received that message. Another positive force must be counted in: the patronage of the papacy. From the earliest days, popes had seen the value of these newcomers and adopted them as favored sons. And the friars had recognized the benefits of papal protection. As a result, an understanding developed: the popes would shield and empower the friars, and the friars would put themselves at the service of the papacy.

It was a forceful alliance, and it came at just the right time. Ever since major church reforms had begun in the eleventh century, the influence of the papacy had been on the rise. Gradually, the local hierarchies were losing ground to Rome, and gradually, together with reforming the Church, Rome was expanding and centralizing its power base.

But expansion and centralization depend on manpower. If the papacy was to succeed in all its additional endeavors, it needed workers, and capable ones at that. It found them, in large numbers, among the friars. They served as specialists in the Vatican's judicial system; they were sent out on diplomatic missions, or to preach crusades; they raised money for Rome; and they helped to staff the Inquisition.

The Inquisition had come late upon the scene. The heretics of earlier centuries, few in number and not very influential, had been more or less sloughed off as a problem for the bishops to solve. They were seldom punished severely. In fact, those executions that did take place were often the work of mobs, who hated all things "foreign" and were not averse to a good lynching. But as the heretic presence grew, the authorities took note, and a process of ecclesiastical inquiry was established. The process remained in the hands of the bishops, but because killing was forbidden to clerics, responsibility for punishing the guilty was transferred to the lay rulers. These rulers had their own reasons for suppressing heresy, which they looked on as a form of treason. By the 1220s they had agreed, with the pope's assent, that the punishment for heretics should be burning at the stake.

One further step was to be taken. Given the seriousness of the Cathari menace, and the notorious incapacity of the local clergy to deal with it, it seemed necessary for Rome to assume overall management. So, in 1233, with the cooperation of some of the strongest rulers of Europe, Pope Gregory IX placed the Inquisition on an international footing. It immediately set to work; the prosecutions began. To ensure convictions the safeguards used by previous courts were set aside: torture was introduced as a way of extracting confessions, defendants were made subject to incrimination by anonymous informers whose allegations they were not permitted to see. Those found guilty were "relaxed to the secular arm" — that is, handed over to the secular authorities, who were more than happy to apply the death penalty. It was a tragic slippage in the progress of humanity. The Middle Ages were rough and often brutal times, but never before had there been an equivalent institutionalization of cruelty.

For all that, the Inquisition was not a kangaroo court. Its procedures were carefully laid out, beginning with an offer of mercy for those who chose to recant, then going on to the searching out and recording of evidence, and examining for heretical opinions. For such work, of course, experts were needed. And this was where the friars, and especially the Dominicans, came in. Because their professional abilities connected perfectly with the papacy's need, they would soon become the indispensable agents of the tribunal. Sadly, some of them would be famous for their ferocious zeal. The order's involvement with the Inquisition would continue for centuries, in spite of the public animosity it aroused.

"The Whole World Is Their Cell and the Ocean Is Their Cloister" (Matthew Paris)

The friars shone in other areas of papal service as well. They were used, and used extensively, as special envoys and as diplomats. It is easy to see why: they were well trained, they were mobile, and they were totally committed to the papal cause. So they were sent out in increasing numbers, as Rome's official messengers and exhorters, to a world in which the papacy was playing an ever more prominent part. Whenever a pope decided to launch a crusade (which in the later Middle Ages was often), it was the friars who spread out across the Continent, firing up men's sensibilities and taking their money for the cause.

There is nothing surprising about this. Preaching was their métier, what they were trained to do, and the crusades were, in their eyes, a means of furthering God's work. But another task fell to them that truly tested their versatility, and in which they certainly proved their mettle. This was the work they undertook as the pope's ambassadors, not only to the powers in the known world but also to a completely strange and terrifying people, the Mongols.

In 1200 continental Europe had been free of foreign invaders for over two hundred years. To be sure, it faced Islam to the east and the south, and much of Spain was still in Muslim hands. But "Christendom," from the Atlantic to the Danube and from Scandinavia to Sicily, was solid and reasonably secure within its boundaries. Its troubles were internal, and of its own making. Most of them involved the taking, losing, and retaking of one another's territory. And in this activity Rome, as a small principality threatened both to the north and to the south by its neighbor the Holy Roman Empire, was frequently involved.

In 1241 the papacy was, and not for the first time, in a deadlock with the emperor. The pope had excommunicated the emperor, and the emperor was forcibly preventing the papal envoys carrying the bull of excommunication from entering his domains. And then, in the words of a contemporary chronicler, "Behold, the Almighty sent messengers, but with a quite different message." In early January armed horsemen from the east burst into Hungary, driving all before them. They broke through the puny defenses that the Hungarians put up, and spent the rest of that year and the next rampaging through the Balkans, as far west as the Dalmatian coast. Nothing, it seemed, could stop them, if they so wished, from getting to Vienna.

Fugitives from Hungary, among them the Dominicans who were already active there, brought the news to Rome and pleaded with the pope to launch a crusade. He did so; the powers of the empire mobilized, though without great enthusiasm. So slow were they to respond that before they got there in force, the Mongols had retreated, leaving a shattered landscape behind them. There was nothing for the German nobility to do but spend the money collected for the crusade on other priorities, which they did without much persuading. And that is where things stood in late 1242. Europe still had no idea who these people were, or whence, or why, they had come. In fact, the Mongols retreated for reasons of their own, which had nothing to do with European military power. A political upheaval taking place behind their backs may have turned them around; or perhaps they were discouraged by the shortage of grassland for their horses; or perhaps they had never had any intention of going farther, anyway. But what was clear to everyone in the West was that they might return, and that if that happened little stood in their way.

In those days an impenetrable wall of ignorance stood between West and East. Beyond the great stretches of wilderness to the north, and a hostile Islam to the south, lay a vast region about which Europeans knew absolutely nothing. For lack of real knowledge, they had peopled it with fabulous beings: dog-headed humans; people without heads whose eyes were in their shoulders; fearsome Amazons; and also, more hopefully, lost races of Christians, ruled by the mythical king Prester John. Now for the first time, from refugees fleeing westward, they began to absorb some vague idea of what was really there. One piece of information they received was that the Mongols were known to receive embassies favorably, and not mistreat them. Upon hearing this, the pope decided to act.

In 1245 he sent out three separate embassies, all made up of friars. The most successful of these was headed by a Franciscan, John of Plano Carpini. After spending the winter of 1245-1246 in Poland, Carpini and a companion set out toward the east, "not knowing whether they were going to death or life." In fact, three thousand miles later they found themselves in Karakoram in Outer Mongolia, just in time to witness the enthronement of the Great Khan Guyuk. When they returned to the West in 1247, they brought with them an idea of the extent of the Mongol empire, and of the number of subject peoples within it. They also had some news that would continue to preoccupy them, and other churchmen, in the years to come: there were already Christians in Asia, both indigenous people and slaves brought in from the West.

For all of Carpini's valiant effort, the embassy did not serve much immediate purpose. The pope's message, that the Mongols should embrace Christianity and be saved, was met with a counterdemand from the khan, that the pope, at the head of the other Western powers, must submit to him or expect the worst: "You in person, at the head of the kinglets, should in a body, with one accord, come and do obeisance to us. This is what we make known to you. If you act contrary to it, what do we know? God knows." For the Mongols, their huge conquests both east and west were proof enough that God intended them to rule the whole world, and they had every intention of doing so. It was an ominous message. It cannot have been much consolation to the pope that, in the eyes of the Great Khan at least, he was the supreme ruler of Christendom.

If Carpini failed as a diplomat, as an information gatherer he was highly successful. The published account of his travels was widely read, and he himself, once home again, went on a sort of lecture tour. Knowledgeable people in the West now had some idea of the Asiatic world beyond the horizon. But it was still a very slight idea. The Christian element continued to haunt them. It led to speculation: Since the leaders of the Mongols were not Moslems, could they possibly be open to Christianity? Successive diplomatic missions brought back hopeful hints, suggestions that this leader or that queen was favorable to Christians or willing to be baptized. And always, there was the knowledge that somewhere in those vast expanses there were souls, baptized souls, who must live deprived of the sacraments and of the hope of salvation.

In 1253 another team of Franciscans went out on a mission to the ruler of the Golden Horde. But this time they went as missionaries rather than as diplomats. It was a role more familiar to them, and more in keeping with their calling. The territory into which they traveled was hardly congenial. From the early 1250s the Mongols had been on the move again. They poured southward toward Asia Minor, much to the alarm of both the Franks in Syria and Palestine and the Moslems with whom the Franks were fighting. Then, in 1259, the Mongols invaded Poland, devastated Lithuania, and attacked Prussia. The forces of the West, led by the Teutonic Knights, were badly mauled. Again, there was no knowing how far the Mongols would go: the king of France himself, Louis IX, received a summons from them to come in person to pay homage to the Great Khan. As before, it was only a change in the invaders' own priorities that saved Europe from more extensive damage.

It could not have been an easy time for the missionaries. Nevertheless, through the following years the Franciscans and their Dominican confreres pushed their way into western Asia until, by the 1280s, they had houses scattered far and wide through a region that stretched from the steppes north of the Black and Caspian Seas down into Persia and modern-day Iraq. By the 1320s their network extended all the way to China. But in the final analysis their success as missionaries was slight, and across the Mongol world they were overtaken by Islam and Buddhism. They disappeared almost without trace, and sadly, their effort never received the respect it deserved.

The greatest unsung hero among medieval Christian missionaries was the Franciscan John of Montecorvino (1247-1328). In 1291, already middle-aged, and already living far from his native land, he left his convent in Tabriz in northwest Persia and, with another friar and a merchant to keep him company, struck out for the Far East. Two years later he and the merchant arrived in Khanbaligh (Beijing), the other friar having died on the way. There, with the indulgence of the emperor, he began a mission. In the three decades and more remaining to him, he built several churches and baptized thousands of converts, a number that, according to his letters home, would have been far greater had he had more help. And yet, back in Italy, the Franciscan order and the papacy remained unresponsive to his pleas until finally, in 1308, a small delegation set out with special powers to consecrate him bishop of Khanbaligh. In time other friars followed. For several decades the Christian church seemed to make headway in China; then, as swiftly as it had built up, it disappeared. By the late fourteenth century it had been eradicated so completely that for centuries no memory of it remained. Only a few inscriptions in stone, recently discovered, survived to mark its passing.

"They Have Put Their Sickle into Another Man's Harvest"

To return, now, to Europe: no matter how much the friars owed to their connections, the fact was that they were "made" not by the favor of influential men but by the extraordinarily fervent response they received from the people. If the popes took the risk to sponsor these new and unconventional orders in the first place, it was only because they saw that they were able to draw Christians back to the Church. It was something of a gamble, and it paid off. Within a few decades, towns and cities that had rarely heard a sermon, let alone a sermon of any substance, were invaded by scores of trained preachers. And they were more than preachers; they were examples. They lived simply, in unpretentious housing, and in contrast with the prelates and monks who were accustomed to ride when they traveled about, they went on foot — barefoot. They drew people to confession, in numbers not known before. Following the pattern set by Francis, they put great effort into reconciling feuding families, an especially valuable service in the burgeoning cities of Italy, the stomping grounds of innumerable Montagues and Capulets. They cared for the poor and attended the sick. They were everywhere. The impact they made can be judged from the crowds they drew to their sermons and their confessionals, and the donations and recruits that came flooding in.

But therein lay a problem. For neither the first time nor the last, Christian society faced the disruption that came when a new and superior force burst in upon an established way of doing things. The diocesan system was creaky and in need of serious repair, but it was *there,* and had been there for a long time. What was more, it could claim direct descent from the apostles. These new men were intruders into the sheepfold, all the more dangerous because they were so good at stealing the sheep. The parish clergy were unhappily aware of the implications for themselves. After all, who lost out when donors decamped to the friars? Who pocketed the funeral fees when devout Christians demanded burial in mendicant graveyards? And when crowds flocked to hear the friars preach, who was left to fill (and support) the parish churches?

The friars could (and indeed did) answer that they succeeded only because the diocesan clergy was so inadequate. And Rome backed them up. "If you lived as they live," said Gregory X to the seculars, "and studied as they study, you would have the same success." For too long, parish priests had been appointed with little regard to training or moral worthiness, and they had fulfilled those low expectations to perfection. They had no right to complain if others came in to do what they had failed to do. Nor should they be allowed to impede the work of the Lord. In this matter the friars were dealing from strength. If, as happened more and more often, they were denied the use of the parish churches, well, then, they would build their own churches. One by one, as the thirteenth century went on, the mendicants' churches began to rise, some purposely larger and higher than every building nearby, some sporting magnificent domes and interiors decorated with beautiful frescoes, everything paid for by a devoted laity. And everything, in a sense, a watering down of the founders' original message. No longer did the friars intend to be "the least of men."

The bishops had their own problem with the mendicants, that of authority. In the early days they had welcomed them, and it is easy to see why: the friars were superior, both in training and in motivation, to run-of-the-mill diocesan priests. They were also few in number at that time, and poor, and happy to take direction. But what was perhaps not apparent at first was the orders' fecundity, the favor they enjoyed with the papacy, and the way they were ready to use that favor. By rights any preacher entering a diocese had to have the authority of the bishop before he could preach and hear confessions. From 1231 onward, however, successive popes began eroding that authority, now granting the friars freedom from episcopal control, now modifying that freedom, now granting it again. Taken to extremes, the privileges that the papacy offered would have meant that the mendicants could enter dioceses at will and set up their own parallel pastoral systems. The bishops, quite reasonably, saw it as a stealth attack on their jurisdictions. The problem grew as the friars multiplied. In addition to the two great orders, which continued to increase by leaps and bounds, there were now lesser orders: Carmelites, Augustinian friars, Crutched friars, friars of the Sack, and others too numerous to recall, all wearing out their welcome with their oratory and their activism.

By 1246 there were enough angry bishops to start talking about a possible solution: the abolition of *all* mendicant orders. The idea came to nothing then, but in 1274 it surfaced again. At a church council in Lyons, a proposal was made to close the friars down. It was an outrageously radical suggestion and had no chance of success, given that there were by now too many Franciscan and Dominican prelates in the ecclesiastical power structure to let it see the light of day. So a compromise was struck. The two great orders were exempted from the decree, by reason of their manifest usefulness to the Church. The Carmelites and the Augustinians were given a lease on life that later turned out to be permanent. The smaller orders of friars went to the wall.

But the sniping went on, and the shifting policies of successive popes kept the bishops on edge. Finally, in 1300, another papal bull, *Super cathedram,* laid the quarrel to rest — more or less. From now on the mendicant orders had the right to run their own churches and to assist elsewhere when invited, while the bishops retained their powers of surveillance over their dioceses. On the surface the bull looked like a draw, but in fact it marked the triumph of the friars. They were now recognized as an accredited arm of the Church. No longer were they beggars and vagrants, living from hand to mouth while preaching the love of God. They were dwellers in large convents, managers of fine churches, acknowledged leaders in academia, still spending their days in the Lord's service and still observing a worthy austerity, but returning at night to the sort of security that Francis had so emphatically rejected. The mendicants who entered the fourteenth century were, in many ways, a far cry from their predecessors.

"Great Is Poverty, Greater Is Chastity, but the Greatest Good of All Is Obedience"

This reproach, delivered in 1317 by Pope John XXII, was directed at all those Franciscans who clung to their founder's way of life and questioned the path that the order had since taken. To make his point, he condemned as heretics four friars whose disobedience was made plain by their stubborn adherence, in defiance of his explicit instructions, to the primitive principle of poverty, and burned them at the stake.

Within the order of Saint Francis there had been, from the earliest days and continuously thereafter, men who bitterly opposed what they saw as the drift away from the founder's ideals. As the order grew richer, more learned, and more influential, the dissent of these naysayers became more disruptive and, in the minds of the majority of friars, more scandalous. It was a quarrel without end: what one side saw as a reasonable and beneficial evolution, the other saw as a betrayal of the founder. Bonaventure, minister general from 1257 to 1274, one of the greatest saints of the order and one of its greatest minds, worked hard to find a common ground, but his work did not long survive him. The gulf was simply too deep.

The question was: What is meant by poverty?

For Francis it had meant making a positive out of what the majority in the world considered a negative — an existence without possessions, or comfort, or ambition — and endowing it with a mystical beauty that few but him could see. He had desired to share it with his disciples, but only a handful had been able to embrace it in its entirety. Not that anyone rejected it altogether: poverty was the foundation stone of the order, it was what made it shine like a city on a hill. But, many argued, it must be an ordered poverty that did not obstruct their principal purpose, the saving of souls. How could they study and teach without books? How could they preach without churches? How could they take their proper place in urban society if they wore rags and lived in hovels? The papacy concurred wholeheartedly. In 1230 Pope Gregory IX offered a solution. "Use," he pointed out, was different from "ownership." The friars could *use* material things without *owning* them, just as servants used, but did not own, their masters' property. Other bodies could assume the ownership of the Franciscans' churches, convents, schools, and libraries. The friars would then be allowed to use them, but only sparingly, as befitted poor men.

This ruling was the bone of future contention. For who was to decide what was meant by "sparing"? Before long the friars' woolen habits became less coarse, less scratchy, and a little more becoming; their food became more attractive and varied, their living quarters more commodious. They no longer worked with their hands but, instead, employed servants in their kitchens and gardens. Whereas most of the first friars had been laymen, the majority were now priests, leaving the rest to be lay brothers, creatures of a lower order. Inevitably, the "least of men" took on many of the characteristics of monks.

Bonaventure had no quarrel with modifications in the practice of poverty, as long as the *vita apostolica* was upheld as the order's central purpose. He rebuked the brothers for their excesses and their outright infractions of the rule, and he reminded them that as Franciscans they should embrace the founder's "smallness" and "lowliness." But what really mattered, he insisted, was that nothing should get in the way of their teaching and preaching vocation. During his thirteen years as minister general he set the Friars Minor onto a clear path toward greater stability and security and, one may argue, a more conventional kind of respectability within the society they were vowed to serve. For years to come, however, the primitive ideal of poverty flickered on in the "Spirituals," small groups of men who continued to argue that the order had gone most dreadfully wrong. They were harried from pillar to post by the order, shut out of its convents, and even imprisoned. And always the charge against them was that of prideful disobedience. What right had they to go against the will of their superiors? What right had they to set themselves up as judges over their brothers? What right had they to make a mockery of fraternal unity? The old question reverberated: Which was more pleasing to the Lord, obedience or sacrifice?

As the thirteenth century wore on, dissension in the order grew deeper. Rome's attitude toward the controversy wavered, as one pope succeeded another. But on the whole, the papacy favored the majority, the men of moderation. How could it not do so? The Order of Friars Minor as now constituted was one of the strongest, most persuasive forces for good that the Church had at its disposal, and its internal health was important for the health of Christianity.

In 1317 matters came to a head. The papacy was now in Avignon, and after two years of uncertainty a new pope had been elected, John XXII, a canon lawyer and able administrator, but a man without much theological training. He called a number of the friars together, consulted with them, and very swiftly came to the conclusion that the Spirituals must be brought into line with the rest of the order. It was because they defied his ruling that the four men were burned to death. But the brush fire that flamed up among the Franciscans took longer to die out. In 1321 a new controversy arose, again around the question of poverty. The friars had always maintained that Christ and his apostles had lived in perfect poverty. Even though they themselves might be falling short, that conviction lay at the heart of their vocation. But now a lively debate developed, with any number of learned men offering their opinions for and against. Was the Lord really as poor as Francis and his followers believed? The Gospels themselves are not too clear. But the pope came down against. In 1323 he published a bull declaring that it was heretical to deny the Savior and his apostles the ownership of property; any friar who continued to do so was liable to arrest. From that time on relations between the papacy and the Franciscans became ever more tense, and in fact did not improve until after the death of John in 1334 and that of his successor in 1342. Through all those years the order had to struggle to survive. And the Spirituals were still there on the fringes, a constant thorn in its side.

The Franciscans were not the only people to feel miserable. The population in general was beginning to suffer stress. The golden years of the thirteenth century had allowed it to increase to levels that, it was now proving, were unsustainable. Europe, somebody said, was "as full as an egg." The evidence is there in the land records, which tell us that more of the Continent's surface was under the plow than ever before. This means that the forests on which peasants depended for firewood and for food for their pigs were being cut down; that grazing lands, the animals that lived upon them, and the manure that the animals produced were sacrificed to the more basic need for cereals; and that marginal lands had been brought into cultivation by a people doomed to live forever on the edge. The fertility of those people during the recent good years was part of the problem: to provide for sons and daughters, peasant holdings had been divided and subdivided until they could no longer support the families that grew up on them. The cities were full and overflowing with the surplus. And then, with the early years of the fourteenth century, signs appeared of demographic contraction. Something was not right. Just how wrong it was about to be, no one could possibly have imagined. No one except, possibly, a prophet with the perspective of a Malthus.

A prime culprit was the weather. A new long-term cycle was beginning, of cooler, wetter seasons that prevented seed from germinating and grain from maturing. For a world that depended on cereals and had almost no fallback capability, one crop failure was a disaster; two or three in a row were Armageddon. And this is exactly what happened. In the years 1315,

1316, and 1317 the rain came down in floods, the harvests failed, the price of grain soared, and people starved. Upwards of 15 percent of the population disappeared.

But what did this deepening distress have to do with the difficulties of the Franciscans, which were all about doctrine and discipline? Or were they? Only by remembering how close, physically, the first friars were to the common people, how inextricably their fortunes were intertwined, can we imagine the many ways that these later friars' morale was undermined by the evil times around them.

They must have known that they no longer enjoyed the people's unalloyed admiration. The distance that had grown up between them could only be to the friars' disadvantage. At a time when social distress loomed large, it appears that they had more or less given up their charitable work. One of the complaints made against them was that they were more interested in currying favor with the rich than in serving the poor. And to add insult to injury, they continued to talk a good line about poverty even while failing to observe it. What right had these men to call themselves mendicants, and actually go about soliciting donations, when they themselves lived in comfortable lodgings and ate adequate food? Whatever tolerance the public might have had for such doubletalk was strained by the prevailing economic distress. The bitter commentary about the friars that would later surface in great literary works such as the *Decameron, Piers Ploughman,* and *The Canterbury Tales* must already have been gathering strength. Add this to the continuing internal criticism coming from the Spirituals and their sympathizers, and it is not hard to imagine that within the convents, too, a dour mood was taking hold.

"The Lord Has Called Us to Do Great Things, That in Us Others May See an Example and Mirror" (Clare of Assisi)

So much had happened in a century. When the great famine struck in 1315, Franciscans ought by rights to have been celebrating the centennial of their order's birth. They should, also, have been commemorating another major event that took place in the same epoch: the revitalization of feminine monastic life.

In the aftermath of the confrontation with his father, Francis had cut a strange figure, wandering the countryside, begging for his food and consorting with outcasts and lepers. His only gainful employment seemed to be the labor he undertook in rebuilding one or two of the local churches that had fallen into disrepair. This involved coming into town to beg for the necessary materials, which, considering his ragged appearance, could not have been easy. But if his eccentricity repelled some, his shining personality attracted others. One by one, men came to join him, and together they worked with the poor and preached, while all the time carrying the stones and mixing the mortar to build up broken-down church walls. When they reached the sacred number of twelve, Francis drew up a rule, a very simple set of principles drawn straight from the Gospels. Then, quite suddenly, he decided to take the group to Rome, to ask for the pope's blessing on their way of life. And this only two years after he had stood alone and naked in the Assisi town square! Together they marched off across country to the Lateran Palace.

The presumption of this ragged little band of brothers was breathtaking. But even more remarkable was Innocent III's response. The pope, when he looked out across his church, saw pockets of heretics everywhere. In many ways, Francis and his crew bore a worrying resemblance to them. And yet, despite considerable reservations among his more conservative cardinals, Innocent saw their possibilities and blessed them with the words: "Go, brothers, and preach penitence to everyone." As it turned out, his endorsement of the twelve was the *laissez-passer* for what was to become the largest religious order of all future centuries to date.

The group returned to Assisi, where they, and especially their charismatic leader, were now the talk of the town. Among the citizens who flocked to hear Francis preach was a seventeen-year-old girl, Chiara [Clare] di Favarone. The daughter of one of Assisi's noble families, she would likely never have known this man of commoner parentage had it not been for his fame as a preacher. But she was so entranced by his words that she took the brave step of meeting with him secretly, to learn more of his message. It is safe to say that over the following year Clare fell in love, not only with Francis, but also with Lady Poverty. In 1212 she gave her dowry money to the poor, left her family home, and went under cover of night to the brothers' church, the Portiuncula. Here she made the same vow of obedience to Francis that he required of the brothers. And as a seal on her commitment, she received the tonsure from his hands.

At this point, though, Clare's future must have seemed very much in doubt. She clearly could not stay with the brothers, nor could she go home. Francis took her to a Benedictine nunnery some miles away; it appears that at this point he himself had no idea what to do with her. There was certainly no intention that she should become a Benedictine nun; nor, in any case, could she have done so, seeing that she had given away her dowry. If he had hoped that she would be safe there, he was mistaken. Before long, members of Clare's family came for her and tried to drag her away by force. A vivid picture remains for us, of Clare clinging to the altar cloth and then, finally, baring her shorn head to show how final and how shameful was her decision. They left in anger. The violent scene was repeated later, when her sister came to join her. Somehow, both girls were able to resist their family's rage.

By this time Clare had left the nunnery and was living with a group of hermit women. Thus within a brief time she experienced the two alternatives then open to her: life in an established nunnery, fully canonical but hardly poor; and a more austere life in an informal community of unvowed religious women. Neither offered her the life she desired. Just how long she and Agnes remained in their limbo is uncertain, but it was long enough to convince Francis of their constancy. "After that," Clare would write, many years later, "he wrote us a Form of Life saying above all that we should persevere in holy poverty." And he gave them a place to live, a set of buildings by the church of San Damiano, close to Assisi.

What did Clare really want at this moment? Is it too far-fetched to think that in some way, perhaps never expressed, she wished to be like Francis, to travel the road he was traveling, to live among the poor and beg for her food? It is impossible to say. What she got in the end was very different: a cloister, and the Benedictine Rule. It could not have been otherwise, given the facts on the ground. In 1215, at the very time that her new life was unfolding, Innocent III was convening the Fourth Lateran Council to bring more regularity to the Church; one of its decrees prohibited new religious orders — all existing communities must adopt one of the existing rules. The brothers had escaped the ban, thanks to the timing of their visit to Rome and also to the favor of the pope, but it would have been pushing their luck to propose a life for women that paralleled their own, even had they wished to. Francis was fully aware of the danger of consorting with women, and from the beginning warned his brothers against it. Clare, in her unquestioning obedience, accepted his prescription for her, which meant enclosure.

But he had promised her that she could share his poverty, and to this she clung, through thick and thin, for the rest of her life. It was a difficult course to follow, since a cloistered community, by its very nature, had to depend on *something* for its daily bread, and that *something* was, by long convention, wealth-generating property. Clare and the women who joined her rejected property, and instead threw themselves on the charity of their neighbors, the friars first, and then all the other folk who lived close by. It was not that the sisters were idle. After their first occupation, which was prayer both liturgical and private, they valued work, which for them was the work, traditional to women, of textile production. But what they produced, they gave away. And they waited in silence and trust for the loaves of bread, the baskets of eggs and vegetables, to appear on their doorstep.

The community's radical lifestyle must have raised many questions, even among its friends; this we can infer from the fierceness with which Clare continued to protect it. Fortunately for her, she had friends in high places. Innocent III himself gave her a written endorsement, which is known as the Privilege of Poverty. "We confirm with our apostolic authority, as you requested, your proposal of most high poverty, granting you by the authority of this letter that no one can compel you to receive possessions." That, and the obedience she owed to Francis, were the arguments she needed more than once against well-meaning prelates who were concerned for the community's security. When a later pope, Gregory IX, offered to absolve her from the poverty that his predecessor had granted her, she answered: "Holy Father, I will never in any way wish to be absolved from the following of Christ." And, graciously conceding her point, he renewed the Privilege of Poverty. Another pope, in 1247, gave her community a set of constitutions that, for the first time, mirrored the rule not of Benedict but of Francis. But still Clare was uneasy. By this time, with Francis long dead, the brothers had accepted a mitigation of the practice of poverty; might not the sisters be forced to do the same? So she set about writing her own rule. As her health declined, she became more urgent in pressing the Curia to confirm it, along with the Privilege of Poverty. Her audacity crashed headlong upon Rome's reluctance. Finally, in August 1253, Innocent IV, "for reasons that are obvious to me," signed the necessary bull. Two days later his reasons became obvious to the world. Clare died, but not before learning that her prayer had been granted. From then on, her community of "Poor Ladies," as they were then called, enjoyed the Privilege of Poverty. The bull for which she had fought was buried with her, folded into her clothes.

However, Rome soon made it clear that the privilege was not to extend to every community that adopted Clare's rule. With only a few exceptions (Assisi being the most notable) they were to be endowed. No matter how austere the nuns' daily life, it was to be underpinned by property and income. Those were the terms under which Clare's order spread across Europe.

The subsequent history of the order was one of success on one level, failure on another. The Poor Ladies (now called "Poor Clares") flourished. By 1400, it is reckoned, some four hundred convents were scattered across the Continent, housing perhaps as many as 15,000 nuns. But with the passage of time the Poor Clares went down what seems to have been the preordained path for cloistered nuns in the Middle Ages: they became more aristocratic. They no longer did housework as Clare had done, but left such demeaning activity to lay sisters and hired servants. Their houses grew rich on the dowries of entrants and the donations of their families. More unsettling was the fact that individual nuns were permitted to hold on to their estates, and to own jewels and books. Some communities took on the character of retirement homes for ladies of quality. There was not necessarily any harm in all this, but it was a far cry from the life Clare had intended.

A great abbot of Cluny, Peter the Venerable, long ago remarked that it was easier to found a new order than to reform an old one. What happened to the Poor Clares was not unusual; the fading of early ideals was something that most religious communities experienced at one time or another. What mattered was whether they possessed the will and the ability to rejuvenate themselves. Almost two hundred years after Clare took her vow of poverty, another woman, Colette of Corbie, began to undertake a serious reform of her order. One by one, as the fifteenth century went on, communities of Poor Clares across Europe returned to the poverty and simplicity that their foundress had so loved.

*   *   *

The same strong attraction to the friars' message that had made Clare and her followers into Franciscan nuns also drew other women toward the Dominicans. In 1206, a decade before the Order of Preachers was created, Dominic opened a house in southern France for the benefit of a group of ladies he had converted from Catharism. In time other houses were opened, and in more time, as the rulings of the Fourth Lateran Council took hold, they became monasteries, following the Rule of Saint Augustine complete with Dominican nuances. There was never any question of the *vita apostolica* for these nuns. Contemplatives from the start, they seem never to have resented their enclosure, believing (as did Dominic himself) that their prayers were as vital for the salvation of souls as were the friars' actions. To our eyes their shuttered lifestyle seems boringly close to that of the Benedictine and Cistercian nuns who came before. But then, we cannot from our distance traverse the monastery walls to spot the differences between communities. In the thirteenth century both Franciscan and Dominican "Second Orders" (the First Orders being those of men) opened up new possibilities for women, and women responded with enthusiasm. In Germany alone, between 1245 and 1250, thirty-two Dominican nunneries opened their doors. It was serendipity, long before that word was invented: "tinder which took fire as soon as the spark of Dominican preaching fell on it," in the words of a Dominican poet. The men at the top looked on with trepidation — understandably, given that there were then only twenty-four men's houses in the whole order. But the women kept coming, and no matter how hard the authorities tried to stem the tide, at the local level the friars found it hard to resist.

It almost seems that some higher force led the friars to divide the world of religious women between themselves. Franciscans dominated in the south, above all Italy; Dominicans in Germany and the Low Countries. In the south, the women continued to follow the banner of Lady Poverty. In Germany they took a different path, that of mysticism. They articulated a vision of the Divine that was passionate and loving, and reflective of their experience as women. They poured that vision into written words, and thus were able to pass it on to a wide readership among their contemporaries. In spite of monastery walls, in spite of all the enduring prejudices that male society felt against women, a distinctively feminine element began to enter the mind and soul of the Church.

The Mendicant Second Orders have survived for eight hundred years, and their history is secured by the many tomes that grace Catholic library shelves. But they should not obliterate the memory of the many other initiatives that failed to survive but were nevertheless significant in their own time. One female community was as famous in its day as it was short-lived: the Cistercian monastery of Helfta in Germany, founded in 1229 and destroyed in 1343. We call it Cistercian even though, like many other female communities, it was never formally adopted by Cîteaux. It simply took over many Cistercian practices, chose its spiritual guides among Dominicans, and developed in its own way.

Nuns of the thirteenth century had the opportunity to be better educated than their forebears and, thanks to the general improvement in religious instruction and direction, more capable of a deep and balanced spirituality. Helfta certainly proved that. The women of Helfta were trained to be studious as well as holy. They maintained high standards of liturgical observance and community life, but they also followed an advanced course of studies; and they boasted a well-stocked library. How much did the nuns profit from all this excellence, and how much did they communicate to others? We cannot tell; so much depended on the spoken word, which melted away with the generation that received it. But among the hundreds who lived in the monastery during its short existence, three have left a legacy in writing: Mechtild of Hackeborn, Gertrude of Helfta, and Mechtild of Magdeburg. Their works survived the destruction of Helfta, and we can read them today: soul-warming testimonies to the love of God, as these women experienced it some seven centuries ago.

But from the great majority of nuns who entered, lived, and died in the monasteries of Europe, we have no testimony at all. We have forgotten them. Like so many soldiers in foreign graves, they are "known only to God."

The *Frauenbewegung* — the "Women's Movement"

The era that we have been following — the thirteenth and fourteenth centuries — was a time of challenge for the Catholic Church. Fortunately Rome, though traditionalist to its very core, showed that it could be innovative. The encouragement it gave the mendicant orders, and the opening to the world that entailed, was one of its inspired moves. But in one area of its responsibility the Church was determined not to innovate. This was with regard to women. From the ruling of the Fourth Lateran Council in 1215 against the creation of new orders to the papal bull *Periculoso* in 1298, Rome's official stance remained the same: religious women belonged where they always ought to have been, confined behind high walls and away from the sight of men.

It would be wrong to see these merely as retrogressive steps, or as acts of pure, undiluted misogyny. To be sure, churchmen did tend to view women in a negative light, considering even the best of them to be flighty creatures, weak of intellect and susceptible to the temptations of the devil and the flesh. Seen in that light, the cloister was a protection for people who could not be trusted to protect themselves. But the Middle Ages also knew another reality. Prayer was essential; it was what snatched Christians from the jaws of hell. Convents were the places where most of the praying went on; they were the hot spots, so to speak, in an otherwise cold and sterile world. One would have had to be extremely cynical not to value the prayers of holy women.

However, throughout all the Christian centuries thus far, the holiness of women had been little more than a sideshow. The central stage belonged to men; it always had. Nuns simply did not have the same power, either in prayer or in action. And there were always fewer of them, because women had less access to institutional life. The anchorite lifestyle was not for everyone, and the alternative, entry into the traditional Benedictine nunnery, was an expensive business, beyond the reach of ordinary folk. As the opportunities for men increased and diversified, women were left standing outside. There was no question, though: they wanted in. They clustered around Cistercian monasteries; they flocked to charismatic preachers like Robert of Arbrissel, Gilbert of Sempringham, and Norbert of Xanten, just as, when the friars came to town, they flocked to them. Wherever a new house was established, they were ready to fill it. But there were never enough institutions to satisfy the demand. So for lack of adequate accommodation, the women started to create their own religious communities, complete with their own rules, their own officers, and their own habit — all of this anathema in the eyes of the canon lawyers, because it was outside the system and might easily lead to heresy.

This was the situation when the Fourth Lateran Council met in 1215. The "women's movement" was becoming a problem. The church simply did not have the structures in place to absorb the ardor of its faithful members. The best it could do was to try to contain it by putting an end to all experimentation. From now on, it decreed, only those orders that followed the established monastic rules were to be allowed. The only state that the Fourth Lateran Council envisaged for religious women was to be found within four walls.

However, almost as soon as the council ceased to sit, its rulings were subjected to qualification. In 1216 a young canon from Reims, Jacques of Vitry, asked for and received from the pope an assurance that "religious women, not only in the diocese of Liège but also in France and the Empire, were permitted to live in the same house and to incite each other toward the good by mutual exhortations." His ardent support of these women, who would come to be known as beguines, won them a tenuous foothold in the Church. Official papal permissions followed, giving a certain authenticity to what had until then been an unauthorized movement. Numerous beguinages appeared in the cities of the Low Countries, Germany, and northern France.

In a world that really liked categories, these women were difficult to categorize. They were not nuns, though in many ways they acted like them. Nor were they just pious laywomen, of the sort who stayed quietly in their homes and attended unobtrusively to their devotions. These women lived together under the direction of a superior, but went out and about freely. Like other laypeople, they attended the parish church. Though they promised to be chaste as long as they remained in the community, they took no vows.

They were poor by intention. In the early days of the movement, the beguines were more than likely to come from wealthy, or at least comfortable, backgrounds. But the passion for holy poverty that swept across Europe in the late twelfth and early thirteenth centuries caught them up as well. Knowing their Bible, they knew how the early Christians had lived, and they desired to imitate them. That meant being genuinely poor and working for a living. Some of them found employment in hospitals and leper houses; others made their livelihood in the cloth industry. Their self-sufficiency, together with the holiness of their lives, won them the respect of their neighbors. Before long, they were being sought out for spiritual advice and direction.

This was how Jacques of Vitry came to know the beguines. A canon in his own city of Reims, with a master's degree from Paris, he heard of a holy woman living in Oignies, close to Liège, and arrived there in about 1211 in order to learn from her. He was not disappointed. Mary of Oignies was not the first beguine, but she was certainly a perfect type. Married at fourteen but soon persuading her husband to join her in a semireligious life of chastity and austerity and service to the sick, she later spent some time as a recluse and ended up as the leader of an informal community of women in Oignies. Jacques of Vitry knew her only for a short time (she died in 1213), but he was so impressed by her sanctity that from then on he was a vigorous defender of the beguines' way of life. "It is, in my judgment, not only those people who renounce the world and go into religion who can be called 'regulars,'" he wrote, "but all the faithful of Christ who serve the Lord under the rule of the gospel and live under the orders of the one highest Abbot of all." For this one churchman at least, the ancient monastic monopoly on holiness was beginning to break open.

In the early days the beguine communities received warm support from the Cistercians, and many beguines were friendly with Cistercian nuns. Then, as the Dominicans moved into the region in the 1220s, the two groups began to gravitate toward each other, and the friars became the women's preferred counselors and directors. It was a fruitful match. The beguines, unschooled in theology and naive in matters of church discipline, had much to learn from the Dominicans. Many Dominicans, in return, caught fire from the beguines. The women spoke in a mystical language far removed from the learned discourse of the schools, and there was an intensity in their feelings that contrasted vividly with the dryness of contemporary scholarship. Using not Latin but their own tongue, they spoke of love and the agony of being separated from God; they used emotional, even erotic imagery to describe their relationship with the Divine. It was a powerfully feminine approach to theology, practical and transcendent at the same time, and it left its mark, both on the men who assisted them and on the lay population that surrounded them. It is a striking irony: at the very time the framework of the official church was being tightened up in Rome and in the schools, ordinary Christians here and there were chipping away at its edges.

The beguines had their day in the sun, but it did not last long. By midcentury there were signs of trouble. From the beginning, experts in canon law had had reservations about these women, unharnessed as they were by any rule or obligation of obedience to higher authority. As long as the women maintained themselves in exemplary piety, virtue, and modesty, it was difficult to condemn their form of life. But nothing remains perfect forever, and soon beguines here and there overstepped the boundaries of female propriety, walking abroad in an undisciplined way, flaunting their piety, annoying their neighbors. There were other problems too: their close association with the Dominicans put them at odds with their parish priests, and their indeterminate legal status — partly lay and partly religious, taxable or perhaps nontaxable, subject to civil law or perhaps not subject — caused headaches for many city officials. Most unsettling of all to the church authorities was their readiness to pronounce on matters of religion, and in an uncanonical language. The prelates at the Council of Lyons in 1274 took note of the doings of this "unbridled multitude." "They have interpreted the mysteries of Scripture and translated them into the vernacular, although the best experts in Scripture can hardly comprehend them." It was important to destroy such works, so that "the speech of things divine be no longer stained by common, vulgar utterance."

So spoke the canon lawyers and professors of theology. They were probably not at all surprised when, a few years later, some cases of heresy came to light. That was all they needed. At the Council of Vienne (1311-1312), the beguines' way of life was denounced and their piety questioned. From then on, the women were subjected to increasing harassment, even persecution.

Whatever the learned men had to say, however, the beguine population continued to flourish. The cities of northern Europe saw things differently from Paris and Rome; they saw social and economic, as well as religious, value in their beguinages. The women who were flocking in from the countryside looking for employment were, by general agreement, more unconstrained in their behavior than their sisters to the south, but they were pious enough, and hardworking. They were perfect fodder for the booming textile industry, but they needed a respectable place to stay. Between 1240 and 1400 some 250 beguinages were founded in the southern Low Countries (what is today Belgium) alone.

There was, however, a marked change in the social composition of the beguine population. Once the great spiritual awakening of the thirteenth century faded, the upper-class element began to drain away, and with it the high-minded tradition of sacrifice for the sake of holy poverty. The middle- and working-class elements that took over may have been just as devout, but they were undoubtedly more practical. In fact, many beguinages were built purposely as charitable enterprises, to provide poor women with lodgings from which to pursue their frugal, laborious lives. The clusters of modest dwellings can be seen to this day in several Belgian cities, testimonies to an interesting chapter in the story of Catholic spirituality.

The beguine "movement," if we may call it that, was the first movement in the Catholic Church that was inspired and advanced by women for the sake of women alone. But its promotion of a spirituality steeped in love would leave its mark on the souls of Christian women and men alike. Beguine mysticism would influence the thinking of future theologians, foremost among them the great Dominican Meister Eckhart (1268-1329). Beguine devotional literature, because it was written in the mother tongue, would reach the laity in a way that Latin never could. For all that, however, the movement did not last. Beguines never gained official status; they never became a religious order. Many individual beguines ended up as nuns, and many communities sought incorporation in established orders (usually the Dominicans). But the beguine movement as such lost its high religious purpose and became little more than a worthy feature of the urban landscape.

"There Came a Privy Thief Men Call Death . . ."

Halfway through the fourteenth century, Europe experienced a natural disaster of dimensions never equaled in its history, before or since. In 1347 twelve Genoese galleys docked in Messina, Sicily, and disgorged their cargo:

sailors already dying of a disease so lethal "that if anyone so much as spoke with one of them he was infected . . . and could not avoid death." The symptoms of their disease were buboes (swellings the size of an egg in groin or armpit) and high fever, and agonizing pain that soon gave way to death. Within days the sailors' affliction became the Great Plague, the Black Death, the Scourge of Europe. It moved deliberately, unstoppably, at the speed of a walking man, through Italy, over the Alps, and across the Continent until it reached the British Isles, Scandinavia, and finally Russia. By 1350 it had run its course for the time being, though not, as it turned out, for long. It left behind it a continent in shock. No exact accounting is possible, but historians estimate that out of the seventy-five million then living in Europe, at least twenty-five million were struck down in this first visitation of the plague. One in three died, often within hours of the appearance of the symptoms. In the cities where people were packed together, where rats teemed in the accumulated filth and dead bodies were often left to fester in the open, the mortality rate could be even higher. In Siena, Marseille, Avignon, London — to name but a few — one out of every two inhabitants is thought to have died.

Europeans would learn from experience that the only protection against the plague was "to take flight soon and far, and to return after a long time." But for ordinary people who lived in crowded conditions and lacked the opportunity to move, the disease's first appearance in their midst was a virtual death sentence. This was as true for people in convents as it was for people in city tenements. Whole communities were stricken together, as in Marseille, where 150 Franciscan friars died, leaving their priory standing empty, and Montpellier, where out of a community of 140 Dominicans, only 7 survived. Nobody escaped entirely. In Paris, the nuns of the central hospital, the Hôtel-Dieu, continued to nurse the sick "sweetly and with great humility" until they, too, were carried off in their numbers. Every part of Europe saw a decline in the religious population of between 30 and 50 percent, according to the records that survive.

The physical effects of the Black Death are to some degree measurable, thanks to land records and a smattering of postplague demographic information. Across the Continent, great tracts of farmland fell into disuse for lack of laborers; entire villages disappeared for lack of men and women to inhabit them. The population did not reconstitute itself for a hundred years. These facts we can know with reasonable certainty. What is less clear is how this catastrophe, which overwhelmed all human understanding, affected people's spirits. After all, in the medieval mind all good things and all bad came directly from the hand of God, and for a good reason. So why was he angry with his people? And how could he be placated?

One response came with the welling up of a pathology that was endemic in the bloodstream of Europe: anti-Semitism. In many parts of the Continent, most notably in Germany, communities of Jews were attacked and massacred. The pretext was that they had poisoned the wells and thus caused the plague. But surely a deeper motivation was also at work here, the need for scapegoats with which to appease the divine anger. Another response appeared with the flagellants, bands of men, sometimes several hundred strong, who wandered from town to town, village to village, publicly scourging themselves until the blood flowed, in choreographed rituals that called the onlookers to penance.

Such activity was not new to Catholics. It had appeared about a hundred years earlier — and the friars had been there at its birth. The Franciscans, particularly, were moved by a strong belief that the world was living in the end-time, and that to turn away the wrath of God it must do penance, much as Nineveh had done penance in biblical times. They often used the flagellants to enhance their preaching campaigns. But this was a powerful force that sometimes — above all in times of deep social distress — escaped control, and the Church's response swung from support to condemnation. The phenomenon was too widespread to be eradicated; whenever times were bad, the flagellants reappeared. Slowly, however, they were tamed. Confraternities of penitents were formed up, complete with discipline and rules, and usually chaplained and led by friars.

There were other reactions to the Great Plague. If its literature, art, and architecture are to be believed, Europe fell into a long obsession with death. From the Church's earliest days Christians had spent time contemplating the end of life, but never like this. The new mood is well illustrated in the *danse macabre,* a theme that now came into vogue. It depicts a ghoulish ring-dance of living and dead together: the nobleman, the cleric, the scholar, the burgher and his lady — and, holding their hands, the skeleton and sometimes the half-decayed corpse with worms issuing out of its eyeholes. There are various other, similar themes: the nubile young woman embracing the grinning death's head, the three young knights in the prime of life who suddenly confront their three skeletal counterparts while in the background their friends play on, unaware that their turn is next. The same story is told in funerary sculptures that we can still see today. No longer does the deceased lie in solemn dignity, clasping the sword or the crosier that symbolizes his office. Instead, he gapes with slackened jaw, his bones protrude, and his flesh falls back to reveal his decaying entrails. Images such as these appeared and reappeared for more than a century, as of course did the plague. Death was not easily exorcised.

It has been argued that the Great Plague injected a permanent strain of fear into the European psyche. It should not be difficult to imagine this, having witnessed the lifelong trauma that has oppressed the survivors of the Holocaust. And it is not difficult to see how, in a God-fearing age, this fear would bring guilt in its train, and how the two together would permeate the religious discourse. From that point on, in sermons and in writings, life on earth would be described as a valley of tears, which could only end with the terrible event known as death, and the even more terrible reckoning known as judgment. As a natural consequence to this, Europeans moved in force toward the practice of praying for the dead. The souls in purgatory, never absent from the medieval mind, became a major preoccupation. This could only help to swell the crowds when the preachers came to town.

The widespread angst about purgatory also led to a serious distortion in late medieval religious practice: the traffic in indulgences. Western Christianity had long held the belief that the punishment due for past sins could be lightened by the performance of a meritorious action such as pilgrimage or penitential fasting. However, with time the definition of "a meritorious action" shifted. The people who effected the change were the popes. From the time that Urban II preached the First Crusade in 1095, it was promised that all who took the cross, as long they were true to their commitment and felt sincere contrition for their sins, were granted "plenary" (full) indulgences, that is, the canceling out of *all* the punishment waiting for them as a result of the evil they had done. No matter what we may think about crusading, it certainly was an arduous way to pay for one's sins. For a century it was more or less the only path to the reward. Then in 1300 Pope Boniface VIII lowered the bar: he proclaimed a "jubilee year" in Rome, and extended the same indulgence to all Christian pilgrims who during that year made confession and visited the holy places in the city. In another significant departure, the benefit of the indulgence earned by one person became transferable to another soul in need — almost by definition a soul in purgatory. And all the time the requirements became lighter, with the result that inexorably, as the century went on, the granting of indulgences became more and more commonplace. But the greatest change came when Clement VI removed the requirement for penitential action altogether, and allowed Christians to gain indulgences, for themselves or for others, with cash payments.

This is where the friars came in. They had long been the papacy's favored preachers. Now they were drawn into this new activity. When the popes turned to the sale of indulgences as a means of raising money, they turned the friars into fund-raisers. Not all the friars were happy with this, but some were, and it was they who carried the message to the people, a message as simplistic as it was debased: "When the money in the coffer rings / The soul from purgatory springs." A century and a half later the Catholic Church would pay a heavy price for that slogan.

But back to the fourteenth century. It might be expected that experience of the plague would lead to a rush into religion; that, vividly aware of the fragility of life, people would flock into the monasteries and convents as though into sanctuaries. This is not what happened. Too much had been lost with the plague. The cloisters emptied by death were slow to fill up, and when they did it was often with substandard candidates, or with youths well below the acceptable age. The fourteenth century saw a trend toward mediocrity and relaxation in the religious life, and that trend was amplified by the Black Death.

The Great Schism

There was more trouble to come. Hard on the heels of the plague came another crisis that, while not so devastating for the population as a whole, caused lasting harm to the Church. This was the Great Schism (1378-1417).

The papacy had been in Avignon since the early years of the century, when it had been virtually kidnapped and carried there by the king of France. These years had done the institution no good. It was not that the seven popes who succeeded each other there were unworthy. But in the mind of much of the world they did not belong in Avignon; they were the bishops of Rome, and Rome was the see of Peter, the center of the Catholic world. No matter that the French party, now riding high in the papal court, was determined to keep it in Avignon; no matter that conditions in Rome, and in Italy at large, had become so violent that the very thought of going back filled the popes with dread. Public pressure continued to mount until finally, in 1376, Pope Gregory XI took the brave decision to reenter the lions' den. What he found there was every bit as bad as he expected. Even if things had gone well, he would have needed time to reestablish a semblance of order. Unfortunately he died in Rome in early 1378, and the vacancy he left was all that was needed to create turmoil both inside and outside the Vatican palace.

The Roman crowds were determined to dominate the election, by force if necessary. To the sound of their angry shouts, "We want a Roman," the cardinals hastily elected the next best thing: an Italian from Naples. Almost at once they regretted their action, for Urban VI turned out to be tyrannical, even sadistic. (Some historians suggest that he was suffering a mental breakdown.) The cardinals fled Rome, and once safely out of his reach declared his election null and void, because it was conducted in an atmosphere of fear. Before the year was out they had elected a new (French) pope, Clement VII. The two popes promptly excommunicated each other. The years of schism had begun.

Christendom was now faced with two pontiffs, two colleges of cardinals, and two papal administrations, one based in Avignon, the other in Rome. For a world accustomed to the idea of one supreme pontiff, it could not have been more disorienting. Several times in the next forty years influential men attempted to find a solution, either by deposing one or the other of the popes, or by persuading both to resign so that someone else could be elected canonically. The parties in question would have none of it. When one or the other contender died, there would be a moment of hope that perhaps this might allow a negotiated end to the stalemate. But then his faction would elect a successor, and the schism would go on. There were four popes (or antipopes, depending on one's point of view) in the Roman line, three in the Avignonese line, plus, in the later years, when the Council of Pisa (1409) tried to make things better but only made them worse, two "Pisan" antipopes. Finally, in 1417, the Council of Constance put an end to the scandal by deposing one pope and forcing the resignation of the other, making way for a brand-new, unencumbered election.

During these contested years Christendom divided along regional lines. France, Spain, Scotland, southern Germany, and the kingdom of Naples supported Avignon; England, the Low Countries, Scandinavia, Poland, Bohemia, Hungary, and the larger part of the German empire supported Rome. For most of the locally based clergy the choice was not too difficult: they went along with their region. For the mendicant orders, however, the schism presented a painful dilemma. They were supranational organizations, answerable first and foremost to the pope. So who was the true pope? The Franciscans and Dominicans both split down the middle. Just as there were two papacies with two sets of officials, there were now, for each order, two opposing sources of authority: two heads and two general chapters, with the provincial chapters breaking down along national lines — and at loggerheads with each other. Any progress, any internal reform that might have been hoped for, was drowned in a sea of mutual bitterness.

The damage went even further. Ever since the popes had taken up residence in Avignon, their need for new sources of income had ballooned. They met this partly by increasing taxation, partly by merchandising their favors. Their supporters and clients were routinely rewarded by appointment to lucrative benefices, bishoprics or wealthy abbeys or other church offices that might be anywhere in the known world. The lucky recipients were not required to visit their new holdings, or even care about them; they only needed to siphon off their wealth. This was the destructive practice of *commenda,* and it became widespread, and the monastic communities suffered. With the schism, matters grew worse. Searching for ways to gain new supporters and gratify old, the rival popes took to handing out all sorts of dispensations. Thus a community could buy the right to eat meat; an individual monk or friar could purchase the right to own private property, or keep servants, or ride a horse instead of walking. And so on. The consequences for the religious life were inevitably harmful. The slippage toward relaxation of the rule, already under way before the Great Plague and seriously accelerated by it, gathered speed.

Despite their failings, however, the friars remained the Church's best auxiliaries. In 1351, when prelates in Avignon arrived carrying, along with their usual complaints, yet another petition to abolish the mendicant orders, Pope Clement VI burst out in anger. "What can you preach to the people?" he asked them. Did any of them have the moral authority to speak about humility, or poverty, or chastity? And who would do it, if not the friars?

In general, the people shared the pope's opinion. For better or for worse, they supported the friars. Boccaccio might rail against them, so might Wycliffe, Langland, and many others. But the records tell us another story, of innumerable bequests still coming their way, of many demands for burial in their graveyards and in the habit of their order, of new friaries being established. They were "as thikke as motes in a sonne beam" according to Chaucer, and they were still active in society. But in fact, deficiencies in quality were causing the brothers concern. They knew they had problems of long standing, and that these had been exacerbated by the Black Death. In its aftermath the survivors, rattling around in their large, empty houses, had looked for recruits wherever they could find them, with little regard to suitability. This meant that they were often saddled with men without genuine vocations, and boys who were much too young to know what they wanted. Morale suffered. Then, during the years of the Great Schism, when the contending popes were looking for support, the communities, still not fully recovered, allowed themselves to be tempted by privileges and exemptions. Individual friars gained the right to own and manage their own money, and with it they furnished apartments for themselves, and abandoned the common life. Nobody went begging anymore. Regular duties were neglected; the choir was left unattended.

But there were always men in both orders — Minors and Preachers — who wanted to change things. Toward the end of the fourteenth century they started to press for reform.

The Return

A century and a half before, at that critical general chapter held in Assisi, Francis, seeing that his order was diverging from his chosen way, had cried out to the brothers: "Henceforth I am dead to you." But he was wrong. Though with the following years many details of his life were suppressed and his image was "deradicalized," there were always people here and there who kept alive the memory of the *Poverello,* the knight-errant of Lady Poverty. These were the "Spirituals." Insofar as they were out of step with the majority, they caused serious friction within the order, and that friction hardened into something close to civil war. The Spirituals eventually broke into small knots of angry men, heretics in the eyes of the church and nothing but trouble where the order was concerned. But there was never a time when their voice was stilled altogether. Then, in the fourteenth century, the original and unvarnished Francis came alive once more to his people. Various written "lives" of the saint and copies of his own writings, long buried in friary archives, were discovered, transcribed, and circulated. There began, in a quiet way, a reappraisal of the order's true purpose.

In 1334 a friar named John de Valle gained permission from the minister general to retire with four companions to a remote corner of Umbria, a wild place called Brugliano, and there to follow the rule to the letter, in poverty and simplicity. They succeeded in doing so without interference, so long as their community remained small and invisible. But as word spread and more men were drawn in, and the single community multiplied into five, the authorities took fright. In 1354 the general chapter ordered the men to obey all the order's statutes, including those that mandated the very relaxations that they opposed. When they refused, they were condemned as rebels, their privileges were revoked, and their independence was taken away. Some of their leaders went to prison. It was the end of that movement.

But in 1368 Paul de' Trinci, a friar who had spent some time in Brugliano before its dispersion, returned to the hermitage. In time he, like John before him, was joined by others, and they set up a little community they called "the family of the observance." This was the beginning of the Observant movement, which after a long and difficult gestation became the main wing of the Franciscan order. The difference between these Observants and the rebel Spirituals was that the Observants were initially determined to continue in obedience to the order. Only gradually as the century wore on did it become obvious that this was impossible, that the disparities between them and the mainstream Franciscans (now known as "Conventuals") were too deep to be bridged. But by then they were so strong that they could not be sidelined. In 1517, after many futile attempts at unity, the papacy divided them, and Observants and Conventuals went their separate ways.

Naturally the Observants of those early days had enemies. But they also won friends, some of them friends in high places. And better even than friends, they attracted talent. It is easy to see why. The main body of the order of Saint Francis was in the doldrums, tossed about between those members who were satisfied with the way things were and those who looked for something better. The Observants had high standards, high ideals, and a clear purpose. For some years they continued their quiet, steady growth. Then, at the turn of the century, they got their champion — the man who was for them what Bernard of Clairvaux had been for the Cistercians — and from that time on they never looked back.

When in 1403 Bernardine of Siena joined the Observants, he already had the makings of a religious leader. He was a well-born (definitely an asset), well-educated, pious, and courageous young man. During an outbreak of the plague in 1400, he led twelve friends into the city hospital where fifty priests and 120 helpers had already died, and worked there among the sick for the duration of the epidemic. Following that, and after some time spent nursing a sick aunt, he entered the Franciscan friary in Siena. But soon afterward, disillusioned by the relaxed life he found there, he moved on to a remote Observant community. There he received formation in the primitive life of poverty as Francis had lived it; in return, he restored an element of the founder's vocation that had so far been missing from the Observant life: preaching. For forty years he traveled barefoot through Italy, preaching with a brilliance and fire that drew thousands to hear him.

To our modern way of thinking, Bernardine's preaching — against Jews, against homosexuals, against gaming, against every form of self-indulgence — was intolerant in the extreme. But this was an age that appreciated intolerance. Everything was clear-cut. Sin was sin, no matter how attractive it might be; not only the friars, but the people, too, saw it that way. When one rejected sin, one did so with panache. In Florence in 1424, when Bernardine called for "a bonfire of the vanities," the crowd cooperated with gusto: thousands of packs of playing cards, hundreds of backgammon tables, as well as great bundles of false hair, rouge pots, high-heeled shoes and mirrors went into the flames. The event was so successful that it was repeated many times. And if Bernardine was hard on frivolity, he was hard also on the feuding that was endemic in many Italian cities. He preached against it vehemently, describing the blood spilt, the women raped, the children orphaned. He took action against it. Like the gangs of our day, the factions marked their territory with their own emblems, a reminder to their rivals of who was in charge. Wherever Bernardine found the emblems he had them torn down, to be replaced by the sacred banner of the Lord. It was an uphill and dangerous battle, and ultimately a losing one. But the image of this brave little man, withered and worn but forever fighting the good fight, resonated far and wide through Italy. Bernardine was not the only great friar to arise from the ranks of the Observance, but he was certainly the most famous.

*   *   *

The recovery of the Dominicans in the century after the Black Death was not nearly as painful as that of the Franciscans. But it was arduous, nonetheless. They, too, were split down the middle by the Great Schism. Ironically, two of their most famous saints, Catherine of Siena (of whom more later) and Vincent Ferrer, were on opposing sides during the schism — Catherine for Rome, Vincent for Avignon. But somehow the order managed to emerge from the crisis in one piece. More challenging, perhaps, was its experience of the same kind of Conventual versus Observant standoff that so convulsed the Franciscans.

The order as it emerged from the midcentury crisis certainly needed a housecleaning. It was in decline, both numerically and morally. Community life was more or less dead, and in its place a class system had grown up, in which an elite — masters of theology and preachers general — were able to live in their own apartments on rich stipends, dispensed from all the duties of common life, even from divine office, while the hoi polloi of brothers subsisted as best they could in what remained of the convent buildings. And the worst of it was that most of the friars were content with the situation, or at least anxious not to rock the boat.

Reform came to them incrementally, after the election in 1380 of a new master general. Raymond of Capua was sensitive to the complaints of the men who wanted change, but also to those of the men who did not. Recognizing how far the order had to travel to regain the high standards of Saint Dominic, he decided that reform would work only if it was not too abrupt or too massive. Those who sought stricter observance of the rule should be encouraged to regroup at some distance from the rest, in their own houses where they could observe the discipline they desired. In time, he hoped, they would be invited back into the communities of their errant brothers, where their example would act like leaven, "and thus the whole Order might be strengthened and reformed." Under his guidance observant "congregations" — semiautonomous groupings within the order — were set up. Unfortunately, the leaven did not work as fast as he had hoped, and the unreformed majority continued on its way, all the time showing a sour hostility to the "do-gooders" in its midst. The Observants responded by becoming even more observant, with the result that, in time, they were responsible for a certain hardening of minds and an aggressive promotion of orthodoxy. Not surprisingly, Dominicans continued to dominate the Roman Inquisition.

That was not the end of it. The fifteenth century was convulsed by another sort of plague, when out of the depths of the European psyche there arose the mass hysteria that has been called the "great witch craze." Thousands of "witches" — more often women than men — were targeted and put to death. Sad to say, the panic was exploited by professional witchhunters, and many of them were churchmen. For the benefit of these witchhunters, and to increase their efficiency, a useful manual appeared in 1486, the *Malleus Maleficarum,* the "Hammer of Witches." The authors of this infamous book were Dominicans.

Yet even while its friars were doing their part in the witch-hunting frenzy, the Order of Preachers was nurturing some of the spiritual giants of the fifteenth century, both among its own members and among those it directed.

The Third Orders

The lesson to be learned from the beguines' story was that the medieval church could not brook independent movements. It was struggling too hard to establish law and order within itself, to break free of the many interests that threatened its structural soundness, and to counteract the very real threats of heresy. One of its most potent weapons was its demand for obedience, obedience that could be enforced by threats of excommunication. The man or woman, no matter how virtuous, who did not answer to higher authority was always in danger of being branded a heretic.

What this meant was that there was no adequate means of containing the ebullience of religious sentiment. As European cities grew, so also did various unofficial religious groupings. Going, often, by the name of penitents, they acted out their devotion in different ways. This lay activity was new to the medieval church. After all, it could hardly have taken place in the scattered rural society of earlier ages. The authorities regarded it with ambivalence. It held great possibilities for good, but also for disorder, at a time when disorder came so easily to people. Should it be curbed or channeled? That was a question that had germinated in the early years of the thirteenth century. The friars provided the answer.

Francis of Assisi had seen the gathering piety of ordinary people, and he had recognized how ready they were for greater participation in the work of the Lord. Around 1214 he wrote a "Letter to All the Faithful." In it he laid down guidelines for devout laymen and laywomen to follow: regular reception of the sacraments; an austere, unluxurious form of life; systematic almsgiving. Follow these, he promised, and you will surely go to heaven. There was as yet no serious attempt at organization (which was hardly Francis's strong suit). But a few years later, at the pope's behest, a rule was constructed, which set out not only the practices that the members were to observe, but also the form their associations were to take. There were to be officers and chapter meetings and outside advisers. And overall supervision by the friars. In 1221, what had been a somewhat amorphous collection of groups of penitents became the Franciscan Third Order, a religious corporation subject to the ecclesiastical courts and protected by privileges and exemptions that came straight from Rome. The Dominicans followed suit some years later, as much because of popular demand as through their own initiative. People who had been close to them for years wanted their guidance, not the Franciscans', and so the Preachers complied, and a Dominican Third Order came into being. The other major mendicant orders, the Carmelites and the Augustinians, also created their Third Orders.

Once the institutional framework was in place, the religious devotion of the laity poured into it. The Third Orders became, and remained, a highly dynamic movement within the church. Whether its founders anticipated such success, it is hard to tell; the original rules do not seem to have demanded anything exceptional of its members. Yet in time some of them soared to extraordinary spiritual heights. One of the most famous mystics of the Middle Ages (and, incidentally, one of only two women given the title "Doctor of the Church") was the Dominican tertiary Catherine of Siena. Born while the Black Death was raging, and dying in 1380 at the age of thirty-three, she plunged from a very early age into a life of prayer, penance, and visions. Even for an era well acquainted with asceticism, hers was proverbial: she ate little or nothing, and slept almost not at all. Yet she lived at high speed, visiting hospitals and prisons in the company of other Third Order ladies, and, later, dashing around the cities of Italy and as far afield as Avignon in a battle to bring the papacy back to Rome. Her influence was phenomenal. She bullied and cajoled Pope Gregory XI until he complied, then, after his death, she rallied to the side of the much-despised Urban VI in an effort to heal the schism that followed.

Throughout her life Catherine had Dominican directors, the last of them being Raymond of Capua, soon to be master general of the order. But she never became a nun. It is an interesting commentary on the age, that a laywoman of no great learning could rise to such a commanding position over princes and prelates. For all that it was a man's world, sanctity could still outweigh all other considerations.

The Third Orders gave the fourteenth-century church a number of canonized saints — twenty-five Franciscans alone, not to mention those belonging to the other orders. They also provided their cities with improved social services. They ran hospitals and hospices, schools for poor children and homes for prostitutes. Because of the many prominent men and women in their ranks, they could be a power to be reckoned with, as in Perugia for instance, where for years they supervised the municipal services and finances as well as seeing to the distribution of food. In Italy especially, and in Spain and southern France, their management of major public occasions, such as the magnificent processions in which all citizens were called to take part, helped to move religious observance to the center stage of cities. They were, in many ways, the friars' surrogates in the day-to-day business of saving souls.

The story of the Third Orders is, first and foremost, the story of how Christianity opened up to include the laity, not just as hearers of the good news, but as its bearers. For a body as traditionalist as the Church, it was a huge psychological step forward to allow that men and women could undertake the *vita apostolica* while living in their own homes and continuing with their worldly tasks and professions. But even as this laicization was taking place, the monastic life was still tugging at the hearts of many members.

It was a gradual development. For practical as well as spiritual reasons, some Third Order members chose to leave their homes and live together. In due course some of them, if so inclined, would adopt a mild version of the religious common life. In time the commitment to the common life could gain strength, to the point where the members decided to take religious vows. With the vows came a new standing in society: monastic, in the sense that the community had a corporate identity and the recognition that went along with it, yet not strictly monastic, because its members were still involved in work outside the house. An example would be various groups of women who appeared in the Low Countries in the later fourteenth century. The Grey Sisters, as they came to be called, lived in common and observed the Rule of the Franciscan Third Order while going out to work among the sick and poor. Acknowledged as full religious communities, they became major actors in hospital care in years to come.

And that was not the end of the evolution. During the fifteenth century some communities of tertiaries went further still, asking to be enclosed — in other words, to become contemplatives. With the blessing of the Church they shut themselves off from the outside world and gave themselves over to the full monastic regime of prayer and penance. And thus the Third Order came full circle. It was a strange inversion of Saint Francis's original purpose, but it was a clear indication of the powerful hold that monasticism still exercised over medieval men and women.

By the 1400s the Third Orders were everywhere, drawing in men and women from every class and profession, and offering them a wide choice of vocations, from the devout life lived at home to the fully religious life lived in the cloister. They were a mendicant success story. The friars had capitalized on the huge religious exuberance of the thirteenth century and created an institution that was able to survive the religious downturn of the years to come.

*   *   *

In 1417, with the election of a single pope, Martin V, the schism was ended, and the Catholic Church was again at peace with itself. But peace did not bring it well-being. As an institution it was much enfeebled. The turmoil in the papacy over the past forty years had disillusioned people, and led them to argue that supreme authority in the Church should belong not to the pope but to the ecumenical council. They had grounds for their argument. After all, the Council of Constance (1414-1418) had decreed as much, and several prominent thinkers continued to argue the case. It was a sort of parliament-versus-king debate, except that this time it was related to church governance. Gradually the conciliar movement lost traction; however, the papacy did not gain correspondingly. Rome remained a small Italian city-state, deeply and sometimes violently immersed in Italian politics. Many of its interventions beyond its borders reflected its local priorities. Meanwhile, power structures in the rest of Europe were changing. Countries were consolidating themselves and moving toward something like nationhood. France, England, Spain, Portugal, and Habsburg Austria would all be major powers in their own right before the end of the century. And there would be a constellation of smaller powers, all with their own ideas on how the church should operate within their borders. Given the steep decline in the papacy's prestige, these ideas were often negative.

The Holy See also fell hostage to another power, the Renaissance. For all its beauty and intellectual splendor, the Renaissance caused deep disturbance in Rome. Embracing it wholeheartedly could well mean denying the old truths of Christendom; denying it altogether could lead to obscurantism. Some people managed the compromise, while others simply split their personalities, adopting the new thinking while continuing to pay lip service to the old Catholic forms. The result was spiritual decrepitude. Though late-fifteenth-century Rome was already preparing for its future magnificence, morally it was in tatters.

The cry was being heard for "reform in head and members." There is no argument about the head; it was, by the end of the century, incontestably sick. The man who has been called the worst pope in history, Alexander VI, came to the throne in 1492, and with him came his disreputable children and a dreadful record of mayhem and murder. But even if he had been the angel Gabriel, it is difficult to see how he could have cleaned out the deep-rooted corruption in the institution. The people who were the pillars of the church, especially those at the top, were too rich, too deeply immersed in secular affairs. What of the members, though? Rome was not, and never had been, the sum and substance of Christendom. Throughout the fifteenth century Europe as a collectivity remained extremely devout. The laity was still pious: people still went on pilgrimage, gave money for masses, built beautiful churches. They had said the rosary before; now they said it more often, with greater intensity, thanks to the inspiration of a Dominican, Alain de la Roche. Preachers still preached, and crowds still flocked to hear them. What was more, the preachers' spoken word was receiving more and more reinforcement from a new quarter, the printed page. By 1500, some twenty million books had been printed in Europe, most of them with religious themes.

Here and there men and women still undertook great things. One of these was the reform in 1419 of the abbey of Santa Giustina, in Padua. A group of reformers sought to return to the authentic Benedictine way of life. As long as they were subject to *commenda* this was impossible, since every effort to change could be thwarted by abbots who did not want to upset the functioning of their cash cows. The reformers found their way around the problem: while keeping to the Benedictine Rule, they adopted a system of governance like that of the Dominicans, in which there would be no abbots-for-life, but only a general chapter that would oversee the entire congregation, appointing its abbots for a limited term and moving them regularly. Thus the commendatory abbots were eased out, leaving the monks free to return to strict observance. The reform was so successful that it spread to scores of other monasteries in Italy and Spain. In 1504 it reached Saint Benedict's own abbey of Monte Cassino, so that from that time on the congregation was known as the Cassinese Congregation. Another successful Italian reform, that of Subiaco, was carried across the Alps, and by the end of the century more than two hundred Bavarian and Austrian monasteries, male and female, had adopted its strict version of the Benedictine Rule. These movements were only a drop in the bucket amidst the prevailing monastic decadence, but they were brave undertakings nonetheless.

The intention of all these reformers was always the same: to return in their way of life to a more perfect past. The same can be said for the Minims, a new society of friars established in the late fifteenth century. They followed their founder, Francis of Paula, in practicing the most ferocious asceticism together with the most ferocious self-abasement, assuming, thus, the role of "the least of men" that Francis of Assisi had desired for his own brothers. For this they were rewarded by the rapid expansion of their order, at a time when most other orders were vegetating. Even in this modernizing century, the world still warmed to the medieval forms of sanctity.

But new forms of holiness were also in the making. In 1432 Frances, the wife of a Roman nobleman and the mother of three children, led a group of companions to establish what she called "a new spiritual edifice," a nonmonastic order dedicated to the service of God and the poor. Her community, the Torre di Specchi, would be an inspiration and a model for others to come. Elsewhere other women, often members of the Franciscan Third Order, were also exploring the uncertain terrain between full monasticism and full lay status. By the end of the century the Grey Sisters in France and the Netherlands, numbering close to a hundred communities, had formed themselves into an order, complete with their own statutes. In Cracow a group of Third Order women took over a monastery and began caring for the elderly and sick. Many such half-nuns were on the move in the fifteenth century. Though they would be reined in later by the Counter-Reformation church, they were still on the side of the future.

"To Love God and Worship Him Is Religion, Not the Taking of Special Vows" (Geert Groote)

One of the great shining lights of late-medieval spirituality was the *Devotio Moderna,* a religious movement born in Holland in the late fourteenth century. The *Devotio Moderna* turned away from extravagant rituals, from mysticism and ecstasies, from excessive asceticism, from the sterile theology of the schools and the puffery so often associated with high office in the church, and proposed a simple piety focused on the life of Christ. It was Catholicism stripped down to its essentials, a perfect fit for the bourgeois spirit of the Low Countries. By melding humanist learning with a deep religious devotion, it helped northern Europe to achieve a renaissance that was also Christian.

In 1374 Geert Groote, a recent convert from a misspent youth, renounced his two prebends, turned his house in Deventer into a hostel for poor women, and started to search for his vocation. After two years in a Carthusian monastery, he became a preacher of repentance. Though he was hugely popular, he spared no one, clerical or lay. In the words of his follower Thomas à Kempis, he was like John the Baptist, "laying the axe to the root of the tree." His downfall as a preacher was not as final as that of the Baptist, but it was serious enough. The secular clergy and mendicants whom he had castigated complained to the bishop of Utrecht, and he was silenced. He died two years later, in 1384.

Groote died without knowing what was to be achieved through his influence: the creation of the Brothers of the Common Life and the Sisters of the Common Life. The women who lived in his house had formed a community, and he had given them a rule; elsewhere groups of followers, both men and women, had formed up spontaneously. But it was all still highly informal. Only in 1402 was their way of life approved by the bishop. Essentially, brothers and sisters undertook to live in community, working for their living but sharing all things, attending their parish church while also following their own communal observances. They were to instruct themselves, both as a group and by private reading, but they were not to seek after learning for its own sake. They were not to take solemn vows, or adopt monastic practices, but they were to train themselves by daily exercise in the virtues of humility, simplicity, and love of neighbor.

The movement found wide acceptance in the Netherlands and the Rhineland. But it was not welcomed by everyone. Among the brothers' most strident enemies were certain Dominicans, who used the same arguments against them that they themselves had once had to endure: that the newcomers were taking on the trappings of monasticism, thus usurping the position that belonged to the proper authorities (the Dominicans, for instance). This, according to one line of argument, made them heretics. The debate went all the way to the top of the church before it was settled in the brothers' favor. As for the sisters, were they not beguines, and had not Rome condemned all beguines? Only the women's solid orthodoxy, and their defense by influential friends, saved them from disbandment. In the course of these fights an important principle was finally hammered out: that community life did not belong to monks and nuns alone, that ordinary men and women could profit by it in their search for a greater perfection.

As was often the case with lay communities, some of the brothers did eventually opt for a wholly monastic life under the Rule of Saint Augustine, and thus was born the Congregation of Windesheim. By 1500 the congregation numbered more than a hundred houses, spread out through the Low Countries and Germany. It was of course at ground zero during the Reformation, and suffered accordingly; it survived, however, only to disappear in the general destruction of the Napoleonic years.

The Brothers of the Common Life took up a cause that was dear to the hearts of their humanist contemporaries: childhood education. From the start they took in poor boys and found ways to get them to school. Before long they began running schools themselves; these schools became highly successful. Of the thousands of boys they educated, two live on in history: Erasmus, one of the great minds of our civilization, and Thomas à Kempis, to whom is credited *The Imitation of Christ,* which has been named the most influential devotional book ever written in the West.

Thomas died in 1471, at a time when the medieval church, having passed from adolescence to a ripe old age, was still holding on to its enormous brood of children, the good, the bad, and the indifferent. Erasmus died in 1536, in a very different world. The Christendom that he had once known was gone, shattered; the Christianity for which he had hoped — a gentle, learned, humanist Christianity — was receding over the horizon. He had decided to stay with the Catholic Church, though he was fully aware of its faults and shortcomings. Others were taking a different path.

Over the past several centuries the civilization we know as "Christendom" had come to full flower, and now it was going to seed. A great historian, Johan Huizinga, has described the fifteenth century as "the waning of the Middle Ages," an era of low spiritual vitality and little freshness of thought. There was no shortage of piety, he argues; indeed, so much piety was on display that it had become devalued. The atmosphere was "saturated" with religious imagery, crowded with so many saints and angels and devotional practices that for the ordinary faithful there was scarcely space left for a serious relationship with God. This was the danger that the *Devotio Moderna* warned against, but across large parts of Europe the warning went unheeded. One might say that longtime familiarity with things sacred had bred a kind of careless contempt, a sludgy ennui that serious Christians found difficulty in overcoming.

Late-medieval civilization was a complicated mixture of beauty and cynicism, casual religiosity and deep spirituality; enjoyment of life and a fascination with violence. Public executions were as frequent and as well attended as religious processions. Public festivals were more gorgeous than ever before; at the same time, the severed heads and body parts of executed men decorated countless city walls. On the brink of a new age, society was still carrying the baggage of the past. Four centuries earlier the Church had looked for ways to prevent Christians killing Christians. In the intervening years the world had learned a lot, but not how to stop the slaughter. Before many decades passed, the slaughter would be resumed with new intensity, and this time it would have the full blessing of the Christian leadership.

But at least there would be no problem with ennui. A very different day was about to dawn.

Suggested Reading for Chapter 2

Many of the works on the medieval orders that I signaled in my first chapter apply to this chapter, notably the contribution by David Knowles to volume 2 of *The Christian Centuries*. With the thirteenth century, however, a new element enters the picture — the friars — and there is enough written about them to fill whole libraries. A good place to start would be *The Friars*, by C. H. Lawrence (1994). For an English perspective, there is a further work by David Knowles, *The Religious Orders in England* (1962-1971). Saint Francis of Assisi is a phenomenon in himself — one of the most written-about men of the Middle Ages. A brief outline of his life will be found in almost every work on the thirteenth-century church. For his order as a whole, there is J. Moorman, *A History of the Franciscan Order from Its Origins to the Year 1517* (1986). For the *Poverello's* most distinguished disciple, there is, among other works, Marco Bartoli's *Clare of Assisi* (1993).

The "women's movement," so-called, had been in evidence since the twelfth century, but in the later Middle Ages it became a conundrum for the ecclesiastical establishment, and a force to be reckoned with. For a sense of the conundrum, read Elizabeth Makowski, *Canon Law and Cloistered Women: Periculoso and Its Commentators, 1298-1545* (1997), and her more recent work, *"A Pernicious Sort of Woman"* (2005). For more on the beguines, read W. Simons, *Cities of Ladies* (2001).

CHAPTER 3

The Sixteenth Century: The Age of Reformation

The Reformation, when it came, came like a thunderbolt. The speed with which Luther's message flew across Germany, and then spread into other parts of Europe, was a phenomenon for which no contemporary, not even Luther himself, was prepared.

And yet for a long time, and imperceptibly, society had been undergoing structural adjustment, and as a result was able to absorb the shock, and grow with it.

Had a person been sent into orbit of the earth in the year 1000, and had he, like Methuselah, enjoyed a life span of hundreds of years, he would have observed significant physical changes in the continent of Europe by 1500. Most dramatically, its forests — those great, dark abodes of the supernatural — had shrunk perceptibly. Patches of cleared land had spread out, had run together, sure signs of the growth of human settlement. Once the good arable land was used up, marginal lands were brought into cultivation, costing tremendous effort yet yielding less than was hoped for. Looked at in one way, the conquest of Europe's raw earth was a triumph of human endeavor; in another, it was a harbinger of hard times ahead. The population, after shrinking drastically during the Great Plague, was on the climb again, and there would soon be more mouths to feed than food to feed them. Out of this imbalance would be born one of the great challenges of the early modern period: the demographic overflow that agriculture could not sustain, the flotsam of desperate people moving to and fro, carrying with them hunger, disease, and crime.

Some of the settlements had become villages, or even small towns. For the most part, people still lived directly off the land. Across the great northern plain of Europe, their open fields stretched as far as the eye could see; in other parts where the terrain was more broken, hedges and stone walls demarcated peasant holdings no matter how small. Elsewhere, across wide swaths of land, agriculture had given way to sheep, the unwitting engines of the economic growth of much of Europe. Their wool sustained a burgeoning cloth industry and an expanding trade network that reached from north to south, from west to east, as far as the Mediterranean and beyond.

The Mediterranean was the hub of this universe. Around its coastline were settled the oldest, richest civilizations known to Western man: the finest cities, the most advanced cultures. All the luxury goods of the Orient came through its ports or were created in its workshops. What it did not use it sent north, up rivers such as the Rhône or on mule trains across the Alps to the Rhine. In return, as its own natural resources were exhausted, it reached further and further afield to gather in raw materials: grain to feed its people, whole forests of wood to build its ships.

The space traveler would have seen in inchoate form in 1500 what he would see today: a concentration of human settlement running up the spine of Europe, with the Mediterranean at one end, the North Sea at the other. Along its path, this south-north trade route stimulated demographic growth, and, in turn, gave rise to some of the finest towns outside Italy. Elsewhere, wherever conditions were favorable the same process was taking place: towns springing up and becoming cities, turning their adjacent countrysides into food banks, so to speak, from which they drew the wherewithal to eat, drink, and become rich.

One of the basic conditions for growth was access to water. In sixteenth-century Europe, land travel was barely better than it had been in the days of the Romans, on whose roads it still depended. Once off these great thoroughfares, movement became difficult. For travelers on foot — traders, peddlers, pilgrims, or broken men seeking subsistence — the roads were scarcely better than trails, passable only when the weather was not too inclement. Horses and mules were few and far between, and wheeled traffic rare. Even for important people movement was painfully slow. From Venice, for instance, the very fastest courier service to London took three weeks; to Lisbon, five. "The struggle against distance," as it has been called, seemed unwinnable. What is amazing is that so many people undertook it anyway. From all over Europe, pilgrims on foot converged on Rome, or Santiago in Spain, or Loretto in Italy, or, less ambitiously, the hundreds of lesser shrines that dotted this Christian continent. But for practical purposes water was the way to go. Though very few traders braved the dangers of the open sea, small ships by the thousands plied the coastal waters, putting in at night to harbors along their route. Great rafts carried goods down the major rivers, to be unloaded at destination and then broken up into saleable lumber, leaving the raftsmen to make their way home on foot.

In every way that human ingenuity could devise, Europeans were striving to make a living and, if possible, to get rich. Land ownership was still the surest path to wealth, but more and more there was opportunity in the cities and in the activity these cities made possible. More and more, the people who mattered were city dwellers. We see them in a thousand paintings, complete with their furs and velvets, their jewels, their money bags, their pet dogs, their books. They have left us their image in the statuary and stained glass windows of countless churches. Look beyond the patron saints at center stage, and you will see the donors kneeling on the side, pious, complacent, justly proud of the association with holiness that their affluence has made possible.

Many of these people owed their wealth to trade or banking. But not all the elites of cities were merchants. Men of law, doctors, university professors, artists also gathered in the cities, because that was where their professions could be practiced. Grand seigneurs, too, recognized the advantages of city life and used their landed wealth to build themselves sumptuous residences. The ecclesiastical ruling classes — bishops if the city was important enough, secular canons in most cases — lived close together in handsome enclaves. Even the monasteries, once repositories of learning in the countryside, now owned houses in the city, joining the innumerable urban convents that had always been there. Then, in certain highly favored cities such as Florence, Paris, or London, there gathered the princely courts with their concentric circles of aristocrats, hangers-on, and servants, and their growing armies of functionaries. These last had their roots in the provinces, but for some time they had been flowing toward the centers of power, establishing their families, forging alliances, building their own town houses, acquiring country estates, making themselves an indispensable part of the social structure. As they increased in number, so also did the laborers and domestics required to serve them.

This great urbanizing movement, already well begun before 1500, underlay the momentous changes of mind and spirit that were taking place. Scholarship requires leisure, and a standard of living well above subsistence level. Art requires patrons, people who have money to spare for the finer things of life. Beginning in Italy, the cities, as they grew in wealth, were able to provide these things. The new elites were more and more likely to be cultured, literate, and demanding. Consciously or unconsciously, they were outgrowing the economic and mental structures of the Middle Ages. They were like new wine, swelling and seething inside old wineskins.

It would be a mistake to describe the changes as a function of wealth and nothing else. The development of cities also had its effect on their less exalted members, the artisans and tradesmen. City living made them different from their country cousins. It released them from the iron grip of village custom and opened them to a wider view of the world. It allowed them to practice new and potentially subversive skills, reading and writing, for instance, which gave them a certain openness to new ideas. It drew them, on occasion, into mass action, even mass violence. In days to come, in city after city, when the religious reform movement faced hesitation and prevarication from the elites, the "lesser people" were ready to embrace the new faith and provide the boots on the ground to enforce it.

Then there were the truly poor. They also had a role to play in the drama of the sixteenth century. The great mortalities of the recent past, plague, famine, war, had wrought havoc in many parts of the Continent. For the dispossessed the cities were a last faint hope, and they came flooding in, seeking work or charity. But in 1500, no city was equipped to accept them in their numbers. In one great theater of war, Italy, their desperate condition did more to spark religious activism than did any other problem, including heresy. The sequence of events — crisis first, soul-searching next, and with it the definition of an apostolate — played out in Italian cities, and was repeated in later years in other parts of Europe. Compassion was the mother of the religious inventiveness that so distinguished the sixteenth century.

The wealth of cities was made visible in their churches. The later fifteenth century had seen a flurry of church building. We can be cynical about that, putting it down to a temporary convergence of devotion and disposable income. No doubt the rich took a worldly pride in their endowments. But feeling, in fact, ran much deeper. This was an age of tremendous piety. People of all walks of life went on pilgrimages, marched in religious processions, prayed the rosary, followed the stations of the cross, celebrated the great new feast of Corpus Christi. They joined confraternities, attended sermons, visited miracle sites, and bought indulgences. They read the religious books that were now flowing off the printing presses. They funded masses for the dead in such numbers that a whole army of "mass-priests" (clerics with no other purpose or source of income) came into being just to recite mass after mass in the chapels, or "chantries," built for that end alone. "These were the anxious gestures of people in distress and in need of help," writes a historian, who suggests that the root of their anxiety was an enormous fear of death. And certainly, if we go by the literature and art of the times, death and the corruption of the body loomed large on their mental horizon, to a degree that is difficult for us to rationalize. Was it simply because they were still haunted by the memory of the Great Plague, and panicked by its periodic reoccurrences? Or perhaps because, as life became sweeter and more enjoyable, they were ever more attached to it, ever more reluctant to leave it? Whatever the reason, the faithful smoothed their anxiety by multiplying their acts of devotion. In their desire to storm heaven, they used a strategy of quantity rather than quality. Prayers, prayers, and more prayers. What their behavior lacked in originality, it made up in spirit.

"The Sheep Look Up and Are Not Fed"

In all this, where was the clergy?

In later years, preachers and publicists of the Reform would make a great case of the pre-Reformation clergy's moral decay. There was some truth in what they said, but also some exaggeration. Of course, the situation varied from region to region, as it did between cities and the countryside. The priests who served in city churches were quite likely to be university-educated and tolerably moral. By and large they do not appear to have been the roistering, woman-chasing ignoramuses that their detractors depicted. But their pastoral activity tended to be perfunctory, and their preaching prosaic, to say the least. Luther would comment that it was not their morals that scandalized him, but their carelessness with the Word of God. And in addition to that, there were just too many of them. It would not be uncommon for 10 or even 20 percent of a city's population to be clerics of one kind or another, enjoying a privileged life and giving little in return.

Thus, while the faith of city dwellers was not dead, we may conclude that it was ill-served and, in some as yet unexpressed way, frustrated. "There was a tremendous appetite for all that was divine," writes one of their most distinguished historians. "But at the same time, as far as we can see, there was a feeling of unrest and disquiet and there were confused aspirations for something better."

What about the people of the countryside? In 1500, anywhere between 90 and 95 percent of Europe's sixty million people lived on the land. Almost to a man and woman they were Catholic, if by Catholic we mean baptized and living within a circumscription, or parish, under the ultimate authority of Rome. They were bound to support their parish financially; in return, they could expect to receive the sacraments of baptism and extreme unction, and burial within the sacred space of the churchyard. Penance and Eucharist were minimally practiced, and confirmation and matrimony were optional extras that many of the faithful never experienced.

The peasants of the sixteenth century were certainly religious. The question is: Was their religion truly Christian? Numbers of historians have explored their beliefs and practices, and concluded that these sprang from a much older, pre-Christian past. Christianity may well have been as much a camouflage as a replacement for much more primitive forms of religion. The peasant world was rife with spells and incantations, and rituals to appease the angry spirits. In time to come, reformers both Protestant and Catholic would be shocked by the discovery of this subterranean stream of what we now call "popular religion" and they called "superstition." But given the uncertainty of life, and the knowledge of what the forces of nature could do, the peasants' practices made sense. The old church had understood this and become complicit. Led by the clergy, processions formed up regularly to pray for rain, to bless the fishing boats, to exorcise the insects and rodents that threatened the harvest. Church bells were rung to ward off thunderstorms. On the feast of Saint John at midsummer, fires were lit to scare away the evil spirits. Ancient sacred springs, which people still visited in great numbers, retained their magical powers, even though they were now baptized with the names of Christian saints.

Within this world, divided by a chasm of understanding from the Christianity of the urban elites, there lived a sluggish parish clergy. Parishes were, of course, "benefices," in the sense that they came with an allotment of land and a salary that in theory derived from the tithes paid by the parishioners but in fact often amounted to a great deal less. By that time most benefices had fallen under the control of strangers — laymen, ecclesiastics, monasteries — who appointed the priest but appropriated most of the income. (Indeed, numbers of fine town houses were built with the tithes of peasants.) As a result, the serving priests were often forced to make money where they could, by cultivating their own lands, by charging for their services, or by taking on outside work. A depressing number of them simply went elsewhere, subcontracting their parishes to even poorer vicars. In some dioceses the great majority of parish priests were nonresident, and their parishes were served by a sort of clerical proletariat.

For those who remained on the job, what incentive was there to perform well? Many rural pastors lived only a notch above their flocks; they were unlikely to have anything more than a rudimentary education; often they barely knew the words of the Mass or of the sacramentary rites. They frequently took concubines; this may not have upset their parishioners as long as the women were modest and the children did not enjoy undue social advantages. What truly disturbed the people was their priests' failure to be there for the established rituals. And, of course, the collection of the tithe, with all its flagrant injustice.

With all this, there was still a deep loyalty among countryfolk, if not to the Church then at least to the parish church, the structure their ancestors had built, the statues and symbols it sheltered, the bells that hung above it, the graveyard around it where the living could still know a fellowship with their dead. Everything about it was sacred, and the onslaught that would later come against those sacred things would be deeply offensive to the people who treasured them. More than anybody else, as the great movements of reform lashed the countryside, the peasants of Europe would remain faithful to the old religion as they knew it.

"We Have All Withered Like Leaves"

Where, in this picture, did the monks, friars, and nuns of pre-Reformation Europe fit?

Whether in the cities or in the countryside, monasteries had over the centuries acquired enormous holdings. The extent of these holdings varied greatly from region to region, but it is reckoned that, overall, one-sixth of Europe's property was in ecclesiastical (and much of that in monastic) hands. Insofar as rural society had experience of the black monks and the white monks and their female counterparts, it must have been as landlords.

Here, their record was not particularly good; or, perhaps more accurately, it was too good. In Germany, at least, it appears that from 1450 onward many Benedictine monasteries refined their management practices and regularized their accounts, so that their tenants were more squeezed than they would have been as tenants of comparatively feckless lay landowners. Increased efficiency in record keeping allowed for more ruthless collection of rents; a more adept practice of law led to the forced reversion of many half-free tenants into serfdom. And to add grave insult to injury, ecclesiastical landlords were also responsible for much of the tithe collection, and the diversion of it away from the parishes into their own pockets that so greatly enraged the peasantry. It was no wonder, then, that when a great peasant rebellion broke out in Germany in 1525, much of the violence was directed against the monasteries.

This antipathy does not seem to have existed everywhere, at least not to the same degree. In England and Wales some eight hundred religious houses, large and small, were to suffer forcible dissolution between 1535 and 1540 — but for reasons of state. In two parliamentary acts, the Crown simply pronounced their elimination and confiscated their property. The pretext for this act of plunder was the unworthiness and decadence of the monastic population. But in fact, what attracted the attention of Henry VIII and his minister Thomas Cromwell was the monasteries' wealth, which taken together was greater than the annual income of the Crown. If the monks were guilty of a sin, it was, according to a Cistercian historian, "not general immorality but general mediocrity," and perhaps that is the key to the quiet way they sank below the surface. They do not seem to have attracted the hostility of their neighbors in the countryside, but neither, for that matter, did they garner much support. Despite some armed uprisings on their behalf, notably the Pilgrimage of Grace in 1536, they went down easily, and thus, apart from a brief moment of restoration under Henry's Catholic daughter Mary, and a hiccup, a hundred years later, under Charles I's Catholic wife Henrietta Maria, monasticism ended in England for centuries.

Whether in France or in England or elsewhere, the appearance of wealth could be misleading. Monastic communities could be rich in property and at the same time dangerously poor in their day-to-day living. The previous centuries had been troubled times. Religious houses had suffered their share of pillage by marauding soldiers, and outright extortion by secular magnates. War and plague and periodic crop disasters took their toll. But far more damaging in the long run was the practice of *commenda,* the assigning of a religious institution, both its personnel and its property, as a gift to a favored individual. For this destructive practice the monasteries had to thank the Avignon papacy. Ever since popes had begun giving abbacies as sinecures to their own partisans — cardinals or curial officials or papal nephews — the wealth of monasteries had been siphoned into the purses of strangers who did not necessarily have any interest in the communities' well-being. Occasionally the partition of goods between commendatory abbots and monks was fair, but this depended on the good will of the abbots rather than on any overarching moral imperative. In particularly egregious cases, monks and nuns were literally starved out of existence while their so-called superiors took possession of their incomes. The practice, widespread in Italy, was also flagrant in France. In season and out, protests were made, both to the Crown and to the papacy, against the abuse; at the start of the new century it looked in France as though the old grief might be redressed. But alas, international politics got in the way of domestic reform. With the Concordat of Bologna of 1516, King Francis I promised Pope Leo X his political support, and received in return the right of appointment to ninety-three bishoprics and 527 abbeys, virtually all the higher ecclesiastical positions in France. He and his successors were free to reward whomever they wished (even, sometimes, courtiers or the young children of favorites) without any regard for the needs of the communities. For the rest of the *ancien régime,* this would be a powerful source of patronage for the Crown, a bonanza for the noble families who were more or less given carte blanche to loot the monasteries, and a cause for despair among would-be monastic reformers. The Cistercian general chapters could do no more than record the impoverishment of their houses and the misery of their members.

For various reasons, then, monasticism did not shine brightly at the end of the fifteenth century. Here and there significant reforms took place: the Cassinese congregation in Italy, the congregation of Bursfeld in Germany, the congregation of Valladolid in Spain, as well as a number of other efforts. In Carthusian houses the rule continued to be obeyed, quietly and faithfully. But reform remained local and incremental. Most monasteries were mere shells of what they had once been. And this seems strange, considering the deep religiosity of the age. The chasm between the aspirations of the Christian world and the actual practice of this, its long-cherished elite, was deep and wide. The verdict of the previous historian is apt: "In no other epoch of church history was so much said about reform and so little accomplished."

With regard to the friars, the story is more complex. Where early-sixteenth-century monasticism was suffering decay, the mendicant orders were still thriving, and their impact on the lives of the faithful continued to be great.

In 1500 there were six orders of mendicants, or friars: the Franciscans, the Dominicans, the Augustinians, the Carmelites, the Servites, and the newly created order of Minims. The major difference between them and the monastic orders was that whereas monks turned inward to the communal work of praising God in the *Opus Dei,* friars considered their principal role to be evangelization. The practical outcome of this was that they became, essentially, urban dwellers. Their vocation as preachers made that almost inevitable. After all, Francis himself had insisted that his brothers live "not for themselves alone but for the salvation of souls" and had set the example in his own life, by preaching here, there, and everywhere until blindness and ill health bore him down. But he had been a wanderer, content to sleep wherever he found himself when night fell. His followers came to look for something more stable. The "desert," that place of solitude and penitence, continued to draw them, but the cities drew them more powerfully still. By 1500 there was not one European town, however small, that did not have its convent of friars, while quite a few of the larger cities had three or four. Whereas the monks lived, by tradition, within their walls, the friars were highly visible to the new urban populations.

The friars specialized in preaching repentance, and in a powerful style. The best known to us, perhaps, is the Dominican Girolamo Savonarola, and his "bonfire of the vanities" in Florence. But in their time there were others, and their reputation ran before them. Of one of the greatest of them, the Franciscan Bernardino of Feltre, it was said that "when he attacks vice, he does not speak, he thunders and lightens!" To heighten people's sense of dread and repentance, the friars allowed crowds of flagellants to accompany them. Furthermore, skilled preachers as they were, they also used other techniques: jokes, songs, dramatizations. The most famous of them were able to attract huge audiences. In Florence Savonarola is said to have preached to crowds of 20,000. In Orléans, the crowd that came to hear the Franciscan Olivier Maillard was so large that it overflowed onto the roof of the ducal palace, which caved in and later had to be repaired.

The friars did more than preach: they taught in the universities, they assisted in hospitals, and they won respect by their service in times of plague. They specialized in reconciling competing factions. They were also instrumental in setting up *Monti di Pietà,* or small lending institutions, to assist the urban poor. But for all their good works, they were by no means universally popular in this year 1500. A number of people disliked them, and for different reasons.

The methods of evangelization that formed the very core of their mission caused annoyance to some. There was now an intellectual and religious elite, modern and humanist in its thinking, that saw that kind of hellfire preaching as a throwback to a darker time. But here, of course, was a problem without a solution, as long as there was diversity in the Christian population. For the rank and file, the friars' great rallies against sin were an important part of life, as can be seen from the crowds that attended them and from the gifts and legacies that the public showered upon them. As the sixteenth century opened, new friaries were still being established, a sure indication that the mendicant orders were alive and well and active. Yet, paradoxically, their very success was a source of friction. Beggars by self-description, and "the least of all men" according to the earnest desire of Francis of Assisi, they were now, in fact, comfortably well-off and sometimes unbearably cocky. They were still active on the turf of the secular clergy, and when the bishops tried to take action against them, they claimed papal exemptions and continued with their poaching. And they sometimes raised money in questionable ways, bartering spiritual benefits for cash. The Dominican Tetzel, who so offended Martin Luther with his indulgence preaching, was just one of a number of friars who specialized in this kind of work.

There was another complaint against them: that they were womanizers. This grievance had been voiced for many years, as anyone knows who has read Chaucer's *Canterbury Tales*. But in the Reformation years it became a deafening roar. After the Romish Babylon itself, friars were the favorite target of the Reformers' outrage, "being Devils at Women," as a complaint to King Henry VIII of England put it, applying themselves, "by all Sleights they may, to have to do with every Man's Wife, Daughter, and Maid; that cuckoldry should reign over all your subjects; that no man should know his own child" and so on. Clearly such material had a polemical intent, but it was responding to a deeply held prejudice. The question is, was the prejudice justified?

Yes and no. In some cities, especially where young friars gathered to attend university, their riotous behavior became a byword. And further afield, those many friars who had license to wander abroad as itinerant preachers had plenty of leeway to misbehave if they so wished. Their superiors could have great difficulty reining them in. Their very activity, even when sexually blameless, could be unsettling. Europe was a patriarchal society. Husbands and fathers ruled. But certain male outsiders were able to intervene in family affairs: priests. And therein lay the rub. Because in confession they could receive confidences of the most intimate kind, priests could be privy to other people's domestic problems; it appears that this was, and would be for centuries to come, a cause for unease among men. Friars as confessors, especially itinerant friars, who were here today and gone tomorrow, must have aroused suspicion. What else passed between the priest and his penitent? How much the suspicion was justified can never be known, but we see it appearing here and there, whenever women became "too religious." Later, as the Jesuits established themselves, they found that they, too, attracted enthusiastic female followings. Prudently, they reversed course and made it a policy to keep as much distance from women as possible. The devotion of women was to be avoided, if it meant incurring the hostility of men.

In one final way the friars were a scandal, even to themselves. The many divisions that had arisen among them over their rule and way of life had not been healed. For some, as for instance the Franciscans, the rift had become toxic. Observants and Conventuals fought like cats. They hurled scurrilous diatribes at each other; they raided each other's communities, they even took over each other's houses by force, sometimes calling on the civil authorities to eject the opposition. The violence of their quarrel had far-reaching consequences: it drew in relatives and benefactors of the respective communities, who followed the battles with fervor, while it left less involved onlookers shaking their heads in disgust. More significantly, it created vacuums that the civil authorities were only too ready to fill. In the early modern period, the orders would become more and more beholden to the ruling elites for protection and patronage.

In the final analysis, all generalization is inadequate to describe the mendicant orders of the early sixteenth century. Living in their thousands across Europe from Ireland to Hungary, the friars were too numerous and too diverse a population to be so simplified. They differed in purpose, in lifestyle, in national consciousness. Their level of discipline was often a function of local accident: economic circumstances, the character of the men in charge, their proximity to or isolation from central authority. The Augustinian friars of Canterbury ate and slept in taverns, played at dice and chased women, while their brother friars in Piedmont lived on alms, slept on straw, and put on shoes only when they were ordered to do so by the prior general. In France the Dominican Jean Clerée preached against corruption in the church and the selling of indulgences, while in Germany the Dominican Johann Tetzel preached indulgences, and sold them, too. But for all their lights and shadows, the friars remained an important part of society, and arguably the most vibrant element in the pre-Reformation church. There were still donations and legacies coming in from the faithful; there were still new convents being built. But note: the outstanding success story of these years was Francis of Paula and his Minims, the brand-new order of friars that breathed life into the old virtues of poverty, humility, and austerity. By 1550, twelve houses of Minims had been established in France alone. Lay society responded, as it ever had done, to the call of the other world.

"And So It Came About . . ."

In Germany, in the early years of the sixteenth century, the Augustinian friars were facing the same "reformed/unreformed" difficulties that bedeviled other mendicant orders, though they tackled them in a generally dignified manner. The priory of Erfurt was a center of academic excellence and a thriving observant community, one of seventeen reformed houses within the larger, unreformed Saxon congregation. In 1510 the superior of the congregation, Johann von Staupitz, in an effort to improve observance across the board, proposed to amalgamate the observants with their weaker brethren. In this way, he hoped, the good yeast would leaven the unenlightened mass. But the Erfurt community saw it differently, as a threat to its own reform and a headache it did not need. Together with other like-minded houses, it sent two friars to Rome to argue the case against Staupitz's project. One of these was the young Martin Luther. He and his companion went to Rome, spent five months there, and came back, a total journey of some 1,500 miles that, we assume, they made on foot. Their effort paid off: Staupitz failed in his cause. It says a lot for this good man that he recognized the potential of the young friar, had him transferred to the University of Wittenberg, made him a doctor of theology, and authorized him to preach.

Luther never forgot the impressions of that journey: the people he met along the way, the different landscapes he passed through — and the unholiness of the Holy City. As he grew more independent in his thinking, he came to regard Rome and all its works as blasphemous. Even before his break with the Catholic Church, while still a monk in Wittenberg, he would write that "the Roman Curia is thoroughly corrupted and infected, a colossal chaos of all conceivable debaucheries, gluttonies, knaveries, ambitions and sacrilegious outrages." But his final rejection of the church and many of its practices (including monasticism) cannot be attributed to his disgust with Rome. Even less can it be put down to disillusionment with his own community, to which he owed a careful, comprehensive theological formation, which included serious study of the Bible and a grounding in Greek, the new language of humanism. He had wise and sympathetic directors. To one of them, Staupitz, he later wrote: "I cannot forget or be ungrateful, for it was through you that the light of the Gospel began first to shine out of the darkness of my heart." Thus when he came to part company with his community there were no lapses in discipline, no failures in observance, to blame. If anything, the rigors of the rule had only aggravated his natural tendencies to anguish and scruple. He later wrote: "I was indeed a good monk and kept the rules of my order so strictly that I can say: If ever a monk got to heaven through monkery, I should have been that monk.... I would have become a martyr through fasting, prayer, reading and other good works had I remained a monk very much longer." The life Luther left behind was a virtuous religious life, fully faithful to tradition. But that tradition was at odds with his own developing theology.

The Luther phenomenon put a nail through the heart of the Augustinian order in Germany. From the time he started teaching and preaching, this brilliant doctor gained a following among his students, and his ideas struck a sympathetic chord. Once he was openly at odds with the church, his followers had to choose between their loyalties. In 1521, thirteen religious left the Wittenberg convent. Other friars from other Augustinian houses followed suit. In time, more and more men left their houses. Then, as the Reformation spread, the communities in its path collapsed. By midcentury there was little left of this once-prosperous central European order. But it should be emphasized that destruction did not come to the German Augustinians through their own failures in observance and moral behavior.

Ecclesia Semper Reformanda

"The Church forever in need of reform." It was a cry that predated Luther by a hundred years and more, a cry that had been growing stronger and more insistent with the passing years. And the cry went further, adding "reform in head and members." Reform movements, of which there had been many in the past, were not enough. For the Church to be truly whole, its reformation must extend throughout its entire body, including the Roman Curia and the papacy itself.

How to effect this? At the start of the sixteenth century the Holy See was little more than a minor Italian principality, torn by the intramural conflicts of powerful Roman families, threatened by the territorial interests of outside powers. For its popes, survival depended on political alliances, patronage, and on occasion force of arms. The Swiss Guards that tourists admire today did not always have so benign a role! To be sure that they had people they could trust, popes surrounded themselves with members of their own families, notably the famous papal nephews, the Latin word for whom, *nepotes,* gives us a word that we can all understand. They awarded the remaining jobs (along with substantial perquisites) to their friends and clients. The Curia as then constituted was filled with prelates who drew their wealth from multiple benefices that they rarely, if ever, visited. And their immorality trickled down through the city. Rome, the city that so horrified Luther, was a sick mixture of religiosity, conspicuous consumption, and corruption.

The only remedy, in the opinion of many, was to call an ecumenical council. An ecumenical council, then and now, is made up of prelates and theologians from the whole Catholic world. Such councils had been called periodically since earliest times, when matters of faith or discipline required a special solemnity. It was not their purpose to supersede the papacy. The trouble in the early 1500s was that the popes suspected them of doing exactly that. The prospect of a council horrified the Renaissance popes, and they shied away from calling them.

As the Luther revolt developed and spread in Germany, Rome remained frozen in its tracks. Of course, it had its own troubles to contend with, troubles that, in its own mind, dwarfed the problem of a faraway mutinous monk. Since 1494 France and Spain had been fighting up and down the length of Italy. Later, when Spain was joined to the Habsburg Austrian empire, the hostility between the two great powers became even fiercer. The consequences for the peninsula, including the papal states, were disastrous. Whichever power the popes sided with (and they changed sides frequently), the other power threatened them. In 1527, because Pope Clement VII was too pro-French, an imperial army entered Rome and put it to the sword. The city was sacked, four thousand people were killed, and the pope himself was, for a time, imprisoned.

This trauma, combined with the natural disinclination of human beings to do anything counter to their natural interests, was certainly enough to keep ecclesiastical Rome in a state of suspension. However, to the insistent urgings of reform-minded clerics was added another voice: that of the Holy Roman emperor, Charles V. After the scandalous sack of Rome by his troops (which he himself, staunch Catholic as he was, denounced), Charles was very much the master of the papacy. And he was mightily concerned by the spreading Lutheran revolt through his territories. He believed, as did many others, that the problem lay in the Church's lack of discipline; that if it took serious steps to reform the clergy's morals, peace and unity would return to Christianity. Successive popes were not convinced. They feared any concession that might indicate weakness on their part. Finally, in 1545, Pope Paul III was persuaded to move. But the council he convened was very different from the council that the emperor desired. There was now little, if any, hope of reconciliation with the Protestants; things had gone too far. In a sense, the pope wrote off the schismatic regions and, instead, concentrated on affirming the Catholic remnant — in other words, southern Europe. For the papacy, the task of the council was to be the defining of Catholic doctrine, especially in those matters that were under attack.

So the bishops and theologians who met in Trent had a double agenda: the definition of orthodoxy and the reform of the Church. The location, Trent, was, like everything else, a compromise. The emperor wanted the council to be held in his territories, and the pope wanted it close to Rome. Trent (or Trentino), a town in the foothills of the Alps, was Italian in character but juridically a part of the Holy Roman Empire. Its drawback lay in the fact that it was small, subject to a severe climate, and close to the action of foreign armies. The fathers of Trent labored under hot sun and cold winter weather; they dispersed during a typhus epidemic and when the fighting got too close. The intervals between sessions were long, so long that there were few, if any, of the original fathers left to celebrate the closing of the council in 1563. By this time Lutheranism had consolidated its hold on much of the north, and a new religion, Calvinism, had taken hold in Switzerland and in France. But Catholicism had defined itself and set out an agenda for reform. Trent, for all the obstacles that had faced the participants, was to become the template for the Catholic Church for the next four centuries.

"If We Are the Sons of Saint Francis, Let Us Do the Works of Saint Francis"

In 1517, the very year Luther's revolt began, the Franciscans' schism had grown so deep that nothing could close it, and the pope pronounced the two parts divided forever. What he was in fact doing was handing the victory to the Observants. They were by now, in most countries, more numerous and more dynamic than the Conventuals, and for that reason able to take over a large part of the Conventuals' property. But their triumph came at a cost. Having fought for the principle of poverty, they now found themselves in possession of large houses, with growing communities whose care and maintenance required prudent planning. History repeated itself: simple hermitages became full-bore conventual institutions. Inevitably, the old pattern was repeated, as here and there, small groups began to break away in search of stricter observance. Some managed to gain permission to live apart, to practice increased austerity in specially erected "houses of recollection." But others simply threw off their obligations and took up a wandering life; men such as these must have been highly threatening to their communities' good name. Against them the Observant authorities reacted with violence, threatening them with excommunication, arrest, and imprisonment, and labeling them, as their own people had once been labeled, "apostates."

It was against this tense background that in 1525 a simple friar, Matteo de Bascio, left the friary of Montefalcone in the Marches of Ancona and headed for Rome, to ask the pope for permission to "observe the rule to the letter." He had no intention of starting a fight; all he wanted was the right to live as Francis had lived, as a wandering, penniless preacher.

It was not that his convent was a den of iniquity. It was following the Observant way of life as legitimated by custom and authorized by papal decree. A life like this, one could argue, served the great majority of the brothers who desired to live under vows but had no stomach for heroic austerity. No doubt Matteo heard the line, often quoted in religious life, that "obedience is better than sacrifice." He, however, was appealing to an older obedience: obedience to the founder, and to the primitive rule. As a first step he made himself a habit of coarse cloth, with a simple square hood of the kind that Francis had worn. Even this annoyed the other members of the community, who saw it, probably correctly, as a reproach to their more comfortable way of dressing. And so he got up and left, and became, in the eyes of his superiors, an apostate, subject, if apprehended, to severe punishment. In Rome his cause was forwarded by a stroke of good fortune — or an act of providence. Quite by accident, while wandering the corridors of the Vatican, he bumped into the pope, who in what seems an off-handed manner gave him the permission to live as he desired. But this first papal endorsement was verbal and therefore highly fragile. It did not prevent Matteo, once he left Rome, from being caught and imprisoned by his Observant brothers. He was saved by the intervention of an influential woman, Caterina Duchess of Camerino, who knew him already and admired him for his work in her territories during an earlier visitation of the plague. She wrote a letter to the superior, Giovanni da Fano, threatening to banish the Observants from her territories altogether if her protégé was not immediately released. So Matteo was let loose to take up his wandering life, under the distant but potent protection of the House of Camerino. Within a short time he was joined by other men, enough to create an informal community. But they still lived under threat from the Observants, until the duchess, in 1528, procured a papal bull that conferred canonical status on the group. From then on the fraternity would be known as the Order of Friars Minor Capuchin.

The Observants continued to seek the suppression of the Capuchins. Their motives were understandable: their own members had begun deserting in droves to join the new order. Of the seven hundred members the Capuchins acquired in their first ten years, most were ex-Observants, whose departure from their old communities caused serious damage to morale. "They live a life so exceedingly austere and rigid that it is hardly human," an Observant brief to the Roman court complained, "and thus greatly disturb the minds of other members of the Order who in consequence doubt whether they themselves are equally satisfying the obligations of the Rule: thus are many scandalized." The battle that ensued in Rome, under the tired and distracted eyes of Pope Clement VII, drew in a number of powerful people and almost cost the Capuchins their order. Fortunately for them, some powerful people were on their side. So were the ordinary people, who had their own way of bringing pressure to bear when something displeased them. A story is told of a small Roman community of Capuchin friars who were rudely confronted, while eating dinner, by an officer bearing an order for them to leave the city. Rising at once from the table, they picked up their breviaries and marched in procession out of town. It was a dramatic action, and it had its effect. The word ran through the streets: "The harlot and the wicked are made welcome; the men of God are driven forth." Feeling in Rome ran so high that the pope decided to reverse his verdict

In the response made to the Capuchin inspiration, both by the men who flocked to join the order and by the crowds who made common cause with it, we get a glimpse of that mood, that "tremendous appetite for all that was divine," that so marked the age. An English traveler who met with them later described the Capuchins with disdain, as unbearably dirty, smelly, and unkempt with their rough robes and ragged beards. But for Catholics of the sixteenth century, they represented something uncompromisingly beautiful: a return to the pure vision of Francis, who was (and probably still is) the most beloved man in the calendar of saints. The favor they found can be measured in their numbers. By the 1580s they were six thousand, in twenty provinces.

When their order began in Italy, it had nothing to do with the Reformation. Indeed, in consequence of the 1542 defection of their vicar general, Bernardino Ochino, to Protestantism, they became highly suspect in Rome, and they were not given formal permission to cross the Alps until 1574. But once let loose, the Capuchins were not slow to take on the role of preachers of the Counter-Reformation. They had, of course, a rich tradition to draw on, a whole array of practices such as processions and public prayers, to which they now added, as a preface to every preaching mission, forty hours of continuous adoration of the Blessed Sacrament. The fervid atmosphere of the Counter-Reformation years provided the perfect conditions for their emotional style of preaching. They knew how to work the crowds. "Raise up a storm in [their] spirits," a prominent Capuchin preacher recommended — and so they did, in a style that was peculiarly their own. They deliberately cultivated simplicity of content and speech, and so gained a reputation as preachers to the poor.

In the way they rose to the challenge of the times, and in their fierce dedication to the Catholicism of Trent, the Capuchins were men of the modern age. But in another sense they belonged to the past. They modeled their spirituality on that of Francis the *Poverello,* the quintessential medieval holy man. Their way of life still reflected the eremitical ethos that, to a greater or less degree, had colored religious life for the past five hundred years. Their apostolate was based on preaching, and on living what they preached. Though there came to be learned men among them, they did not perceive education to be a part of their vocation, and they did not invest themselves in schools. And yet, as it turned out, education was to be the key to the regeneration of Catholicism and its adaptation to the modern world, and the people who took it up were to find a sure footing in the new church militant.

During the same years that the Capuchins were defining themselves, other groups of men were seeking an apostolate that would avoid the constrictions that came with the traditional religious life. Monasteries, as expressions of the aspirations of the medieval world, had been built on the principle of flight from the world; friaries, responding to the changing spirit of the high Middle Ages, were built within the world, but also served as sanctuaries to which their members could withdraw, though temporarily, from its entanglements. Divine office and community life were seen as antidotes to the contamination that came from association with the world. Now a new form of religious life was to develop, which was ready to engage more aggressively with the world. "Leaving God for God" would be its rallying cry.

"The World Is Our House"

A prominent Jesuit historian has written that "ministry in the Catholic Church in the sixteenth and seventeenth centuries was perhaps the most innovative and exciting in history." This innovative spirit was fostered in large part by men and women in religious life. But it also carried within it the DNA of that unfamiliar, and somewhat disreputable, progenitor, the "world." Not the world of high living, the eat-drink-and-be-merry crowd, but the suffering world, the godless world, and the people who cared about it. In the early sixteenth century, while it was still largely unaware of the threat of heresy, Catholicism was already concerned with the spiritual dangers of a torn and tormented society.

The awakening took place in Italy. For decades the region had been the scene of heroic efforts by pious laymen and laywomen on behalf of the poor and the sick, using as their organizational model the medieval confraternity. Of course, as devout Christians they did not doubt that the ills of the soul were as dangerous as those of the body, and so their charitable work always contained a strong dose of evangelization. What was new was the awareness that the opposite was also true: that to be successful, evangelization required a strong dose of charity. People came to see that the healing of the faith must go hand in hand with the mending of the torn fabric of society. And so charitable confraternities appeared in several Italian cities: centers called "oratories," where clergy and laity — men and women — joined together to deepen their spiritual life with communal prayer while, at the same time, ministering to the poor: serving in orphanages, working in hospitals for incurables, caring for the many girls and women who had been victimized during the war. These groups took the basic pattern of medieval sociability and intensified its religious component. Then they served as springboards, which in time launched both men and women into more ambitious, more structured ministries. An impressive number of future religious congregations found their inspiration in the oratories.

In the most outstanding advance of the times, groups of men appeared who were ready to take their commitment further: to combine the apostolate and social service with dedicated community life. These men came to be known as "clerks regular": men (though not necessarily priests) who took religious vows and lived under a rule that mandated not retreat from the world, but involvement in it. Their particular vocation was developed during what may be called the "prereform" years, when the official church in Italy was talking the talk but not yet walking the walk of self-regeneration. The wars that had created so much social dislocation had had dreadful consequences for the spiritual state of the faithful, yet nobody seemed able to do anything about it. One after the other, but quite independently, small religious communities sprang up whose main purpose was pastoral but whose secondary purpose was care of the destitute, the sick, and the orphaned.

How many such groups were there? For all we know, scores, even hundreds, may have gathered, survived for a while, and then faded. We find them mentioned here and there in the literature: Humiliati, Fathers of Peace, Oblates of Saint Ambrose, and so on. But the names that have come down to us are the Theatines (Rome, 1524), the Somaschi (Venice, 1528), and the Barnabites (Milan, 1530). Each of these groups worked, in its own way, to combine pastoral care with social service. They had considerable success, mainly in Italy, and added together, their membership numbered in the hundreds. But they were overtaken by the greatest of all organizations of clerks regular, the Society of Jesus. The rise of this society, first in Italy, then across the Catholic world, was so meteoric that it sucked the oxygen out of the lungs of the competition. To their eventual scores or hundreds of members, it answered with thousands.

Iñigo López de Loyola, whom we know as Saint Ignatius, was first a courtier and then a soldier in northern Spain. In 1521, during a battle against the French at Pamplona, a cannonball crashed into his legs, ending his military career and almost his life. During a long and painful convalescence, with nothing to read but devotional books, he found himself gradually turning toward a different kind of vocation. By the time his body had healed, he was ready to set out on that quintessential Christian endeavor, a pilgrimage to Jerusalem. The road to the Holy Land turned out to have several stopping places: first, Monserrat, the monastery where he made his general confession, exchanged his fine clothes for those of a beggar, and hung up his sword and dagger, then Manresa, where he experienced months of spiritual illumination, and of alternating peace and anguish. From there he went to Rome, then Venice, then, finally, the Holy Land. He had thoughts of remaining there, to serve his Lord among the Muslims, but the resident Franciscans persuaded him to change his mind. Iñigo returned to Spain, still a wanderer.

He decided to go to school, and 1526 found him at the University of Alcalà. It was there that his unusual behavior, which included preaching to a motley (and mostly female) crowd, brought him to the attention of the Inquisition. Imprisoned, examined, and then released under caution not to preach until he had completed four more years of study, he traveled on to Salamanca — and again into prison. Quite clearly, Iñigo was not going to be allowed to pursue his calling of "helping souls" as long as he remained a layman, and in Spain. So he set out for the University of Paris. There, at the age of thirty-seven, he settled down to a long course of studies, financed by begging trips that took him around northern Europe, and even to England. Finally, in 1534, he received his master's degree.

Throughout these years Iñigo continued his work of helping souls, and he gathered about him a group of seven young men, who looked to him for leadership and spiritual direction. Years before, he had begun to lay out "Spiritual Exercises," a method of meditation and self-examination that to a large degree replicated his own spiritual journey. Under his guidance these young men took the exercises (as would all future Jesuits through the centuries). And on the Feast of the Assumption in 1534, the seven joined together as a band, vowing to go together on pilgrimage to the Holy Land, or if that failed, to offer their services to the pope, "that he might use them in whatever way he deemed most to the glory of God and the good of souls."

They would not make the pilgrimage. Weather and the dangerous political situation blocked their way. Then, according to a later account by one of them, Pope Paul III directed them onto the other path. Why travel afar, he said, when souls were in such need closer to home? Rome could be their Jerusalem. Thus it was in Italy that they began their ministry, preaching, catechizing, and serving the sick — a charismatic band, living in any way they could, until in 1540 they received formal status from the papacy and became the Society of Jesus.

The Society grew up in tense times, haunted by the loss to the church of much of Europe, and the possibility that even more of Western Christendom would fall to the Reformation. The Catholic mood was darkening; the hard days of the Counter-Reformation were close at hand. In 1545 the Council of Trent began its first session. One might expect the Society, which was to become the Counter-Reformation force par excellence, to be deeply involved. But that time was still to come; it would be some years before it officially added "defense of the faith" to its program. It seemed at first to be little concerned with the church's high struggle against heresy. At about this time the first Jesuits to enter Germany sent back warnings of the parlous spiritual condition of Catholics there, but Ignatius was slow to follow up. Nor did he initially identify with the council's agenda. The fathers of Trent were taken up with institutional and disciplinary reform, while Ignatius looked for the enlightenment of individual souls. Yet inexorably the two paths — that of the Jesuits and that of the Counter-Reformation papacy — converged. The four Jesuit theologians who were sent to Trent impressed everyone with their mastery of the issues, and they, in turn, were struck by the degree of influence they could exercise in such exalted circles. Something was happening within the Society: it was learning that the friendship of prelates, and especially of the pope, paid off.

Not to mention the friendship of princes. Ignatius acknowledged this in 1552, when the king of Portugal requested a Jesuit to be his confessor. Ignatius saw at once that in guiding the consciences of the powerful there was opportunity for far-reaching influence. The Society, he ruled, should "retain the benevolence" of temporal rulers, "whose favor or disfavor does much toward opening or closing the gate to the service of God and the good of souls." In the years that followed, more and more frequently Jesuits took up the role of court confessors. Inevitably, and often against their will, they became embroiled in affairs of state. For in a time when politics and religion were so closely entwined, where was the line between the spiritual and the secular? Was it not legitimate for Jesuits to have a say in the French religious wars, or the mounting of the Armada, or, later, in the conduct of the Thirty Years' War, or, later still, in the expulsion of the Protestants from France?

The Jesuits took another direction that modified their original character. In their early days the companions had followed in the footsteps of the friars, unencumbered by property and endowments, ready to travel wherever they were called by God. But as the number of men desiring to join the Society began to grow exponentially, the need to give them training also grew, and houses were opened in places where young Jesuits-in-the-making could combine university courses with instruction by their own faculty. The houses were poor, however, and benefactors hard to find, and so the Jesuits decided to broaden their appeal by opening the facilities to other youths in the vicinity. The local elites were delighted to obtain schooling for their sons, and attendance swiftly swelled into the thousands. The Jesuit leadership was equally entranced by the success, and the potential, of their educational enterprises. From the time the first Jesuit college opened in Sicily in 1546 to the year of the Society's suppression in 1773, eight hundred colleges were opened across Europe and in the world beyond. They became the Jesuits' most powerful means of evangelization. But they also diverted the Society's energies into new channels. "Thus began an engagement with secular culture, modest enough at first, that became a hallmark of the order and an integral part of its self-definition, not present at the beginning." In other words, while the colleges enabled the Jesuits to Christianize the world, they also enabled the world to humanize the Jesuits.

Operation of the schools also led to ownership. A society that had been dedicated at the start to an itinerant lifestyle now found itself more and more tied down by property. A price had to be paid for the amazing dynamism that its movement into the ministry of the schools unleashed. By the early seventeenth century membership in the Society had surpassed 15,000, and the numbers continued to grow. Other religious congregations opened colleges, but overall the Jesuits reigned supreme until the onset of their political troubles in the eighteenth century. In the meantime, the hold their colleges gave them over the social elites of Catholic Europe allowed them to exercise considerable political influence. By the beginning of the seventeenth century, a sizable fraction of the ruling classes, including princes and bishops, were alumni of Jesuit colleges. Many of the early modern states' civil servants owed their formation to them. The stemming of the tide of Protestantism in Germany, in Poland, and in the rest of central Europe can be attributed largely to the cooperation that the Society of Jesus created with the political classes. But this association, too, exacted its price.

Anyone who has studied the history of early modern Europe has come across the "black legend" of the Jesuits, those "Spanish Devils" who personified everything that Protestants hated about Catholicism. The polemical literature churned out for many years by English and Dutch presses is, to our eyes, almost comical in its wild hyperbole. Perhaps we can see it as a backhanded tribute to the sheer strength and power of the Jesuit "system." The Society organized itself to be effective and flexible; it attracted men of intelligence and imagination, then trained them in obedience and sent them out on mission across the known world. They took on the most forbidding adversaries, and often paid heavily in blood. But accounts of martyrdom only served to enhance the Society's public image and bring it new recruits: more preachers, more teachers, more missionaries. Without them, it is hard to see how the Catholic Church of the early modern period could have made its successful comeback. And for that, the Protestant world did not forgive them.

What is more remarkable, though, is the enmity the Society aroused within the Catholic world. Here too, the power it amassed, and the way it used it, was bound to cause offense. The Jesuits' tactics were sometimes unethical, and they often used their political connections to further aims that were not (at least in everyone else's eyes) "for the greater glory of God." We can argue that others used the same tactics, but since they lacked the same power, they did not incur the same rage. It was, in part, a question of visibility. However, there must have been more to it than that, because the animus against the Jesuits was building from the very start, while they were still few in number and relatively vulnerable. Ignatius had to fend off a constant barrage of accusations, that his little organization was heretical, that its mission was subversive. "This society appears to be a danger to the Faith, a disturber of the peace of the Church, destructive of monastic life, and destined to cause havoc rather than edification." So spoke the theologians of the Sorbonne in 1554. Opposition was equally strong in Spain, where, according to the eminent Dominican theologian Melchior Cano, the Jesuits were as dangerous as Luther had been in Germany.

Some of these attacks can be ascribed to rival theologians (and rival religious orders) protecting their turf. Furthermore, the Jesuits seemed in some eyes to be too "friendly" with women and (in Spain, where purity of blood was a major issue) too accommodating to Christians of Jewish ancestry. But there were other, more substantive, issues. In their "way of proceeding" the Jesuits roundly rejected monastic practice, such as the singing of divine office and the obligation of stability. They also avoided monastic austerities, even modifying the vow of poverty to ensure their effectiveness in the field. They rejected the organizational model of the mendicants, the system of chapters and election of officers that had worked so well for centuries. Their superior general retained power for life, a practice that even the pope was to call "tyrannical." What it all amounted to was that while many serious Catholics were calling for a return to tradition, the Jesuits were proposing a new pattern for religious life. No wonder they caused alarm.

And then there was their spirituality. There had long been a movement within Catholicism toward a more interior approach to God, a heart-to-heart discourse between creature and Creator. So the Jesuits had history behind them when they made this one of their founding principles. But for their critics, mired in the paranoia of the early Counter-Reformation years, it smacked of Lutheranism, Erasmianism, and the teaching of the *alumbrados,* the Spanish "spirituals" so suspect in the eyes of the Inquisition. Ignatius and others after him had constantly to demonstrate their loyalty to the dogma, discipline, and formal practice of the Church. Faced with repeated challenges to their orthodoxy, they had to be continually on the defensive.

This atmosphere of hostility explains another characteristic of the Jesuits: their close ties to the papacy. At the very outset, the first companions had taken a vow of obedience to the pope, to be prepared to go wherever in the world he sent them. In return, the pope granted them a generous allowance of privileges, including exemptions from episcopal oversight — a poisoned chalice in a way, because outside Rome all sorts of regional church authorities were ready to bridle at anyone who invaded their jurisdictions. Nowhere was this resentment more dramatic than in France, where the Jesuits brandished their papal privileges and were met with a roar of rage from the Gallican church. When unpleasantness arose and the Jesuits invoked papal protection, it was natural that in return they would advocate papal power. Inevitably, their ties to Rome tightened; they became, in the eyes of their adversaries, *papistissimi* — more papal than the pope.

This was the obverse of the unprecedented character their allegiance to the pope imprinted on them, as missionaries to everywhere. In its very beginnings the Society of Jesus escaped local restrictions; it was multinational, and in its vision it transcended the boundaries that had long carved up Europe and the known world. In this way, at a time when Catholicism was yearning for a more perfect past, it pointed to the future.

"And So, Dear Friends, When Are We Going to Start Doing Good?" (Philip Neri)

The institutes of clerks regular evolved out of the confraternities, and ultimately became something quite different. Their departure does not mean that the fecundity of the confraternities was exhausted — far from it. At century's end, in a major city such as Rome, there must have been a confraternity for every known holy purpose. The devout might well belong to several. We have an example in Joseph de Calasanz, an up-and-coming Spanish priest in the service of two cardinals of the noble Colonna family. It appears that his duties as their household theologian were not enough for him. Between 1596 and 1600 he entered six confraternities, one to visit the poor in the slums, one to catechize children, one to promote devotion to the Blessed Sacrament and to assist pilgrims, one to accompany the Sacrament to the beds of the dying, one to prepare the sick for a Christian death, and one simply to deepen his prayer life in imitation of Saint Francis of Assisi. Nor was his membership a mere formality: in one confraternity, that of the Holy Apostles, he is recorded as having attended 239 meetings and making 157 visits. It was during these visits that he came face-to-face with the terrible material and spiritual deprivation of children in the slums and decided to do something about it. And thus, after much effort and contradiction, the first free elementary school in Rome was opened. Success led to success, as children came crowding into the school (never, it seems, did the urban poor reject the possibility of schooling if it was offered to them), and before long new schools were opened. In due course — perhaps inevitably — Calasanz's schoolmasters formed an order, with themselves as religious. The Piarists, as they came to be known, were to have a distinguished future as educators, first in Italy and later in Poland and the Habsburg Empire.

But those were developments for the future. For the sixteenth century, and the confraternities of Rome, it is essential to understand how much these organizations with their loose structure and their inclusiveness and their multiform aspirations meant to the development of the new Catholicism. Though Calasanz was a priest, his work in the confraternities was done side by side with laymen. This was characteristic of confraternity membership: it was composed mainly of laymen and laywomen, and only in small part of clergy. This must have meant a broadening of vision for a man who might otherwise have lived out his life in purely clerical circles. The demands of the confraternities allowed him to step from the palace of the Colonna cardinals into the slums of the Roman suburbs. Here, deep in "the world," he found a calling that otherwise might have been denied him.

Of course, his new vocation drew him away from his confraternity pursuits into a life much more disciplined and dedicated, and it is the second life, not the first, for which he is remembered. It is to our detriment that the memories of the confraternities come to us almost entirely from those members who "moved on" to greater things, who gained recognition in the church as founders and perhaps, like Calasanz, as saints. We would understand the spirit of the age much better if we could reach back into the lives of those lesser folk who never went beyond the everyday but nevertheless took their faith seriously.

The Rome of the later sixteenth century claimed many such people. It is ironic: the city known to half of Europe as the Scarlet Woman of Babylon, and to the other half as the grim guardian of the keys to the kingdom of heaven, was also the venue for a new and refreshing kind of Catholicism that escaped the rigidities of the past and pointed the way to a more open future. The man responsible for this "awakening" was Philip Neri, one of the most remarkable figures in the history of the Catholic Reformation. In a city of monuments to heroes he was a deliberate antihero; in a society that reveled in ostentation he made himself a figure of fun, a true fool for Christ's sake in the spirit of Saint Paul. And yet he gained a following that included all levels of Roman society, from members of the papal court to the poorest street people. After his death the clamor for his canonization was so insistent that the pope was induced to grant him the honor. He has the distinction of being the last saint of the Catholic Church to have been canonized by popular acclamation.

Philip, a Florentine by birth and the son of a merchant, came to Rome in search of a future. The year was 1534, and he was nineteen. He tutored for a living, studied a bit, and joined several confraternities. Seventeen years later, in 1551, he was ordained a priest. But even before he took that step, he had found his future, and the confraternities had helped him find it.

One was the *Compagnia del Divino Amore* (the Company of Divine Love), a confraternity in the new style. Here Philip was introduced to the idea that laity and clergy could work together for the good of others and for their own personal sanctification. And here, while still a layman, he began to preach short homilies to his colleagues. Another, in which Philip, once a priest, would find his permanent home, was the *Confraternità della Carità* (the Confraternity of Charity). This confraternity was headquartered in the church of San Girolamo, where a number of priests (secular priests, not members of a religious order) boarded together and went about their duties without having any community obligations. Philip, always the individualist, took to this form of life, and held on to it, later bequeathing it to the community he created, the Roman Oratory.

An oratory is not a church. It does not have the status, or the functions, of a church. It is simply a place where people gather to pray. Philip's first "oratory" at San Girolamo was his bedroom, where a group of young men came to listen to and talk with him. Sometimes, when things got crowded, he had to sit on his bed. Later, he found a larger space in the attic of the church. As attendance increased, the gatherings took on more structure, and the time was divided between prayer, colloquy, music, and long walks to different pilgrimage sites.

Anyone seeing the devout crowd trailing down the road, following the eccentric figure of Philip in his highly distinctive cloak and hat, must have wondered what Rome was coming to. But the sessions had their appeal. Not least was the music, composed by distinguished musicians of the papal court, Animuccia and Palestrina: orchestrated declamations of biblical texts, which came to be known as "oratorios." The most extraordinary features of the gatherings, however, were the colloquies. Philip did not preach in the fashion of the time. He spoke simply and with deep feeling. And he went further: he encouraged dialogue, a to-and-fro between leader and followers as the Spirit moved them. The main topics of these discussions were passages from the Scriptures. Philip encouraged his young disciples to pro-claim the Word — and this in the Rome of the Index, the Inquisition, and the fearsome Carafa pope, Paul IV. Even when the Counter-Reformation was at its most intolerant, there was more to Rome than meets the eye.

In 1575, the group of men whom Philip Neri gathered around himself became a congregation, the Oratory. In keeping with the spirit of the times, there was pressure to model it after a religious order. But Neri would have none of that. He insisted that his priests should keep their independence, should dispose of their own funds, and should not be hindered in their day-to-day activities by community observances and duties. He believed that their organization should be as flexible as possible, that there should be as little hierarchy as possible, and that major decisions should be taken in con-sultation with the whole community. Also, that the houses of the Oratory should be independent of each other. He was not thrilled by the idea of a rule; he loved living for the possibilities of each moment. If heroes have their antiheroes, founders should be able to have their antifounders; and in that case, Philip Neri was the consummate antifounder. It was said by some-one who knew him that he had become a priest in spite of himself, and it is equally true that he was a founder in spite of himself. In time the Oratory developed the necessary constitutions, but what Philip provided was a model for living, not a set of rules.

Philip Neri has been called "the second apostle of Rome" (the first, of course, being Saint Peter himself). This is because he inspired reform, not only among the citizens, but also within the Curia. By all accounts, while the people who flocked to his side came from all walks of life, he held a spe-cial attraction for the literate classes, including the papal court. He acted as confessor and spiritual adviser to bishops, cardinals, and even to popes. It was said that when the court left the city in the summer, the Oratory's church was almost empty.

But his influence extended much further. To a church that was hardening and closing in upon itself, he brought the possibility of gentleness and open-ness. To its growing clericalism and to its defensiveness about Bible reading, he brought confidence in the laity's ability to understand and serve the Word. In years to come, these qualities would help to "modernize" Catholicism.

* * *

In 1563 the Council of Trent closed its doors, to the triumphant strains of the *Te Deum*. It had achieved great things — on paper. The basic tenets of the faith had been defined and a program of church reform laid out. Yet had the fathers of Trent been able to look out across all the great stretches of Western Christendom, they would have been met with a depressing sight. Across the north, from Scotland to Poland, near-total ruin, with the shoots of vigorous new religions pushing up from the debris of the old church. Within the territory still called "Catholic," disorder and discouragement: church buildings degraded, the cult debased, the secular clergy demoralized, the religious orders in disarray. The abuses were so deeply embedded in the structure that there must have seemed little hope of rooting them out.

In the same year, a small event took place in Ávila, in Spain. A middle-aged Carmelite nun, Teresa de Ahumada y Cepeda, finally put aside the comfortable convent life she had followed since her youth. To signal her intention, she dressed herself in a habit of coarse wool and put on *alpargates,* the hemp sandals worn by the poor. In an age when dress was a guide to status and lifestyle, this shabby footwear was the outward sign of a profound conversion. From then on she and her small group of sisters, soon to be known as the "discalced," or unshod, intended to live as contemplatives, following the austere, solitary life of prayer that had been practiced by the hermit fathers of Mount Carmel centuries before.

The Order of Our Lady of Mount Carmel had an unusual trajectory. It started in Asia Minor. A handful of monks, veterans of the Second Crusade, deciding to become hermits in the eastern manner, withdrew into the caves and crevices of the mountain overlooking the Bay of Haifa. There they flourished and multiplied, and in the early thirteenth century received a rule. However, only a few more years passed before they were overtaken by the Saracen conquests, and by midcentury they were emigrating to Europe. There they received a frosty welcome until, with the backing of the pope, they retouched their rule and officially became a Western-style mendicant order. Henceforth, the Carmelite brothers built convents like other friars, and preached and taught in universities. Yet the eremitical tradition endured, straining against the life of ministry they now professed.

The fourteenth and fifteenth centuries were as unkind to the brothers as they were to the rest of society. The Black Death left them reduced and fearful; the schism and the general demoralization of the Church took away any taste they might have had for "the perfect life." Even the mitigated version of the rule they obtained from the papacy in 1432, which allowed them to eat meat, own property, and chat in the cloisters, seemed too much for them. By the beginning of the sixteenth century, in many houses, the silence and austerity of Mount Carmel were a distant memory. And the cry for reform was making itself heard.

Reform efforts began seriously in the wake of the council. In 1564 the order's general chapter issued a series of decrees designed to enforce a respectable level of observance, "a sincere dedication to religious life within the framework of existing obligations," as its historian has described it. But it was much too moderate for the awakening spirit of the times. As the same historian points out, "in the post-tridentine church this sort of 'observance' failed to impress." It was Teresa's reform, fashioned for her tiny community of sisters but reaching for the heavens, that soared.

Because in the Carmelite order the sisters depended directly on the brothers, there was an immediate need, once the nuns had adopted a strict contemplative rule, to find suitable spiritual directors, members of the order who shared Teresa's ideals. There were such men available, and Teresa knew it. She persuaded the prior general to allow them to hive off from the main body and join the reform. In 1568 the first three friars received the habit of rough undyed wool, and the hemp sandals that henceforth gave them their name, "Discalced Carmelite friars." From then on they followed a rule based on that already observed by the sisters. And like the sisters, by the holiness of their lives they attracted others to their side.

But it was their Lord, *their own Lord,* who had said, "I come not to bring peace but a sword." Reform movements were bound to cause disruption within orders, and to set up crosscurrents of jealousy and hurt feelings. Within the Carmelite order this happened with a vengeance. The friars who lived by the original, mitigated rule were infuriated by what they saw as the "holier than thou" attitude of their reformed brethren. They resented their efforts to impose austerities on them. Indeed, they regarded the whole reforming movement as an exercise in pride and disobedience. The Discalced, in their turn, feared that the main body of the order would gladly do away with them. Nor were their fears groundless. In 1575 and 1576 successive chapters attempted to legislate an end to the movement. Its leaders, including John of the Cross (the great mystic who was later to be canonized), were imprisoned; Teresa was forbidden to leave her convent.

But the Discalced had a powerful friend in the king of Spain, Philip II. Through his influence the pope was persuaded in 1580 to grant them their own province. "Had it not been for the king, all our work would have come to nothing," wrote Teresa. In 1588 Philip helped them yet again: the Discalced Carmelites, by papal authority but through his prompting, became a congregation, answerable to no one but the prior general. Finally, in

1593, the congregation became an independent order and Teresa (dead since 1582) was named its foundress.

The two orders continued on their separate paths, and both thrived. By the end of the seventeenth century Carmelite friars numbered in the thousands, across Europe and in the Americas. In spite of the bitterness that surrounded the separation, the spirit of Teresa came to suffuse the whole body. The old eremitical ethos was reinvigorated: starting in 1592, here and there "deserts" were created, places to which friars could retire for a time to regain the spirit of prayer in solitude.

Some features stand out in this story of the rebirth of the order of Mount Carmel. First, the extraordinary influence of a woman on what was, at the time, principally an organization of men. "She profits the order more than all the Carmelite friars in Spain," wrote the prior general, Rossi. By the force of her personality and the depth of her holiness she was able to win over the powers that be, the pope and the king included. But more than that: she profoundly affected the religious who knew her, the men who longed for perfection but felt disabled by the practical demands of life. Had she not inspired them to undertake the internal reform of the order, her political influence would have stood for nothing.

In second place: while it is not an exaggeration to say that the great Teresa would come to bestride her world like a colossus, her reform movement was initially fragile and could easily have been smothered at birth had it not been for the support of the ruling powers: the bishop of Ávila and the king himself. And though both were respectful of her reputation for holiness, both had other motives. Bishop Alvaro de Mendoza was not sorry to bring the Carmelite reform under his wing, thus extending his episcopal powers at the expense of the order. Philip II was wholeheartedly dedicated to his role as number-one champion of Catholic reform — and for good reason. At mid–sixteenth century, despite widespread desire for reform, the actual process often seemed stalled, and it was often the Crown that gave it the push it needed to start moving. Carmel was not the only order in Spain that needed regeneration, and the king was commissioned by the pope to deal with them all. Sometimes his interventions were useful, sometimes problematic. In either case, while the immediate result might be beneficial, the longer-term effects were questionable. In an age of expanding state control, the religious orders, through their own weakness, were brought more closely into dependency on civil authority. This was a trend not only in Spain but also across Catholic Europe, and the consequences were far-reaching.

*   *   *

And so to Teresa's other, even greater work: the development of a reformed religious life for women, which would in time reverberate far beyond the walls of her Carmelite convents.

During the sixteenth century Catholicism experienced a deep sea change. The burst of humanist reform that marked the early years was overtaken by a severe, unbending determination to enforce orthodoxy at all costs, the reaction of a church that felt itself deeply threatened by forces without and within. The Index, the Inquisition, the burning of heretics in countless marketplaces: such were the distressing hallmarks of the Counter-Reformation. However, within this hard shell there was a huge force for good, of which Teresa, a native of the most militant of militant Catholic societies, was a living example.

What the Carmelite reform offered, and the Catholic world came to approve, was a life of prayer without conditions, prayer as a value in itself. For the active orders, prayer served the practical function of energizing action. In other words, it fueled the apostolic engine. But for Teresa and those of like mind, prayer was in itself the highest form of Christian activity, and the only way in which the world could be saved. Paradoxical as it may seem to a modern secular mind, she saw the contemplative life as a missionary labor, absolutely necessary for the conversion of heretics and the salvation of souls. Her emphasis on prayer, especially private prayer, became as characteristic of the Catholic Reformation as was the call to active ministry.

But it was not without its naysayers. Spanish Catholicism at mid-century was at war with itself. On the one hand, it was alive with mysticism. All up and down the country, people were living (or claiming to live) in their own close communication with God. Known as *alumbrados,* or "spirituals," these people were the objects of suspicion because they seemed to be bypassing the established structures of the church. What was worse, many of them were women, and therefore, by definition, easily duped by the devil. An establishment party, led by the Dominicans, cast serious doubt on such charismatic activity, insisting that vocal prayer and public rituals were the only forms of piety suitable for the faithful. And backing them was the Inquisition, ready at the drop of a hat to root out any practices that smelled of heterodoxy. It was in this unfriendly climate that Teresa, who was both a mystic and an ecstatic, composed her spiritual works and built her reformed convents. She herself was under constant surveillance by the Tribunal (she was investigated twice for heresy), and her *Vida,* or spiritual autobiography, was withheld from publication throughout her lifetime. If on her deathbed in 1582 she was able to say: "At the end, Lord, I am a daughter of the Church," perhaps, to borrow the words of the duke of Wellington after the battle of Waterloo, "it was a close-run thing."

But already times were changing, and in her direction. One of the most striking features of the century that followed Trent was the inclusion of women, and their spirituality, in the Catholic Church's agenda of reform. This was certainly not the council's aim; the council gave little thought to religious women, apart from ordering them to return to their cloisters and behave themselves. In defense of the council fathers, one must say that wayward nuns had become, for Protestants, a source of scandal and ribald merriment; it seemed essential to any self-respecting prelate that in the future religious women must conform to established standards. But in the pursuit of respectability, a great deal of genuine female piety suffered collateral damage. "Beatas" in Spain, beguines in the north, and countless women in the Third Orders who had developed a semireligious form of life while remaining in the world found themselves in an ambiguous position. If they wished to be considered nuns, they had to enter, and stay in, enclosure. Teresa herself was admonished by Rome for leaving the walls of her convent. No matter that she was dragging her frail, tired body around Spain only for the purpose of founding new communities. "Gadding about" was still an inappropriate thing for a woman to do.

To all appearances, the council had reduced the role that women could play in the reform of the church. In fact, the opposite happened. The century after Trent witnessed the deepening and enrichment of female religious life, first within the cloister walls, and then, as well, beyond them. To understand this, we can return to Teresa.

The Carmelite Monastery of the Incarnation that the young Teresa entered in 1535 could not have been called a den of vice, but then, neither could it have been called a school for perfection. About a hundred nuns lived within its walls, in a style that would have befitted any unmarried ladies of quality, which, of course, was exactly what they were. The more fortunate among them had allowances from their families, enabling them to live in well-furnished apartments complete with their own servants (or, sometimes, slaves). The less fortunate had lean pickings, and this, of course, led to jealousy and bickering. The community demands upon the nuns were slight, whereas the demands of founders and patrons continued to be heavy. As in other female monasteries, the Incarnation's daily schedule was loaded with obligatory prayers, to be recited for the intentions of its bene-

factors. Another way in which its nuns were expected to repay those benefactors was by acting, when called upon, as live-in companions to ladies of
their acquaintance. It was a role that Teresa herself played. "Some persons
to whom the superiors couldn't say 'no' liked to have me in their company
. . . the superiors urged me to go," she later wrote. There was no way to escape these special interests. Even within the monastery, the hours spent
with friends and relations stretched out and dominated the sisters' thoughts
and conversations.

It was a "half-monastic, half-hidalgo world," the extension of a society
deeply concerned with status and lineage. It was everything Teresa would
put aside when she put on her coarse wool habit and her *alpargates*. For her,
the reformed religious life was a liberation. The cloister was not a prison; it
was a barrier against all the distractions and demands of secular society.
Poverty, if accepted voluntarily, meant independence from the impositions
of that society. The women in her communities were free to love the Lord
to the exclusion of all others. As for family honor and that peculiar Spanish
obsession "purity of blood," Teresa, the granddaughter of a converted Jew,
would have nothing to do with them. In the face of much disapproval, she
welcomed women of limited means and doubtful ancestry, requiring only
that they have the necessary qualities for the consecrated life.

So both the fathers of Trent and the *madre* of Ávila insisted on enclosure for women, but for different reasons. For them, it meant control. For
her, it meant freedom to pursue an authentic contemplative life, free from
worldly ties. The cloister was going to be embraced by thousands of women
over the next century, and it must have been in part because of the value and
dignity with which she invested it.

Teresa's reform was, without a doubt, the most striking achievement of
feminine monasticism in the sixteenth century, but it was not the only one.
There were other reforming groups, some of them newly fashioned like the
Annunciades or the Feuillantes, others long-established like the Poor
Clares. But for all of them, renewal meant return to the past: to strict observance, austerity, and self-discipline. For consecrated women, the road to salvation lay not in the world but within the walls of the cloister. To us, it
seems an intolerable constriction. To them, it was a life worth living. Even
when, many decades later, women started experimenting with an outside
vocation, they continued to glance back toward the cloister, to feel what
was identified at the time as "the monastic temptation."

Thus it was with a clear understanding that sixteenth-century Catholicism sought to shape its religious orders. It stuck with the traditional order

of things. Men went out to do battle; women kept the home fires burning. While Jesuits, Capuchins, Dominicans, Recollets, Theatines, and countless others took on the forces of heresy and ignorance, cloistered nuns prayed and fasted and mortified themselves, their task being to keep the lines open between God and sinful humankind. To our modern eyes, the women's potential, in terms of energy and dedication, appears to have been compressed into a very small corner of the Counter-Reformation. But in that God-drenched century, the prayers and acts of reparation of the few were considered absolutely essential for the salvation of the many. In the battle for souls, contemplative nuns were a precious resource.

However, other immediate needs could not be satisfied by prayer. The disruptions caused by war, the influx of destitute people into the cities, the rocketing costs of foodstuffs, the recurrences of plague and the irruption of that new and terrifying disease, syphilis — all this, viewed through the prism of deep religiosity, was a demonstration of divine wrath on a godless world. Somehow, society had to be salvaged, body and soul. Nowhere was this perception stronger than in Italy, long the battleground for French and imperial troops. The damage was so critical that it needed all the help available.

Catholicism had never objected to women's active service in the community, or to the principle that this should have a strong religious underpinning. Much of the hospital nursing that was done in medieval and early modern Europe was done by women, members of confraternities or of beguinages or of the various uncloistered communities that had developed over the years. Women visited the poor and buried the dead, and sometimes even dispensed spiritual counsel. The problem for the fathers of Trent was that some of these women seemed to be developing a "middle way of life," claiming a semireligious status while remaining part of the laity. One of the council's firmest determinations was to draw a clear line between the sacred and the profane. The cheerful blurring of the two that had taken place over the centuries was to end. For women, the implications were severe. Shortly after the council closed, two papal constitutions ordered all these semi-nuns to accept solemn vows and full monastic discipline, or disperse. If you were a laywoman, all well and good; you should not pretend to be something else. If you were a nun, then you belonged in the cloister and under the discipline of a rule.

However, by the time these orders were handed down, a significant step had been taken in the opposite direction, by someone deeply concerned with the unmet needs of devout women. In the turmoil of early-sixteenth-century Italy, many such women felt the pull of religion while lacking the means, or perhaps the physical strength, to become nuns. What was needed was an alternative that allowed for a fully consecrated religious life *outside* the cloister. And this was achieved, in the teeth of ongoing public disapproval, by an elderly woman with a handful of followers.

Angela Merici had been a Franciscan tertiary for most of her adult life, and a model one at that, leading an intense prayer life even as she worked for a living. But in 1532, at the age of sixty, she embarked on another course. She gathered a small group of women in her little room next to the church of Saint Afra in Brescia, and turned them into "a company of virgins" under the patronage of the virgin martyr, Saint Ursula. What she envisaged for them was a life "active, but with the mind always raised heavenwards," in the world, but completely consecrated to the Lord. They were to continue to live in their own homes and to support themselves by their own labor; they were not to wear distinctive clothing, and they were not to take vows. In the beginning, it does not appear that they were directed toward a particular activity — nursing, or teaching, or preaching the Word. Their originality lay not in what they did, but in what they were: nuns who belonged to the world, living under a rule but facing all the toil and danger that the cloister was meant to forestall. They had no specific apostolate. Angela herself never seems to have focused on a specific ministry. But since her sisters were bound, as Christian women, to give charity where charity was needed, they soon found themselves engaged in the care of orphan girls at Brescia's Major Hospital. Thus, without anybody intending it, the future life of the Company of Saint Ursula as a teaching order was set, if only in outline.

The company grew by leaps and bounds. In 1544, with a membership of 150 women, it was officially approved by the pope. But already there were difficulties. Angela had died in 1540, and almost immediately her project had come under attack. Italian society still held emphatically that a woman, to be respectable, needed either a husband or a convent — *aut maritus aut murus.* But here were all these virgins on the loose, "in the midst of the perils of the world where they could not help falling into danger!" The pressure was on, to turn the company into a monastic community. This was a more than likely fate; other nuns who aspired to an unenclosed life, such as the "Angelics" (no relation) of Milan, were being sent into the cloister. We cannot lay this at the feet of the council, because it had not yet spoken; the driving force here was social custom parading as the will of God.

The Ursulines avoided enclosure, but only at the expense of a modification of their way of life. In 1568 Archbishop Borromeo of Milan invited twelve of them into his diocese to teach catechism. There he "congregated" or gathered into community those who so wished. Interestingly enough, this turned the women into half-nuns of the very sort that Trent had sought to eliminate: free, still, to move around, but living in a disciplined and protected environment. Borromeo, enormously influential within the church, was able to some degree to exceed its boundaries. He used his influence to modify the Company of Saint Ursula. In 1580, in the course of his pastoral visit to Brescia, he adapted Angela's Rule, making the women subject not to their own "mother" but to the bishop. Thus a company that had at first been designed and ruled by women was brought under the control of the hierarchy. The best proof that these adjustments made sense to the public lies in the fact that the Ursulines prospered, so much so that by 1584 there were six hundred of them in Milan alone, living in five communities, teaching in eighteen schools. And in this form they spread, eventually, into southern France. As the sixteenth century ended they were already there, living in community, wearing a uniform habit, but still free to move about, to visit the sick, to teach in public places.

But not for long. Before these young women grew old, the move would be on to enclose them, to subject them to solemn vows, and to make them into the kind of nuns that Trent had mandated. Though the Brescians and some other local groups continued in their uncloistered form of life, the Company of Saint Ursula as a whole was destined to be a monastic order in every juridical sense, retaining of its original good works only the right to teach, as long as this could be done within enclosure.

The first generations of religious women, if they wished to engage in the apostolate, could hope for no encouragement from Trent. This was the way that Catholic society as a whole, and not just the hierarchy, liked it. Only in the following century would there be a shift in attitudes, as more and more of the church's mission opened up to women.

"All Mankind Is One"

In 1492, Christopher Columbus came upon the shores of America. Six years later, Vasco da Gama reached India by sea, thus bypassing the Turkish blockade that had closed traditional west-east land routes. With stunning suddenness, Europe broke out of the boundaries that had for so long enclosed it. With the sixteenth century came discovery after discovery — more territory in seventy-five years than in the previous one thousand years. In 1521 Europeans gazed with amazement upon the magnificent Aztec city of Tenochtitlan; at about the same time, other Europeans began to wonder if China, now close enough to reach out and touch, was in fact Cathay, the faraway land of dreams and fables. The possibilities seemed endless. Nothing was going to stop their march across the world.

In how many ways could Europeans now get rich? With gold and silver, at first simply torn off the surfaces of idols and temples, and later mined by what amounted to slave labor; with silks and spices that, once transported to Europe, could command a thousand times their initial value. The Age of Discovery was a heady time for those daring enough to profit by it.

In the course of their pursuit of riches, the adventurers in the New World made another massive discovery: of *people,* so many of them, and so diverse, that it boggled the mind. What exactly were these people? Were they human? Did they have immortal souls? In that case, they all had to be children of Adam. But how could this be, given that they lived so far beyond the circumscription of the biblical world? And if they were human, did that mean they were the equals of Europeans, or, perhaps, something less? Contemporary readings of Aristotle had provided a convenient category, of *homunculi:* "little men," a sort of substandard breed, eligible for immortality but unfit for anything in this world except enslavement. Some explorers found this idea very appealing.

One thing was decided early on. In 1493 Pope Alexander VI decreed that the people of the newly discovered territories were indeed human, and did have immortal souls, which meant they must be brought into the church. But how could this be achieved? Renaissance Rome, both physically and morally little more than a puny Italian state, was certainly not capable of organizing such a massive effort. In 1494, with the Treaty of Tordesillas, the pope delegated the task to the two Catholic powers that had made the discoveries. He drew a line dividing the world in half. To Portugal went the east — and, inadvertently, that large chunk of the west, as yet undiscovered, that we now know as Brazil. To Spain went the rest of the New World, stretching in theory from north to south, east to west, including the Caribbean islands, the bulk of the American mainland, and, once they were found and recorded upon the European map, the Philippines.

The Iberian monopolies stood for a long time, until other European powers began to eat away at them. What lasted even longer was the exclusive power that each country received to manage the business of converting "its" natives. Known in Spanish as the *Patronato Real* and in Portuguese as the *Padroado,* this meant that the mother country was in charge of the local church, both its personnel and its policy. The limited influence that the papacy was able to exercise in instructions and appointments had to be channeled through the government in question. From the beginning, missionary work in Africa, in the Americas, and in the Orient was subject to direction by the state.

Spain took its responsibility seriously, Portugal less so. But in both cases the governments began by drawing their missionary manpower almost exclusively from the various mendicant orders. Though the first religious to touch American soil was the Mercederian chaplain to Columbus, the friars pioneered the great evangelizing drive of the sixteenth century. From 1500 on they were active in the Antilles. Then, in 1524, the major missionary effort began on the mainland with the arrival of twelve Franciscans who, famously, walked barefoot all the way from the coast to Mexico City, where the *conquistador* Cortés greeted them on bended knee. After them came the Dominicans and then the Augustinians. For many years these religious orders did all the work of the colonial church, administering the sacraments, preaching, organizing parishes and confraternities. They worked fast. By 1550, it is estimated that as many as ten million people had been baptized in the Americas.

It is said that the first friars, in their exuberant drive to Christianize the Mexican Indians, were carried along by a sense that here, in the New World, a society of faith could be built to make up for the faith that seemed to be withering in Europe. Whatever their inspiration, they certainly accomplished great things. Decades before other countries — France, England, Holland — began even to think seriously about responsible colonization, they had established schools and hospitals and a college for higher learning (the college of Santa Cruz at Santiago Tlatelolco). Their linguistic achievement was stupendous. Almost at once they set to mastering the Indian languages they encountered, not out of academic interest, of course, but because without language, how could the people be converted? The translation of Christian concepts into a non-Christian idiom turned out to be a challenging business, which balanced fidelity to the faith against sensitivity to the thought processes of the catechumens. Today the effort may seem to have been inadequate, but in the context of the sixteenth century it was a considerable advance. And there were other adaptations. Much of the friars' early success was achieved because they co-opted the Indian elites, tolerated some of their shortcomings, and took a serious interest in those aspects of Indian culture that did not, in their minds, conflict with the truths of Catholicism.

And yet there is a dark side to the Spanish conquest of America, and the missionaries do not escape historical blame. In the years following the arrival of the Europeans, millions of Indians died, either from disease or from brutal treatment at the hands of the *conquistadores*. The friars were there from the start; they witnessed their countrymen's behavior and the plight of the natives. Yet they were ready to benefit from the force of Spanish arms to build their own power bases. It was common missionary practice to sequester "their" Indians, in villages that were off-limits to Europeans. This was an anticipation of the later and more famous "reductions" of the Jesuits, and it served the same purpose: the protection of the Indians from Spanish depravity. But it was also a way of controlling the native people. Though the friars' rule was less rough, it was rule nonetheless. In the course of establishing the kingdom of Jesus Christ, they were ready to discipline and punish the Indians, and to destroy their idols and temples. American native culture suffered massive destruction during the conquest years, much of it at the hands of the Christian missionaries. And beyond their immediate areas of control, the missionaries watched as the ugly business of despoiling and reducing the indigenous people went merrily on.

So why were they there? Their answer would have been "to save souls." We should recognize that for any devout Catholic of the sixteenth century, this was reason enough for vigorous action. But in the immediacy of the conquest years, the ways and means were still to be decided. "Compel them to come in," Saint Augustine had said, quoting the Gospel text. It was an ancient argument for forcible conversion, and there were people on the ground in these new times who were ready to put that principle into action. In the early days, the *conquistadores* presented the native people they met with a manifesto requiring them (in Spanish!) to acknowledge the supremacy of pope and king, or suffer enslavement and the loss of their property. There was an understanding that in the event of noncompliance, the invaders were immediately free to do more or less what they wanted, a made-in-Spain theological justification for murder and rapine. The missionary friars protested this, all the way to Rome, and their arguments decided the pope to rule that Indians were "truly men," entitled to "enjoy their liberty and the possession of their property, even though they be outside the faith of Jesus Christ." The newfound peoples were to be converted not by force but by persuasion.

But how should this persuasion be exercised? Here the friars differed. The Franciscans baptized en masse, following their conviction that the sacrament was key to salvation; the Dominicans, by and large, insisted that their catechumens receive instruction first. In either case, the small cadres of missionaries ended up with huge congregations, spread over miles of rugged country, of souls that had received only the slightest smattering of the Catholic faith. Then, as the century wore on and the Indians, demoralized by the death of their peoples and the destruction of their societies, began to fall apart, the missionaries, too, were touched by disillusionment. Their millenarian expectations had not been fulfilled; their flocks were still only half-Christianized. Some of them reflected that they had moved too fast.

Too fast and, we would say, not far enough. Throughout that century (and the next, and most of the one after that), not one Indian became a priest. The college at Tlatelolco had been founded in hopes of training a local clergy. But times and attitudes changed, and in 1568 a provincial council prohibited the ordination of Indians. For all their defense of the native people, the missionaries could not shake the idea that they were, in some way, not fully adult. For this paternalism the church in Spanish America was to pay a heavy price.

So how are we to judge them?

First, we should acknowledge the depth of their conviction, that the freeing of the Indians from their previous idolatry justified all the earthly pain and misery inflicted on them. In the minds of the missionaries, "the spiritual conquest" was akin to an exodus that, like the biblical exodus, was a time to be endured on the way to better things. Second, we should recognize that, faced with the challenges of an unfamiliar world, and with no recent missionary experience to draw on, the friars naturally assumed that Christianization meant imposing Spanish forms of governance and worship. In their mind, there was no separation of church and state. For them, the Spanish conquest of America was a fulfillment of the will of God, in which, as God's servants and the king's, they were doing their part. They could all have echoed the claim of the Dominican Bartolomé de Las Casas, that all his labor for many years had been "to serve my God and to assist in the salvation of those whom he bought with his blood and that the state of my king might grow immensely."

The mention of that name brings us to an aspect of the missionary effort in America that broke through the constrictions of contemporary thinking: what has been called "the Spanish struggle for justice." Las Casas, with support from many other friars, mounted a campaign on behalf of the Indians that has been called "one of the greatest attempts the world has ever known to make Christian precepts prevail in the relations between peoples."

The campaign began in 1512, when, only twenty years after the discovery, Spanish rapacity was running wild in Hispaniola. Another Dominican, Antonio de Montesinos, used the pulpit to condemn the colonists for their abuse of the natives: "Are they not men? Do they not have rational souls? Are you not obliged to love them as yourselves?" To add insult to injury, he threatened to withhold the sacraments from his hearers if they did not make restitution. His challenge to the colonists, and their enraged response, marked the beginning of decades of intramural conflict over the question of Indian rights. On one side were the friars, or most of them; on the other, the adventurers who had come to get rich and needed the labor of a subjugated people to do so. The quarrel rippled back to Spain, where serious thinkers (many of them Dominicans) debated questions of Indian capacity and Spanish responsibility. The outcome was legislation that brought about a limited improvement in the Indian condition — but only limited, because the colonists' main argument, the gold and silver flowing back in shiploads to Spain, was irresistibly attractive to the Crown.

Bartolomé de Las Casas participated, at one time or another, in both sides of the argument. In his early years in Hispaniola he was an *encomendero* (a landowner entitled to the labor of native people); he held slaves, he worked Indians in the mines. In 1515 he threw it all away and became a lifelong champion of Indian rights. After entering the Dominican order, he became a missionary, experimenting with various schemes to make his people's lives more bearable. Then he became a propagandist, crossing and recrossing the Atlantic to make his case, bringing with him to Spain practical observations — volumes of them — of Indian culture, to counter the theories of scholars who knew their Aristotle better than they knew America. His most famous confrontation was the debate with the respected humanist scholar Sepúlveda, held at Valladolid in 1550-1551 in the presence of the emperor Charles V. The result was a stalemate: Sepúlveda's harsh arguments for the inferiority of the Indians and the justification for use of force against them failed to sway official policy, but Las Casas's plea for a more evenhanded treatment of the emperor's new subjects also fell short.

Here was a genuine attempt to save not only souls but also social structures. Yet historians are divided in their judgment of Las Casas. Some see him as a great prophet of social justice. Some are less laudatory, while conceding only that even if he did not achieve the perfection he desired, he did secure something positive. Others dismiss him as a ranter who did more harm than good with his impossible dreams. Nothing, it seems, could have saved the native people of America from their tragic fate.

So the fact remains: whatever line the missionaries took up, they were participants in the conquest. How are we to judge them?

Who are we to judge them?

In our times, religious proselytism is definitely out of favor. It is seen as intolerant of other religious beliefs and disrespectful of other cultures. But the values that we hold dear in our secular societies — democracy, women's and children's rights, basic education, advanced farming practices, and so on — are seen to be eminently exportable. Our modern "missionary" organizations are called NGOs, and many of them are Western in inspiration and in provenance. They, and the people who work in them, can be counted among the redeeming features of a basically selfish first world. But are they not also the spiritual descendants of the early friars of America? What differentiates the motive of saving lives from that of saving souls? And if, in the course of their mission, they become entangled in the larger agendas of nation-states, how much are they responsible for the outcome? In several areas of conflict today, NGOs are struggling to stay free of association with their sponsoring countries' activity. But it is an unequal struggle, as was that of the missionaries against the *conquistadores* and *encomenderos*. Will history condemn them for trying?

Where the missionaries were concerned, the passage of time made it a moot point. By the end of the sixteenth century, the mood in the Spanish American empire had changed and the turbulence of the mendicant friars had quieted. The critiques of Las Casas were no longer read. The soul-searching had come to an end. The Indians were marginalized. This boded a sad future for the church in Latin America.

"Our Christian Relation Is Suitable for and May Be Adapted to All the Nations of the World"

These were the words of Las Casas, and no missionary would have argued with them. The question was, how much adaptation was permissible? How could the relation of the faith be altered without endangering it? To a Catholic culture long unused to missionary work, it was a perplexing question. The friars of Spanish America struggled with it and developed their own answers. At the other side of the world the same question was being explored, with a very different outcome. The Iberian pattern of conquest and evangelization proved no match for the societies of the Orient.

Portugal was responsible for this sector of the globe. All missionary activity took place under its watchful eye; all correspondence, even that with Rome, was expected to pass through its hands. It was naturally expected that the *Padroado* would dictate things there as elsewhere; natural, too, that evangelization would be made to serve the country's agenda. Portuguese Franciscans began work in India in 1518, largely as chaplains to their own merchants and soldiers, and to the Indian clientage that built up around their enclaves. They also worked among the poor, much in their established tradition. But the name that dominates the history of the Asian missions is that of a Basque Jesuit, Francis Xavier, possibly the greatest Christian missionary since Saint Paul. With him, Christian evangelization began to move into uncharted territory.

Xavier arrived in the Portuguese stronghold of Goa in 1542, and spent the next few months preaching and catechizing wherever he could gain a hearing. Early on he learned what other missionaries also experienced: that the preaching of the gospel to the native peoples was severely compromised by the behavior of the European expatriates. "Spices and souls," the byword of the Portuguese adventurers, did not hold out a very healthy promise for evangelization. "There is here a power," he wrote, "which I may call irresistible, to thrust men headlong into the abyss, when besides the seduction of gain, and the easy opportunities of plunder, their appetite for greed will have been sharpened and there will be a whole torrent of bad examples and evil customs to overwhelm them and sweep them away." Such men, he vowed, must someday face the judgment of God. "Let them be blotted out of the book of the living, and let their name not be written among the just." Yet for all his disgust, his mission was always dependent on Portuguese power; it always had to travel along Portuguese trade routes.

He was sent to the Coromandel Coast, to work among poor low-caste fishing communities. From there, during the following years, he traveled to Portuguese outposts on the Malayan and Indonesian coasts, everywhere making converts and establishing Christian communities. Up to this point he remained very much the traditional evangelist, the only difference being his readiness to translate his faith into the local language. In spite of his obvious love for the people, he showed little sympathy for local cultures and none at all for other religions. The faith he taught was still the faith of Europe, couched in European concepts.

Then in 1547 he met Yajiro, a Japanese samurai temporarily on the run from trouble back home, and was invited by him to go to Japan. In 1549, leaving the various missions he had built to other Jesuits who had now come east, Xavier took ship with three Japanese Christians and two confreres, and landed on the island of Kyushu. From there, slowly and painfully, he made the journey to the imperial capital, Kyoto. Along the way he came to understand the present reality of Japan: that the *daimyo,* or feudal lords, were the real power in the land, and that if he wanted to gain influence for his society, he needed to approach them on their own level, as a personage of some importance. Consequently, when the occasion demanded, Xavier abandoned the humble, unpretentious soutane that for Europeans marked the man of God, and took on the guise of an aristocrat, wearing fine clothes and bearing expensive gifts. In this way he impressed his hosts, and gained permission to preach the gospel in Japan. But more: he himself became attuned to Japanese culture; he learned to esteem Japanese values and to recognize that they were not all antithetical to Christianity. And he came to realize that Western scientific knowledge was intriguing to the elites of the East, so much so that it might be used, in a way, as bait to draw them to the faith.

He also became aware of the enormous respect in which the Japanese elites held their neighbor, China. If Christianity was all-true, all-powerful, they argued, why did the Chinese not practice it? In time, Xavier concluded that the key to the conversion of the whole region lay in China. He resolved to travel there and to create a bridgehead from which to preach the faith. So, leaving Japan and the successful missions there, he made his way to an island at the mouth of the Pearl River and settled down to wait for permission to enter the Middle Kingdom. But China, unlike Japan, was a firmly closed society, and the permission did not come. Francis Xavier died in 1552, still short of his ultimate objective.

Xavier's insight, that the Christian message could be delivered in a non-European form, represented a huge departure from what has been called "the *conquistador* tradition of the Iberian missions," and it continued to cause divisions among his successors. In particular, the Portuguese members of his society tended to act as though the expansion of Christianity must involve the expansion of their motherland's influence. And in 1583 a serious crisis developed, as Spanish Franciscans arrived in Japan from Manila, thoroughly determined to challenge what they saw as the Jesuits' ambiguous methods of evangelization. There developed an open rift between the two orders, the Franciscans seeing the Jesuits as timid and equivocating, the Jesuits seeing the Franciscans as human bulls in a china shop. The Jesuits had good cause for their nervousness. The power behind the imperial throne, the regent Hideyoshi, was already turning threatening eyes on the Christian community, which, in his opinion, was becoming too powerful. The combustible situation blew up when a Spanish sea captain whose ship was wrecked on Japanese shores tried to bully his way out of his predicament by boasting of Spain's worldwide power — and intimating that, somehow, the missionaries were agents of this power! When Hideyoshi heard this, he immediately ordered the execution of all Franciscans in the country. They, together with a number of Japanese helpers, were crucified in Nagasaki in February 1597.

It was during these dangerous years that a brilliant Italian Jesuit, Alessandro Valignano, laid out the course that his society was to follow in the East. In 1573, upon being appointed visitor to the region and while preparing to lead out a Jesuit mission, Valignano challenged the principles of the *Padroado,* insisting that the men he took with him be as free as possible of Portuguese influence. Once in the East, he proceeded on the path that Xavier had opened, insisting that the Japanese need not become European to receive the faith. He wrote: "Japan is not a place which can be controlled by foreigners, for the Japanese are neither so weak nor so stupid a race as to permit this. . . . Therefore there is no alternative to relying on training the natives in the way they should go and subsequently leaving them to manage the churches themselves." He drew up a code of behavior for his fellow Jesuits, instructing them in Japanese etiquette and, more significantly, in respect for Japanese culture. With this gentle and sensitive approach the missionaries made good headway, and if left alone might have avoided Hideyoshi's wrath. But the arrival of the Spanish friars and, at the same time, the dawning in the Japanese consciousness of the dangers of European expansionism marked the beginning of the end for the Catholic mission in Japan. In the next forty years, the crucified Franciscans were joined by another 2,126 martyrs. More than 37,000 Christian peasants died in an uprising in 1638. As Japan closed its doors to the outside world, the Christian project withered away.

In the meantime, Valignano's policy of "gentle conversion" was taken into the heart of China by another extraordinary Italian Jesuit. Matteo Ricci was the personification of everything that the visitor had requested for the Eastern missions: he was strong in the faith, and he was also learned academically, with a lively interest in the sciences, a flair for languages, and a skill in such things as watchmaking. He was a true Renaissance man. At Valignano's order, he started learning Chinese before he even entered the country. Then, dressed as a Buddhist monk, he with another Jesuit, Ruggieri, took up residence in a provincial town in 1583. Ruggieri's health soon broke, and he had to withdraw, but Ricci stayed on. Through eighteen years, as he preached and heard confessions, he also studied and read, and tried his hand at translation with growing success. His patience paid off: the literati class, fascinated by this Westerner's technical skills and scholarship and his evident respect for their customs and culture, accepted him into their company. In keeping with his new status, Ricci now put off the robes of a monk and put on those of a mandarin. He gained the tolerance of the court and a residence in Beijing, and the right to preach and practice his religion. When he died in 1610, hundreds of mandarins came to pay their respects, and the imperial governor erected a plaque in his honor.

Ricci's method, which has been called a "pastoral of technology," won him and his religion great respect in China. And yet, what did he have to show for all his brilliance? Some 3,000 Chinese Christians, compared to about 300,000 in Japan at the same time, and a deep ambivalence among his fellow missionaries, both Jesuit and other, over what were seen as his accommodationist methods. What made these methods even more suspect, perhaps, was that they were not merely tactics adopted to make his message palatable to the Chinese. His long immersion in Confucian learning had brought Ricci to believe profoundly that this was a base onto which, with sensitivity and patience, Christianity could be grafted, much as, centuries earlier, Christianity had been grafted onto Aristotelianism. In the meantime, he advised that missionaries should proceed painstakingly, and not give in to the temptation of effecting mass, uninformed conversions.

Ricci was far, far ahead of his time. In the years following his death, disputes would break out between missionaries over what was the proper, even permissible, way to evangelize. Were the preexisting rituals of the Chinese — the veneration of ancestors, for instance — compatible with Christianity, or were they pagan practices, to be rooted out in the cause of true religion? And just because Eastern minds were offended by the concept of a deity in disgrace, was it acceptable only to preach Christ in glory, while downplaying the crucified Jesus? And what about the effect of this hybrid life on its practitioners? A Jesuit visiting from the Philippines in 1582 described it with disapproval: the silk clothes and comfortable mattresses and frequent baths, the general slackness in observing the rule. Ignatian spirituality was built on discipline, obedience, and self-abnegation. How much could this discipline be watered down without losing its soul? With time all these arguments heated up, until finally, in the eighteenth century, the papacy came down against the Jesuits, in what has become known as "the Chinese Rites controversy." The Eurocentric model prevailed, and continued to do so into modern times.

Taken as a whole, sixteenth-century Catholicism's missionary endeavor suffered from many flaws and shortcomings. Paternalism, racism, complicity in the evils of conquest — there was plenty to criticize. But perhaps these ills were inevitable, given the blank slate with which the Westerners started, the size of the challenge with which they were suddenly faced, the conditions under which they had to proceed, and their lack of preparation for what lay ahead. What is undeniable, however, is the creativity the overseas missions released, which in turn helped to invigorate the mother church. This was almost entirely the work of the religious orders. It was they that provided the personnel and energy for the missions. It is difficult to exaggerate what their pathfinding meant for the future of the Church.

And, indeed, what it meant for the knowledge and understanding of civilizations. The discovery of so many new societies existing, so to speak, outside the Christian pale gave rise to serious discussion in Europe regarding their legitimacy and their rights. The Spanish Dominican Francisco de Vitoria laid the foundations of international law precisely because of the issues that the newly discovered worlds presented. And after him, many other thinkers took up the debate.

We can argue, then, that imperfect though they were, and ineffectual though their work often turned out to be, missionaries were the best, the most sensitive mediators that sixteenth-century Europe could have found, as it set out to take hold of the rest of the globe.

*   *   *

It is suggested that in the evolution of a species, a crisis may sometimes occur, a sort of disruption that knocks it sideways and alters its course. If we accept that Christianity has been evolving over these last two thousand years (and surely that is what we mean when we speak of a pilgrim church, moving through history), then it is not hard to see the sixteenth century as that sort of rupture, throwing the established order sideways and reworking its moving parts. The innovative thinking born of the Renaissance, the growing power of the monarchies, the impact of European exploration overseas, the challenge of Luther, the amassing of Protestant power, the rebounding of Catholic power, the religious wars, the Council of Trent — all these events combined to change the scenery in the Church, to alter the mood, so that what we call post-Tridentine Catholicism was a different thing from what had been before.

Central to this change was of course, as the word suggests, the Council of Trent. The fathers of the council clarified Catholic doctrine. They defined the chain of command in the church while, at the same time, calling bishops and priests back to their pastoral duty. They emphasized the importance of education, both of priests and of people in general. They cleaned out many of the medieval excrescences that, over time, had come to clutter the practice of the faith. They pointed the way to a new regime of law and order, very similar in spirit to the law and order being established in the secular world. It was strong medicine that they offered to Catholics, and it took a while for Catholics to accept it, but the result was, in time, a church sturdy enough to face the challenges of the coming age.

But the sixteenth century saw another development that cannot be credited to the council, a spontaneous burst of activism and creativity that was to last well into the seventeenth century and permeate Catholic society for the rest of the modern age. Some of this creativity originated in the hierarchy, some in the laity, but more came from the religious orders, both men and women. This was in spite of the fact that their contribution had been devalued, almost to the point of disapproval, by the council.

Only later, as the Catholic Church turned to the huge task of restructuring itself, of training its clergy and educating its people, did it turn more and more toward the religious orders. They did not fit into the Tridentine blueprint, but they were the force behind reform, and the spirit that suffused it. It is hard to imagine how the church's regeneration could have succeeded without them.

Suggested Reading for Chapter 3

For a general overview of the period, the relevant volume in *The Christian Centuries* is useful. Of course, the reform of the church did not end in 1600, as Robert Bireley's *The Refashioning of Catholicism, 1450-1700* (1999) and Ronnie Po-Chia Hsia's *The World of Catholic Renewal, 1540-1770* (1998) make plain. Jean Delumeau's work, *Catholicism between Luther and Voltaire* (1977), gives the same long view, with particular insight into the grassroots religion of the age and the problems the church faced in its efforts at reform.

Albert Einstein once said that "Imagination is more important than knowledge." It is difficult, almost half a millennium later, to imagine the psychological makeup of the age of reform. Yet without the help of imagination it is well-nigh impossible to put our knowledge into context.

H. Outram Evenett offers us a glance into the Catholic mood in the years after the Council of Trent in *The Spirit of the Counter-Reformation,* a groundbreaking lecture series that was published posthumously (1968).

For an introduction to the two most influential new religious orders of the sixteenth century, you can read Father Cuthbert, O.S.F.C., *The Capuchins: A Contribution to the History of the Counter-Reformation* (1971), and John O'Malley, *The First Jesuits* (1993). (If you want to know more about the Jesuits, keep looking out for John O'Malley.) As for Teresa, there has been a great deal written (some if it by herself); if you are also interested in the background to her extraordinary life, a good place to start would be Jodi Bilinkoff, *The Avila of Saint Teresa* (1989). Teresa's achievement is all the more impressive in view of all the social and cultural imperatives that had long hedged around the lives of nuns. For more on this, see Mary Laven, *Virgins of Venice* (2002).

Two books that deal with the challenges facing the church in the missionary field are the classic work by Lewis Hanke, *The Spanish Struggle for Justice in the Conquest of America* (1949), and the newer work by A. Ross, *A Vision Betrayed: The Jesuits in Japan and China, 1542-1742* (1994).

CHAPTER 4

The Seventeenth Century: The Age of Confessionalism

The sixteenth century had brought seismic change to old Europe. The seventeenth century would be a time of following through, of settling accounts, of bringing the world back under control. And this was no easy undertaking: after so many years of fighting and of persecution, violence continued to course through the European bloodstream. Feuding was endemic, so was banditry, and a general lawlessness. And there was, as yet, little hope of peace at the top. The dynasties were wrapped up in their own feuds, and those feuds had spawned marauding armies that ranged unchecked back and forth across the Continent.

So it makes sense, before looking at the new age, to look at the legacy of the old. In 1600 Spain, the great Catholic protagonist of the sixteenth century, was in decline. Its revenues, massive though they were, had not kept pace with its military expenditures. Since the 1560s it had been struggling to scotch a rebellion in the Netherlands; this war was still costing it heavily in blood and treasure. In 1588 it had undertaken to send an invasion army to England under the protection of a mighty naval armada; the destruction of the armada had delivered a mortal blow to those ambitions. In the 1590s, Spanish troops had been engaged in the French wars on behalf of the fanatical Catholic League and its desperate design to put a Spanish princess on the French throne, both of which projects collapsed with the accession of the Protestant (but French) king Henry IV. Even if Philip II refused to recognize the fact, his days, and those of superpower Spain, were numbered. When he died in 1598 his country was already becoming too weak, both politically and economically, to continue his crusade. His dynastic ambitions

161

in France had already crumbled to dust. Peace with England came in 1604, a truce with the seven rebellious Dutch provinces in 1609. Though fighting still lay ahead in this latter arena, Spain's mastery was doomed. At midcentury the United Provinces were recognized as a sovereign — and thoroughly Protestant — state, divided by the Rhine from the southern — and thoroughly Catholic — "Spanish" Netherlands.

What western European Christianity had in 1600 was a de facto partition. Across the north, England, Scotland, the Dutch provinces, Scandinavia, and most of northern Germany were firmly in the Protestant camp. Catholic holdouts in these countries had to shift for themselves, in whatever way they could. Facing them were the major Catholic powers, the Austrian Habsburgs, Spain/Portugal, Rome and the other Italian states, and Bavaria. Dotted here and there across the face of the Continent were territories still in dispute: Switzerland, where small Catholic cantons jostled against powerful Protestant strongholds (foremost among them Calvinist Geneva), and a scattering of minor German principalities and independent cities, some Catholic, some Protestant, that bucked the general trend of their neighborhoods. But the great uncertainties lay to the east and to the west: in the Austrian Habsburgs' troubled territories and Poland, and in France.

Given the staunch Catholicism of the Habsburg rulers, it is ironic that so many of their subjects were Protestant. In some regions, like Bohemia, Protestantism was deeply entrenched, with roots reaching back two centuries to the days of John Hus. In others, Austria for instance, the reformed religion was largely an affair of city people and of the nobility, who valued it as a weapon in their struggle against their Catholic overlords. The same identification of Protestantism with noble "liberties" is found in Poland, where a landed gentry together with a powerful minority among the bourgeoisie were using it to hold their own against the central government. If in these regions the rulers dealt carefully with the problem, it was because they had to, given the power of the opposition.

Un Roi, Un Loi, Une Foi (One King, One Law, One Faith)

France had been torn by a series of religious wars since 1562. The new, dynamic form of Protestantism that we know as Calvinism had entered the kingdom in the 1530s. Though it came from Geneva, its leader and many of its most ardent protagonists were French exiles; on returning in secret to their homeland they found a ready following. The Huguenots, as they were called, presented a serious threat to the Catholic establishment, and the consequence was over forty years of bloodshed and mutual destruction. Peace finally came when the Protestant Henry IV inherited the throne and converted to Catholicism. But the end to hostilities did not by itself heal the country's divisions. In 1598 Henry issued the Edict of Nantes, which guaranteed a limited security and freedom of worship to his Huguenot subjects. This was his personal, and highly political, solution to a difficult problem, and for the time being it worked. Though tension continued, and there was fighting still to come, the extremism of the war years faded away. But the Protestant minority stuck like a bone in the monarchy's throat. The following decades would see a steady erosion of their rights until finally, in 1685, Louis XIV revoked the Edict, leaving the Huguenots of France with no choice but to convert or get out. And many got out, taking their skills with them to more congenial religious climates.

Louis's action was brutal, and it came somewhat late in the day. By 1685 the age of religious absolutism was drawing to a close. Not that people stopped hating each other (that would take many years more), but a few of them, here and there, were beginning to realize that toleration bore positive economic advantages. At the start of the seventeenth century, however, religious dissidence was still considered treasonous. The people in power saw it as a foreign body, and doubted that a state could truly thrive with such a foreign body planted within it. The problem was that the reformation years had left the grass roots of Europe in a sectarian tangle, with men and women of different persuasions living side by side, sometimes harmoniously, sometimes not. It was up to the powers to sort the tangle out, one way or another.

The process by which this was achieved has come to be known as "confessionalism." Its root is the word *confessio,* coined in Germany to describe a public and official statement of religious belief. Starting in the 1520s, the various faith communities of Europe had drawn up these confessions — hard-edged and specific versions of what we might loosely call "vision statements" — to which the people living within their ambit were required to subscribe. There was a general understanding, which Luther had expounded at the very outset of his revolt, that the civil powers had the responsibility to implement these confessions, even, if necessary, by using force on the less willing members of their communities. This understanding received legal endorsement with the Peace of Augsburg (1555), the agreement that ended the German religious wars. The principle of *cuius regio eius religio* (he who rules [a territory] determines [its] religion) meant that each territorial power of the empire was entitled to impose its faith on its own people. Dissidents could accept that faith or emigrate.

And emigrate they did. Thousands upon thousands left their homelands for the sake of religion. As a result, the map of Europe was redrawn. Geneva had been a fairly easygoing part-Catholic, part-Protestant city until, in the 1550s and under Calvin's firm hand, the Catholics departed and a flood of observant French Huguenots came pouring in. The southern Netherlands had been a hotbed of "heretics" until Philip II's forces sent them fleeing north to Holland and Zeeland. There, beyond the reach of the Spanish army, they built a new Protestant republic, while their native land, which today is Belgium, became a fortress for Catholicism. In various territories of Germany and the Habsburg Empire, thousands were made to leave their homes. Those who remained were required to submit to the discipline enforced by state and church together, to attend the official services and receive the official sacraments, to be subject to the church courts and to a general oversight of their everyday behavior. In this way, through eviction of some and coercion of others, numerous territories became more religiously homogenous.

The Thirty Years' War

So seventeenth-century Europe believed in coercion. And on occasion, coercion led to war. In 1618 a war began in response to coercion in the cause of religion, which led to the devastation of much of Germany. And all for naught. When it finally sputtered out, the religion of the Counter-Reformation was left in a much weakened state.

The Holy Roman Empire stretched from the Baltic Sea to the Alps, from the borders of France to those of Poland. What today comprises Germany, Austria, the Czech Republic and Slovakia, and the west bank of the Rhine was then a collection of some three hundred autonomous entities, ranging from major principalities such as Bavaria and the Palatinate down to pocket-size statelets. There were sixty self-governing cities and sixty-five sovereign bishoprics, as well as dozens of "imperial knights," rulers whose miniterritories extended, perhaps, for only a few miles — all of them leftovers from a medieval world system in which power had been widely dispersed. Whereas in many parts of Europe there had been consolidation over the years, and the outlines of modern states were beginning to appear, the empire knew no such progress. The only tie that bound this jumble to-gether was the Holy Roman emperor. According to ancient custom, his was an elected office, but for time out of mind he had been a member of the Habsburg family, master in his own right of Austria, Bohemia, Silesia, Moravia, and the Tyrol.

For many years in the sixteenth century the Habsburg dynasty had been even more powerful. Through a series of shrewd marriages it had col-lected into one empire not only the Austrian heartland but also Spain, the Spanish territories in the New World, most of southern Italy, and a broad strip of territory running along the Rhine from Savoy through the Nether-lands. The heir to this vast domain was Philip's father, Charles V, a half-Spanish, half-Burgundian, slow-moving, conscientious, and ultimately ill-starred man. As a Catholic through and through whose ill fortune it was to preside over Luther's rebellion and all that followed, he naturally made a lot of enemies. But even without Luther he would have been hated. He had too much power, and too many people felt threatened by him, most signifi-cantly the lesser rulers of the empire, whether Catholic or Lutheran, and the king of France. So compelling was their sense of threat that they were ready to join together across sectarian lines to bring him down. And this is what happened. In the end, after years of back-and-forth warfare, Charles ac-cepted that he could never force his subjects into Catholic orthodoxy, that it was inevitable that the Lutherans would gain the right to enforce their faith in their own territories. This they did, with the Peace of Augsburg in 1555. Rather than face the bitter moment himself, he abdicated, and divided his empire. To his son, Philip, went Spain and all its possessions; to his brother, Ferdinand, went the Austrian lands and, by arrangement, election to the imperial title. And the intractable problems that came with such a di-vided realm.

When Ignatius Loyola first sent Jesuits into central Europe in the 1540s, the situation looked grim indeed for Catholicism. Whole stretches of Germany were solidly Protestant, and seemingly well beyond their reach. The duke of Bavaria and a cluster of prince-bishops were the only major rul-ers still in the Catholic camp. Several of the more influential states, many of the imperial cities, and some bishops had moved to the reform; others were teetering on the edge. The Habsburg lands were in no better shape, with large and powerful territories completely in Protestant hands and Protes-tant influence elsewhere on the rise. Beyond the boundaries of the empire, Poland was a hotbed of sectarianism, with multiple religious groups, main-stream and otherwise, pressing their advantage against a weak Catholic monarchy. Across the region, the ancient religious orders were smashed almost to pieces. Everywhere there was debility and a sense of surrender. But as long as the situation was fluid, it was capable of being changed. After the Peace of Augsburg an uneasy quiet took hold, which lasted until 1618. It was during this time that the Jesuits built their forces.

The Jesuits would later say that it was they who "saved" the empire for Catholicism. There is much truth to their claim. Of course, there were other players in the game: reforming prelates, powerful ministers and functionaries, the Catholic rulers themselves. From the 1570s on these men began to exercise their muscle. But if the perspective is broadened to include the previous generation, one thing becomes clear. Almost to a man, the Counter-Reformation leadership of central Europe was educated in Jesuit colleges, either in Rome or in their own countries. The first German college was established in Cologne in 1544. Before the Council of Trent closed in 1563, six more had opened in Austria and Germany. It was here, more perhaps than anywhere else, that the fact was borne out: education was the key to the modernizing of Christianity. Not that everybody got an education; far from it! But the people who mattered in politics did, and along with their courses in rhetoric and philosophy they absorbed a new form of Catholicism, dynamic and militant. Then, when the opportunity arose, they turned this new spirit into power.

The period of peace ended in 1618 when a group of Protestant noblemen, angry at what they saw as a power grab by their Habsburg king, forced their way into the Hradschin Castle in Prague, confronted his representatives (Catholics, of course) who were meeting there, and threw two of them out of the window. This event, known to history as the defenestration of Prague, was followed at once by the establishment of a new representative government and a decree banishing all Jesuits from Bohemia. Within a few months several more territories joined the rebels, fighting broke out, and the most murderous European war to date, the Thirty Years' War, began.

At the outset the prospects for the king (who coincidentally had just been elected Emperor Ferdinand II) were dire. Surrounded by enemies, and with his capital city, Vienna, under siege, he might well have thought that only God could save him. And indeed, when his fortunes did turn, and when his armies won a resounding victory at the battle of the White Mountain in 1620, this was exactly what he and his Catholic supporters believed. From this moment on, the war became for them a holy war, in which God had signaled that his design for the re-Catholicization of the empire must be pursued, no matter what the cost in human suffering.

From very early on voices counseled compromise. But they were not Jesuit voices. From the superior general in Rome, Vitelleschi, and others came warnings that any concession to the Protestants would be tantamount to apostasy. But possibly the voice that mattered most was that of Ferdinand's confessor, the Jesuit William Lamormaini. Over the following years he consistently urged unyielding militancy. For seventeen years Ferdinand, a devoted alumnus of a Jesuit college, listened to him.

We should remark here on the phenomenon of the royal confessor. Every Catholic prince had one, and in almost every case he was a Jesuit. It had begun in 1552, when Ignatius Loyola encouraged one of his men to become confessor to the king of Portugal, arguing that this could work to the betterment of the Catholic cause. Later, the Society put limits on the mandate: confessors were not to make their opinions public, and they were not to exercise any commissions on behalf of their prince-penitents. They were not to meddle in secular affairs or seek advancement for friends and relations. The advice they gave was to remain private, and to concern only affairs of conscience. All these restrictions were overstepped at one time or another. But the real rub lay in the last one. Where, for a prince, did private conscience end and public duty begin? Especially at a time when religion and politics were so tightly fused together? Ferdinand and Lamormaini saw eye to eye. The way Protestants were to be treated within the empire was a matter for the emperor's conscience, informed by his confessor. The goal, they agreed, was total elimination. A mass expulsion of Bohemian religious dissidents, among them many of the country's nobles and intellectuals, took place. Their estates were given to Habsburg loyalists, in an enormous, unprecedented transfer of property. Thus began what is remembered in Czech history as "the time of darkness," of backwardness and stagnation under the rule of foreign landlords. The practice of the Lutheran faith was forbidden within the Habsburg hereditary lands. Some prominent Protestants were executed "to encourage the others" (to anticipate Voltaire's words, spoken a century later).

For all that it was framed as a holy war, this was in fact a war full of grubby motives. Ferdinand's genuine religiosity was sharpened by the thought that victory might allow him to smash the local representative bodies and establish absolute control over the Holy Roman Empire. Of course, the leaders of the various factions wanted the opposite. Foreign interveners (and this would in time include Denmark and Sweden) saw their chance for a land grab in Germany. The generals of the mercenary armies that ranged back and forth across the ruined land were less interested in achieving peace than in enriching themselves. Cardinal Richelieu of France weighed religious solidarity against political gain, and decided that by assisting the Protestant cause he could make serious trouble for the old Habsburg enemy. As for the Jesuits, they identified the cause of religion with the recapture of the vast monastic landholdings that had fallen into Protestant hands after the Reformation. Some of this wealth, they hoped, would come to them and allow them to finance more colleges and exercise more influence in hostile territory. For this end, much as they deplored the devastation taking place, they were prepared to let Germany go to the wall.

In 1629 Ferdinand, with the backing of the militant wing and his confessor, issued his Edict of Restitution, banning Calvinism from the Holy Roman Empire and requiring the Lutherans to give back all the church properties they had taken since 1552. It was an act of supreme political ineptitude, in that it galvanized and united all who feared his power. The war went on, and on, and on, and finally reached deadlock. As the emperor's prospects failed to improve, the vision of "holy war" began to evaporate, and voices of reason began to be heard. Theologians were heard arguing that a peace of compromise might not, after all, be a mortal sin. Finally, in 1648, the Peace of Westphalia was achieved, its terms not unlike those of the Peace of Augsburg in 1555. The Holy Roman Empire remained as fragmented as it was before; the difference was that great stretches of it lay in ruins, and its population was diminished by some six million souls.

Another casualty of the war was the Catholic Church, or at least that concept of church as monolith that had been developed in the Middle Ages and defended with ferocity for more than a hundred years. The war had shown with painful clarity that when forced to choose, the powers of Europe put national interests before those of the universal church. Rome continued to speak out, but with much less effect. In the later seventeenth century, state power was no longer "rising"; it had risen. From then on, state churches were very much under the control of their princes.

The Jesuits, whom we think of as the great champions of papal power, had unintentionally done a great deal to advance the cause of princely absolutism. And they were only the foremost among many churchmen who thought to enhance their own power by championing that of their royal masters. Certainly, their actions on behalf of their princes, which may have served their own purposes in the short run, helped in the long run to enhance those princes' claim to supreme moral authority. Sadly for the spiritual advisers, the day would come when the princes were ready to treat their advice much more lightly.

The Art of Persuasion

The Thirty Years' War showed how much, a century after the great confessional rupture, the European powers were ready to kill and destroy, allegedly in the name of religion. Coercion was still favored as a weapon: seizures of property, imprisonment or exile, even death. But coercion was not the whole story. Rulers both secular and ecclesiastical also used persuasion. The authoritarianism of the regimes was interlined, so to speak, with a determination to reach into the very core of the people, to capture their minds and, if possible, to inflame their hearts. It made good practical sense. The princes of Europe, Catholic and Protestant alike, reckoned that religion could make their subjects more deferential, more orderly, and even more industrious. There were, of course, the old means of persuasion: church rituals, preaching, processions, and other mass demonstrations of religious solidarity. To these a whole gamut of new techniques was added: community hymn singing (often to the tune of old folk songs); religiously inspired art, from Bernini's sculptures to the crudest of woodcut illustrations; edifying stories and legends; and a mass of printed literature — Bibles, books of devotion, household guides, almanacs, pamphlets. The emphasis varied but the process was remarkably uniform. Whatever the prevailing religious culture was, the people were to be immersed in it. Architecture spoke volumes, as did religious symbols. Where was the pulpit placed? Where the altar? Or was there an altar at all? Should there even be a crucifix? Was the church interior uncluttered and austere and lit by clear daylight, bespeaking the nakedness of man before the Protestants' transcendent God, or was it rich in stained glass and the statues of saints, glimmering with candles, redolent with incense, a monument to the greatness of the Catholic Church Triumphant? The visual differences helped to entrench differences in belief. In the very tenor of their everyday life, the men and women of Europe were subjected to a process of "confessional acculturation."

And it was in this process, in the Catholic regions of Europe, that the religious orders played a major part.

The Council of Trent had set out the framework. It had clarified doctrine, and it had laid out a program of reform. Everything, according to the fathers of Trent, was to depend on improving the quality of the clergy and returning them to their duties. Only bishops who took their work seriously should be installed. A sluggish lower clergy had to be galvanized and enlightened. Monks and nuns who had lived for years in comfortable slackness had to be persuaded to give up their comforts and embrace austerity.

Once all these people began to practice what the church had long preached, the world would fall back into its proper place. But for this to happen, there must be no more clerical concubinage, no more absenteeism, no more pluralism, no more worldliness — a tall order, given the habit of many generations.

And no more ignorance of the faith. The council subscribed to the prevailing spirit of the age, that instruction was essential to salvation. It demanded that priests be trained in the knowledge of their faith, and that they pass the knowledge on, at least in rudimentary form, to their people. But herein lay the rub. First, for the thousands of priests across the Continent (an estimated hundred thousand in France alone) there were, as yet, no established educational standards. Second, Europe, even with the Protestant regions subtracted, was a complicated babel of languages and dialects, of cultural crosscurrents and conflicting traditions and prejudices. And there was a huge urban/rural divide. While the cities at least had the structures upon which to build this new Catholicism, enormous peasant populations still lived in remote areas and practiced a form of religion more or less ignorant of orthodox Christian doctrine. How could their priests teach them what they themselves did not know? Training cost money; where was the money to come from? It required teaching personnel. How were they to be found? It was one thing for Rome to speak, another for the world to listen. The fact was that the church needed more than a knowledgeable priesthood; it also needed the support of a laity prepared to commit both effort and money to the cause — and this, at the moment, was largely lacking.

Nowhere was the dilemma more acute than in France. The religious wars, which lasted from 1562 to 1598, had left the country close to anarchy, its population insecure and divided. Its political situation was perilous, to say the least. The last Valois king had died in 1589 by an assassin's hand. The heir by rights, Henry of Navarre, was — horror of horrors — not only a Protestant but the leader of the Protestant armies. His full accession to the throne was delayed for several violent years, and then only made possible by two conditions: the crushing war-weariness of the French people, and his own pragmatic grasp of what was needed. "Paris is worth a mass," he is supposed to have said, as with his conversion he pulled the rug out from under his ultra-Catholic, pro-Spanish adversaries. Then, by the force of his personality, he pressured the official institutions into granting religious freedom and a limited civil status to the Protestant minority. And so peace came to France at last.

But the years of warfare left many gaping wounds. The countryside was impoverished, the population rebellious and often criminalized. As for the official religion, Catholicism, things were in serious disarray, with churches standing empty, monasteries sacked and ruined, and a clergy that had little idea what it was supposed to do, and no money to do it with. It was as if the entire reforming movement around the Council of Trent had passed the country by. Henry did not do much to help. He used the power of his position to fill high posts in the church with favorites and the relatives of favorites. And he was partial to young nuns, whose favors he sometimes repaid by making them into abbesses.

And yet, even before his assassination in 1610, things were beginning to change. France was rising from its ashes, to become the great powerhouse of Catholicism in the seventeenth century. Many of the holy men and women of the age, and many of the religious congregations that are now known around the world, were born within its borders.

Within the political class of 1600 was a small but politically influential group known, and not affectionately, as the *dévots*. They had supported the Catholic League in the recent wars, shared its fervor and suffered its traumas. The power and vigor of the Protestant cause had shaken them; the margin of its defeat had been much too close for their comfort. And now that the peace had come, they were seeking answers. Was all the bloodshed of the past years not a judgment of God upon their country for its infidelity? How could they make amends for all its previous failures? And how could they tap into the spirit of regeneration that they saw elsewhere in the Church?

Sixteenth-century France had not lacked for religious impulses. Throughout its worst years there had been active preachers, and dedicated churchmen, and occasional stabs at monastic reform. Sanctity, especially if accompanied by austerity, never lost its appeal. A case in point is the Feuillant Congregation, a Cistercian offshoot. In 1573 Jean de la Barrière, a young nobleman who was also the commendatory abbot of a totally degraded monastery in southern France, experienced conversion, entered the order, and undertook to reform his community. After a rocky start during which a number of the old hands were forcibly expelled, he managed to install a regimen of the strictest austerity. His monks went barefoot, slept on planks, engaged in heavy manual labor, ate nothing but bread and vegetables (and, during Lent, nothing but bread). What is striking is that at a time when most monastic communities were foundering, this way of life drew in a flood of novices, so that within two decades there were enough Feuillants (and, later, Feuillantines) in enough monasteries to form an independent congregation. Eventually their austerities were scaled back somewhat, but the fact that they were attractive for so long indicates that for some French men and women at least, there was an intense spiritual need waiting to be satisfied.

The "Mystical Invasion"

Satisfaction came with a rush, and from an unexpected quarter. In 1604 six Spanish Carmelite nuns arrived in Paris. They were met by a group of high-born ladies, who conducted them with great fanfare to the convent that had been prepared for them. The nuns were followed in, almost at once, by a cluster of French aspirants, the first of scores who would soon be clamoring for admittance. Thus, twenty-two years after her death, Teresa's reform began its surge across the Pyrenees.

This foundation was the work of the *dévot* party, which had to use considerable political clout to secure it. Since the war, all things Spanish were regarded with deep suspicion in France, and the *dévots* were openly pro-Spanish. Furthermore, public opinion in Paris harbored a sour hostility toward what was considered their extreme religiosity. It took some daring to hope that the new community would be able to put down roots. Nothing, however, could have prepared the founders for the great wave of feminine fervor that broke over the capital, and from there, over the country. Within two years the Paris house was forced to use its overflow to open new convents in two other cities. In the next forty years, fifty-five discalced Carmelite convents were established in France alone, while further foundations took place in Italy, Lorraine, the Spanish Netherlands, and Poland. Confounding the humble beginnings of the order, these communities came to occupy a privileged place within the upper echelons of society. Queens and duchesses patronized them, and the daughters and widows of elites — and even an ex-mistress of the king of France — knocked on their doors demanding entry. Carmelite nuns gave advice to prominent churchmen, who, buffeted by political forces that they could not avoid and compromises that they had to make, seemed to find refreshment in the women's clear, uncluttered vision of holiness. This was one way in which cloistered women who never saw the outside world powered the engine of Catholic reform. The "Europe of the devout," as it has been called, had not lost its "tremendous appetite for all that was divine." Nuns in their cloisters were thought to bring that divine a little nearer.

The religious revival of seventeenth-century France came about through what has been called a "mystical invasion," and the Carmelites were certainly the spearhead of that invasion. But they were by no means alone. In Paris, forty-eight new monasteries of women were built in the first half of the century, most of them contemplative. As fast as they were built they were filled with aspirants. It was a contagion, nothing less. Within a half-century, the cities of France were bursting with women's convents. Significantly, behind the stones and mortar (and the huge investment of capital they represented), and behind all the young women in their white novice veils, there was a broad population of fathers and mothers who now saw religious life as a desirable end for their daughters. We can question their motives (convents were more than retreats for the devout; they were also a cheap and secure solution to a surplus-daughter problem), but we cannot deny that French society, at least in its upper echelons, had "got religion" in a big way.

However, in this first great flush of religious enthusiasm, which we can date to the early decades of the century, a major problem needed to be solved. As we have seen in the development of the orders of clerks regular, such as the Barnabites and the Jesuits, the Catholic Reformation had allowed the new male congregations to modernize by moving away significantly from the traditional monastic model. But for women, the religious life as envisaged by Trent had nothing to offer but the status quo ante: the cloister, and within it, a life of contemplation, mortification, and self-denial. Without a doubt, the numbers of women now flocking into the reformed convents proved that this regimen had great appeal. But even more women were left standing outside, for the simple fact that they were physically incapable of enduring the rigors of the monastic life. "Some are constrained, because of the austerity of the Rule and the weakness of their bodies, to remain in the world," complained a prominent *dévote*, Jeanne de Lestonnac, the widowed baroness of Montferrand. Their only alternatives, the unreformed monasteries, were in her opinion positively dangerous, and she advised women against entering them, "for fear of finding spiritual death where they looked for life." The new age was for women one of bounding religious affectivity and, as yet, only limited means of sustaining it.

Another widowed baroness (who, as it happened, lived on the other side of France) was caught in the same dilemma. Jeanne de Chantal, left by her husband's death with four children, found herself at odds with her life and drawn toward a more spiritual path. Her first thought was for the new Carmelite community in Dijon, and she spent many hours talking with the prioress. However, any hope of entering there was thwarted by two stubborn realities, her children and her own delicate health. Jeanne did her best to live the devout life in the world. But she continued to feel the pull of the monastery.

A solution for her, and for many women like her, was devised by her spiritual director, Francis de Sales. An alumnus of the Jesuit college of Clermont, and later the bishop of Geneva, de Sales had a distinguished political/ecclesiastical career that took him to Rome and to Paris but did not prevent him from preaching, visiting the 450 parishes of his mountainous diocese, and giving counsel to a growing number of laymen and laywomen. In this last activity, as is so often the case, the teacher became a learner; Francis developed a deep appreciation of his disciples and of their spiritual potential. He came to believe that they were capable of great service to God. Yet he saw that in the mind of the times, they were trapped in an inferior state; they belonged in "the world," which conventional religion regarded as a den of iniquity. What use was all their piety as long as they remained in the den?

Francis's answer came in his book *Introduction to the Devout Life,* published in 1609. It must be regarded as one of the most influential books of its time, in that it opened the possibility of personal holiness to all people, whatever their calling. "God commands Christians . . . to bring forth the fruits of devotion, each according to his position and vocation. Devotion must be exercised in different ways by the gentleman, the worker, the servant, the prince, the widow, the young girl, and the married woman. Not only is this true, but the practice of devotion must also be adapted to the strength, activities, and duties of each particular person." The devout life, for Francis, was not an exterior state, but an orientation, in whatever circumstances it happened to be, of the soul toward God.

These words implied interiority, and it may be difficult for us in this age of individualism to appreciate how new this idea of interiority must have appeared to the majority of seventeenth-century Catholics. In a simpler time, the practice of religion had meant (at least for most people) little more than the observance of outward ceremonies; the concept of an inner, private creature/Creator relationship would have seemed passing strange. However, there was now a lettered elite, and they took to it gladly, if we can judge from the fact that the book was reissued forty times before the author's death in 1622, and translated into several languages. One of its effects was to uncouple the holy life from the religious life. For centuries, "flight from the world" had been the ideal. Francis de Sales never ceased to respect the monastic forms, but he insisted that God could be loved and served in this world too, in many different ways.

This brings us back to the baroness de Chantal, the most eminent and the dearest of all his disciples. Together they developed a little community in the tiny Alpine town of Annecy, in which they gathered a handful of women together to follow a life of prayer and charity. It was called the Visitation, in honor of the hidden, kindly life of the Virgin. With women like Jeanne in mind, de Sales did away with the more stringent demands of a monastic rule: physical deprivation and self-mortification. "For the infirm I hope that this congregation will be gentle, gracious refuge," he wrote, "where without many corporal austerities they can practice all the essential virtues of devotion." Furthermore, for widows and other women with family obligations (again, like Jeanne), he allowed for the occasional absence from the house. In any case, he ruled, the cloister should not be so inviolable that the sisters could not go out on occasion to help the poor and sick of the neighborhood. What he looked for was a "mitigated" enclosure. "If the spirit of true devotion reigns in a congregation, a moderate enclosure will suffice to make true servants of God," he argued.

Thus with one fell swoop, Francis de Sales took on the two great shibboleths of medieval female monasticism, *clausura* and mortification of the flesh. On both counts he was criticized, and in the end he suffered partial defeat. As long as the community confined itself to Annecy, in Savoy, it escaped notice. But in 1615 another house was opened in Lyons, and thus within the reach of the French hierarchy. In 1616, at the insistence of the archbishop of Lyons, the two communities were turned into full monasteries, with formal vows and full enclosure. As if to prove how appropriate these changes seemed to contemporary society, the Visitation now entered a period of rapid expansion. Before the end of the century thousands of women had entered its doors, and there were 149 monasteries in France alone.

Certain characteristics of the original foundation survived. Although the lifestyle was now fully contemplative, it remained physically gentle, suitable for delicate constitutions. But it was not an easy life for all that; the nuns exchanged exterior austerity for mortification of the spirit through humiliation and self-abasement. They became powerful exemplars of the new spirit of interiority. Secondly, though their lives were now cloistered and inward-turning, they retained one opening to "the world": they were allowed to let laywomen in temporarily to take part in spiritual retreats. In a subtle but significant way, the Visitation opened the female contemplative life up to modernizing forces.

These two congregations, the Discalced Carmelites and the Visitation, are only the best known of the contemplative orders for women that opened their doors in the seventeenth century. There were others. The rush of women into the cloister during those years is recognized as an unusual phenomenon, a response to what is sometimes referred to as "the monastic temptation." But it has its skeptics. Was it really an expression of something sublime? Could the movement not have owed its force to hard-nosed economic considerations, or to a shortage of marriageable men as a result of the wars? And was this spike in devotion just a "woman thing"?

Perhaps it can be explained thus, but only partially. The women's communities were, above all, manifestations of the wave of religious sensibility sweeping through the upper reaches of French society. It did not last for many decades, but before it faded it fueled a massive investment of people and money in all sorts of laudable enterprises: in institutes of prayer, in education, in the promotion of the faith, in improvements in hospital care, and in attempts to reconstruct a damaged society. The contemplatives benefited from the wave, but they also contributed to it, by touching a chord in a public that longed to do well before the Lord. In their own way, they were that public's cheerleaders.

And yet . . .

The traditional cloistered life of prayer and physical austerity, or the newly conceived cloistered life of prayer and inward mortification: these remained, in the early 1600s, the officially sanctioned choices for women with a religious vocation. But they still did not answer to all possible circumstances; they still did not satisfy every type of woman. The fact was that attraction for the religious life did not lead everybody to the cloister. Some people were just made for action. This became clear in Pontoise in 1605, when the Carmelites arrived to establish their first house outside Paris. Their fame had, of course, preceded them, and no one was more excited by their coming than the local group of *dévotes* who had lived in a prayer community since 1599. Some of the women now decided to break ranks and join the new convent. For those left behind, who felt no vocation to the contemplative life, the future looked bleak, and several advisers suggested that they disband. But their director thought otherwise. "What, gentlemen; just because the hen has laid one good clutch of eggs, do we need to strangle it?" With his help the women survived as a community, and eventually became Ursulines.

Being Both Mary and Martha

They were not the first Frenchwomen to call themselves Ursulines. In fact, the Ursuline way of life had first been imported from Italy into the papal enclave of Avignon and its surrounding areas in the late 1590s. It was not Angela Merici's Ursulinism, in which the women committed themselves to a religious rule while still living at home, but the version developed by Cardinal Borromeo in Milan, in which the sisters were congregated into communities and worked under obedience to the bishop. The important thing, however, was that since they were not cloistered, they were able to combine their religious exercises with works of charity. As one of their admirers recalled, "They frequented the Sacraments and the exercises of Christian doctrine; they assisted the poor, visited the sick, and devoted themselves to all the other works of piety which their age and their sex allowed." And above all, they catechized. They were given the name of *congrégées,* but they were, in fact, half-nuns. In this form, Ursuline communities began to pop up in different places across southern France — twenty-nine of them by 1610: tiny groups, often, of three or four women, encouraged perhaps by a sympathetic priest, supported perhaps by a benevolent patron or two. On the advice of some of these patrons, their multiform charitable activity gave way to a heavy concentration on religious instruction and the basic ABCs. Since their good works depended on what the world still considered to be an unfeminine mobility, they were greeted by a mixed chorus of approbation and condemnation. All in all, however, their supporters outnumbered and outmuscled their detractors, and their numbers continued to grow. Regardless of church law, the Ursulines were simply too useful to be dispersed.

But success brought its own problems. The more they entered the big cities, the more visible they became, and the more the question of their half-nun status began to surface. The old adage was still in force, *aut murus aut maritus* (either a convent wall or a husband). Women at large were women in peril. The hierarchy had to be anxious, since any contravention of church law and/or public morality would certainly be laid at their door. Fathers and mothers had to worry that their daughters might lose their reputations. The higher the family's social standing, the greater the worry. The convent was — or at least was supposed to be — a haven where ladies of good family were safe from scandal. Whether or not they behaved themselves therein was not, in the France of Henry IV, a matter of prime concern, as long as they were invisible. What mattered was that women of quality should not roam the streets like commoners. There is a story told in the seventeenth-century literature about Catherine de Veteris, Ursuline of Aix, meeting her father as she walked with her students to church, "her veil drawn down, her hands in her sleeves, her eyes lowered to the earth, her walk exceedingly humble." Her father turned away in shame, but Catherine was followed by the young gallants of the town, chanting, "Mademoiselle de Veteris has gone mad!" Inside a cloister somewhere, Catherine could have been a credit to her family, but out on the streets of Aix she was an embarrassment.

The *congrégées* presented their contemporaries with a dilemma. On the one hand, they were performing services that society badly needed. On the other, by their exposure to the public they were violating established standards of respectability. The problem came to a head in Paris in 1607. A small Ursuline community set up, amidst a warm welcome. The sight of the young women openly conducting their catechism classes captured the interest of the elites, to the point where even the queen and the princesses came to watch. The more conservative were divided, however. Some of them approved of the community in its present open form, while others insisted that to conform to church law it must be enclosed, and the *congrégées* must become full nuns. The "others" included the woman who was prepared to fund the community, Madame de Sainte-Beuve, and of course her opinion prevailed. It was agreed: the Ursuline community of Paris must become a monastery. And so it did, in 1610.

The example of Paris was followed in the provinces, sometimes willingly, sometimes unwillingly. By 1658 all the Ursuline congregations in France were fully cloistered. They had, however, won a major concession from Rome. They had begun as teachers, and teachers they would remain. They were allowed to keep their free schools, as long as these were enclosed in the monastery walls, with their opening to the outside carefully controlled. The sisters' contemplative life, with its daily round of prayer and community activity, was made to fit around their teaching. Their austerities were moderated so as not to damage their effectiveness in the classroom. The "mitigated" cloister that Francis de Sales had proposed became, in their convents, an established fact. It was a compromise that worried the purists, but it worked because it was needed. Early modern society was getting serious about educating its girls, and there was no one around who could do it as well as these women. By the end of the century there were some ten thousand Ursulines in France.

Nor were they alone. In the southwest the Company of Marie Notre Dame, founded by Jeanne de Lestonnac, and in eastern France and Lorraine the Canonesses of Notre Dame, founded by Pierre Fourier and

Alix Leclerc, served the many thousands of young girls who came flocking into their free schools. A smaller congregation in the Cistercian tradition, the Bernardines, also set up schools. All these nuns were cloistered. By the 1640s it would be a rare town that did not have at least one monastery of teaching nuns. Within their newly established perimeters they proved to a skeptical world that they could combine the contemplative with the active life. That was an achievement in itself. They also proved that their enclosure need not prevent them from contributing to the improvement of society. They became skilled catechists. They pioneered a pedagogy specifically for girls, and they remained, for many years, its foremost practitioners. Through the children, and the adult women's associations that formed up under their guidance, they were able to touch a restrained but influential circle of sympathizers. And meanwhile, they gained access to what their generation considered the most perfect form of life, the penitential life of the monastery.

On the other hand, the time when they could move freely among ordinary people was gone. Three centuries would pass before they left their cloisters.

"Women in Time to Come Will Do Much"

Most of us would say that these women in search of an apostolate experienced more setbacks than advances. But in fact, they were standing at the commencement of a long journey toward validation within the Catholic Church.

It is a strange paradox: the society of the seventeenth century was about as patriarchal as any in European history, and the reforming church that the Council of Trent designed was about as free of women as a reforming church could be. Throughout most of the Western Catholic world, women continued to accept that the only role open to them within the church was that of cloistered nuns. In Poland and Hungary, in Austria and Germany, in Italy to a lesser degree, and most emphatically in Spain and Portugal, religious women kept within their walls and very rarely aspired to active apostleship — and this to the very end of the *ancien régime*.

But the Catholic Reformation was, from the very start, infiltrated by women in three countries: France, Lorraine, and the Spanish Netherlands. In all three countries their opportunity lay in society's need for female teachers.

The Netherlands were, in the late sixteenth and early seventeenth centuries, one of the most densely populated parts of Europe. The region experienced a long sequence of troubles, and untold bloodshed, under an imperial Spain struggling to keep control and Calvinist rebels in the north struggling to break free. Eventually, of course, the region split; the north went its way and the south remained within the Spanish, and Catholic, orbit. But a residue of Calvinism remained in the south, which, the authorities decided, would have to be eliminated by gentler means. One of the Calvinists' clear superiorities lay in the field of education. So there needed to be Catholic schools, for both boys and girls.

The first groups of "half-nun" schoolteachers took shape in the mid–sixteenth century. By the start of the seventeenth, they were present in a number of Belgian towns. They had a name, *filles de Sainte Agnes,* and a set of rules to live by. But they did not wish to enter the monastic life. In their own words, theirs was "a state a little lower, of honorable and virtuous life ... neither a church nor a religious order, but secular." They were enthusiastically supported by their bishops and their municipalities, and by the local Jesuits. Indeed, they earned the nickname "Jesuitesses," and this was going to be a source of trouble for them. Within a few years they would be caught up in a campaign launched in Rome against such feminine presumption.

It was not one of theirs who caused the trouble, but Mary Ward, an English émigré. She made the mistake of flying too high, of brushing against the sun, and for this she suffered a painful fall.

When Mary came to the Spanish Netherlands in 1606, England had been officially Protestant for some fifty years. Over that time the Catholic population had dwindled to some 40,000 holdouts, known as recusants because they resisted attendance at Church of England services, even at the cost of fines and confiscations. They lived, for the most part, in the northern counties (Mary herself was a Yorkshirewoman). Serving them was a tiny army (less an army than a small regiment, actually) of secular priests, Benedictine monks and Jesuits, who moved from place to place and conducted services where and as they could, in secret. For these men, discovery meant severe sentences, up to and including death, for the crime of treason. There was an anti-Catholic paranoia in England, fed for many years by plots and rumors of plots against the Crown, and brought to fever pitch in 1605 by the Gunpowder Plot, in which Catholic conspirators were discovered in an attempt to blow up Parliament, together with the king and his ministers.

So it was not easy to be a Catholic in England. The sons and daughters of the wealthier recusants had one option: to retire to the Continent and, if they wished, enter religious life. Before long there were numerous English monasteries in various cities of the Low Countries and France, whose communities were content to wait and pray for the conversion of their homeland.

But not Mary. After experimenting with life in a Poor Clare convent, she decided on something more ambitious. She and six companions set up a school in Saint-Omer, where young girls could learn to "read, write, and sew for the honor of God." The school was an instant success, and received plaudits from the authorities. But no one was yet prepared for Mary's deeper purpose: to build a community of women who would return to England to work in the mission field.

This project would, of course, entail a surreptitious lifestyle, far beyond what continental Europe considered appropriate for nuns. It would require the sisters to move around freely within society, and to dress as the well-born ladies that they were. There would be no cloister, no religious habit, no hours spent in choir. In other words, it would entail a complete break with female monastic convention. Mary saw this, and proposed to solve all difficulties by modeling her society on that of the Jesuits. The plan she submitted to Rome in 1615 provided for a Jesuit-like structure, with members free to travel to where they were needed, and with a superior-general subject only to the pope. She received a provisional approval and went to work establishing communities of "English Ladies." By 1628 ten houses had been opened on the Continent, and an English mission had been initiated.

But time worked against the English Ladies. For all the good they were able to do, and all the schools they were able to open, they could not escape accusations that they were behaving in a manner inappropriate for women, and, worst of all, that they were aspiring to be "Jesuitesses." As the years passed their critics became more vocal and their friends faded away. Even the Jesuits, who already had enemies of their own to deal with, tried to stay clear of them. Official Catholicism was not yet ready for female apostles.

Mary was a woman of extraordinary grace and charm, and had a natural air of authority that impressed all whom she met. She was also totally frank. "I so greatly . . . loved integrity," she wrote, "that unless I had gone against my nature, it would have been impossible for me to act by halves in things of the soul." Integrity, for her, meant carrying a rosary openly while in London, and speaking her heart to the pope, and refusing to compromise on her plan for an uncloistered, self-governing order of women. And for this, in 1631, her institute was suppressed by Rome, its members condemned as "noxious weeds" to be rooted out of the church. "They went about freely, without submitting to the laws of clausura, under pretext of working for the salvation of souls. . . ." So ran the Bull of Suppression, arguing that this arrogation of the male prerogative was tantamount to heresy. The communities were dispersed. Mary herself was imprisoned for a year. It is worth noting that the pope who condemned her, Urban VIII, was the same pope who condemned Galileo.

Recently, Pope John Paul II reversed his predecessor's condemnation of Galileo, thus apologizing for the church's mistake. For Mary Ward, an equally striking reversal had already taken place. In 1951, Pope Pius XII paid tribute to her as one of the great figures in Catholic history: "this incomparable woman whom, in the darkest and bloodiest hours, England gave to the Church." His predecessors had not been so gracious. Mary's rehabilitation, and that of the English Ladies, was gradual and grudging. Although she was absolved personally of the crime of heresy, she remained in bad odor, and her institute was allowed to continue only by dissociating itself from her.

The affair of the English Ladies had further repercussions. The papacy now took note of the "Jesuitesses" teaching school in the Low Countries, and included them in its condemnation. However, in doing this Rome ran afoul of the archbishop of Cambrai, a strong supporter of the *filles de Sainte Agnes* and a power to be reckoned with, and the ruler of the Spanish Netherlands, Archduchess Isabelle. Before their combined protests, Rome quietly drew back, and the sisters continued to teach until war between France and Spain came to disperse them.

As for Mary Ward's sisters, they outlived their troubles, and we find them teaching to this day.

"The Amazons of Almighty God"

In his tribute to Mary Ward, Pope Pius XII spoke of "the progressive introduction of women into the modern apostolate." It was an uncommon form of introduction. The Rome that condemned Mary had no desire at all to see women enter the apostolate, and it did what it could to prevent it. But as fast as it pushed them out through one door, they entered through another, and the war of wills began again.

From the earliest years of the seventeenth century, France had been striving to establish a foothold in North America, centered on a high spur of land overlooking the Saint Lawrence River that they called Quebec. It was hardly a fertile field for colonization; in 1635, after thirty years of effort, the European population of the colony counted only 320, in a region that counted some 100,000 Indians. But of the 320, 9 were Jesuits. After the fur trade, the missionary enterprise was the most absorbing occupation of early New France.

In 1632 one of the Jesuits, Paul Le Jeune, began sending home a record of his community's work among the natives. This was traditional Jesuit practice: since the days of Loyola, written reports were the nexus that held the far-flung Society together. But these letters were different. They were written with the public in mind. Published annually in France, the Jesuit *Relations* became the "must read" of *dévot* society, and a clarion call for greater involvement in this difficult, dangerous territory. The response was huge, both in money donations and in recruitment into the Society. And in female enthusiasm.

Le Jeune, incautiously as it turns out, wrote in the 1632 *Relation* about the need for someone to work with Indian girls and women. How nice it would be, he mused, if "some brave schoolmistress . . . with a few companions of equal courage" would brave danger and hardship for this noble purpose. But as the saying goes, we should be careful what we wish for. Not long after publication, offers started pouring in from the cloisters of France. Le Jeune was taken aback, and somewhat appalled. "They write to me with such great fire and in such great numbers and from so many different places that if the door was opened to their desires, we could make a city of nuns, and there would be ten mistresses to every scholar." Try as he might, he could not damp the women's ardor. Nor could anybody else. The hierarchy disapproved; the families were horrified; the Jesuit general, Vitelleschi, was displeased. What could cloistered women do in such a primitive place? Would they not be a burden to the mission? But still the offers came, and the clamor for inclusion finally paid off. In 1639, thanks to the support of Cardinal Richelieu's niece and other ladies of quality, two small communities of women were allowed to board ship for Quebec: three Augustine nurses and three Ursuline schoolmistresses.

From that moment on these women, obedient nuns though they were, had to live on the outside edges of church convention. Trent had sought to make female monasticism separate and safe; here it was neither. In the poverty-stricken and dangerous conditions of Canada, their separation was less than complete and their protection from danger less than adequate. In the Indian wars, when six of their Jesuit co-missionaries were murdered, there was no guarantee that they would not share their fate. But in the mind

of the Ursuline Mary of the Incarnation, this gave new value to her vocation. "I was able to risk my life for God, to render him this little token of my
affection," she wrote. It was something that up to then nuns had not been
allowed to do.

They earned their right to be recognized as part of the mission. It was
Paul Le Jeune himself who, setting aside all his initial reserve, came to call
them "the Amazons of Almighty God."

Other women joined them and, not many years later, other communities found a footing in Canada: the Sisters of Saint Joseph from La Flèche,
who established a hospital in Montreal in even more perilous conditions,
and the Congregation of Notre Dame, a gathering of secular schoolmistresses established by another remarkable woman, Marguerite Bourgeoys.
These little communities marked the first step of women into the female
missionary apostolate, which would be such a force in the later expansion of
Catholicism across the world.

"In Your House, Jesus Is Sick, He Has Need of Your Care"

If any story in the Gospels has ruffled feminine feathers over the centuries,
it is the story of Mary and Martha as told by Saint Luke. Did Mary, sitting
at the feet of the Lord, really have a better part than Martha, who was doing
all the work?

In the main, seventeenth-century Catholicism thought so. No matter
how commendable the active religious life, a greater perfection was attain-
able in the life of contemplation. So when the nuns of a hospital in France
questioned their superior on the matter, she answered in the words given
above. When the Lord admonished Martha that day, she said, he was feeling
well. If he had been sick, he would have appreciated her services — as did
the patients now lying in the hospital wards.

Hospital nursing was another field in which religious women were trying to reconcile the rulings of the church with the demands of their work.
Unlike school teaching, nursing was a time-honored profession for women,
whether laywomen, beguines, or nuns. France boasted monastic nursing
communities that dated back to the early thirteenth century. The women in
them lived under a rule (usually that of Saint Augustine); underwent a novitiate; took the solemn vows of poverty, chastity, and obedience; and were
attached to the same house until death. Years before, in a more open time,
they had worked with men, side by side in the same communities, and their

enclosure had been fairly permeable. But by the seventeenth century the men were mostly gone from their company and the Tridentine rule of *clausura* was brought into force. The transition from the more open form of religious life to the cloister was not always easy. Some nuns, like the Sisters of Saint Joseph of La Flèche who nursed in northwestern France and in New France, resisted it hard and long. In the end, however, they were no match for their bishops and the full authority of the Church.

But nobody could stop them from nursing. The need to reconcile public service in the wards with the privacy of the cloister led to awkward compromises. Nuns were expected to work in close proximity to patients, male and female, but were otherwise cloistered, which meant separation from their families and friends by the traditional grille. This, at least, was the theory of things. Conditions often fell far short of the ideal. The cloister might be nothing but an upstairs floor above the hospital. In smaller hospitals, with no money to put into walls and grilles, the principle of enclosure could be stretched to the breaking point. Thus when the first nurses in North America, the Augustines of Dieppe, arrived in Quebec in 1638, they were faced at once with a full-blown epidemic among the native people. It was natural that they should take the sick in. Their little house was soon so crowded that they were forced to put some of their patients into the kitchen — "which bothered us not a little, because . . . it was the smallpox, a very disgusting disease." In this case the Augustines had to live cheek by jowl with "the world," and a sickening, dangerous world at that.

Could such nuns really be considered contemplatives? Yet that was what they were, and continued to be, thanks to what their historian has called "their fierce determination to adjust the realities of nursing to the demands of the cloister." The improbable compromise worked. Although never as numerous as secular nursing sisters, the cloistered nuns continued their hospital service well into the twentieth century, in Europe and America, and in other parts of the world.

*   *   *

While the appearance of apostolic women held deep significance for the future, in the immediate perspective of the seventeenth century it had a limited impact. It was men who rescued the church from the doldrums and reinvigorated the Catholic faith.

The overwhelming concern of early-seventeenth-century French *dévots* was the reform — or, better said, the upgrading — of the secular priesthood. Religious orders were all well and good, but how much influence could they have on the daily lives of the faithful? This still depended on ordinary parish priests, many of whom were not only ignorant but almost indistinguishable in lifestyle from the people they were supposed to lead. It is significant that one of the first campaigns of the early-seventeenth-century reformers was to reinstitute the tonsure and a suitably clerical form of dress, to mark a clear separation between clergy and laity. It is significant, too, that most of the masculine congregations that appeared in the first half of the seventeenth century were dedicated to the education and edification of the secular clergy. To this end, the design of their institutions departed even further from the monastic model than the Jesuits had. Essentially, their members were secular priests who lived in community but retained their civil standing and their private property. Some of them took simple vows, some did not. They did not take on monastic obligations; instead, they worked in parishes and answered to their bishops. By their virtuous lifestyle, they aimed to create an ideal of "the good priest" for others to follow. And they became the educators of priests for the whole of France.

The leader of these groups was the congregation of the Oratory. It was an offshoot of the Roman Oratory of Philip Neri, brought to Paris in 1611 by Pierre de Bérulle, almoner to the queen, cardinal-to-be, prominent theologian, leader of the *dévot* party — all in all, one of the most influential churchmen of his time. In 1618 the bishop gave him an old abbey just outside the city walls and told him to create a seminary for twelve young scholars. It was easier said than done, however: it took some years, and considerable effort — to find the funds, for one thing, and to counter the resistance of a clergy stuck in its old ways, for another — to get the seminary up and running. And even then, how important were a dozen priests with seminary training, given the hundred thousand priests still without? There was a huge shortage of facilities and cash, and generations would pass before all the parish clergy reached a satisfactory standard. But the movement was under way.

Like many others before and after them, the Oratorians were diverted from their original purpose when Pope Paul V imposed upon them a second obligation, to open and run colleges for boys. This side of their work soon became more demanding than their seminary work. In 1630, a year after Bérulle's death, they were running thirteen colleges and only four seminaries. But in the meantime, other congregations were entering the field. Two more companies of priests, the Sulpicians and the Eudists (both Oratorian offshoots), were formed specifically to train priests, and a third, the

Lazarists, or Priests of the Mission, undertook the work as part of their larger service to the countryside. From a very modest formation to start with (a two-week retreat before ordination), seminary training eventually became both rigorous and mandatory. But it took more than a century for this to happen: for enough seminaries to be built, and enough money to be found to support all the young men studying for the priesthood. Much of this money would come from private donors.

This brings us to an interesting aspect of the seminary movement in France. It was not nearly as monolithic as most histories of the Catholic Reformation would make it appear. These usually name three, four, or more congregations working in the field. The famous names crop up, over and over. But they do not complete the list. Many communities appeared, operated for a while, and then either disappeared or were absorbed — and, consequently, have been forgotten. A pioneer in the training of priests was the seminary of Saint-Nicolas-du-Chardonnet; who today would remember that at a time when the rural clergy had almost no access to training, it was already turning out fifty or sixty priests a year? Who today has heard of the Gillotins, poor clerks fed, boarded, and trained in parish work by a benefactor called, oddly enough, Germain Gillot; or the seminary of the thirty-three, founded in 1638 to prepare worthy but needy young men for the priesthood; or the seminaries of Providence, created for the benefit of men who "for lack of means, could neither do their studies nor be admitted to the priesthood"? These and other communities even more ephemeral, most of them supported by private benefactors, contributed mightily to the improvement of the priesthood. But like so many other unknown soldiers, they have no known grave.

These institutions provided something that the Oratory and Saint-Sulpice largely lacked: a path to the priesthood for men who were talented but poor. It cost a lot to educate a priest, and in the greater seminaries the cost was borne by the students themselves. Consequently these more prestigious institutions became the preserve of the well-to-do, and their syllabus reflected that reality. "[They] make every effort to raise minds and to detach them from earthly affections, to bring them to great enlightenments and lofty sentiments," said Vincent de Paul. More useful, in his mind, was the preparation offered by Saint-Nicolas-du-Chardonnet, which took in poor men at no cost and turned out "hard-working journeymen in the functions of the priesthood." This point was being increasingly made. The reform of the French church had begun with the elites, but it could not end there. The lesser folk had their part to play, and they must be included.

"The Love of Christ in the Person of the Poor"

This brings us to the man who is perhaps the most loved of seventeenth-century saints: Vincent de Paul, the priest of obscure peasant origins who rose to the highest circles of the French court, becoming adviser in spiritual matters to the Crown. Influential though he was in his own time, his most lasting work was the foundation of two religious congregations for the express purpose of rescuing the rural poor from spiritual and material deprivation. The first of these was the congregation of Priests of the Mission, or Lazarists, as they came to be called, after their headquarters in the Parisian church of Saint-Lazare. The second was a company of women, the Daughters (or Sisters) of Charity.

First, to the word "mission," which we associate with being "sent out," usually to "somewhere else." Wherever explorers went in the sixteenth century, missionaries were quick to follow. Around the turn of the seventeenth century, however, another concept of mission took form. At the risk of oversimplification, we can say that this shift of focus marked the progression from "Counter-Reformation" to "Catholic Reformation." Catholicism turned its eyes inward and was not happy with what it saw. The church perceived with alarm that while it had been fighting its Protestant neighbors and proselytizing the pagans, thousands if not millions of souls waited on its doorstep to be saved. It is ironic but true: what started in the outskirts of Christianity spread, in reverse fashion, to its old heart. Their experience in the overseas missions led the religious orders to draw an analogy between the heathen masses they found there and the un-Christianized masses they had left at home. Souls "on the point of being lost," wrote a Capuchin preacher, were every bit as important as those "which were already lost." How could they go abroad to save souls and yet leave so many in danger of perdition in their own country?

And so the internal mission came into being. It was an experiment in evangelization, aiming not so much to make new Catholics as to reclaim those who were already baptized. The method it used might be called religious blitzkrieg. A preacher, or a group of preachers, would travel to a designated town or village and there set up an intensive schedule of events — sermons, catechisms, confessions, disputations, and mass demonstrations of Catholic devotion, in the form of processions and prayers. Once satisfied that the local population had got the message, they would move on, leaving the follow-up to the resident parish priests. By this means, it was hoped that over time the official Tridentine church would find its way into the countryside.

One way or another, most of the new orders took part in these missions. They used different tactics. The Capuchins, true to their tradition, alternated thunder and lightning with tender appeals, all designed to stir up the emotions of their hearers. They employed all the techniques that we associate with the baroque: theatrical presentations, massive penitential processions, dramatic rituals in darkened churches or in churches aglow with lights. They counted on the crowd effect to amplify the emotions they aroused. The Jesuits were usually more subdued, though not always; they, too, had their famous fire-and-brimstone preachers and their sound-and-light shows. Whatever method the missionaries chose, the fact is that internal missions were highly successful, at least in the short term. But once the missionaries left, how could anyone be sure that their work had staying power?

Vincent de Paul came to see that if the countryside was to be converted, a much more sustained effort was needed. Like everything else in his life, it was a slow, laborious process of discovery. He would have said (and who can argue with him?) that it was a discovery forced upon him by God.

He came to the mission field, and the problems associated with it, more or less by accident. In 1616, while serving in Picardy as almoner to one of France's great noble families, the Gondis, he was asked to hear the confession of a sick tenant on the estate. The man later declared that the confession had saved his soul, which otherwise would have been damned. The declaration shocked Vincent's patroness, Madame de Gondi. "Ah, Monsieur Vincent, how many souls are being lost! What remedy is there for this?" She asked that he do the same for her other tenants, and so he set to work to conduct a mission, with help from the Jesuits of Amiens. The undertaking turned out to be enormous, requiring them to preach and instruct and hear confessions late into the night. It became clear to both Vincent and his patroness that there was a need here waiting to be filled. She was the first to move. She offered a legacy of 16,000 livres to any religious community that would promise to mount regular missions on her estates. After the offer was turned down by the Jesuits and the Oratorians, Monsieur Vincent accepted it. Thus in 1626 was founded the Congregation of the Mission, specifically for opening the eyes of the rural poor to the religion in which they had been baptized. And from going on mission into the countryside, the congregation was very soon drawn into the work of training the parish priests who were destined to live there. By the eighteenth century, it had become the principal operator of seminaries in France.

As the missionary movement took hold, other eyes were also opened:

those of the missionaries themselves, who had never before comprehended the profound gulf between their own Catholicism and that of the peasant world. One of them wrote, "I did not learn about the state of these poor people from someone else; I discovered it for myself. . . . When we spoke to them about God, and the most holy Trinity, and the Nativity, Passion and Death of Jesus Christ, and other mysteries, it was a language that they did not understand at all." In the seventeenth-century mind, ignorance of the faith — the faith that had been laid down by Trent — meant damnation. And for men and women of good conscience, it followed that if they failed to fight that ignorance, the judgment of God would descend on them, too. "If you have not fed them, you have killed them," warned Vincent. "How shall we answer to God if through our negligence one of these poor souls comes to die and is lost?" It was this uncomfortable thought, as much as any policy of "confessionalization" imposed from above, that impelled so many members of high society to contribute time and money to his cause.

Vincent's missionary method was marked by gentleness. He instructed his priests to avoid polemics, to treat nonbelievers with consideration. He urged them to see that the way to convert skeptics to the faith was by living that faith blamelessly. From early days, too, he understood that the needs of the people were physical as well as spiritual. The France in which he exercised influence — the France of the 1630s, 1640s, and 1650s — was racked by war, disease, food shortages, unemployment, and vagrancy. He saw, and insisted, that it was not enough to preach to the poor; they must also be fed, cared for in sickness, and given decent Christian burial.

To accomplish this, Vincent reached back to that ancient institution, the confraternity. Wherever a mission was preached, he dictated that there should also be a *charité* established, a confraternity of laymen and/or laywomen whose purpose was ministering to the poor. The rules he designed for these confraternities exist to this day, testaments to that blending of religious devotion and social activism that was a striking feature of seventeenth-century French Catholicism.

"For Cloister, the City Streets,
Where You Must Go in the Service of Your Patients"

The *charités* worked best in villages and small towns, where people of different social status could share the responsibility of visiting and assisting their less fortunate neighbors. But the appeal did not end there. Before long the rich were drawn in — even the *grandes dames* of Paris, who created their own highly exclusive confraternity. This exclusivity created a problem, however. No matter how well meaning, ladies of high society simply could not go visiting the homes of the Parisian poor. So they sent their servants instead. And in Vincent's eyes, that was not good enough: true charity could not be exercised in this way, by proxy. Again, the path he was to follow was presented to him by someone else, in this case a young peasant woman, Marguerite Naseau, who approached him, offering to serve the ladies' *charité,* to do the work they would not do. In time she was joined by other young working girls. Since they needed both spiritual guidance and job training, Vincent placed them in the care of one of the ladies, Louise de Marillac. Under her supervision they developed new skills, adding simple nursing and basic teaching to their original work of visiting. They succeeded so well that they were soon in high demand by *charités* across the region. Before long, they were being invited to serve in hospitals. Where they were asked to do so, they also opened small schools. In time, as their numbers grew, it was inevitable that they should acquire organization and a rule. Thus began the company of Daughters of Charity, whose many descendant congregations are spread across the world today.

To the modern mind, the way the early sisters mixed their vocations — school teaching, nursing, and home visiting complete with spiritual counseling — suggests a sort of riding off in all directions, bound to reduce effectiveness. But that only shows how far we with our concern for specialization have moved away from our ancestors. In the Catholic world of the seventeenth century, people thought, and tradition taught, that the various works of charity were indissolubly bound together in one great whole. Nurses taught and teachers nursed, in whatever way was necessary. In time, as their numbers grew, their communities became more formal in structure and their responsibilities became more clearly defined. Then they began to specialize, as was only sensible. The results were impressive. The seventeenth and eighteenth centuries were virtual black holes in the history of medicine, but within the limitations of their day, the sisters worked hard at the profession of nursing. Long before Florence Nightingale was born, the Daughters of Charity were known for their model hospitals.

Louise de Marillac had not desired this outcome for her sisters. They had originally been intended to visit the sick poor in their homes, to take them food and medicine and give them comfort and spiritual counsel. The hospitals she saw as dehumanizing and cold, and antithetical to the more humane home care that she wished to promote. But this sort of diversion away from the founders' original purpose was not unknown to religious orders: Philip Neri had wanted his Roman Oratory to steer clear of the trappings of formal religious life but had lived to see his first plan under threat. The Jesuits and Oratorians had not envisioned the education of boys as a primary purpose of their companies, but so it had come to be. Angela Merici's simple design of a life of service to God performed by women living in their own homes and without solemn vows began to unravel soon after her death. The fact was that, sooner or later, society dictated the need, and the religious orders had to act at its dictation.

In France the proliferation of nursing sisters coincided with a huge explosion of interest in hospital care. Of course, hospitals had been a part of the scenery since the Middle Ages. Rare indeed would have been the town or village that did not sport its leper house, or hospice, or almshouse. The same institution often served different purposes, sheltering local indigents or pilgrims on their way through town, nursing the sick poor, caring for orphans and the handicapped. It was usually administered by the municipality, which hired and fired whatever staff was necessary. But time, and most especially the religious wars, had taken a severe toll, so that by the early seventeenth century many of these small hospitals lay in ruins, incapable of fulfilling even their original purpose. And now, with the coming of further wars, epidemics, and years of poor harvests, the need to do something about the poor (if only to control them) weighed heavily on the public mind. As in Italy in its terrible sixteenth century, the sheer desperation of the situation in seventeenth-century France demanded action. The socially conscious elites, led by the Crown itself, looked at ways of dealing with the problem. The solution, they decided, lay in bigger and better-organized institutions. Across the country, *hôtels-dieu* (hospitals) and *hôpitaux-généraux* (workhouses) proliferated, as also did orphanages and homes for the aged and the insane. And in the running of these the nursing sisters played a major part.

In former years, the hospitals had usually been staffed by laypeople. Men had figured prominently. But by the start of the seventeenth century, the male presence was seriously diminished and the lion's share of the work was being done by laywomen. They were attractive to the municipalities because they could be hired and fired at will. But their performance could be inconsistent. As communities of sisters formed up and consented to serve in hospitals, they came, more and more, to edge out the competition. It was a win-win situation: the municipalities got good service at a reasonable price, and the sisters got the opportunity to minister to the poor and, through them, to Jesus Christ. The arrangement lasted well. In 1789, on the eve of the French Revolution, 6,500 women belonging to twenty-nine different congregations were serving in more than 1,500 establishments, all across the country.

None of these were nuns by the seventeenth-century definition of the word. Because they were not cloistered and did not take the solemn vows of religion, they did not meet the criteria that the Council of Trent had set down. They were "secular sisters." But in one way or another they adopted the characteristics of nuns, living communally, performing set devotions, obeying a rule and a superior — all of which made them, in a sense, half-nuns. It amounted to a blurring of the clear lines so recently drawn between the lay and the consecrated states. The fact that they were accepted, in spite of some hesitations, shows that tradition can give way before new demands. The sisters served the needs both of civil society and of the church's apostolate; that was all the justification they needed. The fact that Rome did not give them full official recognition until the late nineteenth century did not slow them down.

But the secular sisters needed another permission, and without it they were unable to act. This was a cultural permission. In some societies the prejudice against open, free-ranging female activism remained strong, and in those societies almost all religious women remained cloistered. In Spain and Portugal and their dependencies, in the Holy Roman Empire and in Poland, uncloistered nuns were rarely seen, and that until the end of the *ancien régime*. In their promotion of the female apostolate, France and its immediate neighbors, Lorraine and the Spanish Netherlands, stood head and shoulders above the rest.

"It Is a Sublime Employment, Worthy of the Apostles"

The teaching of young children had never before enjoyed much respect. During the seventeenth century it became an honorable profession.

The rulings of the Council of Trent, and their implementation in the following decades, led to a number of significant changes in Catholic society. One of the most important was the obligation now imposed on every believer to know his religion. Ignorance of the faith had not before been an impediment to salvation, which was just as well, given the nature of premodern, massively peasant European society. Of course, there had always been centers where learning was prized: the monasteries, the cathedral schools, the universities, the municipally funded colleges, and more recently, the palaces and town houses of educated urbanites. But for the plowman, or the woodcutter, or the woman working her spindle, nothing had been demanded except baptism, a not-too-sinful life, and adherence to a parish church. There were those who prayed, those who fought, and those who labored, and they did not intrude into the territory of the others. That was the medieval way of looking at things, and in the early medieval world it worked.

But the invention of the printing press and the growth, in the cities, of a class of readers who could take advantage of it, changed the dynamic. More people than ever before could follow their own thoughts and, if they wished, challenge the ancient certainties. Protestantism, the religion of the Book, gave impetus and justification to their progress. Numerically, this literate class was still insignificant. Strategically, it was extremely powerful. It resided in the cities, and it controlled a large part of the Continent's power and wealth. Princely courts and burgeoning civil services were centered in the cities, as were the various parliaments or diets. Prominent churchmen had their headquarters there. Lawyers, doctors, and artists came there to find fortune and advancement. Great magnates started spending less time in their country châteaux and more time in their city mansions. A growing army of merchants and bankers was ready and willing — and rich enough — to enjoy the good life. All in all, it was a formidable force. In a hundred different ways, rural Europe, scattered as it was, illiterate, and almost voiceless, was in its thrall. It made sense that in the fight against religious ignorance, this population of the already-literate should be the first to be targeted.

As far as a direct approach to the problem of mass ignorance of the faith was concerned, the church was already a laggard. Luther's catechism had appeared in 1529. It was not until after the closing of the Council of Trent in 1563 that Rome followed suit. But the Counter-Reformation had not been idle. In 1546 the Society of Jesus opened its first college. By the early 1600s it was running over 400 colleges in cities across Europe, and the number was still growing. The education of Catholic youth (male, largely urban) was now clearly a priority.

The strategy paid off. From Brittany to Bohemia, from the Spanish Netherlands to Sicily, the elites of Catholic Europe were treated to the same Christian and humanistic education. Furthermore, the Jesuits soon realized that their colleges were more than institutions of learning; they were excellent bases from which to engage the local noncollege populations. While some of the fathers were in the classroom, others could be out proselytizing the neighborhood. And they had auxiliaries to help them do it: their students, whom they nurtured and trained in a militant form of lay apostleship.

One of the Jesuits' most successful instruments of evangelization was the lay sodality. The brainchild of a young Belgian priest, Jan Leunis, it took that old standby, the confraternity, and remodeled it into a much more dedicated institution than the medieval *fratres* would ever have known. No more patronal feasting, no more elaborate costuming, no more conviviality. Members pledged themselves to an exacting program of prayers, devotions, good works, and aggressive propagation of the faith, all under the guidance of their Jesuit directors. And in the fervid atmosphere of the times, people joined by the hundreds of thousands, not only students, but also men and women from all walks of society, from nobles to artisans. By the start of the seventeenth century, as much as 20 percent of the population of some cities was enrolled in one sodality or another.

This huge infusion of energy, magnifying a hundred times anything that the priests could have managed on their own, had a powerful effect on public religious practice. Where there were active sodalities, attendance at Mass went up, as did the frequentation of the sacraments. Crowds of people came to their processions and public spectacles. Heretics, ladies of ill repute, tavern-frequenters, and eaters of meat on Friday cowered before them. They tore down immodest pictures and burned inappropriate books. They remonstrated with people who failed to say grace before meals. But activities like these had their naysayers, not only among Protestants but also among many austere Catholics. Devotion, these people could point out, was not the same as understanding. People could pray to their patron saints, beat their breasts at penitential ceremonies, march in Corpus Christi processions, and still know no more than they ever did before about what the Church held to be its immutable truths.

Fortunately, the involvement of the laity in the re-Catholicization of society had another important consequence. It fostered a conviction among the comfortable classes that the world would be a better place if the poor — especially the urban poor — were instructed in religion, their ABCs, and a modicum of good manners. College education was all well and good, but it served only boys who already had a certain level of schooling. At the other end of the spectrum, the workhouses offered a training of sorts, in manual skills and religion, but only to their own paupers. Grammar schools were to be found in the cities, but they cost money, and in any case, they were insufficient for the numbers of people who swelled the urban population. For the many young ragamuffins now thronging the streets, untaught and unchurched, something else had to be done. It was a productive convergence of motivations. Where churchmen saw a problem of religious ignorance, laymen and laywomen saw, also, a social problem. Their solution came in the form of "little schools": classrooms where the children of the working poor could receive the benefits of a basic instruction without having to pay.

For a more systematic instruction for the poor, something beyond Sunday schools and catechism classes, there would have to be significant investment. That was met, over the years, by a great increase in bequests and donations in favor of free schools for the poor. And there would have to be teachers. The problem here was that school teaching had traditionally been held in very low esteem. Literate young men had other, more promising careers, above all, the priesthood. School teaching as a profession and a vocation did not hold much appeal for them. On the other hand, plenty of women were ready and willing. This is the reason why, in France at least, the first successful experimentation with "charitable schools" was female. Just as the public's new interest in hospital services created a space for a new kind of noncloistered nursing sisters, the public's new interest in free schooling for the common folk created a space for a new kind of noncloistered teaching sisters. In both cases, the peak in the creation of communities of service came in the later seventeenth century, when Louis XIII, the Most Christian King, was dead and Louis XIV, the Sun King, was in his full splendor.

In 1662 a Minim friar named Nicolas Barré set out to preach a mission in a poor neighborhood of Rouen. Among the auxiliaries that he took with him was a small group of women, whose job it was to catechize the children and to prepare women for the sacraments. These helpers were, according to the record, "women with free time," which means they were unmarried and most likely from the more prosperous bourgeoisie. For them the mission was a short-term voluntary commitment, and after it had achieved its purpose they went home.

But Barré did not let it end there. He saw that the women had been able to move beyond the range of any priest: into homes and neighborhoods where a priest could not go without giving scandal. And there, among women and children, they were able to communicate with a freedom that a priest could not enjoy. What might they not do if they were allowed a long-term commitment?

A few years later he was able to prove his point. Under his guidance, five or six young women began teaching school in one of the parishes of Rouen. A description of those early days comes to us in a memoir written by one of the sisters. They were not yet a community; they lived in different homes and taught in different places, often in the rooms of their benefactors' houses. Once school was over for the day the women went out to private homes, "to instruct the people, teaching them the principal mysteries." On Sundays they held catechism classes, which were so popular "that it was necessary to . . . break down the walls to make enough space."

Within a few years the original few had grown to 30 and had become a community. Ten years after that they were 200 and had spread to other towns and villages in Normandy. One small colony had been invited to Reims. In the meantime, Barré had been transferred to Paris, and there, immediately, he looked for opportunities to set up more charity schools. The expansion continued until, by the early eighteenth century, Barré's sisters were teaching in every parish in Paris and were being sent out, as the Daughters of Charity were sent out, to work in places, large and small, across the country.

It was the Ursulines' story, repeated some sixty years later. The same enthusiasm among women for the new challenge, the same positive response from the public to the opening of the free schools, the same generous funding from private benefactors. And, sad to say, the same negativity from the same quarters. As the founding sister recalled, "there were great difficulties (I find it hard to speak about them) on the part of the parish priests, the ecclesiastics, the religious and the laity, which caused our very reverend father much suffering." Some elements in society still disapproved of women appearing in public and meddling in the teaching of religion — the male, and priestly, preserve. However, attitudes had changed over the years, and these women would not be pressed into the cloister. The "charitable schoolmistresses" not only thrived in their secular form of community life, but they also served as the model for numerous other women's teaching congregations across France.

There were, of course, some hurdles to overcome. In an age when coeducation was officially frowned on, they could teach only girls. And because of small budgets and an adverse student-teacher ratio (as for instance, up to 100 children to a mistress), the course of studies was, to begin with, extremely basic. However, the well-worn analogy of "takeoff" might be useful here. Just as a plane starts up laboriously, then gathers speed along the runway and, finally, lifts into the air, so the society of the seventeenth century began the ponderous movement that would end, long after its time, with takeoff into mass literacy. The first charitable schoolmistresses worked with virtually no teaching aids, with children who had no sense of school discipline and little or no experience of the written word. If their progress was slow, it was nevertheless steady. Gradually, very gradually, female literacy rates began to rise.

*   *   *

For some years, efforts to provide similar schools for boys continued to stumble. It was not for lack of trying. Barré himself, and several others, struggled to find men who would enter the same life that the sisters were leading. But few came, and those who came did not stay. The problem was one of status, and of pay: if a young man was prepared to remain celibate, he would do better in the priesthood; if he was married and had family obligations, he would do better in a grammar school. Teaching the children of the working poor was hard work, and paid badly. It was also, possibly, illegal, if it infringed on the lawful rights of various established interests. Above all, it offended the deep conservatism of *ancien régime* society.

A few words about that term *ancien régime.* It means, first of all, the old political order — kings, nobles, bishops, and royal ministers — that ruled Europe in "the old days." But it means much more than that. *Ancien régime* society was a society of orders, of slots into which people were fitted at birth, of privileges and exemptions that came with those slots and remained a barrier to any kind of equality. Thus a noble, if convicted of serious crime, had the right to be decapitated; a commoner could only be hanged. A noble did not, in principle, engage in commerce; that was the sign of a commoner. A noble did not have to pay the same tax as a commoner (nor did a churchman). A noble could wear flashy clothes and a plumed hat, and carry a sword; a bourgeois should be dressed in sober black; the working poor were expected to wear plain undyed cloth. So much did clothes make the man that in 1789, anyone who wore knee britches was marked as an aristocrat, and the revolutionary people of Paris took pride in being "sans-culottes."

It was not just a matter of noble versus commoner. Among commoners there were scores of barriers that separated the bourgeoisie from "the people" and from each other. One of the great instruments of social control was the guild, a closed shop, so to speak, that held the monopoly to a trade or profession and was entitled by law to pursue anyone who trespassed on its turf. There was a hierarchy of guilds, for goldsmiths, for cobblers, for soap makers, and so on. Their stratification did not end with their trades; they took care not to mix, or marry, across boundaries. And there were guilds for grammar school masters and for "master scribes." A grammar school master could teach boys up to the age of nine, at which time they were ready for college. A master scribe, and nobody else, was allowed to teach advanced subjects such as writing and mathematics. The schools run by these two guilds were fee-paying, and anybody who was not indigent was expected to pay. Free schooling of a sort was available for paupers, but they must be true, certifiable paupers, even to the point, sometimes, of wearing their identification on their clothing. At the end of the day, all schools were designed to keep children in the station into which they were born.

Then along came Jean-Baptiste de La Salle, who was ready to challenge the system by offering free quality schooling, complete with writing and mathematics, to the children of the working poor. What he wanted was to give these children the benefits of a good education; what he did was threaten the *ancien régime*'s system of privilege and exclusion. For that he suffered no end of trouble.

Born in 1651 in Reims, La Salle had become interested in educational questions through his acquaintance with the Barré sisters from Rouen, brought to the city by his friend Nicolas Roland. His efforts to establish similar schools for boys began there in 1679, and spread out into the countryside. When he expanded his work to Paris in 1688, his community of teaching brothers and his ideas about the way they were to teach were already well formed. The most striking originality of his plan lay in the fact that the brothers were *not* to be priests. Teaching, and teaching alone, was a sufficient vocation. And yet they were to be religious, taking vows and living in community under obedience. La Salle believed, with justification, that no candidates of quality would undertake the thankless task of poor-school teaching unless they had both strong formation and strong support.

His move to Paris came at an opportune time. The Edict of Nantes of 1598, with its provisions for religious toleration, had been revoked three years previously. The Crown had brought the question of schooling to the forefront, as part of the aggressive action it was now taking against its Protestant subjects. Since education was thought to be the key to the re-Catholicization of the country, Louis XIV and his ministers were ready to promote, and perhaps even subsidize, Catholic schools. Yet almost at once La Salle ran up against fierce opposition from the vested interests, the grammar school teachers and the master scribes. He was taken to court, sued, and fined; his schools were closed down and the furniture in them confiscated. When he died in 1719, his institute had not yet been approved, either by the king or by Rome. But in the end, quality trumped privilege. For the children of shopkeepers, artisans, and laborers, the Brothers of Christian Schools offered the best education at the most affordable price. And they received their reward. By the end of the eighteenth century they numbered 800, in 121 houses. In the nineteenth, after the Revolution had run its course, they returned in force and soon numbered in the many thousands.

*   *   *

If we were to think of the Catholic Reformation as a series of news stories, most of the headlines would be devoted to the new "active" orders. To them belonged the freshness and the inventiveness, and the long string of successes that helped to restore the Church and bring it into the modern age. But in the background, quietly and steadily, the ancient monastic orders were also rebuilding.

In France alone in 1600, there were about a thousand monasteries practicing various versions of the Benedictine Rule — Cluniac, Cistercian, and so on — and a lesser number of Augustinian houses. A century of chronic warfare between England and France, known as the Hundred Years' War (1337-1453), had undermined these old orders in much of the country, as soldiers and freelancers roamed at will, destroying many houses and enfeebling others. The Black Death that struck Europe in 1348 had resulted in a drop in personnel that could not easily be repaired. The Great Schism (1378-1429) had caused loss of morale, here as elsewhere. But nothing in all those years compared to the devastation caused by the sixteenth century's religious wars. Because they were favorite targets of the Huguenots, as well as being singularly defenseless, many monasteries had been sacked and destroyed, and the people inside them murdered or dispersed.

The battering caused by sectarian violence was compounded by the creeping sickness of *commenda*. A century before, with the Concordat of Bologna in 1516, a pro-French pope had delivered the abbeys of France into the hands of their king. That meant abbots were no longer canonically elected members of the community, but people appointed by the Crown. There had once been an understanding that these people would be monks (or nuns), twenty-three years or older; but this had long been forgotten. Now many commendatory abbots were royal favorites, or the young children of royal favorites "appointed while still in their nurses' arms," as one contemporary complained. The problem was that much of the time their interest in monasticism extended no further than the monastic revenues.

Efforts had been made to limit what they (or, more likely, their agents) might extract from the monasteries, but these provisions, too, had proved ineffective. Short of litigation, which many communities could ill afford, little could be done to enforce fair distribution of the monastic goods. In too many cases communities lived at starvation level while the abbots drained away their monasteries' riches. In the meanwhile, as long as the struggle over resources went on, it was in the interest of neither abbot nor community to increase the number of mouths to feed; in other words, no more novices. As the size of communities diminished, so did their ability to defend themselves. And so the hollowing out of the monasteries went on. It is hardly surprising that in many places the regular life collapsed.

Though the monasteries of France were in particularly bad shape, they were not alone. Across Europe, apart from a few shining exceptions, monasticism was in trouble. The Council of Trent had recognized the problem, and reached for a solution. It had decreed that all men's monasteries were to gather into congregations, small groupings of houses that would still live under their order's rule but would function autonomously. This had been done before, and successfully, as congregations such as that of Monte Cassino in Italy, or Melk in Austria, had shown. Now the council ruled that the practice was to become general. In this way the unreformed power structures would be pushed aside and *commenda* would be undercut. Slowly its word became law. By the end of the seventeenth century almost all men's monasteries across western Europe belonged to one or another congregation.

The French monasteries, for the usual reasons of war and general dislocation, were slow to move. The first nudge toward reform came from Lorraine, which was at that time an independent duchy. In 1604, with encouragement from the local bishop, the reformed congregation of Saint-Vanne was set up. Based on the Cassinese model, it established what amounted to self-rule. Then, with its commendatory abbots out of the way, it reinstituted the Benedictine Rule in its primitive rigor. As was usually the case in the seventeenth century, this strictness was warmly welcomed. The Saint-Vanne reform prospered and spread through Lorraine into Franche-Comté, and from there into eastern France.

There it hit an obstacle. No self-respecting French king, and no self-respecting French parlement, could tolerate a religious takeover from Lorraine. But there was no objection to creating what amounted to a clone. As a result, a new congregation, similar but French, appeared. The Benedictine Congregation of Saint-Maur was given pontifical approval in 1621, and before long came to outshine its neighbor. By the end of the century it numbered some two hundred monasteries across France. Its monks acquired a Europe-wide reputation for scholarship, especially for their advances in the methods of historical research. In fact, if historians are looking for a patron saint (and why not? — the lawyers have Thomas More), they should adopt the Maurist Jean Mabillon, a man of vast learning and a pioneer in the critical study of early medieval documents. The historian, Mabillon insisted, was as responsible for the interpretation of things past as a judge was of things present. He must act ethically; he "must present certain things as certain, as false, things false, and as doubtful, things doubtful; he must not seek to hide facts that tell for or against either party to an issue." Piety and truth, he argued, could not be separated, "for honest and genuine piety will never come into conflict with truth." The integrity he demanded in his profession shone forth in his own life; he was a humble, gentle, totally observant monk.

Both congregations owed their prosperity to the fact that they were reformed. But reform had its problems. In creating their new communities the congregations were not building from the ground up; they were taking over existing properties and buildings, and these came complete with monks who had lived in them, perhaps for years. Often, and quite reasonably, these men resisted changes to the relaxed lifestyle they had undertaken in good faith. The reformers had two options: to evict them, even using force, or to accommodate them, by allowing them to remain in place without accepting the new discipline. Each option had its drawbacks. Force (which was actually used quite often) created bitterness. Accommodation risked years of intracommunity tension, as the two groups of monks, reformed and unreformed, jostled against each other within the same space. However, time, and the eventual funerals of all the old guard, smoothed over the difficulties, and the two congregations went on to achieve distinction for their religious discipline and their learning.

Where most Benedictine monasteries had previously had nothing in common but their rule, the order of Cîteaux was a true order in every sense of the word, in that it was unified by both a rule and an organization. Cistercian monasteries all belonged within an organic body, a sort of family tree in which the Burgundian motherhouse, Cîteaux, was the root, her four principal foundations (La Ferté, Pontigny, Clairvaux, and Morimond) the branches, and subsequent foundations the offshoots of the branches. The offshoots were subject to oversight and discipline from the abbots of their founder houses, and so on back down the line. Overall governance fell to the abbot of Cîteaux and an executive council of other abbots; a general chapter met regularly to report on the state of the order and to mandate changes or reforms.

Within this framework, individual monasteries were designed to be largely self-standing. Local abbots were to be in control of their communities, assisted by their priors, and it was left up to them to ensure both the observance of the rule and economic viability. Each monastery was to be responsible for the recruitment and training of its own novices. And the vow of stability, which Cistercian monks had taken since time immemorial, by which they promised to live out their lives in their own monasteries, acted as a moat, safeguarding the essence of their own particular version of community life: simplicity, silence, perpetual abstinence, and the daily round of liturgical duties.

Although five hundred years old, it was an excellent system. But it was no longer working. The same flow of events that devastated the Benedictine monasteries also caused havoc among the Cistercians: war, plague, schism, and finally, more war. Of the approximately 200 houses functioning in 1550, only 150 had survived to 1600, and of these only a few were intact. When visitors from the order went on an inspection tour, they found scores of severely damaged buildings and pathetically diminished communities — often, no more than one or two elderly monks, too few and too decrepit even to sing office. And in many cases, there was neither the will nor the wherewithal to repair the damage.

At the start of the seventeenth century, then, the Cistercian order in France was in a dangerously weakened state. Visitors to the outlying monasteries found "an infinity of disorder and abuse": monks who were ignorant of the rule, who did not know Latin, let alone liturgical chant; who lived on private pensions and wore secular clothes; who ate and drank wherever and whatever they wished; who hunted and gambled and allowed women into their enclosure; and who wandered the countryside in complete disregard of their basic vow. And yet, at the same time, one visitor was able to report in 1607 that he had "found scarcely any monastery of men where monks desirous of regular observance were lacking." Men of conscience, including the order's leadership, agreed that it was time to introduce reform.

It was at about this time, in the Cistercian college in Paris, that three young monks joined together in a solemn pledge to observe the rule in its primitive purity, cleansed of all compromises and dispensations. This meant a rededication to community life as the founders of the order had known it, with stability, silence, austerity in clothing and furnishings, and perpetual abstinence from meat. To show their absolute commitment to their pledge, they added that, rather than give it up, they would even defy their superiors: "we are determined to bear the Cross of Christ and every tribulation, rather than to abandon our resolution." It was rather an intemperate declaration, considering that those superiors themselves were already considering reform. It drew a line in the sand that, in time, became an obstacle to understanding and good governance within the order. Two sides formed up, the "Strict Observance" and the "Common Observance," and their mutual antagonism destroyed any hope for a united reform effort.

As usual, the devil was in the details. First of all, many of the dispensations that the young tigers denounced were perfectly lawful. For instance, the dispensation from total abstinence had been granted by Pope Sixtus IV in 1475. In monasteries across the country there were monks who had eaten meat all their lives. How, all of a sudden, could they be deprived of that right? Or of all the other comforts they had come to enjoy? From the broader vantage point of the abbot of Cîteaux, it was obvious that reform had to be handled carefully, lest it cause serious disturbance. Perhaps new rules could be introduced gradually: abstinence for half the year, for instance. This way the order could maintain its unity while it moved to a greater austerity. The problem was that the Strict Observance men would have none of it. For them, "total abstinence" became a clarion call. There was a problem, too, with the "ancients," those monks who clung obdurately to their old ways: they could be grandfathered, to use a modern term: given the choice of accepting pensions and moving to other monasteries, or staying in their houses but living apart. In time, it was anticipated, they would die out. But in the meantime segregated communities within the same walls were hardly a prescription for success, even if both sides exercised charity. Which they didn't. As time went on, attitudes hardened. The champions of Strict Observance, or "abstinents," gaining in numbers and armed by a sense of their own righteousness, tried to take over whole monasteries. The champions of Common Observance fought back. Sometimes force was used, and sometimes royal officials were called to intervene.

For the greater part of sixty years they fought each other, in the privacy of their chapters and in the public forum provided for them by their parties in Paris and Rome. In the end, which came with a meeting in 1683, little had been gained. The Strict Observance held the high ground, but not very firmly. It controlled sixty-one monasteries, many of them acquired by force. In those monasteries lived about 800 monks, an adequate but hardly imposing number, which leads to the conclusion that this reform movement had not resonated among the faithful.

There was, however, one community that was able to do just that. It was the monastery of La Trappe, a house of the Strict Observance, ruled by the famous abbot Armand-Jean Le Bouthillier de Rancé.

He was, in his youth, a rather stereotypical seventeenth-century *abbé*-about-town. Born into a wealthy and influential family, tonsured at the age of nine, commendatory superior of five different religious houses at the age of eleven, ordained at twenty-five, he was a serious scholar, an accomplished preacher — and a passionate horseman. "This morning I'll preach like an angel, this afternoon I'll hunt like a devil," he once said. He lived comfortably on his country estate. For several years he paid court to a lady of questionable reputation, Madame de Montbazon. Her death in 1657 devastated him and, it is conjectured, started him on a slow road to conversion.

In 1658 he set off on a tour of his five benefices. One of these was the abbey of La Trappe, a sad spectacle of crumbling walls occupied by seven impoverished, demoralized monks. Rancé went home and gave the situation much thought. A few years later both he and La Trappe underwent a transformation. First the abbey was rebuilt, and stocked with monks from a nearby monastery of the Strict Observance (much against the will of the original residents of La Trappe). Then in 1666 Rancé, having rid himself of his possessions and having entered the Cistercian order, became its abbot — not a commendatory abbot, but a true abbot, the father and guiding light of his community.

La Trappe became a radical exemplar of strict observance. Its monks labored, fasted, and prayed in the silence and poverty that, in their minds, was the inheritance of the Cistercian founders of the eleventh century. But because they, and their abbot, belonged to the seventeenth century, they gave the monastic life a seventeenth-century coloration. In the long shadows thrown by the Great Reformation, most major Catholic thinkers had developed a pessimistic view of the world, and of their own human nature. The monks of La Trappe took this view to extremes. For them, the monastic state was, above all, a state of penitence, a never-ending act of reparation to God for the evildoing of men, a "continual crucifixion." "What is the business of a monk?" asked Rancé; and answered: "It is to weep for our own sins and for the sins of others." In this spirit he led his community to multiply acts of self-mortification to a degree that would have been unfamiliar to most medieval Cistercians. Life for the monks of La Trappe was hard — and short. The community's mortality rates were abnormally high, even for an age that was used to early death. But they did not alarm Rancé. In his mind, monasticism was nothing if not a preparation for death.

To be sure, Rancé was hardly typical. Everything about him was larger than life. Very few of his contemporaries followed his discipline to its extremes. But they admired him and his community. La Trappe in its humid and unhealthy valley was, biblically speaking, a city set upon a hill, a light shining out to a generation that felt itself desperately in need of redemption. And the life, for all its harshness, drew a response. Between the time Rancé became abbot in 1666 and his death in 1700, close to two hundred men entered the community. The regimen he laid out continued to prosper until the revolution of 1789; after the revolution had run its course, the Trappists were the only members of the Cistercian order to reenter France.

*   *   *

The long struggle for reform that convulsed the monks of Cîteaux also affected its nuns. In 1600 the Cistercian nunneries of France were, for the most part, in the same sad condition, and for the same reasons: the baneful effects of the war, shrinkage of numbers, failure of the monastic spirit, and loss of morale.

One of the communities that suffered all these ills was the royal abbey of Maubuisson, situated not too far from Paris. Its abbess was Angélique d'Estrées, who was (no coincidence!) the sister of Henry IV's mistress, Gabrielle d'Estrées. In fact, the king had given her the abbey as a way of securing a convenient base for his trysts with Gabrielle. Angélique was not likely to object, given her own alleged record of twelve children by twelve different fathers. Under her the monastery was a lively place, a venue for gambling, plays, and elaborate feasts.

To this monastery, in 1599, there came as a novice a little girl seven and a half years old, Jacqueline Arnauld. Her age upon entering the novitiate — and *that* novitiate! — does not end the surprises: she was also already the abbess-designate of another Cistercian nunnery, Port-Royal. Once she had taken her vows at the age of nine, all that was needed was to apply to Rome for authorization, even if this involved lying about her age. Just before her eleventh birthday, Jacqueline, now renamed Angélique (in honor of her disreputable mentor?), became abbess of Port-Royal.

Her realm was a cluster of dilapidated buildings, offered by the abbot of Cîteaux and accepted by her parents on the understanding that they would repair and restore Port-Royal themselves. In other words, Port-Royal would become the property, more or less, of the Arnauld family, and a powerful status symbol. True to their word, Angélique's parents spent time and money fixing up the property and reorganizing the community.

But they reckoned without the girl, and her total lack of vocation. Her grandfather had arranged the appointment, and she had told him, "I am only agreeing to become a nun because you are making me an abbess." Once the novelty of the situation had passed, she became a sulky and defiant teenager. Her mother, fearing the worst, frequently searched through her belongings for love letters. But in fact Angélique, stranded in the countryside with no company other than a dozen halfhearted nuns, painfully missing the excitement of the Paris scene and lacking, it seems, even the most basic spiritual guidance, committed no greater sin than reading "profane" books, taking long walks, and wishing she was not a nun. And then, at seventeen, she began the painful journey that led to her own and her community's conversion.

At last she found a spiritual adviser (a Capuchin, since there were no Cistercians of quality around) who was prepared to give her solid guidance. What he told her was not comfortable. He warned her that reforming herself was not enough; she must also reform her community. The very suggestion of this brought her into conflict with her father, who insisted that she give up any such ideas. But Arnauld senior reckoned without his daughter's strong will. In 1609 matters came to a head. Angélique decided to take the momentous step of establishing *clausura* at the very moment the Arnaulds were arriving for one of their visits. They found all the entrances barred. Their daughter, standing behind a small window (a *guichet*), explained to them that they could no longer enter. The ensuing confrontation lasted several hours; then the family departed in fury, vowing never to see her again.

This event, known as "the day of the *guichet*," was the beginning of the monastery's return to strict Cistercian observance, and Angélique's rise to fame in the religious circles of Paris. The *dévots* were fascinated by the uncompromising faith of this young woman. In time, she was called upon to reform other houses, notably the scene of her novitiate, Maubuisson. But this required the deposition of the reigning abbess, and Madame d'Estrées was not so easily moved. She belonged to one of the premier families of France, which was ready to treat any slight to her as a slight to itself. When commands and reasonings from the abbot of Cîteaux proved to have no effect, she was ejected by order of Parlement, and Angélique Arnauld was installed in her place. A year later Madame d'Estrées came back with a troop of armed men commanded by her brother-in-law, and Angélique was forced to flee. However, in a final showdown, the Arnaulds prevailed upon the king to send a force of 150 archers to escort the deposed abbess away. Several years later the abbey's reform was complete and Angélique was able to return to her own community of Port-Royal.

In years to come, Port-Royal would become a center for the spiritual movement known as Jansenism, and later still, the scene of a distressing confrontation between the nuns and the state that, of course, the nuns lost. Louis XIV, who saw Jansenism as a threat to his power, ordered them dispersed, their monastery razed to the ground, their cemetery dug up. But this was still many years away, and Angélique would not live to see it.

What she did see, however, was the coming of the reform movement to other women's monasteries. It was to be a slow, painful business. Like their male counterparts, the nuns of the ancient orders found it difficult to change their ways. There were women who resisted, sometimes violently, the introduction of rules and practices that they had not first agreed to; for the sake of peace, they had to be accommodated somehow, until they passed from the scene. However, the younger nuns, who were generally in favor of reform, had the advantage of the leadership of a group of distinguished abbesses. Among other orders, we see that between 1600 and 1660 the number of Benedictine nuns in France doubled, and several new congregations in the Benedictine tradition were founded. In keeping with the character of their times, these new contemplative communities tended to emphasize austerity and mortification. For monasticism, both male and female, this was a time of rebirth.

But in this success story there are some significant ambiguities. In France the monasteries owed their revival as much to the reconstitution of their landed wealth as to their spiritual regeneration. Rancé and the Arnaulds were not exceptional in spending money to set "their" abbeys to rights. A number of noble families invested heavily in monasteries, and received their reward in kudos and in the control of those monasteries' future prosperity. On neither account were they disappointed. With the eighteenth century, land values began to rise, carrying with them the fortunes of the owners of land. The better-endowed houses became extremely wealthy. Furthermore, as the aristocracy's grip on the monastic life tightened, communities came more and more to reflect the class from which they were drawn. Through the rest of the *ancien régime* the great abbeys of France, and indeed many of the lesser ones, were reserved for the highborn. Their abbots and abbesses were expected to be of noble or — even better! — royal blood. This did not preclude genuine religious spirit, but it did limit the pool from which the monks and nuns were drawn. And unfortunately, in the later 1600s that pool began to run dry. Louis XIV, though conventionally pious, had little use for the contemplative orders. Following the king, the nobility lost its taste for devotion. And the monasteries began to lose subjects.

In any case, times were changing. The age of mysticism was giving way to the age of Descartes and the scientific revolution. More and more, as the century went on, people in power came to rate religious institutions according to their "utility." How much were they a drain on the public purse? What did they do to serve the public good? This explains why the new active congregations, offering value for money, so to speak, went from strength to strength. And with them, a huge new source of talent and energy — bourgeois talent and bourgeois energy — poured into the service of the Church.

And this, seen from the vantage point of social history, was one of the great contributions of the religious orders to the modernization of society. They created a bridge over which people of modest background could pass to positions of influence. To Daughters of Charity, peasant or working-class city girls who became managers and semiprofessionals in the hospitals of France, or to Jesuits of humble origins like Lamormaini, a cook's nephew who became confessor to the Habsburg emperor, the religious life offered a means of advancement. During the Enlightenment years, when the mood changed and the critics of the religious orders were legion, this would be held against them: that they allowed "the lesser people" to rise above their station in life. But the damage, if we may call it that, was done. In its higher offices the French church might still be aristocratic, but across the board it was wide open to talent, and incorrigibly bourgeois.

*   *   *

This chapter has concentrated mainly on developments in France. There is a reason for that. Of twenty-two major congregations of men founded in the seventeenth century, thirteen were founded in France. Of the major women's congregations, both cloistered and uncloistered, almost all were founded in France. France, we can say, was where the action was. For one thing, the civil wars of the sixteenth century had stirred the French Catholic community to its foundations and unleashed a myriad of new emotions: anger, aggressiveness, intolerance, emulation, self-examination, contrition. For some, this meant seeking out a life of prayer and atonement. For others,

the grim economic conditions of the century brought home the deprivation, both spiritual and material, of the people. They were shocked into activism, which, in the spirit of the times, had to have a deep religious motivation. Unprecedented numbers of men and women entered the priesthood
and the religious orders. They found allies in a host of laymen and laywomen, seized by the desire, as one of them put it, "to do all the good that
was possible." Together, they made the century after Trent into an age of
religiously inspired activism.

It did not last. Even as the seventeenth century progressed, subtle
changes took place in the Catholic spirit. "The age of mysticism" gave way
to "the age of moralism." This was not altogether a bad thing: people did
not necessarily lose their taste for the divine when they became more socially involved. But other factors were at play: a changing intellectual environment, and a certain measure of boredom with a church that combined
privilege with state-backed powers of enforcement. Before the century
ended there were widespread signs of skepticism and disaffection, especially
among the elites. Without their support, the religious orders began a slow
decline both in numbers and in influence. Before the eighteenth century
ended they would be in danger of total extinction.

Suggested Reading for Chapter 4

The continuing story of the Catholic Reformation is followed in two books
previously cited: Robert Bireley's *The Refashioning of Catholicism, 1450-1700*
(1999) and Ronnie Po-Chia Hsia's *The World of Catholic Renewal, 1540-1770*
(1998). Two works by the same authors have special relevance for the seventeenth century, especially with regard to the Habsburg Empire: *The Jesuits
and the Thirty Years War* by Bireley (2003), and Hsia's *Social Discipline in the
Reformation: Central Europe, 1550-1750* (1989). Also useful is Peter Shore's
The Eagle and the Cross: Jesuits in Late Medieval Prague (2002).

The orders never acted alone. The massive surge in popular devotion,
ignited and directed by the Jesuits first and foremost, provides much of the
context for this period of religious revival. The leading work on the movement is *The Europe of the Devout: The Catholic Reformation and the Formation of a New Society* (1989), by Louis Châtellier. At the other end of the
spectrum, we see extremes of spirituality among some of the elites, well illustrated in David Bell's *Understanding Rancé: The Spirituality of the Abbot
of La Trappe in Context* (2005).

The seventeenth century saw the full flowering of the women's religious orders. Again, it is important to know the context. For this development, and the reasons behind it, see Elizabeth Rapley, *The Dévotes: Women and Church in Seventeenth-Century France* (1990); Barbara Diefendorf, *From Penitence to Charity* (2004); and Susan Dinan, *Women and Poor Relief in Seventeenth-Century France* (2006).

CHAPTER 5

The Eighteenth Century: "A Time to Break Down"

"The worst pest among monks is too many monks." So, at mid–eighteenth century, wrote Pope Benedict XIV. It was a strange irony: monasticism was in trouble because it was too successful. To all appearances, both "old" and "new" orders were at the top of their form. Collectively, Europe's 25,000 monastic communities were sitting on about 10 percent of its land, and more than that of its wealth, which many of them were using to erect the extravagantly sumptuous buildings that we can still admire today, from Portugal to Poland. Convents were packed with nuns. As for the nonmonastic orders, in some of them, such as the Capuchins, the reformed Franciscans, and the Jesuits, membership was at an all-time high, and still rising. Monks, friars, and clerks of various kinds were everywhere to be seen.

If anything, they were too much to be seen. "Ten frocks to every man," the saying went, the exaggeration being a measure of a deep and widespread resentment. In some European cities the proportion of clergy to population was about one to ten. Across the Continent, countryside and cities combined, it was somewhere between 1 and 2 percent. Of these, many were regulars. Taken together, the personnel of the male religious orders matched and sometimes even outnumbered the secular clergy, and certainly outshone them in talent and popular appeal. In 1700 it would have been impossible to imagine the church without them. They were its brains and its muscle and, to a great extent, its spiritual underpinning.

They were not without their problems, however. For the healthy balance of society, there were just too many monks and nuns. And they were unevenly distributed. Whereas medieval monasticism had idealized the remote and lonely places, most orders now showed a marked preference for city living. In Spain, for instance, at a time when thousands of rural parishes were without priests, urban institutions were groaning under an overload of members; the Franciscan province of Santiago, for instance, had so many friars that "it did not know where to put them or to find the means to feed them." The same situation obtained elsewhere: in Portugal, overcrowding and underemployment marred life in the cities, but even the most basic religious services were lacking in the countryside; in Italy, known as "the monks' paradise," towns and cities teemed with clergymen while church officials had difficulty providing parish priests for an impoverished and almost unchurched peasantry.

It was not just that the religious orders were too numerous, or too rich, or not sufficiently useful. There had long been an undercurrent of hostility toward monasticism per se. The political theorists of secular society had been criticizing it for half a century. In France, from the time of the royal minister Colbert in the 1660s, "populationists" had worried that the rush into celibacy was depleting the country's manpower reserves: that too many young men and women were choosing (or having chosen for them) a lifestyle that drained the public purse and deprived the state of future citizens. Where the upper classes — the very people who espoused monasticism so vigorously in the earlier seventeenth century — were concerned, there was truth to the populationists' argument. Given the limited choice of careers open to the younger sons of the elites, the army and the church were two prime options, but the one was wasteful of lives and the other of posterity. When parents placed their surplus children in the priesthood or the religious orders, they were taking a gamble that their one or two marrying sons would carry on the family name. But in an age when infant mortality rates were high, this did not always happen, and many elite houses found themselves facing extinction. As for girls of good family, in some cities in France, Italy, and Spain they were for many decades more likely to become nuns than to marry. When, in time, their family lines sputtered out, it was easy to blame the convents. And yet, what was the alternative? For daughters, a suitable marriage required a generous dowry, and if parents could not afford that the cloister was really the only safe and respectable way to keep old maids out of public view. The option of the religious life was essential to the structure of that particular patrician society. Colbert himself, the archpopulationist, had five sisters in Visitation convents.

There were other constant concerns, mainly having to do with money. All Catholic countries bowed to the principle of mortmain ("dead hand"), by which all property acquired by church institutions was sequestered, to be kept forever in the hands of the church and, therefore, out of circulation. The idea was that what had been made sacred should not be returned to the profane marketplace. But what seemed laudable in theory was frustrating in practice. Institutions under the church umbrella (with monasteries at the forefront) had been acquiring property for seven hundred years or so, and thus had eaten into the amount of real estate available for exploitation by secular society. The thought was beginning to find traction that perhaps this was why Catholic countries had fallen behind Protestant countries in prosperity.

This perception was sharpened by economic trends. In the early eighteenth century many Catholic states felt themselves to be in the doldrums. Their points of comparison were England and Holland, both Protestant through and through, and both expanding mightily. Did these countries' religion have any bearing on their commercial success? And if so, was it because their talent and capital were free-ranging, not locked up in religious communities? For those thinkers on the Continent who already disliked the church, the answer was obvious. The dead hand of religion must be lifted, or at least lightened. For the sake of prosperity, the dense thicket of convents must be pruned back, and their people and their wealth released into the public domain.

And then there was the tithe, a running sore in peasant society. A levy on the produce of the land, it was originally intended to provide for the upkeep of parish churches and their priests, but now much of it was diverted into the pockets of the landlords. This was scandalous in any case, but when the landlords were monks, men vowed to holy poverty, it was infuriating. Many abbeys paid their parish priests a minimal salary, maintained the churches in a minimally satisfactory state — and pocketed the rest. Living, too often, on insufficient incomes, and faced, too often, with crumbling churches, the parish clergy added their grievances to those of the peasants. The contrast between their lives and those of the monks was galling. "We spend night and day in the rain going about the countryside to administer the sacraments, but these gentlemen would refuse to take four steps from their home without a good carriage, or at least a horse to carry them and a well-equipped valet to serve them." This complaint, voiced by the parish priests of Cambrai, could have been repeated by many of their fellows across the Continent.

Later in the century, in regions open to Enlightenment thinking, the criticisms of monasticism would become more virulent. Monks would be described as lazy and vicious, nuns as the pathetic victims of cruel family strategies, and friars as charlatans who by their begging took bread from the mouths of those who really needed it. As for the Jesuits and their ilk, they would come to be seen as the power-hungry manipulators of a credulous populace. In the salons, the academies, the coffeehouses, and wherever the chattering classes met, nothing good would be said about the regulars. But this time was still a few decades away. In the early years of the century most Europeans did not waste too much effort on such thinking. The orders were just a fact of life. They provided schooling, hospital care, social services. They patronized artists and craftsmen. They employed numerous domestics and workers; what would happen if all those jobs were lost? They provided alms and free soup to beggars, and where the beggars were too numerous they staffed the institutions that kept them enclosed. At a time when the religious orders monopolized the colleges, the universities, the free schools, the hospitals, the orphanages, and the asylums, who could talk of replacing them?

This does not mean that ordinary people necessarily *liked* the religious orders. It did not take great intellect to observe that monasteries and convents, by their sheer numbers, were absorbing too much urban space and squeezing out too many productive citizens. "[They] occupy the greater part of the city's terrain," wrote a royal engineer in the French town of Laon in 1701, adding that their building programs had wiped out so many houses "that the number of inhabitants, the only contributors to the expenses of the city, is notably diminished." His complaint could have been made in any western European city. Catholic society's devotion had been expressed over the centuries in the establishment of religious houses: 84 of them in Seville, for instance, more than 150 in Paris and in Rome, almost 200 in Naples. Now, as religious sentiment started to cool, these houses came to be seen more and more as a burden to their cities.

There is a difference, though, between apathy and antipathy. Resentment there might be among the people, for the overabundance of the clergy, for their privileged place in society, for the high-handedness of some of them, and above all, for the "spirit of property" that so many of them exhibited and was such a flagrant contradiction of their vows. There is little sign that resentment reached the point of anger. For most Catholics through most of the century, and throughout most of Europe, the religious orders were simply *there,* as inevitable as death and taxes, and most likely a lot more tolerable. They had their detractors, and they had their supporters. This ambivalence was most marked in France, where the Enlightenment worked to greatest effect. Even in 1788, as the Revolution was about to break over the country, the people of France, upon orders from the Crown to register their complaints about life in general (the famous *cahiers de doléances*), spent very little time complaining about their local religious communities. Some praised them, some criticized them, most had nothing to say about them; only a tiny percentage asked for their outright abolition.

The fact is that the attack on the religious orders came from the top down. It took place over many years, indeed, over most of a century. Although in time it covered almost all of Catholic Europe, it was carried out by different regimes, each with its own agenda and its own rationale. The trend was always toward more severity, the rationale was always more aggressive. And where the leaders led, the people fell into line. In the end war and revolution came, to throw everything into confusion. When the period of suppressions was over in the early 1800s, the great majority of monks, friars, clerks, and nuns were gone, their buildings taken over or destroyed, their lands sold. That is the story of the religious orders in the eighteenth century.

The Harnessing of the Gallican Church

The story begins in France, and it involves the country's cloistered nuns.

When Louis XIV died in 1715, he left his country in the grip of a serious depression. He is said to have apologized on his deathbed for the harm he caused his people; without a doubt, he did have reason to apologize. His pursuit of grandeur had taken him into four costly wars that, at home, had meant heavier and heavier taxes. These, falling upon an already overstrained economy, had led to disaster. "All France is nothing more than a huge, desolate, starving poorhouse," a prominent churchman dared to tell the king. During the first years of the new century the economy almost ground to a halt. Then, in 1720, came national bankruptcy and soaring inflation. The only commodity that retained its value was real estate. Major landowners like the old endowed monasteries suffered no great hardship. But people whose major investments were in the money market lost the greater part of what they had — and this included the majority of the two thousand communities of cloistered nuns. Many women found themselves in intolerable poverty, made worse by the fact that, stuck within their four walls, they could do very little to help themselves.

Before long, cries of distress were rising to Versailles. It was embarrassing. These were respectable ladies, after all, and it was hardly fitting to let them starve in their cloisters or (still worse!) go begging in the streets. So the Regency government made the politically correct moves: it ordered an inquiry and then, in 1727, established a commission. The original mandate of this body, known as the *Commission des Secours,* was to provide alms to deserving communities. But before long a second mandate was tacked on. When the returns from the inquiry were in, the commission's suspicions were confirmed: there was "an excessive number of women's communities" in the country. The commissioners came to the convenient conclusion that these communities were poor not because they had lost everything in the general bankruptcy, but because there were just too many of them. And this was the time to do something about it. A radical surgery must take place: there must be fewer houses in France, and fewer women in those houses. The commission went to work and developed a program of suppressions.

There was no question, in those early years, of breaking with established church practice. It had always been accepted that if a community dwindled in numbers or failed to observe its rule, its buildings, land, and revenues could be taken over. The Middle Ages are full of examples of colonies of monks or nuns moving into abandoned or condemned monasteries. What was more, wealth that had been invested in a monastery for one purpose could be appropriated for other purposes, as long as they were church-related. When in 1518 Cardinal Thomas Wolsey suppressed twenty-one religious houses to finance the building of his college in Oxford, no one thought it improper. Nor did anyone object when in 1618 the bishop of Paris turned the Benedictine abbey of Saint-Magloire into an Oratorian seminary. During the Catholic Reformation, any number of monastic buildings were transferred in this way. The only rule of thumb was that the transfer must not involve the alienation of church property. Everybody still agreed that what had been given to God must not be taken away again; that what the Church had, it must continue to hold. The commission's actions were completely in harmony with this. The properties that came to it through the suppression of one house were normally transferred to another house. All that the commissioners were claiming to do was to adjust the internal economy of female monasticism, so that it could live within its means.

Furthermore, although the commission was a creature of the Crown, it took its action in the name of the Church, and in accordance with canon law. Once the commissioners had decided which houses to suppress, it was up to the local bishops to do the dirty work. Several bishops protested, but in vain. One of them was reprimanded: "If you are wise, and if you are zealous for the public good, you will enter into the views of the commission, and cooperate with it in the execution of this worthy project." The words "or else" were not added, but they must certainly have been understood. The bishop might be the front man, but ultimate power rested with the king. And the king, who had chosen the bishop in the first place, had the power to make his life difficult if he did not fall into line.

One of the problems the commission faced was that very few women's communities met the criteria for suppression. For the most part they were not underpopulated, nor were they unobservant of their rule. So in earmarking some of them for suppression while subsidizing others, a variety of factors were taken into account. Number one: Were they part of the king's patronage system? Number two: Did they have powerful friends at court? Number three: Were they thoroughly orthodox? Number four: Were they submissive to their bishops? And lastly, and above all, were they *useful?* The word "utility," and the values behind it, had now entered into the public lexicon. But what was meant by "useful"? Providing respectable retreats for ladies of quality? Yes. Nursing? Yes. The education of children? Yes. The giving out of bread and soup? Well, maybe. Prayer and contemplation? Well . . .

What had been so precious in the eyes of the seventeenth century was becoming marginal in the eyes of the eighteenth. Social service was commendable; contemplation and the singing of divine office were idle pastimes, of no public value. This is one reason why the authorities, while giving the women's monasteries a hard time, spared the secular sisters. These were seen to work for their living, in a way that contemplative nuns did not. And they cost less per person than the cloistered working nuns. Somehow, their lifestyle fitted more comfortably into the spirit of the century, and indeed, of the century to come. Though the seculars were still heavily outnumbered by their more prestigious sisters in the Lord, and would remain so throughout the rest of the *ancien régime,* the future belonged to them.

The commission continued its work until 1788, but with waning energy. The suppressions, and the endless bickering that went with them, created a lot of bad blood in the country. So in the final analysis, it did not achieve everything it had set out to do. However, close to 250 women's monasteries out of 2,000 were closed down, their communities broken up and dispersed to wherever there was room for them — a heartbreaking end for women who had spent their entire adult lives within the same house. As for the surviving monasteries, they were cut down in size. Through the simple device of suspending new entries for as long as it took, the overall population of cloistered nuns was reduced by about a third. And the Crown had established the principle that, as long as it had the "right" reasons and stayed within canon law, it could do more than just close an errant convent here and there; it could rearrange things in the interior of the Gallican church.

It is worth noting what it did *not* do. It did not abolish any religious orders. And it did not meddle with the monks. In 1727 it had thought of doing so, but had then decided that would raise too many red flags within the church. However, time would put an end to this caution.

*   *   *

> *O blessed and triune God*
> *Grant that for the peace of men*
> *And for thy true glory*
> *This society of Jesus may die.*

In October 1759, 153 men were deposited without prior warning on the shores of the Papal States. They were the first of more than a thousand Portuguese Jesuits who, exiled from their own country, would come seeking refuge — men who only a year before had belonged to the most powerful religious order in the Church.

In 1750 the Society of Jesus numbered 22,500 members, spread out through the entire known world from the Orient to the Americas. Their power was immense. They held a virtual monopoly on higher education; their sodalities and secret societies were still drawing in men and women by the thousands; they exercised influence in many of the princely courts of Europe; they were active as missionaries, at home and abroad. Within their ranks could be found brilliant men: brilliant theologians, brilliant scientists and mathematicians, brilliant diplomats, brilliant polemicists. There was not a religious order that could compete with them in talent, training, and discipline.

It was their power that brought them down. In protecting their turf against all comers they made many enemies within the church: cardinals, bishops, other religious orders. As for the laity, though the intelligentsia found their classical educational system hopelessly out of date, the Jesuits were able by the sheer weight of their influence to rebut all criticism, and continue with the methods that Loyola had prescribed two centuries before. Across Europe, their confessors still held pride of place in royal households, and (according to countless rumor mills, both Protestant and Catholic) whispered self-serving counsels into royal ears. The price the Jesuits paid for their preeminence was that they were the targets of a constant barrage of slander. Stories about their perfidy and greed circulated endlessly, and though many of these were total fabrications, they made their mark. The word "Jesuit" entered the European vocabulary as a synonym for someone sly and underhanded.

Ominously for the Society, in the early years of the century its carapace of power was twice dented, once by a failure, once by a success. The failure was in China. The Jesuit missionaries there, following in the footsteps of Matteo Ricci, had built a form of Christian practice that made room for Chinese thought and customs. In particular, it allowed the cult of Confucius to continue, on the premise that Confucianism contained so much that was good that it must have originated with God. But to other Christian missionaries, notably Dominican and Franciscan friars, these compromises smacked of superstition and threatened the purity of the faith. After long wrangling in Rome, the friars won the fight. In 1704 the pope issued the first of several condemnations of the Jesuits' practices. By 1715 the destruction of their work was complete. By papal decree Confucianism was back to being pure heresy and the church was back to being pure church, that is, untainted by anything not in the European tradition. Two years later the Chinese government retaliated, ordering all missionaries to leave and all native Christians to abjure. What had been a successful mission turned into a shambles. At home in Europe, the enemies of the Society sniffed the air and smelled blood.

The success was in France, and it was in France that the wound was inflicted. Beginning in the 1630s, a dispute had developed within the Gallican church, a very rarefied theological dispute to begin with, but a fierce one for all that. On one side were the Jansenists, a body of highly devout true believers who were as close to Calvinism as faithful Catholics could be. They held to the view that the path to salvation was narrow, and passable only if God ruled it to be so; man was too weak and too soiled by sin to help himself. Like strict Calvinists, they lived by the severest of ethical standards. Theirs was an elitist faith, which left little room in heaven for the majority of Catholics, the very people whom the Jesuits, with their preaching campaigns and their mass rallies, were trying to reach. The Jesuits took after them with a vengeance, and a war of words erupted that raged on for years. The Jesuits scored the most points, bringing both the pope and the king into their camp. But all the while they were losing the battle for hearts and minds.

The Jansenists had a large following, and an even larger circle of admirers. France, even when Louis XIV was at his most powerful, had a politically conscious class, centered in the Sorbonne university, the law courts, and the *parlements*. These men came to loathe the Jesuits and to identify them with an overweening papal power that threatened their own Gallican liberties. How right they turned out to be, when in 1713 the pope, giving in to Louis XIV and the Jesuit party in Rome, issued the bull *Unigenitus,* which condemned Jansenism, lock, stock, and barrel. Jansenism as a religious movement was smashed. There was nothing left now but a mopping-up operation, as the government hounded its adherents from pillar to post across the country. But as the spiritual force for a political movement, it grew stronger and angrier. In time to come, under a weaker king than Louis XIV, this movement would find the opportunity to flex its muscles.

This was the situation at midcentury. The Society was powerful, and to many people, unbearably so. But its enemies did not have the means to do it damage because it enjoyed the support of the rulers of Europe. Then, all of a sudden, that support fell away. In the eyes of princes and their counselors, it became a foreign body living within their realms and threatening to leach away their power. The Jesuits, it was now observed, had their own power structure; they were answerable to a foreign ruler (the pope); they had been known to argue from time to time that tyrants could lawfully be assassinated. Their very existence was seen as a challenge to the eighteenth-century concept of state power.

The trouble for the Society started, strange to say, in Portugal. "Strange," because of all European countries, Portugal was about the most conservative, and the least touched by Enlightenment thinking. In the action it took against the Jesuits it was moved purely by reasons of state.

For two centuries and more, the two great Iberian colonial powers, Portugal and Spain, had coexisted in the South American continent: Portugal to the east, where its viceroyalty of Brazil encompassed the vast basin of the Amazon and its tributaries, Spain to the west, with its three viceroyalties running from the isthmus of Panama down the spine of the Andes and across to the river Plate. It was here, toward the southern end of the continent, that the two powers collided. Amicably enough, they met in Madrid in 1750 and settled their border differences. As a consequence of their treaty, the region called Paraguay, which had up to then been in the Spanish orbit, was transferred to Portugal. With it went territory occupied by a number of Indian settlements run by the Jesuits, known as "reductions." Some 29,000 Guarani Indians, inhabitants of the reductions, were ordered to emigrate to the far side of the river Uruguay. This involved untold hardship, well beyond the imaginings of the authorities in Lisbon and Madrid. When the Guarani resisted, and gained the support of their Jesuit missionaries, the home governments were outraged. A joint force moved in and a small war started, in which some Jesuits took up arms beside the Indians. Eventually the insurgents were crushed. But in the meantime, what was seen as Jesuit complicity in an unlawful rebellion was added to a growing list of grievances against the Society.

The Jesuits had a deep commitment to the Guarani. In the reductions of Paraguay we have another case of their creativity in the mission field. The principle was not original: the friars in Mexico had decided early on that the mixing of European settlers and native Indians never worked to the advantage of the Indians, and they had experimented with establishing reservations that were off-limits to the Europeans. The Jesuits took the idea further, using the separateness of the reservations to create autonomous social systems in which the Indians farmed, were schooled and churched, and prospered — albeit under the highly paternalistic control of their Jesuit overseers, but still more happily than most of their countrymen. The reductions were held up as a model to admiring European supporters.

The settler population was not so impressed. It was growing and expanding, and it was beginning to covet the territory of the reductions that, according to rumor, was incredibly rich both in agriculture and in mining. Local bishops, resentful that they had no authority over these colonies, backed the settlers. And so the word went back to Lisbon, Madrid, and Rome: the Jesuits were building kingdoms within kingdoms; they were sitting on unfathomable riches; there was no limit to their ambition and their greed. For the moment, the Portuguese Crown took no action. But then a change of ministers of the Crown, and an unexpected turn of events, gave it its opportunity.

Disaster can open the floodgates of drastic change. We have seen it in our own time. In February 1933 the Reichstag, the seat of the German parliament, burned down; within a matter of weeks German democracy was submerged in a Nazi tidal wave. In November 1938, in Paris, a German diplomat was shot by a distraught young Jew, and thousands of Jews in Germany saw their livelihoods destroyed, almost overnight. In September 2001, in New York, the Twin Towers collapsed, and from one day to the next the world was rocked upon its axis. In October 1755, while the fighting was still going on in Paraguay, a massive earthquake destroyed the city of Lisbon and took some 10,000 lives. Efforts to rebuild the city took place in an atmosphere of bitter questioning, which led to complaints against the religious orders' wealth. Then, in 1758, an attempt was made to assassinate the king. The Society had nothing to do with it. But by some strange alchemy, and with adroit management by the king's minister plus a huge campaign of disinformation, this all fed into an anti-Jesuit paranoia. In 1759 the Jesuits of Portugal were declared to be in rebellion, their property was confiscated, and they themselves were imprisoned or banished, all 1,698 of them.

Europe sat up and took note. It had happened so fast and, apparently, with so little effort. A small and not particularly powerful kingdom had cut off the arm of the most prestigious religious order in Christendom. More amazing still, Rome had done nothing to save the Portuguese Jesuits. The papacy, it seemed, had been powerless to prevent its faithful sons, its favorite children, from being knocked down and beaten up. The conclusion was obvious: the papacy could no longer stand up to the princes.

Meanwhile, in France, a second disaster for the Jesuits was in the making. It started in the 1750s, in the Caribbean colony of Martinique. The superior of the Jesuit mission there, Antoine Lavalette, had for some years been turning the Society's holdings into a commercial enterprise, growing tropical crops for export to France and Holland, and doing a bit of speculation on the side. In all this he was flouting both French trading rules and canon law; for his misdeeds he was reprimanded by both the government and his superiors in Paris. But the Caribbean was far away, and discipline was difficult to enforce; perhaps the superiors, who were facing money problems at home, were mollified by receiving the occasional sweetener. So Lavalette continued on, and if anything, became more ambitious in his dealings. He borrowed money from scores of financial houses back home, promising repayment in shipments of sugar and coffee. Unfortunately for him, war intervened, and his cargoes were seized by English privateers. He, and the mission he headed, found themselves in debt to the tune of 4,000,000 livres.

In 1760 some of his creditors, seeking redress wherever they could find it, sued not only the Martinique mission but the entire Society of Jesus in France. The French Jesuit superiors contested the suit, but the course they decided on could not have been worse: they appealed to the Parlement of Paris. The Parlement, pro-Jansenist in spirit and mindful of its long-standing grudge, and seeing the chance at last to get even, ruled against them in a big way. In 1762 it sequestered all Jesuit holdings in France for nonpayment of the debt. And it did not stop there. After expelling the Jesuits from their houses, it moved to have the whole order removed from

French territory. As in Portugal, the action was bolstered by a mass of propaganda, against which the Jesuits' friends could make no headway. The king and his ministers were not ill-disposed toward the Society, and they made feeble efforts to save it. But in the depths of the Seven Years' War, with the Crown's debts piling up and a desperate need to ask the Parlement for more taxes, Louis XV could not afford to stand his ground. Unwillingly, he acceded to the Parlement's demand and in 1764 banished the Society of Jesus from France. Some three thousand men were set adrift.

Then it was Spain's turn. The Jesuits had been out of favor with the king for some years, but it took a crisis in the capital to bring matters to a head. In 1766, for reasons totally unrelated, rioting broke out in Madrid. The ministers of the Crown very quickly decided that the Jesuits were behind the riots. Were they not known to foment rebellion and encourage assassination, all for the purpose of taking power themselves? The king was persuaded, perhaps because he wanted to be. He was nudged along by a ministerial campaign of rumors and open accusations, and also by the willing acquiescence of his bishops and the other religious orders. In February 1767 he ordered that all Jesuits be expelled from his dominions, whether in Europe, America, or the Philippines. In April the order was put into effect, and another five thousand men lost everything they had lived and worked for.

By now there were more homeless Jesuits than neighboring states could absorb. Wherever they went, they were likely to find the borders closed. Even the Papal States, already struggling to care for the French and Portuguese Jesuits, could take no more. Shiploads of exiles wandered the Mediterranean, to be put down wherever their captains found an opportunity. For a time Corsica was a favored dumping ground, and the refugees lived there for some months in abject poverty. Then the island was taken over by France, and the unfortunate men were again set adrift.

Worse was to come. The three Bourbon powers, having used their bully pulpit to banish the Society of Jesus from their own territories, now decided, for the sake of their own credibility, that it must be destroyed altogether. For this to happen, the papacy must be persuaded — or forced — to act. The only problem was the pope, Clement XIII. He had made it plain that in his eyes the Society was the work of God and a nursery of saints; he would never consent to its destruction. However, in 1769 he was a dying man. The powers agreed to be patient, to wait for his demise, and then make sure that a more compliant pope was elected. And this is what happened. The ambassadors of France, Spain, and Portugal worked their will on the College of Cardinals. The new pope, Clement XIV, had no great quarrel with the Jesuits. But, faced with an alliance of powerful kings who were threatening schism if he did not comply with their demands, he was ready to accept the idea that for the good of the Church the Society must go. One obstacle remained, however: none of the Catholic countries east of the Elbe had joined in the demand for abolition. And one of these countries was highly important to the pope. How could he make such a sweeping move without the permission of Austria?

The Austrian empress Maria Theresa had always been ambivalent about the Jesuits. They had caused no scandal in her lands, and they were useful, even irreplaceable, as educators. On the other hand, she was not impervious to the drumbeat of criticism rising both from foreign powers and from her own clergy, who, like so many others, had their own reasons to dislike and envy the Society. What was more, since she was in the process of negotiating the marriage of her daughter, Marie Antoinette, to the heir to the French throne, this seemed like the right moment to do the French a favor. So in her official response to the pope she took up a neutral stance, but added that if he decided that for the good of the Church the Society should be suppressed, she would not object. Her only stipulation was that in that case, the state, not the Church, should take charge of its property.

So the way was now clear. In 1773 Clement XIV signed the brief *Dominus ac Redemptor*. The peace of the Church, it said, depended on the extinction of the Society of Jesus, and therefore, "we dissolve, suppress, extinguish and abolish the said Society." The brief was received across Europe with rejoicing, though here and there small demonstrations of loyalty to the Jesuits broke out. Perhaps most touching were the scenes of affection that the Jesuits from the Philippines met as they crossed Mexico on their weary way eastward toward exile. But the pope had spoken, and even though he had spoken out of weakness, the Catholic world obeyed.

Through a strange twist of fate, the Society of Jesus did not suffer the total extinction prepared for it. While Catholic Europe attended to the business of turning all its Jesuits into ex-Jesuits, two monarchs held out: the Protestant king of Prussia, Frederick the Great, and the Orthodox empress of Russia, Catherine the Great. In Prussia, the Jesuits were given another name and allowed to continue their work. Catherine saw no need for such subterfuge. She had recently seized a large slice of Poland, and with it, a sizable Catholic population and a number of Jesuit schools. Since she owed no obedience to the pope, she saw no reason to do away with an order that provided useful services to her people. She refused to publish the brief. So in her territories the Jesuits continued to exist, though in a strange sort of limbo: in obedience to the state but in defiance of the Church. On the other hand, what did the Church really want? In spite of French and Spanish pressure, Rome refused to condemn the Russian Jesuits outright. Finally, in 1814, Pius VII, liberated by the French Revolution from the yoke of the Bourbon kings, gave them his official approval. In the eyes of the papacy, the Society of Jesus was alive again.

For the troubled church of the eighteenth century, the Society of Jesus was a Jonah that had to be cast overboard to save the ship. But Jonah had gone into the belly of the whale and had lived there until cast up on a faraway shore. In the same way, the Jesuits were swallowed up and disappeared, and then returned, to live and fight another day.

"The Religious State in France Is Nearing Its Tomb"

One of the longest-running irritations within Catholicism was that felt by bishops toward the religious orders. In the sixteenth century the Council of Trent had ordered the bishops to take control of their dioceses, but when they began to do so they found themselves facing a multiplicity of monks, friars, and clerks of various descriptions, many of whom could claim exemption from episcopal control, exemption given to them, ironically enough, by Rome. For decades to come the bishops had to seek the help of these men, so ineffective and ill-equipped were their own secular clergy. But this help came at a price: the religious orders were so good at their job that they drew the faithful to their own churches, undermining the parish system. Furthermore, strong in the sense of their own virtue, they challenged the bishops' authority in any number of ways. It would not be surprising if a few bishops dreamed of a time when they could cut them down to size.

In mid-eighteenth-century France they saw their chance to do exactly that. The secular clergy was, at last, in good shape. At the same time, monastic reform was in the air. The *Commission des Secours* had shown the way, with its reorganization of the nunneries. The Jesuits were on the run, and it looked increasingly possible that control of their properties and their colleges would fall to the bishops. On the other hand, the atmosphere was not altogether comfortable for the hierarchy. The antimonastic mood within the intelligentsia showed signs of metastasizing into out-and-out anticlericalism. If this happened, the bishops themselves would be a prime target. *Philosophes* and parlementarians already had the prelates — highborn aristocrats all — within their sights. By being the first to launch a campaign of monastic reform, the bishops might hope to preempt a wider attack, or at least to control it.

In 1765 the General Assembly of the Clergy met in Paris. This was a body composed of archbishops, bishops, and a few ordinary priests, but no monks or friars. It met every five years, mainly to make money grants to the Crown but also to thrash out internal problems. On this occasion the state of the religious orders was high on the agenda. During the session a report was tabled by the archbishop of Toulouse, Loménie de Brienne, exposing their dire situation and suggesting how they could be reformed.

There is an old saying, "Physician, heal thyself." The prelates of France were, at this time, as much in need of reform as were the religious orders. They were appointed by the king, often at the behest of the queen or some court favorite. They were all men of high society, and too many of them were more interested in their careers than in their pastoral duties. They all drew part of their wealth from the vicious practice of *commenda,* which had perhaps done more than anything else to undermine monastic life. With a few exceptions they were immersed in Enlightenment thinking. Some were able administrators, some were not; almost all of them lacked the fire of faith that had burned in the great bishops of the Catholic Reformation period.

Loménie de Brienne was such a man. The younger son of an aristocratic but not particularly wealthy family, he saw that his chance to ascend to power lay through the church, and he worked assiduously toward that end. He studied hard, and cultivated the right people, and spent money in the right places, in the happy expectation that one day he would be able to repay his debts, "through his marriage, as one might say, with a well-endowed church." And so it fell out. Becoming archbishop of Toulouse in 1763, he was within two years able to dominate the assembly, by dint of hard work and sheer ability. From that time on the business of reforming the religious orders was, effectively, in his hands. His career was made. Some twenty years later he became, briefly, a minister of the Crown, and retired a cardinal and a rich man. His last years were tragic. One of only three French bishops to compromise with the Revolution, he then fell afoul of it and died, possibly by his own hand, only hours before he was to go to the guillotine.

As a man of the church, Loménie de Brienne had one serious defect. He was at best an agnostic, and at worst an atheist. Louis XVI believed the latter. In 1787, pressed by Marie Antoinette to name him archbishop of Paris, he refused, protesting that "the archbishop of Paris ought at least to believe in God." That such a man should have pursued the reform of the regulars with such dedication is strange, to say the least. He was accused of having a hidden agenda, that of total destruction, but history does not bear that out. The religious orders were part of the ecclesiastical establishment that he valued, and it would not have been in his interests to undercut them altogether. What is clear, however, is that he had little sympathy for the institutions he set out to redesign. Monastic failures he could understand and deal with; monastic successes were beyond his comprehension. He found the Carthusians to be blamelessly observant of their rule, yet he said it was impossible for a Carthusian to be an enlightened man. And with that, he left them alone.

But to find fault with the man is not to deny the truth he was speaking. In 1765 there were almost 3,000 religious communities in France housing some 26,000 men. Many of these communities were in fact in a bad way. Some were too rich, others too poor. There was widespread laxity, and there were frequent instances of scandalous behavior. Across the country morale was poor, and this showed up in two major ways. First, in diminishing numbers. For some time the male monastic population of France had been dropping, and it now averaged less than ten per house. Many communities that had once numbered twenty or thirty men or more now made do with two or three — not enough to sing divine office, or observe the daily rule, or even take proper care of the monastic properties. The second way low morale showed itself was in internal quarreling and rebelliousness that had an unfortunate way of breaking into the open. According to Gallican law, men and women in religious orders had the right to appeal to the secular authority, the Parlement, against abusive superiors. This they were now doing in unprecedented numbers, giving the impression that the rank and file of the monasteries were the victims of serious mistreatment. Their complaints handed critics of monasticism the pretext they needed to intervene. Clearly, it was argued, the old rules were no longer viable; they needed to be modified and updated, to squelch the "despotism" of the superiors. Another monastic practice that exercised enlightened minds was the early age at which religious profession was allowed. The Council of Trent had set it at sixteen; a proposal existed to raise it to twenty-five. In this way, one might hope that the riffraff that polluted the monasteries would soon disappear.

The assembly subscribed to the idea of reform and recommended that Rome be asked to act on it. But now a strange thing happened: the assembly was suddenly suspended, by the will of the sovereign. When it reconvened half a year later, it learned that a commission was being formed to deal with the problem — but by royal, not papal, authority. In other words, the Crown was taking the matter right out of the pope's hands. The commission was to deal with the religious orders, leaving the pope, as he himself later complained, "in entire ignorance of what had been done and what was going to be done." The *Commission des Réguliers,* to give it its official title, was made up of five councillors of state and five archbishops — one of whom was Loménie de Brienne, who became the moving spirit of the group. From start to finish, there was not a single monk or friar on the commission.

During the following years the commission moved steadily forward with its program of reform. The religious orders reacted in different ways. A few were manifestly decadent and quite willing to be suppressed — as long as they received a golden handshake. Nine small orders, accounting for a hundred houses, disappeared in this way. The major orders put up more of a fight. Nobody had the right to interfere with their rule, they claimed, except their own general chapters, with the blessing of the pope. Some of them, the Dominicans, for instance, pointed out that they were members of larger international orders, over which the French Crown had no authority; an alteration of their rule in France might lead to schism in the order. In any case, what problems there were lay not with the rule but with the failure of too many of their members to follow it. The more ancient orders also appealed to the authority of past kings, citing privileges granted them as long ago as the thirteenth century — an argument unlikely to cut any ice with the enlightened men of the present day, who despised all things inherited from that age of unreason! The commission moved on courteously but with iron determination. Every order and congregation was forced to call a general chapter where, under the supervision of commissioners selected by Loménie de Brienne, it was required to bring its rule into conformity with the royal will. If it refused to do this, it risked destruction. Despite vociferous protests, most orders complied, and very few were left unscathed. Four hundred fifty houses disappeared, and some three thousand men were either secularized or sent off to join other communities.

(Amidst all this effort to reform monastic abuses, no mention was made of the abuse of *commenda.* Nor did anyone suggest that perhaps there was too much money sloshing around within the church. Once the pensions of the displaced monks had been paid, the rest of the suppressed monasteries' wealth was redistributed to the dioceses and to various worthy institutions. The five archbishops on the commission all kept their monastic benefices.)

The immediate consequence of the commission's activities was a steep drop in the male monastic population: a result, in part, of the raising of the age of profession, but also of all the uncertainties that the reforms had created. Curiously enough, however, in the 1780s recruitment began to rise, as though, perhaps, monasticism was being reborn in France. Nobody can be sure, however, where the future would have taken them, because the revolution ended that future.

"God's Foolishness Is Wiser Than Human Wisdom"

The travails of the religious orders in the eighteenth century were the result of state action, but they might not have been so successful had there not been grave permutations in the mind-set of the Gallican establishment. Times had changed since the glory days of the Catholic Reformation. Old certainties had shriveled under the bright light of reason. The heroic religiosity of yesteryear seemed dreadfully passé. In its place were new values, those of the dawning Enlightenment: individual liberty, freedom of expression, equality in the eyes of the law. Where the people of God had once been defined as a communion of saints, they were now also to be a society of citizens. In the rarefied atmosphere of upper-class religious sentiment, otherworldliness by itself no longer seemed particularly valuable or useful.

This kind of thinking would still have been rare in 1700. French men and women were not yet ready to give up the values of the past. But changes were already taking place. The age of mysticism was giving way to the age of moralism. Gone were the frills and folderols of the baroque age; in their place was an austere, no-nonsense spirituality. The official church was close to achieving its aim of a Catholicism stripped of its former exuberances and consisting of a body of the faithful guided and instructed by an educated and well-formed parish clergy. And in the process, the institution was becoming terribly "institutional."

But even in the most orderly parades someone will be marching to a different drum. Such a person was a young Breton, Louis Grignion de Montfort. In 1701 he arrived in Poitiers to begin his priestly career. He had just completed several years in a Parisian seminary. They had been difficult years for him, because he did not fit into the conventional seminarian mold. He was too extreme, too eccentric for the times; in his prayer life and his deportment he belonged more to the seventeenth century than to the eighteenth. He was passionately devoted to the Blessed Virgin, and for this he was twitted by his fellow seminarians. He spent hours locked away in private prayer. He was both intense and maladroit, a combination of personality traits that made him a difficult companion. He had few friends.

His reception by the clergy of Poitiers was equally strained. He was sent almost at once to serve as almoner in the general hospital (what we would call the workhouse). There he wore, instead of modest clerical black, clothes so ragged that the inmates considered passing the hat to help him out. He adopted a lifestyle that matched that of the poor, and the poor loved him for it. "This is our priest," they said. The hospital's board of governors was less enchanted, especially when he gathered up some of the female inmates into a religious community, complete with the outlines of a rule. Everything about him — his intense piety, his identification with the poor, his rejection of the accepted clerical etiquette — struck others as excessive. His was an untidy personality in an increasingly tidy world. His superiors, and he himself, wondered whether he was suitable for the ministry. In the face of a great deal of negativity, he left Poitiers, and eventually decided to join a team working under a famous mission preacher. But here again, his behavior irritated his coworkers. The only course left to him was to strike out on his own. And again he got into trouble. In 1709-1710 he preached a highly successful mission and, when it was over, led his penitents in the construction of a "calvary." Structures such as this were the traditional memorials left behind after a mission; the trouble with this one was that it was enormous, and visible for miles around. Its building took mammoth effort and thousands of volunteers, and because of this, as well as its sheer grandiosity, it irritated the local seigneur, whose complaints went all the way to Versailles. As a result, the formal ceremony of blessing was canceled, the monument was dismantled, and Montfort was cashiered by the diocese. He retired, hurt, into temporary obscurity. But when he emerged, he came with a new understanding of how a mission should be conducted.

The trouble was that the Catholicism of the elites had totally come apart from the Catholicism of simple country folk. The one was cerebral, orderly, tasteful; the other was earthy, demonstrative, and laced through and through with charms and superstitions. The one no longer countenanced the use of blessings and curses as a way of confronting the natural world; the other wondered what use the church was, if not for that. The one condemned dancing, and profane songs, and unauthorized nocturnal gatherings in chapels or barns. The other saw no reason to be deprived of these traditional pastimes. A century of reform effort had left the elites in positions of command, but by driving the people's religion underground it had made them tepid and indifferent. Somehow a missionary must reach out and offer his hearers a faith they could hold on to, and practices they could build into their lives.

This is what Louis Grignion de Montfort did. To paraphrase his own words, he "renewed the spirit of Christianity among Christians." He preached repentance, but more: he showed the people simple ways to carry on and deepen their prayer life. First of all, he reintroduced them to a familiar and accessible intermediary, the Mother of God. Then he taught them a method: hymns set to popular refrains and regular recitation of the rosary. Finally, he captured them with his dynamism and passion, and the solidarity he shared with them.

He was with them for only a short time. When he came back to the missions he had only about ten years to live. During that time he preached scores of missions in the Bas-Poitou region of western France. In some of the neighboring dioceses he was not welcome, but this did not prevent his reputation from spreading. After his death in 1716 pilgrims crowded to his tomb from far and near, asking for relics and seeking miraculous cures for their ills, the very kind of behavior that had bishops and parish priests shaking their heads in disapproval. But for all his great stature, he left nobody behind him to carry on his work. He had hoped to create a congregation of mission priests, and he had even drawn up a rule for it, but his premature death left the plan unfulfilled. That would only happen later, and in a roundabout way.

The odd little community of women that he had built years before in the Poitiers general hospital had of course been suppressed. But one member, a young bourgeoise named Marie-Louise Trichet, stayed true both to him and to his idea. For ten years after Montfort's departure she worked in the hospital, establishing a solid reputation as a nurse and an organizer. When in 1713 he returned to Poitiers, he initiated her and a companion, Catherine Brunet, into a "community" of sorts. They continued to work in the hospital until, two years later, he found openings for them in La Rochelle, where he was based, as teachers in free schools for the poor. As was ever the case, the schools were a success. Before long the community grew to four members.

But they were still, in a sense, wanderers. Montfort, with his busy life as a mission preacher, was seldom close to them; his death left them even more adrift. Paradoxically, though, it led in time to their firm foundation. Their mentor was now at rest, and his tomb in Saint-Laurent-sur-Sèvre was a center of public veneration. It only remained to move close to him. One of his wealthy devotees offered them support if they would establish there, and take up the traditional double task of nursing the sick and teaching young children. This they did, and after some initial difficulties, managed to persuade the bishop to appoint René Mulot, Montfort's onetime associate, as their director. Within a short time Mulot was also authorized to receive their vows of religion. By 1721 the women had become the religious congregation that Montfort had desired, under the rule he had drawn up and the title he had devised: "Sagesse," Wisdom, the wisdom of God that overturns all human wisdom.

Furthermore, their establishment, and the appointment of Mulot as their director, had the effect of drawing Montfort's old disciples to Saint-Laurent-sur-Sèvre. These men had been wandering since his death. Now they, too, agreed to form a community, the nucleus of what we know today as the Montfortian Congregation. The two congregations, the Daughters of Wisdom and the Montfortians, entered into a partnership similar to that of the Daughters of Charity and the Lazarists.

The priest-missioners remained a small but potent group until the Revolution. They continued to unsettle many with their unconventional preaching, which one critic in 1786 described as "a spectacle given by a troupe of buffoons." But they continued to draw large crowds, although they remained limited in number and confined to the west of France. The sisters, on the other hand, went from strength to strength. Evidently their "product" was more successful than that of their male colleagues. Preachers were tolerated as long as they did not keep the peasants from their work. But nurses and school mistresses were in great demand, especially in country districts where girls' schools were few and far between, and doctors rarely set foot.

How much did Montfort's two congregations "renew the spirit of Christianity among Christians"? How closely did they bind those Christians to their Church? Significantly, their area of influence, the Vendée, would be stoutly resistant to the Revolution's plans to remake the church, and it was in the Vendée that the most serious rebellion against the revolution broke out in 1793. Before it was extinguished, some 25,000 Vendéans had lost their lives, and the Jacobins of Paris were more convinced than ever that religion was tantamount to treason. There was reason in their rage. Though the rebellion had serious economic causes, it was fed by strong royalist and religious passions. One of the banners under which the rebels marched was "Our Holy Religion"; one of their demands was for a return of the old church; on their breasts they pinned emblems of the Sacred Heart.

In memoirs of the *Vendée militaire* written down many years later, it was recalled that the rebels sang hymns as they marched and knelt to say the rosary at night.

Sadly the rebellion, broken and resurrected and broken again, degenerated in time into savage brigandage. But even then the cause for which the brigands claimed to be fighting was that of church and king. In the Vendée, religion and royalism fused together, and remained fused into the following century.

Montfort has been called "the father of the Vendée." Was he also the father of the *Vendée militaire?* His priests and sisters were singled out by republican officials as inciters to rebellion. But what was really troubling the regime? The men and women themselves, or the staunch loyalty to the Church that eighty years of service had created in the region's peasants? One thing is certain: whether in 1713 or 1793, Louis Grignion de Montfort and his spirit spoke to, and for, a Catholicism that was prepared to stand up against the changing times.

"Thus Far and No Farther"

Modernity stopped at the entrance to the Neapolitan countryside. The progress of Europeans in the preindustrial centuries was decided primarily by geography. Good harbors, navigable rivers, flat or gently rolling terrain, the remains of ancient roads or the first efforts at new ones: these were the conditions that led to settlement and eventually to towns and everything that towns made possible. Hills and mountains, crags and crevices, roads that were mere dirt tracks (or streams of mud in the rainy season), rivers swollen by spring floods and passes blocked by winter snows: all these things stood in the way of modernity, and literacy, and the spread of orthodox religion. In many regions of Europe the peasant was no closer to "civilization" in 1700 than he was in 1500. He never set foot in a city; he knew no city people. He was as likely as his ancestors to be born, marry, and die within the sound of his parish church bell. And even at that, his life was easier than that of the shepherd, who lived as his forebears had lived for generations, wandering with his flocks from summer to winter pasture and seldom sleeping under his own roof.

So it is not an exaggeration to suggest that even in the eighteenth century, at the very time that men of reason and enlightenment were elsewhere seeking to bury the Counter-Reformation, men such as these had not yet even encountered it. A hundred years of mission preaching had not effectively penetrated to the back of beyond where they lived. Theirs was still a semipagan, magical world, badly served by a parish clergy who were almost as illiterate as they.

This was the case with the further reaches of the kingdom of Naples. Nature had drawn a line, and churchmen, for the most part, did not care to go beyond it. It is not that they were idle: the city of Naples itself was humming with activists, starting with older orders such as the Franciscans, the Lazarists, and the Jesuits, continuing with "the Pious Workers," a local congregation dedicated to evangelizing the ignorant, and including several confraternities of priests, men drawn from different communities who desired to go beyond what their own rules demanded, and to serve the miserable poor in the city and its immediate surrounds. But not too far afield. The remote countryside still went hungry.

In 1735 the Congregation of the Most Holy Redeemer was founded for one purpose alone: preaching to the rural poor. The timing could hardly have been more inauspicious. State power looked out and saw a glut of religious congregations and asked why there should be one more. The existing congregations asked a similar question: How was the newcomer going to fit into an already crowded field? Was it going to siphon off the men and money on which they depended? In any case, what was it going to do that had not been done before? There was little sympathy for the undertaking, and plenty of obstruction. Nevertheless, the company made headway against all difficulty, and showed that there was room for new development, even in the well-trodden field of the interior missions.

Alphonsus Liguori was a lawyer-turned-priest and a native of the city of Naples. Even before his ordination in 1726 he was attracted to missionary work. Initially, the mission field he looked toward was China — an impossible dream, perhaps, given that this was the very time that the Chinese missions were collapsing. Nevertheless, there was an inspiration close to hand. A missionary recently exiled from China, Matteo Ripa, had established a tiny seminary in the city, with the purpose of training men for a possible return to the Orient. As an expression of his hopes for the future, he named his house the "Chinese Residence." Alphonsus lived in the residence for some time and took over the ministry of its church; there were high hopes that he would enter the little congregation. However, an illness in 1729, and an invitation to convalesce at a country residence at Scala on the Amalfi coast, gave him an opportunity to live, and preach, among the local shepherds, and to grasp as never before the depth of their deprivation. From this time on, Alphonsus Liguori was drawn toward the abandoned poor of the countryside, that "China" that, as the saying went, lay "at the gates of Naples."

It is not difficult, in reading the histories of the foundation of the congregation, to imagine oneself back in the glory days of the Catholic Reformation. Here, in the bright glare of the Age of Reason, was an event, or series of events, that would have fitted comfortably into the Age of Faith. Liguori, it seems, had no thought beyond that of taking a group of men out to preach missions. But a nun in a convent in Scala, Maria Celeste Crostarosa, had a different message for him. In a series of visions the Lord told her that he wished her to propagate a new institute for women, "whose rule of life imitated that of Jesus himself"; he ordered her to write out that rule. This she did, and it was Liguori who was sent to examine the authenticity both of the rule and of her revelations. Upon his approval, a new institute of nuns came into being. However, he was more than a little discomfited a year later, in 1731, when Maria Celeste received a further revelation, mandating a new congregation of men, dedicated solely to the evangelization of the poor, with Alphonsus as its head. This was a far cry from his own design, which was simply to continue his practice of going out on mission with anyone who was ready and fit to join him. But because he himself lived close to the supernatural, and was ready with all his being to accept messages from heaven, he could not easily reject the nun's message. He shrank from its implications for himself, but he feared disobeying the command of God. His biographer recalled that he now suffered "a thousand agitations and anxieties."

In the small but select company of founders of religious orders, Alphonsus Liguori might seem to be an uncomfortable fit. He lacked the certainty of an Ignatius or the fire of a Teresa, or the regal assurance of a Mary Ward. He was delicate in body and in mind, sensitive and scrupulous, diffident of his own judgment and dependent on the advice and encouragement of others. A story told by one of his earliest companions, Giovanni Mazzini, illustrates this. After his encounter with Sister Maria Celeste and her revelation, Mazzini found him weeping alone. He spilled out his feelings, exaggerating (according to Mazzini) the impossibility of success. Mazzini tried to encourage him, pointing out that if God willed it, it would be taken care of. "At this he answered: But where are those people who will go with me? I answered: here I am, I am the first. . . . He immediately gave in and came to dinner."

But he did share two qualities with other founders: conviction and charisma. As for conviction, his early comrades testified that the sense of shock he had felt upon meeting the poor shepherds of Scala never left him, and that he believed profoundly that the spiritual care of such folk, and that alone, was to be his mission. As for charisma, the following years gave ample evidence of it. Alphonsus knew how to talk to simple people, how to arouse their religious sensibilities, how to fill them with the love of God *and* the fear of hell. Wherever he went they crowded to him, and in his old age revered him as a saint. He trained his followers in his methods: in simple language and in dramatic effects. They learned from him how to stir the people to contrition, how to train them in community and private prayer. Some of their practices, such as public self-flagellation and self-abasement, will seem abhorrent to us today, as they probably did to their more sophisticated contemporaries. But they worked with the people for whom they were intended. The Redemptorists brought religion back to a countryside where it had been largely lost, and planted it so strongly that it withstood shocks yet to come.

In the beginning the congregation survived politically for one reason only: its work among the peasantry benefited the state as well as the church. Even at that, the authorities' attitude was one more of sufferance than of support. Then, as the years passed, the political environment in which the Redemptorists had to function became steadily more unfriendly. The government of Naples, still a subaltern to the Spanish Crown, was more inclined to suppress existing congregations than to start new ones; this it proved by legislating a cap to the number of priests who could be ordained, and by getting rid of the Jesuits. So while giving Liguori permission to gather men together and go out on mission, it remained highly suspicious of his intentions. And with good reason. The government wanted an association of secular priests who would live together for practical purposes but take no vows. The institute that Liguori envisaged — and built — was a true religious congregation in the old style, whose members would live in community under the three vows of poverty, chastity, and obedience. As he put it, "the Redemptorist is to be a Carthusian at home and an apostle abroad." Witnesses would later recall that "the first house breathed nothing but penance and poverty," the poverty a matter of necessity but the penance self-inflicted. Did the royal ministry in Naples know that the men were sleeping on straw, scourging themselves, kneeling on the floor to eat their food, accepting humiliations from their brothers? If it did, it did not address the matter openly. As long as the Redemptorists went out and brought civility to the uncouth masses, it tolerated their monastic practices.

But it kept them on a short leash. It limited the amount of money they could receive in donations. It forbade them to expand beyond four designated houses, and even these four, it warned, were in no way to resemble monasteries. And it retained the right to close them and disband the congregation, at a moment's notice.

So the Redemptorists' continued existence depended on the king's good pleasure, which wavered up and down as his ministers came and went. Alphonsus decided to build some assurance into things, by establishing a house in the Papal States to which, if things got bad, his company could emigrate. This made good sense, but it was provocative; Naples would be bound to regard it as a contravention of the original understanding, and react accordingly. The later eighteenth century was a time when sovereign states guarded their powers jealously, against each other and against the papacy. In the mind of the Crown of Naples, the Congregation of the Most Holy Redeemer belonged to it, lock, stock, and barrel, and it had no business expanding outside the kingdom. In 1780 a new royal ordinance came down, handing over the governance of the congregation to the bishops, eliminating life in community, and replacing the three vows with simple nonbinding oaths. The unfortunate men had no choice but to obey, even though this threw confusion into their original constitution. And predictably, Rome reacted, forbidding "its" Redemptorists to accept the ordinance and depriving the Neapolitan branch of its canonical existence. With personnel and houses divided between two sovereign states, the congregation was cut in two, with the junior part retaining legitimacy and the original body being shut out in the cold. In his extreme old age, Alphonsus Liguori was no longer, in the eyes of the church, a member of his own order.

There is a happy postscript to this sad story. The two branches survived, and in 1793, several years after the death of the founder, they were reunited. In the meantime, a small band of Redemptorists hived off and made for Vienna. There, and later in Warsaw, they subsisted throughout the Napoleonic years and laid the groundwork for a great expansion in the nineteenth century. They became some of the world's most effective missionaries.

The Redemptorists' experience was not unique. The times did not welcome new religious congregations, and consequently, those that did appear had inauspicious beginnings. In northern Italy a similar institute of missionary priests, the Passionists, was founded in the same years and suffered the same sorts of harassments. These two, together with Montfort's little congregation in France, and a few others, were all that the eighteenth century produced. It was a meager crop, compared to the pulsating productivity of the sixteenth and seventeenth centuries. It was not for lack of good and well-trained men, or because they were poorly received by the people. Rather, the limitation on their activity came from above, from authorities suspicious of their intentions and unsympathetic to their religiosity. Indeed, what measure of toleration they did enjoy came from the fact that the ruling classes saw them as reliable agents of social control. As Voltaire himself put it, "I like my attorney, my tailor, my servants and my wife to believe in God because I can then expect to find myself less often robbed and less often cuckolded." There was no doubt about it: across Catholic Europe, the church had come to be considered an arm of the state.

"I Have a Voice within Me . . ."

". . . which tells me what is proper for me as a legislator and protector of religion to do or leave undone; and this voice, with the aid of divine grace and of the just and honest character that I recognize in myself, can never lead me into error."

So, in 1782, wrote the Habsburg emperor Joseph II to the pope. This powerful man, ruler by inheritance of the lands of Austria-Hungary, and by election of the Holy Roman Empire, was on the point of undertaking a radical reconstruction of the church within his territories. The first stage was the dismantlement of the religious orders.

Joseph was a devout Catholic, little affected in his own mind by Enlightenment thinking. But he was perhaps the most perfect specimen that the age had to show of a benevolent despot, which meant that he took the good of his people to heart and believed that he alone was in charge of procuring that good. Among other goods, he wanted to bring the church into modern times. To do this he decided to redistribute its wealth.

In the larger empire (German lands, for the most part) his freedom of action was limited by the dozens of sovereign powers, both ecclesiastical and secular, that had their own ideas on how to rule and what to do. The Peace of Westphalia, which ended the Thirty Years' War in 1648, had left all these powers in place precisely for that reason: to thwart the emperor's efforts at centralization. So Joseph had to leave these regions out of his calculations. But within the "hereditary lands" that belonged by right to the Habsburgs — Austria, Bohemia, Tyrol, Hungary, parts of Romania and the Balkans and northern Italy, not to mention faraway Belgium and Luxembourg — his only limitations, as he saw it, came from God.

However, doing anything for these lands was always a challenge, because they were such a welter of different populations, traditions, constitutions, and needs. This was as true of their religious structures as it was of their economic, social, or demographic makeup. In the Netherlands and in Tuscany, a relatively wealthy population supported a dense network of parishes, monasteries, and convents. But the farther east of the Elbe one went, the sparser was the population, the fewer the cities. Much of the territory was given over to great landholdings. Central Europe's broad plains had become the breadbasket of western Europe. Its wheat was transshipped through Baltic ports to Portugal, Spain, and the Mediterranean; its cattle made their weary way across land to the abattoirs of western cities, much as, a century later, their younger brethren would walk across America's plains to the slaughterhouses of the Midwest. Labor was provided by an enserfed peasantry. Whereas in western Europe serfdom had all but disappeared, here, starting in the seventeenth century, it had been restored and reinforced. It was a strange and contradictory system, in which powerful landlords grew rich by producing for the free market while their tenants remained trapped in a medieval bondage. A society of serfs and landlords did not make for a vibrant or forward-looking church.

Furthermore, much of Joseph's inheritance was still mission territory, in the sense that it had been regained in the not-too-distant past from the Protestants, the Uniates, and the Turks. The Habsburgs were the Counter-Reformation's most ardent champions, but even they could not undo the neglect and damage of many years. There had been little effort, as the Catholic population grew, to upgrade the parish network. The shortage of parish clergy, especially in Hungary, remained a perennial problem. Yet at the same time, the countryside was dotted with monasteries — few in number compared to western Europe, but for the most part very rich. These monasteries did provide priests for the surrounding parishes, but their contribution was only a drop in an ocean of need. Insofar as the countryside was evangelized at all, it was thanks to those traditional workhorses of Catholicism, the Franciscans, the Capuchins, and other mendicants, and the Jesuits.

As Joseph saw it, the situation could be mended if both monastic and mendicant orders were harnessed to a state-controlled program of church reform. All monasteries that did not serve some useful purpose would be closed, and their wealth turned over to a central religious fund. All mendicants (by Joseph's time, the Jesuits were gone) would be drafted into the secular clergy. With this infusion of men and money, the parish network could be greatly extended. Standards could be set for the training of priests, and their salaries could be raised. Schools could be opened and education made compulsory. Hospitals could be built. In time, the obscurantist devotions of the past, even though much loved by the people, could be cleared away. The emperor's hereditary lands would become a model of enlightened religion.

Joseph's reforms had a different objective from that of France's *Commission des Réguliers*. Loménie de Brienne had aimed to reform the orders, arguing that though there would be fewer monks, they would be better monks. Where reform was not needed, as in the case of the Carthusians, he left things alone. Joseph, on the contrary, aimed to do away in time with *all* religious orders, allowing a stay of execution only to those that were useful to the state. The contemplative orders, and (given that this was a part of Europe where the minuscule number of nunneries that existed were almost all cloistered) all nuns, were in his sights from the start. The Carthusians were among the first to go. Others followed fast: over seven hundred monasteries in all, and thousands of religious. On the positive side of the ledger, money poured into the state's religious fund, and with it several new dioceses and hundreds of new parishes were created. The secular clergy was swelled by thousands of ex-religious. However, reforms, no matter how well intentioned, bring uncertainty, and the short-term consequences for pastoral care were not encouraging. By the end of the reign the number of clergy, and vocations to the priesthood, had dropped significantly.

This ambitious project of church reform, known to history as "Josephism" or "Josephinism," was not, in the end, as thorough as its namesake had wished. There are various reasons for this. First of all, Joseph's window of opportunity was limited. Queens have a way of ruling for a long time, it seems, and his mother, Maria Theresa, was no exception. Joseph was nearing forty when he inherited the crown, and he was to die before the age of fifty. His brother and successor, Leopold, would prove much more conciliatory in his ecclesiastical policies. Second, the inevitable institutional drag that bedevils ambitious undertakings also hindered church reform. People simply could not be shuffled around quickly, especially if they had allies in high places, as the Franciscans did, for instance. Third, some of Joseph's schemes were too radical for the people to live with, as when he tried to dictate change to his subjects in the Netherlands. There, in the summer of 1789, a full-scale revolt broke out, financed and led by some prominent churchmen; Joseph, already a dying man, was forced to back off. Belgium's monasteries emerged triumphant, but for all too short a moment. In 1792 the French revolutionary armies invaded, and were driven out; in 1794 they returned, this time to stay. In 1796, under French occupation, all monasteries and religious houses were dissolved and their goods expropriated.

The French revolutionary armies did not reach Austria, however. There the assault on the religious orders was the work of a Catholic king, who throughout it all maintained his good standing with the pope. When he died, eight abbots could still be found to accompany his body to the grave.

"One of the First Acts of the Revolution Was to Attack the Church"

So wrote Alexis de Tocqueville in 1856. And the question arises: Was the French Revolution, figuratively speaking, an assassin already armed and lying in wait during the critical months of 1789? Was the Church already its victim of choice? Given the hindsight that we share with Tocqueville, the knowledge of the terrible events that were just over the horizon, it is easy to believe exactly that. And yet we can also regard the Revolution as an object lesson in the way that events themselves can take control and send the world tumbling into a vortex that it never intended. Or a monster of the kind that stalks children's nightmares, a benign creature that suddenly swells into a bloated, ravenous beast. "There was reason to believe that the Revolution, like Saturn, might devour in turn each of her children," wrote the revolutionary Pierre Vergniaud. Not long after, on October 31, 1793, he himself went to the guillotine.

Ten days after Vergniaud died, a celebration was held in Notre-Dame cathedral, a great "Festival of Reason," starring an actress dressed up as Liberty. The king was already dead, and the monarchy with him; now the official demise of Catholicism was being proclaimed. Its churches were either closed down or converted into "temples of Reason," its priests, monks, and nuns were in hiding, in exile, in prison, or dead. Across the country, convents were being turned into barracks, prisons, or storehouses; roadside crosses were being pulled down; the saints' names that identified many towns and villages were being erased. Even the calendar was being reworked, to obliterate Sunday and everything that Sunday stood for. The de-Christianization of France was being pushed ahead with venomous energy. A stunning reversal, to say the least, given that only four and a half years earlier this had been, to all appearances, a Catholic country.

How could so much have happened so fast? Was this a bolt out of the blue, or the onset, at last, of a storm that had been gathering for years? It is hard to give an answer. French society during the later days of the *ancien régime* certainly seemed Catholic enough, if we go by the standard measurements: Sunday observance, Easter communions, books of devotion printed and purchased. It did not reach the heights of religiosity seen in the Catholic Reformation, of course, but it was respectable. And in some ways it was infinitely better. The parish system was working efficiently, even in the depths of the countryside. The parish clergy was arguably the best-trained in Catholic Europe — a tribute to the centuries-long effort of Jesuit, Oratorian, Sulpician, Lazarist, and Doctrinaire colleges and seminaries.

But that was not the whole picture. The eighteenth century was in many ways an anti-Christian century. The Church had been taking a battering for many years. The best thinkers and writers of the times, the *philosophes* and *encyclopédistes,* were openly and persistently hostile to Catholicism; and Catholicism, alas, found no one of equal caliber to speak in its defense. It was difficult, when faced with brilliant polemicists like Voltaire and Diderot, to maintain one's dignity. In the fight for the hearts and minds of high society — high intellectually and high socially — they held the upper hand, without a doubt.

How far did their arguments reach into the minds of the French public?

If we go by the evidence, we must assume that the "public" (by which we mean those people, mostly urbanites, who followed the movement of opinion) were not totally won over by the *philosophes.* French men and women were still, by and large, Catholic and churchgoing. But they were not stuck in the seventeenth century. Too much had happened, in astronomy, in biology, in physics, in chemistry, to allow people to think that the world was the same place it had always been. There was a love affair going on with science, and a sort of optimism that in time every question would have its answer. Human behavior had also evolved. There was an intellectual excitement over the possibilities of a new social and political order. The country bristled with learned societies, and in every one of them someone was busy devising a new scheme for the improvement of society. Faced with that effervescence, religion made a poor showing; it offered no new ideas. Even among the faithful, the fervor was gone. Mysticism had given way to good grooming.

The clergy ranged from those of a circle-the-wagons persuasion to the accommodationists who identified, in varying degrees, with Enlightenment thinking. Among the latter were many good minds, but they had a difficult argument to make, in which compromise of any kind looked very much like defeat. Yet they had a case: the Enlightenment was offering important new values, of freedom, equality, and human rights. Why should these not be incorporated into official Catholicism? They were as aware as anyone else of the inequities of the present regime, and they welcomed the prospect of far-reaching reform in both church and state. Only later did they have to make the hard choice between faith and citizenship.

The French Revolution is now celebrated on July 14, the anniversary of the storming of the great fortress of the Bastille. In fact, it started earlier, when the representatives who had been elected to a three-chamber consultative body, the Estates General, forced an unwilling king to accept the transformation of that archaic body into a modern one-man, one-vote legislature. What the storming of the Bastille by the Parisian crowd did was to guarantee the revolution, by fending off possible royalist countermoves. Under the people's watchful eye, the *ancien régime* was systematically dismantled, privileges and ranks were cast aside. The public mood was euphoric. "Bliss was it in that dawn to be alive," Wordsworth would write. And among the blissful and the euphoric were many religious.

This was not surprising: the monastic community as a whole was literate, fond of debate and argument, sensitive to injustice, open to the currents of thought then running through society. A number of monks, in fact, were Freemasons. Many more were Jansenist-leaning, and therefore resentful of "despotism," whether practiced by king or by bishops. And as Gallicans they had no great love for Rome. In a different arena, quite a few of the friars were resentful that their work among the poor did not get the respect it deserved from the hierarchy. So the new call for freedom resonated among them, too. During the summer and fall of 1789 many of them supported the constitutional changes that took place, the renunciation of privileges and the reconfiguring of the National Assembly along egalitarian lines. They attended celebratory banquets, blessed revolutionary flags, and sang the *Te Deum* on special occasions. It was the beginning, they hoped, of genuine reform.

But in October 1789, only four months after the new National Assembly had been formed, the first warning shot was fired at French monasticism. A member rose to his feet and read out two letters from nuns in the city of Paris, both of which alleged that novices in their communities were being forced against their will to take solemn vows. The assembly reacted immediately, ordering that there be no solemn vows taken anywhere in the country until further notice. With this single vote the assembly was serving notice that, whatever path the new nation was going to take, monasticism was not coming along as a fellow traveler. Solemn vows were by their very nature incompatible with the individual liberty promised by the Declaration of Rights. Free men could not swear away their freedom. Furthermore, the new political wisdom dictated that in the all-encompassing state all subsidiary corporations must be liquidated, and religious orders were nothing but private corporations, practicing their own discipline and pursuing their own ends. Added to these arguments were the usual well-worn slurs against lazy, useless monks and pathetic, frustrated nuns. Already, things were not looking good for the monasteries of France. In February 1790 their worst fears would be realized: solemn vows were banned definitively, and the novices of all monastic orders, male and female, were ordered to go home.

But what was new? The *Commission des Réguliers* had suppressed several congregations; the Crown had banished the Jesuits. And the papacy had not protested. In many minds the state was perfectly within its rights to allow, or disallow, religious congregations within its borders. Furthermore, the suppression involved only the true monastic orders, those with solemn vows. The "active" congregations — Oratorians, Sulpicians, Lazarists, Daughters of Charity, and so on — who took only simple vows, or no vows at all, were not being targeted. Not yet.

So the dissolution of the monastic orders did not, in itself, cause too great a stir. But it was in fact a step in a much larger program, that of relieving the church of its property. The Crown was facing bankruptcy; that was why the delegates had been called together in the first place, and that was the problem they now had to solve. The only solution, they agreed, was expropriation of the church's assets — which, it was estimated, accounted for about one-fifth of the country's total wealth. In November the assembly voted that all ecclesiastical property be placed at the disposal of the nation. It was money, or lack of it, that lay at the heart of the confrontation between Catholicism and revolution.

The immediate implications were worrying, but still not fatal. Many churchmen already accepted that for the sake of the country the church must give up some of its wealth. The question was, how much? To determine exactly what its new assets amounted to, the assembly ordered an inventory of church property. Uneasily, the bishops gave orders to their people to cooperate, as across the country officials went from convent to convent, gathering up financial records, counting the spoons, checking the bed frames.

But the long-term outlook was grim. If it no longer controlled its own wealth, the church must look to the state as its paymaster. It must accept its agenda — or defy it. And the National Assembly had very different ideas of what the church should be. An Ecclesiastical Committee had already been struck, with instructions to redesign the clergy along modern lines. The plan it presented in March 1790 to the assembly came as a shock. The committee proposed that dioceses and parishes be reduced in number to correspond to the new administrative districts, that bishops and parish priests be henceforth elected by the voters, and that they be put on a fixed salary. There were to be no further ties with Rome, except those of common courtesy. In other words, the church would henceforth be reduced from pillar of the state to outright servant.

When they enacted this program, called the Civil Constitution of the Clergy, the men of the assembly had no inkling of the trouble it would cause. The previous reform activities of monarchies, including their own, allowed them to believe that anything they did was acceptable, as long as it made good sense (to them). The papacy had been silent about those past reforms, and it was remaining silent now. But as the year went on, opposition became more troublesome. The National Assembly decided to drive a stake through the heart of that opposition by demanding from the clergy an oath of loyalty to the new constitution, with the clear warning that anyone refusing to take the oath would lose his position and his pension. In the winter of 1790-1791, every priest practicing any official function, whether as parish priest or curate, hospital administrator, army chaplain, or college professor, was ordered to subscribe publicly to the Civil Constitution of the Clergy and everything it stood for. The consequences were disastrous for national unity. Across the country, close to 50 percent of all priests rejected the oath. They were immediately fired from their posts, and their benefices were given to the priests who took the oath. But this settled nothing. The people of France were faced with two sets of priests, one legal, one illegal. Matters became even more volatile when finally, in April 1791, Pope Pius VI officially condemned the Civil Constitution. Now the people were faced with the same two sets of priests, one orthodox but illegal, and one legal but schismatic. While the legal priests (called "jurors" because they took the oath) occupied the rectories, the illegal priests, the "nonjurors," said Mass in the convents, and anywhere else they could. Their followers were numerous enough to cause serious disturbance.

The following year saw a deadly sequence of events: the royal family's aborted attempt to flee the country; the threats, and then the actual invasion, by foreign powers; the deposition of the king by force and with bloodshed; and sporadic royalist rebellions in the west. The fact that so many unreconciled priests were roaming free and preaching defiance caused enormous anger among republicans. By September 1792 all spirit of accommodation was gone. France found itself divided within and in mortal danger from without. This was when the damage done by the oath became plain. The nonjurors and their supporters were seen to have cast their lot with the enemies of the Revolution; that made them a fifth column who, if left to their evil machinations, would destroy the country. How could patriots go off to fight the enemy while these enemies were left behind?

It was in this atmosphere of paranoia that the first great massacre of the revolutionary years took place. In early September, in Paris, a mob invaded the prisons where aristocrats, nonjuring priests, and other "enemies of the Republic" were being held. Fourteen hundred prisoners were killed, among them more than 250 priests. Elsewhere in the country, lynch mobs went in search of nonjurors. The writing was on the wall for all supporters of the *ancien régime*.

In January 1793 Louis XVI was guillotined. Catholic to the end, the king had clung to the church and it to him; together they went down to destruction. Ironically, the constitutional church, the church created in 1791 by the Civil Constitution, was soon to follow them. By the end of 1793, even those priests who had taken the oath were forced to relinquish their offices. The powers that ruled France were out in full cry against Christianity in all its forms — indeed, against God himself. It took all of Robespierre's authority to insist that there must at least be a Supreme Being.

"Wrench the Sons of the Republic from the Yoke of Theocracy"

In all this, where were the religious orders, the thousands of monks, canons, clerks, and friars, cloistered nuns, nursing and teaching sisters who had played such an integral part in the country's history?

One after the other their communities fell to the Revolution. The clearing of the monasteries came first, beginning in 1790. At that stage it was courteous, though ruthless. The National Assembly had decreed that all monks and nuns should have a pension to suit their status — that is, generous for ex-abbots and ex-abbesses, modest for the middling sort, miserly for ex–lay brothers and ex–lay sisters. No one who had taken solemn vows should be forced to leave religious life, but those monks who wished to persevere would be consolidated in larger communities, leaving their former properties available for expropriation. Nuns would be allowed to live out their lives in their own houses, though as tenants rather than owners. It was their choice. Not a few monks opted for secularization, some of them gladly, some with great reluctance. Others stayed on, though the shock of being thrown into composite communities with different practices and traditions left them disoriented and discontented. "It is not we who are leaving our Order, but our Order that is leaving us," they complained; and in time, many of them gave up the struggle. Nuns, in overwhelming numbers, chose to stay in their convents, thus giving the lie to one of the favorite canards of the Enlightenment, that they were all "prisoners sighing for release." The nonmonastic congregations, both male and female, were left alone, as were their properties. The Oratorians, the Brothers of Christian Schools, the Sisters of the Holy Child Jesus, and scores of others went on teaching; the Daughters of Charity along with all the other secular nursing sisters went on nursing. The hope from above was that they would find their place and continue their good works, as ordinary citizens of the republic.

In 1791 the oath crisis changed all that. In both monastic and secular congregations there were many priests who performed public service. Now all of them had to take the oath or step down and lose their pensions. They broke both ways, for a variety of reasons, some laudable, some base and self-serving. But one thing was clear: those who saw their way to taking the oath had all sorts of career opportunities, at a moment when nonjuring parish priests by the thousands were being deprived of their benefices. The jurors' future as republicans was mixed; some went on to become willing agents of the Terror, but many served their new parishes in all good conscience until de-Christianization sent them packing. Their justification for staying was a pastoral one. How could it be right to leave the faithful without guidance, without the sacraments? But to be honest, the faithful had their own ideas. In some parts of the country the constitutional *curés* were received enthusiastically, while in others they had to endure harassments and empty churches. In some places the congregations happily blended their religious and republican ceremonies, while in others resistance was so stubborn that the National Guard had to force-march parents and their newborn infants to the constitutional baptismal font. On the subject of its religion, France was hopelessly split.

The nonjurors faced a dismal future. In the beginning they were able to say mass, preach, and administer the sacraments without too much interference, but as the republic's fortunes took a turn for the worse, they were driven into a tighter and tighter corner. Finally they were proscribed by law. Many of them were imprisoned or deported to Guiana. Not a few were killed, either by the law or by lynching. But a significant number of brave souls continued to function, in private houses and in convents, or wherever they could.

As for the nuns, still hidden inside their cloisters, they were limited in the ways that they could defy the Revolution, but they managed to attract the rage of the "patriots" by hiding and supporting nonjuring priests and inviting the faithful to come to hear "real" masses in their chapels. If they ran schools, they insisted on teaching their students according to the old catechism. More and more, the exasperated authorities saw their communities as nests of fanaticism, which had to be cleaned out for the public good. At the same time, the noncooperation of the secular brothers and sisters put a damper on the good will that the men of the Revolution had at first felt toward them. Schoolmasters and schoolmistresses who surreptitiously taught the banned religion, nurses who pressured the sick and dying to repent and return to the fold — what use were they to the brave new world? Better to get rid of them altogether. In September 1792, shortly after the deposition of the king, the first legislature of the First Republic ordered the liquidation of *all* religious communities, male and female, monastic and secular. Thousands of men and women were set adrift, to survive as best they could in a disintegrating world. Many faced imprisonment, deportation, and death; many more quietly composed their differences with the regime and found a way to keep out of sight. Some clung together, in tiny clandestine communities. Some chose to emigrate, and in doing so found footholds in foreign lands.

Robespierre fell in 1794, and with his fall came the end of the Terror. There followed a miserable interim of upheaval, corruption, and revenge killing. Throughout these, the last turbulent years of the century, the religious orders in France had no history; they simply did not exist. Individuals made their mark: at one end of the spectrum was Fouché, the ex-Oratorian turned anti-Christian revolutionary who later became Napoleon's terrifyingly efficient minister of police; at the other, Emery, the Sulpician whose carefully reasoned leadership throughout the whole ordeal earned him the title of "conscience of the French clergy." Some ex-religious became armed insurgents, others became bandits, killing and robbing with the best of them. The vast majority just stayed out of sight. But whatever they chose to do, they were on their own. For about ten years there were no religious congregations in France.

Then, with the new century, came Napoleon and dictatorship. Under him order was restored to the country, and the French church was allowed to come back to life, or at least to a sort of half-life. Napoleon did not share the anticlerical zeal of the revolutionaries; rather, his thinking was in tune with that of his *ancien régime* predecessors. Religion, he believed — and often affirmed — was an essential component of an orderly state. And of all religions, the one most suitable for France, "the single anchor amid storm," as he himself put it, was Catholicism. Furthermore, on a practical level, he realized that reconciliation with the Catholics of France was necessary if the nation was ever to be strong and united. Almost immediately upon taking power, he entered into negotiations with the papacy for a new concordat.

The agreement that was finally ratified in 1801 restored Catholic worship in France, but at a cost. More than ever before, the church was the salaried servant of the state, and subject in many new ways to the state's oversight. It was also going to continue being poor: none of its confiscated property was going to be given back. The concordat caused much bitterness among French churchmen, who felt that after all they had gone through they were being sold out. Among those most certainly sold out were the religious orders, who were not to be invited back into the country. Only those congregations that Napoleon deemed "useful" were to be reconstituted.

With almost half of its clergy gone, the church that crept into nineteenth-century France was impoverished, exhausted, and deeply wounded. But it was still alive.

"Morally, Theft from God; Juridically, an Illegitimate Usurpation"

The destruction of monasticism was over in France, for all intents and purposes, by the end of 1792. Across great swaths of the rest of Europe, it was just beginning. There was a difference. Although there were sporadic bursts of revolutionary enthusiasm here and there, the antimonastic campaigns were nowhere else homegrown as they were in France. They came in the train of the French armies, the "liberators" of much of the Catholic world. The pattern was much the same: suppression of monasteries and nunneries, with pensions for the dispossessed as long as they behaved themselves; a conditional tolerance for the nursing and teaching orders; expropriation and sale of the monasteries' property, but with a difference now, as many of their art treasures were parceled up and taken back to Paris. And more and more draconian measures, as people began to fight back. Before long, the liberators were recognized, and hated, as despoilers, and their message of Liberty, Equality, Fraternity was forever tainted.

Belgium (once the Spanish, now the Austrian, Netherlands) and parts of the Rhineland were the first to fall to French expansionism. The Austrian/Prussian invasion of France, so confidently begun in August 1792, had sputtered within months, and before the end of the year French forces had driven the invaders out and were pouring north and east across the borders. In no time the process began in the conquered territories, of suppressing monasteries and confiscating property. But little was accomplished before the French were forced to fall back. Jubilantly, monks and nuns and other "enemies of the republic" returned to their properties — but not for long. By 1794 France's armies were on the march again, and this time the occupation would last for a long time. Belgian Catholicism's bitter years began in earnest in 1797, with the suppression of the religious orders, the despoliation of the churches, and, a little while later, the imposition on the clergy of an oath of submission to the republic, an oath almost nobody agreed to take. In retaliation, some eight thousand priests were ordered deported to Guiana, and the fact that only a few of them actually took the journey can be attributed to the connivance of their parishioners, and the effectiveness of the British naval blockade that made such crossings problematic. They stayed around and made life difficult for their foreign masters — and of course, reaped the inevitable consequences.

In the Belgian occupation we see republican tyranny at its worst, and its most counterproductive. Belgians did not want to see their churches closed and their holy sites profaned; they rebelled against the persecution of their priests. In Belgium the priests, monks, and nuns who stood up against the occupation were seen as freedom fighters; this identification of Catholicism with national freedom was a legacy that lasted into the nineteenth century, making Belgium one of the most liberal of Catholic countries.

Elsewhere the story varied with the circumstances. The French invasion of Italy, which began in 1796, did not involve the same measure of harshness, in large part because Napoleon was in control, but also because Italy claimed a significant number of churchmen who welcomed the prospect of democratic reform. A policy of co-option seasoned with targeted benevolence and a large dose of outright bullying tended to get the conqueror what he wanted. Even the occupation of Rome and the expulsion of the pope along with most of the cardinals came off with only minor disturbance. A generally unprepossessing pope, Pius VI did not command great loyalty among Italians.

Nor did the monasteries. The suppressions and confiscations began in 1798, and before the end of the French occupation almost all monasteries in Italy had disappeared, leaving only communities of teaching and nursing sisters, and a few brothers, still standing. The confiscations netted a huge haul for the regime, in real estate and tons of gold, silver, and precious stones. Connoisseurs carried off crates of valuable artworks to France — an anticipation of the work of Hermann Göring in another direction, in another century. But the reaction of the common people was muted. Eventually guerilla bands of peasants did form up, often with a priest or a friar at their head. But insofar as their anger had a religious cause, it was not the closure of a monastery or a college of canons, but insults to their own local church, or profanation of some object sacred to them, that fueled it.

Pius VI died in 1799, an exile and a prisoner. He was succeeded by Chiaramonti, the bishop of Imola, a gentle and holy Benedictine, whose chief attraction to Napoleon was his readiness to reconcile Catholicism with the new order. "Our democracy is not in the least in opposition to the precepts of the Gospel. On the contrary, it demands the virtue which only may be won through Christ." These words, spoken in a Christmas sermon in Christmas 1797, earned him Napoleon's remark, that "the Citizen-Cardinal of Imola preaches like a Jacobin." But Napoleon did not fully know his man. Chiaramonti did indeed see virtue in the new order; he did indeed put the words "Liberty" and "Equality" at the head of his letters. But between them, instead of "Fraternity," he placed the words "And Peace in Our Lord Jesus Christ." There were limits to his amenability.

Once elected, Pope Pius VII was swiftly put to the test. He was presented with a draft concordat and more or less told to sign on the dotted line. It was the best bargain he could get, but it came at a price: the church was allowed back into France, but as one religion among several, and placed firmly under the control of the state. Two years later a second concordat was mandated for Italy. In neither concordat was any provision made for the return of monks and nuns. Only the usual teaching and nursing congregations were to be tolerated.

Pius VII would later cross swords with Napoleon, showing that he was much more than "the emperor's chaplain" that contemporary gossip made him out to be. For daring to defy that emperor he, too, was kidnapped and imprisoned in France, but eventually, in 1814, he was allowed to return to Rome. Paradoxically, while the quarter-century between the fall of the Bastille and the fall of Napoleon saw a general weakening of the national churches, the papacy ended up gaining in strength — partly because of the example that this pope gave in adversity. But the Catholic world over which

Pius now presided was profoundly different from that in which he had become a monk so many years before.

*   *   *

In Germany, not only the church but also the entire political landscape was permanently changed by the French invasion. For a thousand years the Holy Roman Empire had been the presence at the center of Europe, a huge jumble of autonomous territories large and small, each with its own ruler, but all harnessed together under the suzerainty of the elected emperor. Since the early 1500s this emperor had been a Habsburg, the ruler in his own right of Austria and its possessions. When they were not feuding with each other, this assortment of statelets was feuding with him. And since the early 1500s, their natural quarrelsomeness had been intensified by the Luther rebellion and the religious divisions that flowed from it.

The Peace of Westphalia that ended the Thirty Years' War in 1648 reinforced the autonomy of the individual powers but otherwise left the Holy Roman Empire more or less intact. In other words, over three hundred "sovereigns" still ruled the roost in their own bailiwicks, large or small, as they had done since the Middle Ages. They held court, taxed their subjects, dispensed justice, conducted diplomacy, each according to his (or sometimes her) own tradition. The imperial institutions that were meant to tie them together were close to useless. An untidy arrangement to begin with, it became more and more ramshackle with the passing years — and more unrealistic. In a Germany that was more Protestant than Catholic, it perpetuated a system that favored Catholic power. It sanctified tradition and avoided innovation. It impeded local efforts to improve infrastructure. How, for instance, could a prince encourage trade and production in his territories if the route to market was interrupted by numerous customs barriers? or drive a new road through his lands if an independent abbey lay across the path?

Bishops and even monasteries held sovereign power in their own enclaves. Twenty bishops and thirty abbots and abbesses were princes of the empire, rulers of extensive domains and all the people who lived on them. Most everybody agreed that these ecclesiastical states were an anachronism, and several Protestant powers had lobbied in the past for their secularization. But it was easier said than done. Then, in a strangely indirect way, the armies of France solved the problem when they invaded and occupied the Rhineland in 1794-1795.

This rich and strategic territory had long been coveted by France, on the grounds that the Rhine itself was the country's natural boundary. France now possessed it, and had no intention of letting it go. It so happened that much of it belonged to ecclesiastical princes, the archbishops of Trier, Mainz, and Cologne, several lesser bishops and a few monasteries. All at once they were divested of their holdings. Unfortunately for them, they were, in the eyes of the major German powers, expendable. In long-running peace negotiations, stretching from 1795 to 1801, Austria and her allies, desperate to end the war, decided that for the sake of peace they must let the Rhineland go. The prince-bishops concurred, but argued that they should be compensated with other territories, farther east. However, the big players had other ideas: they, too, had lost territory west of the Rhine, and they were determined that their own interests must be served first. This could be done only by handing them comparable slices of ecclesiastical territory closer to home. And so the principle of "compensation through secularization" was anointed in the Peace of Lunéville (1801). France kept the Rhineland, and Austria, Bavaria, and Prussia sent troops to occupy the bishoprics in their own neighborhoods.

From there to a general expropriation of church lands was only a short step. In 1803 an imperial committee decreed that the property of *all* endowed foundations should be left to "the free and full disposition of the respective sovereigns." That meant the monasteries as well as the bishoprics. And thus began a scramble to expropriate that, in a few short years, brought an end to the monasteries of Germany. There was no ideological rationale behind the action as there had been in France in 1790. The secular rulers were not admirers of the Revolution, or even of the Enlightenment. Quite simply, they wanted the church's land, and the power that went along with it. The French invasion gave them the opportunity to get it.

Politically, the secularization empowered the greater German states, those able to take advantage of it, and weakened the lesser. By reducing the number of Catholic entities, it altered the balance of power in favor of the Protestant majority. And it gave the coup de grâce to the empire. Without the ecclesiastical states to support him, the emperor lost his hold over the rest. Weak within, and facing enormous pressure from France, he accepted the inevitable. In 1806 he abdicated the imperial crown. From then on he would only be emperor of Austria. The Holy Roman Empire had come to an end.

As for the monks and nuns, suddenly bereft of their monasteries, it was the usual depressing story. For those men who were able, there was alternative service in the parishes. For old monks and for nuns, there was a pension and the privilege of staying in their monasteries until they died. For others, there was secularization, pure and simple.

For some, there was emigration.

"When They Persecute You in One Town, Flee to the Next"

In early 1790, as the revolutionary government's legislation against the monasteries began to bite, a monk of La Trappe, Augustin de Lestrange, began to think about taking the community out of France. He was ahead of his time, though; people still hoped that the antimonastic tide would turn, or that when the country's monasteries were dissolved some of the more exemplary communities would be given a reprieve. La Trappe was certainly exemplary: it was well regarded in its neighborhood, it was still faithful to the life that Rancé had mandated over a century ago, and it boasted ninety-one monks, at a time when most monasteries in France were lucky to have ten. But when he took his thoughts to the prior, Lestrange was dismissed as a troublemaker and censured for his pains. With the passing months, however, his forebodings appeared more reasonable, and finally he was given the commission to go abroad in search of suitable accommodation. He found an abandoned Carthusian monastery in Switzerland, close to the French border, and was given permission by the senate of the canton to settle there with twenty-three of his fellow Trappists.

This was in 1791. Once established, their numbers grew swiftly. Then, in 1796, women began to appear, searching for a community. Lestrange gave them a nearby house, around which the brothers hastily built a wall. Within fifteen months, sixty-two women had entered the house, émigrés all, and most of them ex-nuns drawn from every corner of France, from every conceivable religious order and congregation. On this unusual community-on-the-fly Lestrange imposed the rule that he and his monks had adopted: the strict version of Cistercianism that Rancé had created for La Trappe, but now made stricter still. For the Trappist communities in Switzerland — the only Trappists left in the Western world — it was a life of perpetual silence; fasting for more than half the year; a diet of vegetables and grains seasoned only with salt, and without fat of any kind; five or six hours of sleep, four of work, nine of divine office, with what remained of the day divided between prayer and readings. No beds, just boards on the floor, and one set of clothes in which to live day and night. In the years to come these nuns would face vermin and cold and an extraordinarily short life expectancy of forty-one and a half years. And yet they came, and for the most part stayed, and in time fortified the community with new applicants from across Europe. By late 1797 they were sixty strong and, together with monks and assorted hangers-on, made up a Trappist population of 240, all living hand to mouth in precarious circumstances.

One of the entrants was Louise Adélaïde, daughter of the prince of Condé, and a member of the closed circle of "royals" that included many of the princes of Europe. Her presence was a godsend to Lestrange, in view of the threat that was hanging over his communities. For the French armies were now on the frontiers of Switzerland, and in his opinion it was time to move on. Looking for a sanctuary, his eye fell on Russia, where the ruler was none other than Louise Adélaïde's "cousin." As Lestrange explained: "Since I knew that before entering the monastery she had [known] the Emperor Paul I, I told her, 'You should write to him to see if he would receive us in his states.'" And so it befell. Soon afterward, in the spring of 1798, as French troops began their march on Berne, he led his ragtag army of monks and nuns and women and children eastward, hoping to reach Russia but ready to accept any refuge anywhere.

The trek, which took up most of the year, was an extraordinary feat of management on Lestrange's part, as he shepherded his people through unfamiliar territory, without any sure knowledge of what lay ahead. Divided into three groups, they traveled by water and by land, on foot or in any conveyance that happened to come their way. Several word pictures have been left to us of their journey down the Danube on two great rafts, one for the men, one for the women; and of their efforts to sing divine office as they went, to the fascination of the locals gathered on the banks. When night came they climbed ashore, ate whatever the brothers could scare up, and slept wherever they could — on the ground, if necessary. If there was a church close by, and a Mass to be celebrated, they tried to attend it. Once this led to an embarrassing misunderstanding. The whole troop marched to the church in procession — monks first, children and their attendants second, and nuns last — only to learn that the onlookers assumed that monks and nuns were husbands and wives! From that time on, the nuns were kept in covered vehicles.

What strikes the reader is the remembered kindness of the population, Catholic or Protestant, toward these unfamiliar wanderers in their dirty clothes. The difficulties and delays they did experience came from officialdom, from the rulers of the enclaves through which they passed (for this was still the old empire, broken into scores of states) and from the border guards who flagged them down and kept them waiting, sometimes for days. The official nastiness was understandable. Much of the country through which the Trappists traveled was Josephist territory, which considered itself rid of its monks and nuns — and here they came again, the very epitome of the monkishness that Joseph had most despised. To make things worse, they were far from being the only refugees in eastern Europe; the empire was teeming with émigrés, impoverished and desperate and . . . well, foreign, and therefore possibly subversive. Their presence created feelings that our modern world may recognize.

And to cap it all, the years of the Trappists' exile were the very years when the empire was beginning to cave in under French pressure. Too much kindness now to émigrés might have serious consequences later. If they were allowed to stay at all, it was only for a short time, or in limited numbers. Lestrange broke his community into smaller groups, one in a country house here, another in an abandoned convent there — in fact, wherever he could leverage a welcome, and for as long as that welcome would last. When the welcome grew cold, they moved on. In the end, only a handful of monks and nuns made it to Orcha in Belarus, just ahead of the severest winter in memory. Then, after eighteen months, and for political reasons they could not possibly understand, they were ordered to leave the country within a fortnight. They had to retrace their steps into territory that was becoming more unstable, more insecure by the day.

The experience of the Orcha communities was replicated over and over during those years, by refugees from the French Republic wandering back and forth in search of a safe haven. The history of Napoleon's wars is not a history of constant, uninterrupted French expansion. There were shifting alliances, military advances and retreats; territories were occupied, then liberated, then occupied again. Each ebb and flow provoked a corresponding movement of people, as refugees fled, then flooded back, then fled again.

Finally, with the fall of Napoleon, many of the survivors made their way back to France. Among them were five communities of Trappist monks, four of nuns. But some colonies stayed behind in Germany, Belgium, and Switzerland, and put down roots. Most surprising was the continuing welcome that they, along with some other religious communities, found in England. Although still fundamentally anti-Catholic, this country was even more fundamentally antirepublican, and its sympathy for the victims of the Revolution to some degree wiped out its horror of papists. Thus the émigrés, monks and nuns included, who arrived on its shores were treated gently. And from that time on, England had a Trappist presence.

This is one of the legacies of the French Revolution. In its efforts to destroy monasticism, it in fact metastasized it. It started a practice of out-migration of religious communities that in time would impact the whole world. Nineteenth-century France, though a resolutely secular nation (apart from a couple of monarchist/imperial blips that only reinforced its resolution), was the world's most fertile breeding ground for religious congregations. Sporadically the government would try to get rid of them, and they would pop up somewhere else, in America, in Europe, in Africa, in Asia.

*   *   *

The eighteenth century had severely tested the principle of consecrated religious life. Public support had declined, the intellectual trendsetters of the times had grown increasingly critical, government after government had indulged in policies of slash and burn — and after all this, de-Christianization and the Terror. But the case has been made that the experience had been salutary, that the orders and congregations that went through the trial by fire came out in much better shape to face the future than those — in Spain and Portugal, for instance — that did not. Without a doubt they were poorer, leaner, hungrier. The wealth they had enjoyed, and the social status, was gone. But so were the ennui and the self-questioning. "It is certain, by experience, that those religious who before the Revolution could not be persuaded to wear their habit, are those who are the most determined to wear it now." So complained a republican in 1792. And it continued to be the case. Monasticism, and the different forms of religious life that developed from it, has been shown to thrive on adversity. Nothing in recent history has so galvanized the Society of Jesus as the murder of its six members in El Salvador. No order of nuns in recent years has had the drawing power of the poor nuns of Calcutta.

When Pius VI died in 1799, his authority totally undermined by the major powers, his own realm under occupation, his cardinals scattered and impoverished, himself a prisoner in exile, the papacy had fallen so low that it seemed unlikely ever to recover. But a new pope, in a new century, proved the predictions of gloom and doom to be wrong. The Roman Catholic Church was set to rebound, and with it, the religious orders that were its strong right arm.

Suggested Reading for Chapter 5

The eighteenth century is not a favorite subject for church historians, at least until the revolutionary years at its very end. You can see why if you read John McManners's *French Ecclesiastical Society under the Ancien Regime* (1960). Church life was just too bland, too undramatic to inspire great interest. For a look at the mood of the times, you can read W. Callahan and D. Higgs, *Church and Society in Eighteenth-Century Europe.* While there was considerable public disaffection, the secular clergy had made great progress, as *Priest and Parish,* by Timothy Tackett (1977), points out. But one of the characteristics of the Enlightenment years was a general loss of respect for monasticism. For an exhaustive study of the journey of the monasteries of Europe from heyday into ruin, see *Prosperity and Plunder,* by Derek Beales (2003).

The religious orders still held the high ground in education, hospital care, and social welfare. Some of this can be seen in *The Charitable Imperative: Hospitals and Nursing in Ancien Regime and Revolutionary France* (1989), by Colin Jones.

A great deal has been written on the Revolution. A good introduction is found in *The Oxford History of the French Revolution,* by William Doyle (1989). And for more, read *Citizens,* by Simon Schama. For the most part, however, the reader finds little about the religious orders, lost as they were in the general conflagration.

CHAPTER 6

The Nineteenth Century: "A Time to Build Up"

In 1815, Europe's forward march seemed set toward peace. By midsummer Napoleon, after his brief return to power, had suffered his final defeat at Waterloo and was on his way to Saint Helena, on the other side of the world and beyond any hope of returning alive. It was a time of restoration. Louis XVIII, brother of the executed king and heir to his throne, had been brought back to France "in the baggage of the allies," after promising his wary people that he would rule, henceforth, as a limited monarch with a bicameral assembly. In Vienna, the victorious powers had just reached a settlement that redesigned the map of Napoleon's broad empire. From now on, so the plan went, Europe was going to consist of a checkerboard of sovereign states, well balanced so as not to threaten each other's interests. As international agreements go, the Vienna settlement was highly successful; it would keep the Continent at peace for nearly forty years, until fighting broke out in the Crimea in 1854.

But if the top crust was stable, the same cannot be said for what lay beneath. Here there was a restlessness that could easily turn to discontent, discontent that had all the makings of outright rebellion. Many people who had lived through the revolutionary years had themselves become revolutionary in spirit. They knew from their own experience that the status quo could, in fact, be overturned. They remembered the dreams and the possibilities, and they remembered the grudges. Then there were other people — and many of them — who had lost too much in the Revolution, who hated its very memory and hoped, now that it was over, to erase every trace of it. They longed for a restoration of law and order and the certainties of the past. But even as they longed, the old world that they valued so deeply was fading away. Another revolution even greater than the political one was invading their lives. The wars had prevented the Industrial Revolution from taking hold in continental Europe, but it was there now, and people would soon feel its effects. As the times turned ugly, with overcrowding in the cities and factory chimneys spewing deadly smoke, with the intelligentsia coming up with new political theories and the "dangerous classes" talking revolution, the people who looked to the past looked at it with ever more yearning, dreaming of a golden age in which the rulers ruled and the people obeyed, and everyone feared God. In other words, the *ancien régime.*

There were other people, too, who over the last decades had done very nicely. They had grown rich through the Revolution. But more than that: they had been changed by it; they had internalized its principles of liberty and individualism. They had no desire to return to the caste-ridden society of the *ancien régime.* They accepted the return of the dynasties, but without great warmth. As for the Church, their attachment to it had thinned, or vanished altogether. In their eyes the past was dead and the people who wanted it back were dinosaurs. However, they had not "bought" the whole revolution. The concepts that the old revolutionaries bled for, like equality and sovereignty of the people, they thought chimerical and dangerous. The world they desired would be a meritocracy, forward-looking and liberal, but solidly anchored in wealth and property.

"The Seeds of Civil Discords Are Cast upon the Soil of France" — France, 1800-1900

There is every reason, when considering the nineteenth century's travails, to look first at France. Here was the rest of Europe writ large. Every resentment, every anxiety, every contradictory emotion that Europe felt in the aftermath of the Revolution was felt most acutely in France. The nation's psyche was brimming with anticlericalism, and yet, at the very same time, there was a widespread clamor for the return of religion. Part of society craved the Church's presence, another part dreaded its power. Successive governments struck at the Catholic interests, and then, as power changed hands, turned around and coddled them.

France after Napoleon was governed by five regimes in sixty years. From 1814 to 1830, the last of the Bourbon kings ruled the country: first Louis XVIII, elderly, weary, and, like the English Charles II many years before but in similar circumstances, concerned above all that he should not "go on his travels" again; then his brother, Charles X, a reactionary if ever there was one. In 1830 a brief revolt ousted Charles. From then until 1848 there was the "bourgeois monarchy" of the Bourbon kings' close relative, Louis-Philippe, duke of Orléans. In 1848 revolution led to the establishment of the Second Republic. In 1851 a coup d'état led to the creation of the Second Empire under Louis Napoleon, nephew of the great man. In 1870, after the disaster of the Franco-Prussian War, the overthrow of the empire and a brief interval of disturbance preceded the establishment of the Third Republic. Within those regimes came a giddy succession of ministries. Tempers were too hot, differences were too great to allow the political tranquillity that the country needed. Royalists, republicans, liberals, Freemasons, radical ex-Jacobins, ultra-Catholics: their mutual hostility was sharpened by fear of each other's motives, and by a fierce self-interest. Catholic parties used the new liberal freedoms where they could, but were, in general, perfectly ready to undermine those same liberties if it paid them to do so. Their secular enemies stalked them with the undeviating vengefulness of a Jabert tracking down a Jean Valjean. In the end, victory went to Jabert. In 1901, 1904, and 1905 the National Assembly succeeded in dismantling the Church's privileged position. But not before France had become the powerhouse of the Catholic world.

France, post-Napoleon, seethed with contradiction. This was the country that had killed its king and done its utmost to eradicate its religious heritage. Yet here was another Bourbon king on the throne, and here was Catholicism seeping back in, not the dry Enlightenment-tinged Catholicism of the eighteenth century, but a new assertive no-holds-barred Catholicism that would come to strike alarm into liberal hearts. The Bourbon kings did not last, but Catholicism did. Although the population at large went to church less often, and though the "godless" elements in society were certainly gaining ground, a strong religious revival took hold and continued to gather strength through most of the century. It was fueled by the most massive expansion of religious orders ever seen. In 1800 there were few regulars to be found anywhere; by 1900 they were everywhere, men and women both, in their hundreds of thousands. France produced more new orders than the rest of the world combined, and sent them out in record numbers. Throughout the century, two missionaries out of every three were French.

*   *   *

Their recovery began with Napoleon Bonaparte. The great man, no ideologue himself, had seen the turmoil that de-Christianization had caused in his country, and decided to be done with it. In late 1799, shortly after he seized power, he ordered an end to religious persecution. Within months he was in contact with the papacy, outlining his plans for the reestablishment of the Catholic Church in France. In 1801, after some hard bargaining, a concordat was signed and the Church was allowed to reenter the country, under terms largely dictated by himself. The terms were stiff. Catholicism was no longer to be considered the "dominant" religion of Frenchmen; given the secular nature of the state, other faiths must be respected. There were to be fewer bishoprics, and the men who filled them were to be chosen by the government before being instituted canonically by the papacy. They, and the lower clergy under their control, were to swear an oath of fidelity to the constitution and to instruct the people in due deference to the state. As regards the church's very considerable prerevolution property, there would be no question of return. Too much of it had been put to other uses, or passed into private hands, and no one — not even the great Napoleon — would consider stirring up that hornet's nest. In sharp contrast to their wealthy forebears, the new hierarchy were expected to live modestly on salaries provided by the state.

In all this Napoleon had his reasons. He was counting on the return of religious normalcy to pacify and calm the country, leaving him and his army free to follow his imperial designs. A widely publicized entente with the pope would also play well in the occupied Catholic territories — Italy, Belgium, and the Rhineland. Even better: France, once more the "Eldest Daughter of the Church," could replace the enemy, Austria, as the protector of the Holy See, and perhaps even lead the way to peace in Europe. "With Catholicism, I was sure to succeed in all my great plans," he later wrote. But there was an important proviso: this Catholicism had to be subject to him. "A nation must have a religion," he said, "and that religion must be under the control of the government."

The new pope, Pius VII, also had his reasons. He knew he had a weak hand to play. The Church had no infrastructure left in France, and religious practice everywhere in the country was suffering for it. Half a loaf was surely better than none. Furthermore, French armies were sitting in northern Italy, within a stone's throw of Rome, and it made good sense not to provoke them. Inevitably, some in the Curia urged defiance, but Pius decided to sign the concordat and to swallow all its humiliations. By doing so he gained a place in France for a Catholicism that was fully in tune with

Rome's teachings, and he allowed the ten-year-old schism to end. There would once more be a network of priests to serve the faithful. The dismissal of the bishops was a hard blow, but it ended well for the papacy. They had been a proud lot, those *ancien régime* bishops, with a strong sense of their own autonomy; their replacement by new papally approved men left Rome in charge of the French church more completely than ever before.

The chief losers in the deal, apart from the bishops, were the religious orders. There was not a word about them in the concordat. In the new arrangement of things, it appeared, they were simply not going to exist. Little by little, however, they edged their way back in, partly through their own determination and partly because the government recognized that it needed them after all. In the *ancien régime* a huge part of the country's educational and social services had been provided by them. The ideologues of the Revolution had dismissed them, but at great cost to French society. Now Napoleon took another look at them. His criterion, though, was "utility"; only those that he deemed useful were to be invited in. It was their practical service, not their prayers, that interested him. "You will see what use I shall be able to make of the clergy," he remarked to one of his associates.

Most useful among the regular clergy, in his mind, were the Priests of the Mission, or Lazarists, the congregation named after the Parisian church of Saint-Lazare where Vincent de Paul had first gathered his followers together some 150 years before. Their principal work had been the interior missions and the training of priests for rural parishes. This was something the new government needed to restore if it wanted its policy of pacification to work. But another of their activities was even more interesting to Napoleon. When the Jesuits were suppressed in the eighteenth century, the Lazarists were handed many of their functions, including their foreign missions in China and the Middle East. These, added to the posts they already manned in North Africa, made them useful listening posts for France overseas. Through the revolutionary years, even as the Lazarists in France were smashed and scattered, their colleagues in the missions continued on, protected by distance and by the mother country's absorption in its own immediate problems. Now Napoleon, with his eyes fixed on the wider world, recognized their potential as instruments of soft power that he could use to his advantage. What was more, he feared that if France did not embrace them, the British might, a not unreasonable fear, considering the way the Royal Navy was ranging freely around the Seven Seas.

But in the political climate following the Revolution, any tenderness toward regulars was likely to lead to trouble. Anticlerical feeling still ran high in the nation's ruling circles, and Napoleon had to move cautiously if he wanted to reinstall the Lazarists. The solution was to entrust them, officially, with one task only: that of preparing missionaries for service abroad (no mention being made of work in the mission fields at home, the purpose for which Vincent de Paul had founded them). In this limited capacity they, along with two other foreign mission groups, were allowed back into France.

There was a second powerful reason to bring back the Lazarists. They were the spiritual guides of the religious company that Napoleon really did admire: the Daughters of Charity. The Daughters, of course, had long had a special place in French society. Their company harked back to the 1630s, when Vincent de Paul had begun recruiting women to act in a support role, so to speak, for his priests: to bring physical and material care to the people the priests were evangelizing. Before many years had passed, the sisters were working in hospitals; a century later they were recognized to be among the most capable nurses in the world. The Revolution would gladly have found a way to keep them on, even as it was dispersing most other religious orders. But the sisters' stubborn fidelity to their church made them a lightning rod for the patriot extremists, and they, too, were forced to disband. They spent the revolutionary years working wherever they could: alone, or in groups of two or three, or — more and more as time passed — in little communities that were sometimes clandestine, sometimes open, depending on the tolerance of their neighbors. They survived because they were useful. By 1797, in spite of the waves of repression that swept across the country, they had already opened some two hundred houses.

In 1800 Napoleon gave the Daughters of Charity back their legitimacy, and followed up with a house in Paris all freshly repaired, plus a handsome sum of money. One thing was lacking, however. These sisters belonged to the family of Saint Vincent de Paul; they had always had his priests as directors, and now that they were reinstated they wanted them, and no other. In a gracious gesture to "these good women," as he called them, Napoleon agreed to restore all their previous prerogatives, including the right to have Lazarists as directors. And so in 1803 the Lazarists were brought back, in a support role, one might say, for the sisters, though on the side, and without fanfare, they were allowed to resume their interior missions.

But even with official backing the congregation was slow to take hold. In 1808 the superior general, Dominic-François Hanon, could count a total of only twenty-one Lazarists in Paris, plus a few more in the provinces, who had actually been reunited, while another sixty were waiting in the wings, and this at a time when the French Daughters of Charity numbered over sixteen hundred. As it turned out, even the small foothold that the Lazarists had gained in France was about to be taken from them. In 1809 Napoleon, he of the tidy mind, looked out across his domain and saw that all sorts of communities of sisters — not just the Daughters of Charity — had sprung into being and were doing useful work. He decided that they should be amalgamated into one giant congregation and placed under the direction of the bishops, with his own mother, the powerful *Madame Mère,* as overall protectress. This meant, among other things, detaching the Daughters of Charity from the Lazarists. Monsieur Hanon at once protested, and continued to protest so loudly that Napoleon decided to get rid not only of him but of all his tribe. "I no longer wish any missions," he wrote. And with that the entire French missionary effort was disbanded. The sisters were reorganized, the Lazarists were dispersed, and Monsieur Hanon was carted off to prison.

There was more involved here than Napoleon's pique at being contradicted by a mere priest. By now the pope, too, was giving trouble, so much trouble that in the summer of 1809 he was snatched from the Vatican and spirited away to five years of near-solitary confinement. The action backfired: the gentle Benedictine pope's living martyrdom turned him into a hero in many eyes, so that on the rare occasions when he appeared in public he was surrounded by respectful crowds. The amenability of the Catholic Church, on which Napoleon had counted for the enhancement of his *gloire,* was turning out to be a pipe dream. In reaction, he let loose, upon both the pope and the hierarchy of France, a fearful spate of bullying. While in this foul mood, in 1810, he ordered the suppression of all religious men's communities within his empire.

The French Lazarists had to wander in the wilderness for a few more years. In 1816, with Napoleon finally gone, the congregation was officially reinstated by the Bourbon monarchy. But its circumstances were painfully inadequate. The men had no hope of returning to the house at Saint-Lazare, which was now a prison; they had no money save that which the government gave them, and their nationwide membership had dropped still further. When a house in Paris was finally assigned to them and new seminarists began to trickle in, only fourteen old men were left to receive them.

But the congregation limped on. By the 1840s it had reached a total of eighty priests. It was slow to make progress, with its leadership forever caught in the political tangles of the times: the uncertainty arising from the ups and downs of the government in France, the conflicts over authority that continued to simmer between Paris and Rome, the challenges that came from Lazarists in other countries, notably Italy, who argued that because they now far outnumbered the French they should take charge of the congregation. Actually, these last challenges helped to cement successive French governments' support for the Lazarists. This was a *French* institution, the politicians never tired of insisting; it was *French* in its origins, its spirit was *French,* its leadership was, and must continue to be, *French.* Nationalism, as much as any appreciation of the congregation's intrinsic value, kept the governments' support. The leadership stayed in France, and the congregation, by cleaving cautiously to the secular power, eventually prospered. In 1870, some fifty years after its rebirth, its personnel numbered nearly two thousand — priests, brothers, and novices — working in Europe, the Americas, Australia, North Africa, and China. By 1900 that total number had passed three thousand.

Depending on who was in the ascendant at any given time, the religious orders were sometimes favored, sometimes tolerated, sometimes threatened. On the one hand, even their critics acknowledged that they served the country efficiently and at relatively little cost; also, that in a society that allowed for freedom of opinion, they had as much right as anyone else to exist. On the other hand, their double allegiance, to the state but also to the papacy, meant that their very existence had political implications, implications that grew more threatening as Rome itself became more political.

"The Pope's Legions": Rome and the Jesuits, 1800-1870

Pius VII was known in his own time as "the good pope." His gentle, suffering presence ignited a real affection in people living north of the Alps, an affection that later fed into the single-minded allegiance to Rome that we know as ultramontanism. Something else happened under his watch that had more negative consequences. In 1815 the papacy took back from the victorious allies what it had lost to Napoleon: the Papal States, a broad swath of territory running north and east from Rome that the Holy See had guarded as its patrimony since time immemorial. He and his three successors, Leo XII, Pius VIII, and Gregory XVI, were saddled with a temporal kingdom that they did not know how to rule well, and a subject population that had moved into the nineteenth century while they themselves remained stuck in the *ancien régime.* It was here, in their own backyard, that the popes ran up against all the things they did not like about the nineteenth century: liberalism, freedom of opinion, popular sovereignty; dancing and drinking and games of chance, women in form-fitting dresses, Jews free to live wherever they wished — even, for some reason, street lighting! And worst of all, a population that no longer tolerated clerical rule. The popes sent cardinals to manage these stiff-necked people, and the result was a string of running battles and some executions. The rest of Europe watched in fascination. The liberal-minded world came to the conclusion that the papacy was hopelessly fossilized; the popes came to the conclusion that all rebellion against authority — no matter how pernicious the authority — was damnable. In successive briefs and bulls they sent this message out to the faithful.

Catholics were divided. They were born into the Church but they lived in the world. How could they serve two masters? Was there an insoluble contradiction between their civic ideals and their religion? Some intrepid souls sought out a path to compromise, arguing that they could be liberal and Catholic at the same time. For many more, however, there was only one answer: if they wished to be true Catholics, they must be truer to Rome than to any other master.

To a great extent, the religious orders, both the old and the new, would be ultramontane. And (probably no surprise) the most ultramontane of them all would be the Jesuits.

Return of "the Soldiers"

The Society of Jesus had disappeared from western Europe in 1774. It still existed in Russia, but in circumstances of dubious legitimacy, and at the pleasure of the Orthodox tsars. Individual Jesuits were scattered around Europe and the New World, but with no recognized standing. In 1800 there could not have been more than a few hundred of them in all, dispirited and rudderless, mere shadows of the "soldiers of Christ" that Ignatius had created. But if the actual Society had shrunk, its reputation had not. Its detractors (and they were legion) still saw it as that dark force that plotted to dominate the world. Even the rumor of its return was enough to set their troops on alert. Its admirers saw it as the Church's best hope, and looked for its second coming. While they waited, some of them sought to model themselves along its lines.

Among these was a handful of young émigrés, officers in the royalist army living in Luxembourg, who came together in 1791 to form an informal religious community. There was nothing of permanence in the community's beginnings, neither name nor rule nor objective, nor even stability. Four times the men had to pick up and move, traveling ever farther east ahead of the oncoming French armies. But during this time of migration, which ended in Vienna in 1796, they took two steps toward self-identification. They took the three vows of religion, to which, in true Jesuit style, they added the fourth vow of obedience to the pope; they gave their organization a name, the Society of the Sacred Heart of Jesus.

Few of our contemporaries would grasp all that the title meant in the nineteenth century. For Catholics, the Sacred Heart of Jesus had long symbolized the Savior's loving mercy, and his desire that those who loved him should make reparation for the sins of mankind. In the seventeenth century the devotion gathered strength, after a series of visions to a French Visitandine nun, Margaret Mary Alacocque. It was promoted then and through the following century by the Jesuits, who used it to counter the dry, stern religion of the Jansenists. Later on, in the revolutionary years, it took on a political meaning. After learning that the king in his prison had made a vow to the Sacred Heart, ardent Catholics seized upon the action as a message to them from on high: in a time of godlessness, the link between Crown and religion was divinely ordained; thus when they defended the one they defended the other. The royalist forces of the Vendée were saying as much when they went into battle against the republic with the emblem of the Sacred Heart pinned on their breasts. In the bitter years of government-directed de-Christianization, the Sacred Heart came to stand for counterrevolution.

The king was soon to die, to be followed not long after by his loyal Vendéans. But the devotion to the Sacred Heart — an expression, if you will, of a militantly conservative approach to faith and politics — lived on, and prospered. No fewer than fifty-seven new religious congregations would be erected during the nineteenth century under the banner of the Sacred Heart, and most of them were, in some way, emulators of the Society of Jesus.

The little group of émigrés was among the first to make the connection. They were, as one of their historians has said, Jesuits in waiting. While still in Austria they made the acquaintance of an Italian society with similar leanings, and in 1799 the two groups entered into a brief union, under the more anodyne title of Fathers of the Faith. They were soon numerous enough to create colonies in Germany, Switzerland, England, and Holland. And some of their men slipped into France.

Here they came up against one of the most sinister characters of the period, Joseph Fouché, the ex-Oratorian-turned-revolutionary who was now Napoleon's highly efficient minister of police. It was not long before he knew of the men's arrival, and from that time on he kept them under surveillance. As long as they acted as simple priests they were perfectly legal; but Fouché had no doubts that these were Jesuits in all but name, and that they were going to assume a Jesuit role sooner or later. And sure enough, it was not long before their little company took charge of several secondary schools and began to organize lay congregations, the very activities by which, in the government's opinion, the Jesuits had once illegally sought to amass their power.

There now began a competition for the emperor's ear, with Fouché on one side and the minister of cults, Portalis, on the other. Fouché had certain advantages: first, since the Fathers of the Faith had not been officially authorized, their activity was partly covert, which gave them the appearance of a secret society; and second, Napoleon himself hated the Jesuits. He once wrote to Fouché: "I don't even want the name of the Jesuits spoken; anything leading to discussion about this society should be avoided in the journals. I will never permit its reestablishment in France." All that Fouché had to do was whisper the dreaded word "Jesuit," and his case was made. On the other hand, Portalis, who sincerely desired the restoration of a solid system of schools, argued that in the current broken state of education the Fathers of the Faith were the best teachers available. These two men worked at cross-purposes with each other, and the Fathers were caught in the middle, being called to different cities to set up school, then being thrown out, then starting up again somewhere else. Their resilience tested Fouché's patience, but he finally won the day. In 1807 they were dispersed, each to a different part of the country, where they were, by his orders, kept under permanent surveillance.

That was not the end of them, however. After Napoleon and his dreaded minister of police had departed the scene, and after the Society of Jesus had been restored by the pope, many of them became Jesuits.

In 1814, at last, the event that so many had desired came to pass. Pius VII officially resurrected the Society of Jesus, praising it as "the glory of the Church," calling upon it to come once more to the aid of that Church.

The image, however, far outshone the reality. The Jesuits were few in number, and they were scattered far and wide throughout Europe. The discipline for which they were famous had long since withered away, and they were not all sure they wanted to return to the past. However, the past was what they got. The election of one conservative general in 1820, and of an another, even more conservative, in 1829, and the disappearance from the Society of its most liberal members opened the way to a return to the extremes of sixteenth-century discipline. As time went on, the Society of Jesus was drawn further and further along the path of reaction. Throughout the rest of the nineteenth century it would be a bastion of ultraconservatism, and the strong right arm of an ultraconservative Rome.

People could not get over it. The Jesuit training, its "way of proceeding," seemed so archaic, so out of touch with the times. The insistence on instant, unquestioning obedience; the military precision that guided everything, even posture and demeanor; the submersion of the individual's will in the will of the institution: it all appeared to people to be unsustainable in modern times, and for a while there were questions as to whether the Society could survive. But survive it did, and prosper, because it still held to its high standards. By 1900, with over 16,000 members, it had become one of the Church's largest orders of men, and certainly its most powerful.

And just as it had before, the Society paid the price for its preeminence. For years at a time the Jesuits were banned from certain countries: from Prussia and Bavaria, for instance, until 1848; from Switzerland after 1847; from the Austrian Empire after 1848; from Spain from 1868 to 1876; from Germany after 1872; from France after 1880. They were usually able to slip back in sooner or later, because the men in power found it difficult to do without them — or, on some occasions, because the men in power could not withstand the nagging of their devout wives. But for many decades Jesuits had to live, metaphorically speaking, with their bags packed.

It is impossible to guess how much the presence of the Society of Jesus exacerbated the ill feeling between Catholics and secularists. But we can be sure it did no good. The outcry against the Jesuits began among the political elites. Even before the Society had regained its footing, its enemies were reviving the old mythology, no less dramatic for having lain dormant for so long. We can see this in France in the 1820s, when in the Chamber of Deputies accusations were flying against the Jesuits, and the rumor was circulating that their novice house was being used to train 50,000 members of the order in small-arms drill. It was a ludicrous idea, given that only a few hundred Jesuits were in France at the time. But they had already been branded as the archenemies of the nation, the movers and shakers of a great underground force, the fifth column that would be able to mobilize millions, when they so wished, to subvert the government.

As the Society grew in strength and numbers, the patriotic cries became more shrill, the accusations more hysterical. The Jesuits, it was said, had the whole Catholic population in thrall. Under their hands, good citizens of France were being turned into zombies, unable to think for themselves, "members of this gigantic body, whose will they mechanically perform." The Jesuits were intriguers, spies, seducers. Long before the term "brainwashing" came into being, the Jesuits were being accused of it. Long before the expression "conspiracy theory" was ever coined, they were the victims of one.

Why this extreme reaction?

Underlying it, surely, was the insecurity that secular Frenchmen still felt regarding their country's future. The feeling was reasonable enough, given the ongoing political instability, but anxiety can (and did) transmute into paranoia. With no external enemies on the horizon, the Jesuits became the villains of choice. And who was to say that the fear was totally misplaced? What these men, with the rest of the Catholic party, saw as a noble cause, the return of the people of France to the Church, did, in the nineteenth-century context, have the potential to destroy the legacy of the revolution. Legitimists and ultramontanists, led by the popes themselves, were openly proclaiming that lawful authority came from the top down, that the powers that rulers exercised — even if abusively — were given to them by God, so that there was no such thing as lawful rebellion. This, of course, was anathema to those who believed that sovereignty originated with the people. Between the two camps there stretched a no-man's-land that would not be crossed for many years.

But why the Jesuits? Why did they become, so spectacularly, the scapegoats for reactionary Catholicism?

The first answer is that they *were,* at that time, reactionary. The nucleus of the restored party, the men who came out of Russia in 1820, very swiftly took control of what had become a very wayward Society. Highly conservative, and completely out of touch with the currents of thought in western Europe, they were entrusted by the papacy with the task of restoring discipline; they repaid that trust a thousandfold. The more liberal members of the Society, who for the most part did not reside in Rome, were eased out, or at least constrained to remain silent. The rest submitted to an order of life and a way of thinking as rigid as any the Society had ever known.

The second answer is that they were strong; they occupied the high ground in the Church. As the popes, faced with turbulence in Italy and elsewhere, became more militantly antiliberal, they depended more on the Jesuit party in Rome for support and expertise. Before long the Jesuits were firmly ensconced in positions of power in the Vatican. When Pius IX ascended the papal throne in 1846, he found that though he did not like them much he could not do without them. With time he came to lean on them more and more, as his most trusted counselors and propagandists. As a result, other voices tended to be drowned out. John Henry Newman, even though he admired the Society for its high standards, was nevertheless still able to remark that "the Jesuits tend . . . to swamp the Church."

Pius IX was a kindly, warmhearted man whose fate it was to rule the church until 1878, during a period of deep crisis. He had flaws: an impulsive and none-too-intellectual nature, a tendency to be easily swayed by the advice of whoever happened to be near him. But he also had strengths: a deep sincerity of purpose that seems to have been altogether free of cynicism, and a charismatic personality that made him the idol of his people. He was, arguably, the most popular pope of all time (until the later twentieth century); at the same time, he was the despair of many serious Catholics ("liberal Catholics," he called them, with open hostility). Liberalism, the child of the eighteenth-century revolutions, had come to represent, in his mind, the taproot of everything that was wrong with the modern world; the fact that some of the faithful tried to work with it was reprehensible.

It had started differently. As bishop and cardinal, he had resisted the reactionary tendencies of the Italian hierarchy, and for that reason his election to the papacy had stirred the hopes of progressive Catholics everywhere. But his was a moderation combined with paternalism; he came to power convinced that as long as he governed the Papal States well, and stretched out an olive branch to those who opposed him, the immense restlessness that was roiling Italy would be pacified. He was soon made aware that his moderation was no match for the revolutionary, fiercely secular spirit that was sweeping the country. The Risorgimento, no respecter of papal dignity, rolled across the Papal States and, in 1848, took over Rome itself. The pope's spokesman was murdered; he himself was forced to flee. A republic was declared in early 1849, amid scenes of vandalism and iconoclasm. It lasted only a short time, and Pius, with the help of French arms, was reestablished on his throne. But the event shocked the pope, and he came back from exile convinced that the revolutionary cause must be fought tooth and nail.

The pope's change of heart marked a turning point in church history. From that point throughout his long pontificate, he treated all reformers with the same unrelenting hostility that they showed to him. When forces of the Risorgimento annexed a large slice of the Papal States in 1860 and established a secular regime, he responded by flexing the one great power left to him, his spiritual arm. The *Syllabus of Errors,* published in 1864 and disseminated throughout the world, condemned as heretical everything about liberalism — the good, the bad, and the indifferent. It was an extraordinary document, born out of extraordinary times.

For the many Europeans who were anti-Catholic, the *Syllabus* was a confirmation of everything they already believed: that Rome was hopelessly obscurantist, incapable of adapting to the modern age and therefore marked for extinction. For some Catholics (including some, but not many, Jesuits) it crystallized the dilemma that had been facing them for many long years. They saw the potential for compromise with liberal and democratic principles. Now they were being forbidden to think that way. A great deal of loyalty was required of them in the future, as they quietly fell into line behind their pope. For the great majority of believers, however, there was no dilemma: the *Syllabus* was a powerful rallying cry; it gave them order and certainty at a time when the world was in flux. The Church had become a fortress, but within its walls things were good, religion was safe. After the lean years at the start of the century, Catholicism was enjoying a revival, a revival that drew its strength and its inspiration from Rome.

In all this the Society of Jesus, the defender of the papacy for the past three hundred years, played an important part. Prominent Roman Jesuits became the pope's advisers in his critical decisions. Their hand can be seen in the proclamation of the doctrine of the Immaculate Conception in 1854, the drawing up of the *Syllabus of Errors* in 1864, and the convening in 1869 of the Vatican Council that led to the definition of papal infallibility — all measures that greatly enhanced the papacy's supremacy over the Church. They also provided the pope with a powerful instrument of communication: the newspaper *Civiltà cattolica,* founded in 1849. This was an instance of the papacy making use of a modern convenience, the free press. For the first time a newspaper giving the papal point of view was able to reach directly to grassroots Catholics, and most importantly, to the grassroots clergy, bypassing local hierarchies and thus cementing the alliance between the ordinary faithful and Rome. It was left to Jesuits across the Continent to fan the strong ultramontane spirit that was sweeping across the Catholic world.

And again, they paid the price. The other world, the one moving in a secular direction, took note. The suspicions about the Society that so many people had voiced since the start of the century were being justified: to its power base in Rome it had added enormous local influence, through its churches and schools, its lay organizations, and its political connections. The first thing that any progressive government taking power was likely to do was to get rid of them. In 1870 the pope lost the rest of the Papal States while, in one country after another, the Jesuits lost their footing. The pope became a prisoner within the small circumference of the Vatican; the Jesuits, ever resilient, moved on to new fields in Russia, South America, and the United States.

"To the Least of My Brothers"

The great French historian of the Mediterranean world, Fernand Braudel, has compared the movement of world history to the movement of the sea. On the surface he sees the agitation of the waves, the ever-changing patterns of foam and spume. These are events, he says. They make up most of our daily news, and we attach great importance to them. But they are superficial, and they soon give way to other events. Beneath the surface lie historical currents (he calls them "conjonctures") that move more slowly but create more lasting effect. The world's major economic upturns and downturns could be called "conjonctures." Finally, far beneath the currents lies the deep sea. It also moves, and its movement, though beyond our comprehension and certainly beyond our control, affects us all.

Nineteenth-century Europe was alive with coups, elections, assassinations, alliances, wars — in other words, events. It was also the scene of major structural change, with the destruction of the *ancien régime* and the establishment of the groundwork for modern forms of government: liberal democracy, socialism, fascism, communism. It fostered egalitarianism and capitalism and nationalism. But Braudel would call all of this "conjoncture." He would point to the deep sea of human existence where an even greater movement was under way.

Between 1750 and 1900 the population of Europe almost trebled, from 150 million to 420 million. And it broke free of its moorings, abandoning the countryside where it had lived since time immemorial and making for the cities. By the time the great migration was over, much of western Europe was urbanized. The movement was necessary; agriculture alone could not have fed so many new mouths, while on the other hand industry was able to absorb more and more workers. It would, in the end, create a different kind of world. But in the meantime it threw up huge, intractable problems that were not soon solved. For millions of men, women, and children throughout several lifetimes, progress brought dislocation and distress.

The city of Turin, in Piedmont, is a case in point. In medieval times the seat of the dukes of Savoy, after 1720 the capital of the kingdom of Sardinia, it became during the nineteenth century the second-largest industrial center in Italy. Its population leaped from about 117,000 in 1838 to about 205,000 in 1861. More than a tenth of this population was to be found in the slums that clustered around the industrial centers of the city, living nineteen to twenty families to a dwelling. The conditions, bad to begin with, were made even worse by the heavy influx from the countryside of seasonal workers, rootless, penniless, and often very young.

To its credit, Turin tried harder than most municipalities of its day to provide for its poor. Various institutions were established, including oratories, and free schools run by the Brothers of Christian Schools. But as long as the migrants kept pouring in, these efforts did little more than scratch the surface. In the minds of most citizens, the people of the slums, whether settled or seasonal, were a problem they wished would go away. As for the church as an institution, it was badly situated to deal with the problem. To be sure, it boasted sixteen parishes and a high ratio of priests to parishioners, but fourteen of those parishes were in the old town and only two in the burgeoning industrial districts. Little had been done to adjust to the new realities. Most of the priests that *were* working in the slums were doing so on their own time, out of charity and human concern. There was, as yet, no consensus in the church on how to approach the immense new problem of the urban poor.

Enter Don Bosco, one of the great men of nineteenth-century Catholicism, and a powerful witness to his times. He was born in 1815, three years before Karl Marx, and he died in 1888, five years after him. In 1848, the year of revolutions, he was already well into his life's work as pastor for the abandoned youth of Turin. There was nothing Marx or his comrade Engels could have told him about the miseries of the proletariat that he did not know already. No one could have worked harder than he to alleviate them.

His Christian name was John; "Don" was the title that came with his ordination as a diocesan priest. Actually, the fact that he became a priest at all was extraordinary, because seminary training cost money and he was a poor boy from the country. His father, a tenant farmer, had died young, leaving a wife and three sons, aged nine, four, and two. John, the youngest, grew up to know grinding farmwork and only intermittent schooling. At the age of eleven, he had to become a hired hand in another household. But gradually, thanks to the continuing support of a devoted mother, the kindness of other people, and his own aptitude and hard work, he achieved the goal he had set for himself: the priesthood.

John Bosco had always had something else in mind: a determination to work with the young. Not the rich young either; he was very clear that his calling was to be with poor boys. And in Turin there were plenty of these. He described them in his memoirs: "bricklayers, stonecutters, road pavers and others who came from distant villages"; children from the tenements, dirty, ill-fed, and jobless; boys in prison — "fine healthy youngsters alert of mind" whose future was nonetheless dire. What they needed, he thought, was a friend and mentor, someone who could save them from the streets, give them dignity, and guide them in the right path.

His life's work began in earnest on 8 December 1841, when he was twenty-six. He was preparing for Mass when he and the sacristan noticed a boy who had slipped into the room. The sacristan, realizing that the boy had no business there, berated him, beat him with a feather duster, and chased him out. But Don Bosco had him brought back, put him at his ease, and gently questioned him. The boy, Bartholomew Garelli, was sixteen years old, an orphan, illiterate, a stranger to the city and to the religion in which he had been baptized. Don Bosco invited him to return to the sacristy after Mass, and there he gave him his first instruction: how to make the sign of the cross.

The constitutions of the congregation that Don Bosco later founded tell us that "This Society had its beginning in a simple catechism lesson." Garelli came back for more, bringing with him other boys. Soon the dozens of boys turned into hundreds. "This," wrote Don Bosco in his memoirs, "was the beginning of our Oratory." It marked, in fact, the way the Oratory was to grow: step by step, in response to the needs thrown up before it.

For most of us here and now, an oratory is a place of worship. This was not the meaning that Don Bosco gave the word. For him, as for Saint Philip Neri three centuries before, the oratory was not a place but a people gathered together to share friendship and good times and the word of God. The meeting place could be anywhere — and indeed for Don Bosco and his growing horde of boys it *was* anywhere, because wherever they tried to settle in the early days, the neighbors soon complained of noise and confusion and material destruction. Understandably, as the good people looked at their damaged vegetable beds and trampled grass, they did not much appreciate the saying attributed to Neri: "Let them shout, run, and jump, as long as they do not offend God." It was some time before the Oratory found a permanent resting place.

There is no question: Don Bosco's primary aim was to make his boys into good Catholics. The time given over to religious observance and instruction would, by our standards, be overlong. But the Sundays and feast days when the Oratory was open were leavened by singing and by play, and for the young urchins whose only alternative was idling on the city streets, it was heaven. Above all, the whole unruly mob was bound together by near adoration for their priest. He was, for them, a true superstar, charismatic and warm, as genuinely loving toward them as they were to him.

In time Don Bosco took on additional tasks. When an orphan in dire straits came wandering in one evening, the priest and his mother (who had come to live with him) fed him and cleaned him up, made him a bed of straw, and trusted him not to decamp with the sheets. Before long, a fully fledged orphanage was attached to the institution. Later, workshops were set up to teach the boys trades, and night schools for reading and writing. Once the boys were trained, Don Bosco found them situations with good masters. Then, because some youths showed themselves to be more capable academically, further classes were arranged, and the brightest of them were sent out for advanced schooling. In return, Don Bosco set them to supervising the studies of their comrades. All this fulfilled the dreams he once had, in which a multitude of wild animals were turned into lambs, and then some of the lambs were turned into shepherds. In 1854 he challenged four of his young followers to dedicate themselves to the work of the Oratory. He called them "Salesians," after Saint Francis de Sales, whose "charity and gentleness" were to be their guiding principles.

And indeed, this was the great originality of John Bosco. In an age when the clergy's standards of conduct were still tinged with a Jansenist severity, he proved the truth of the adage that the great French saint had often quoted, that more flies are caught with honey than with vinegar. He "caught" his boys with kindness. Accustomed as they were to the harshness of parents and masters, and the tough mores of the streets, they found it irresistibly attractive. His method, in which he trained his disciples, involved closing the distance between themselves and their charges, and behaving toward them, always, with warmth and a certain informality.

This grated on the sensibilities of some of his fellow priests. They had been schooled in the tradition of Trent, which had sought to distance the priesthood from the laity. A cold aloofness came easily to them. Those of them who actually visited the Oratory saw priests in less-than-formal dress, mingling and actually playing with the boys. In the opinion of some, the Salesians were demeaning the sacerdotal office; they were "a motley crowd of ignorant fellows, good only for making a lot of noise and nothing else." What more could one expect? Their training was highly questionable. Their recruits did not spend a year or two living in isolation, studying theology and learning how to pray, as novices were supposed to. Instead, they were put straight to work with the boys and allowed to study only in their free time. The Salesians' resemblance to a properly constituted religious congregation was thin, to say the least.

But in fact, that was how Don Bosco wanted it. Piedmont in the 1850s was hardly a congenial environment for religious congregations. In 1855 the interior minister Rattazzi introduced a law suppressing all religious orders except those involved in education and health care. Rome immediately responded by excommunicating the sponsors of the law. This was hardly the moment to propose a new congregation. However, Rattazzi admired the work of the Oratory, and wanted the organization established on a firm basis. He himself suggested to Don Bosco that a society of laymen and clerics, properly trained and organized, would have a great future. What was essential in his eyes, however, was that this society should not become a religious order with all the exemptions and privileges that a religious order enjoyed. Its members should continue to be full citizens of the state, subject to civil law. Don Bosco took this to heart. The draft constitutions he presented to the pope in 1859 included the principle that every Salesian was to be "a religious in the eyes of the Church and a free citizen in the eyes of society." And Pius IX approved.

As usual, however, the devil was in the details. Before Rome finished amending the constitutions, the Society of Saint Francis de Sales had become much more "religious" in character than Don Bosco had intended. Its somewhat amorphous structures were trimmed and tidied up to meet canonical requirements. A proper novitiate was introduced, as were perpetual vows. Significantly, his idea that laymen living in their own homes could be full members of the society was a step too far for the authorities. Instead they separated them out and assigned them a distinct status as "cooperators." Other novelties for which Don Bosco was responsible were also sidelined. In many ways the society was recast in the mold of a traditional religious congregation. "My idea was to set up something quite different from what it now is," he said in 1879. "But I was compelled to do this, and there you have it."

But it was on safe ground, and it was flourishing. Because it was more modern in its outlook, perhaps, or more democratic in its structure, or more firmly dedicated to the service of the poor and disadvantaged, it outpaced every one of the other newly formed men's institutes, counting over thirty-five hundred members by the end of the century. Indeed, if we glance ahead to 1970, we see that the Salesians outnumbered all the rest — old orders and new — with the exception of the Jesuits and the Franciscans. And like the Jesuits and the Franciscans, they were active in every corner of the world.

Don Bosco was both a conservative and a progressive. Though he claimed to be nonpolitical, he was the pope's man in a time when so much about the papacy was political. In an era characterized by doubt and questioning, his Catholicism was sturdy and straightforward, anchored in the certainty that God and the Blessed Virgin were guiding and protecting him every inch of the way. His methods were highly paternalistic. On the other hand, in his social views he was much in advance of his times. In the year that *The Communist Manifesto* appeared, he remarked that "the revolutionary movement was not just a passing storm. Not all its promises to the people were unjust; some of them filled real needs. The workers demanded equality of rights without class distinction, more justice, and improvement of living conditions." He recognized, and deplored, the triumph of unbridled capitalism. Where the Church was concerned, he worried about its alienation from the urban poor. To cure this, he maintained, priests must be recruited from among the working classes — "those who labored with a spade or a hammer" — exactly the kind of men he chose to be his first Salesians.

And finally, in his desire to incorporate the laity into his society he was speaking as a prophet. The time was not yet ripe; the Church was still too clerical in its thinking. But in his recognition of the immense good that the laity could do, John Bosco was pointing to the not-too-distant future. The founder of the Salesians was also one of the fathers of lay Catholic action.

*   *   *

Karl Marx championed the proletariat. John Bosco championed the working poor and the unemployed. There were other poor, though: people who were too old and too weak to count for anything. They, too, needed their champion. They found one in Jeanne Jugan, the first of the Little Sisters of the Poor.

This is not to say that such people had previously been altogether neglected. In the old hospitaller tradition, and in the activities of the various charities, there had always been concern for the aged. But urban poverty was ballooning, and the old structures were staggering under its weight. It was not only the larger industrializing cities that were in trouble; even the smaller communes were complaining that the "poverty problem" was overwhelming them. Thus, in 1836, the municipal council of the Breton city of Saint-Servan protested that it could no longer afford to feed its poor, seeing that in a population of ten thousand there were "no more than six hundred families in reasonably easy circumstances." The only recourse it could devise was to forbid public begging.

Only three years later, in the same city of Saint-Servan, Jeanne Jugan took an old blind woman into her home and went out into the streets to beg for the means to support her.

Jeanne had known poverty all her life. Born in 1792 in a coastal village of Brittany, into a fishing family whose father was later lost at sea, she had entered domestic service at the age of sixteen, and from then on had known no other life. The move to Saint-Servan in search of new work was the longest trip she had ever taken. Now, at the age of forty-seven, she was embarking on a much greater journey: like Saint Anthony fifteen centuries before, she was being led step-by-step toward a more fundamental commitment, not in the emptiness of the Egyptian desert, but in a state devoid of material certainty, where even the meager living she had secured for herself was left behind and everything depended on the goodness of God and the charity of her neighbors.

Before long she found another old woman in dire straits. She and the two companions who lived with her took this one in, too. Now, though they continued to work for their living, it became clear that their earnings were not enough to feed five mouths. So Jeanne went back to begging. Soon begging became the household's principal means of support. During the same time the two lodgers increased to twelve, which forced the whole group to a larger (though dark and not very wholesome) space. The three companions formed themselves into an association, which not long after became the first religious community of Little Sisters of the Poor.

All this took place in the same Saint-Servan that had recently protested that it could not afford to feed its poor. What was it about Jeanne's approach that so disarmed people? Begging was frowned upon by a population long grown weary of "the poverty problem." But how to refuse someone who, without possessing anything herself, was ready to give everything to others, whose generosity of spirit far outshone that of her most liberal donors? She and her sisters lived as their poor old people lived, sharing the same food or lack of it, giving up their own beds when beds were needed, wearing the same assortment of patched and mended clothing. The radicalism of their commitment inspired some people, and either annoyed or shamed others, into giving. Whatever the case, the little community thrived and grew, both in numbers and in reputation. Before long it was being invited to open houses in other cities, first in Brittany, then across France and other European countries, then overseas. In 1851 the sisters were invited to London — the same London where paupers like Oliver Twist had no home but the workhouse — to set up a hospice for elderly indigents. There, as in France, they pioneered the practice of palliative care. Then, after several years of obscure service, came a great breakthrough. In 1868 a small contingent was dispatched to America, carrying little more than the clothes on their backs. The welcome they received overwhelmed them. One of them described the experience: "How, arriving with nothing, we ended up being provided with everything." By the end of the century they were serving in some forty well-established houses, from New York to Milwaukee to Pittsburgh to New Orleans.

It was an extraordinary accomplishment for a group of women who were as poor, and as humble, as church mice. It owed everything, in the first place, to the authenticity of their Christian witness. Even after their company grew in numbers and in popular respect, the Little Sisters of the Poor retained their commitment to poverty, solemnly resolving not to accept endowments or legacies, to own nothing but their houses. In other words, they would go on depending on charity for their daily bread.

"Holy poverty" in an age of burgeoning wealth! It turned out to be a winning formula. The sisters' experience in the United States proved that. The milieu into which they came when they stepped off the boat was one in which wealth was exploding, and where philanthropy was taking wing. The rich had money to give away, and a willingness to give it; the sisters and their elderly poor were the beneficiaries of their generosity. When one loyal Catholic admirer struck oil in Pennsylvania, the Little Sisters of the Poor were among the first to share in his good fortune.

Jeanne Jugan and the women who followed her were dedicated, first and foremost, to the elderly poor; their plan was to serve them by enlisting the help of the better-off. This was in the age-old Catholic tradition. One of their most ardent supporters also described it as "good socialism and communism." It is most unlikely that Karl Marx would have agreed; for him and for all true believers, people like the Little Sisters of the Poor were simply bandaging over deep social wounds; they were getting in the way of the progress of the working class.

A hundred years after Jeanne, another great saint of the poor, Mother Teresa of Calcutta, had to deal with the same argument. She was asked more than once whether, instead of caring for the poor, it would not be better to work for an improvement in the conditions that kept them poor: in the popular analogy, instead of giving them fish, why not give them fishing rods with which to catch their own food? Her answer: "They have not even the strength to lift a fishing rod, let alone use it to fish. Giving them fish, I help them to recover the strength for the fishing of tomorrow."

Throughout the nineteenth and twentieth centuries, women like Jeanne Jugan and Agnes Bojaxhiu (Mother Teresa) have been instrumental in defining the Christian message for the modern world. They have made it kinder, gentler, more complete.

The Feminine Invasion: France, 1800-1900

When, in 1799, Napoleon announced, "It is over," he meant that the revolution had been achieved; that it was time to end all internal hostilities, including the visceral conflict between the ideology of '89 and Catholicism. He was wrong. The struggle would last a long time, because neither belief system was prepared to surrender to the other. It was a struggle between titans: on the one side, the modernizing world, strong in its sense of enlightenment and progress, and on the other, the Church, armed with a certainty born of the ages. The one controlled most of the levers of state power; the other continued to exercise an extraordinary hold on the hearts and minds of its people.

Among the Church's most effective forces were its religious orders. And the papacy knew it. Six centuries before, under the great pope Innocent III, it had sought to restrict the multiplication of religious orders; now it welcomed them. Between 1800 and 1900, many of the old orders rebuilt themselves, and new congregations of men appeared almost yearly. Almost all of them received papal approval. The number of European monks, friars, canons, priests, and brothers rose steadily, to reach 135,700 by the end of the century. Combined with the secular clergy, they formed a powerful army. Their political opponents had good cause to fear them.

But most contemporaries, absorbed as they were in the struggle of the titans, failed to observe that a third force was creeping in; or if they observed it, they did not pay it much heed. It remained for historians to point out the obvious, that between 1800 and 1900 the Catholic Church was finally "feminized." Women in ever-increasing numbers became activists for the faith. And in ever-increasing numbers they sought to frame that activism within the religious life.

Though the most anticlerical country in Europe, France was several decades ahead of the rest in the way it opened up to what was in fact a major women's movement. Whereas in much of the Continent the female religious life continued to mean enclosure, in France it swiftly evolved to mean community life combined with active service of one kind or another. The criterion of "utility," already embraced by the *ancien régime,* was made into a rule by Napoleon: no congregation was to be authorized unless it served some useful purpose. But in fact, Napoleon was only putting his stamp of approval on what was already happening spontaneously. Before the end of the century, 400 new active-life congregations would join those already in existence, and of the 200,000 Frenchwomen who became nuns, the majority would enter such congregations.

From that point on, cloistered nuns were in the minority. The monastic attraction had grown dim; it did not seem to suit the modern mentality. In any case, it was extremely difficult, after the destructions of the Revolution, to reestablish a traditional women's monastery. The heavy investment in buildings and in the ongoing financial support that contemplatives required was beyond most people's reach. Consequently, when it finally regained its foothold in France, the cloister remained what it had always been, a retreat for the affluent, or at least financially comfortable. On the other hand, it was easy to set up a community of sisters. All that was required was a cluster of like-minded women, a house of some sort, the support of a willing priest (or better still, a bishop), and some money. And above all, a need to fill: children without a school, invalids without hospital care, people facing the wretchedness of poverty or disablement without help of any kind. In the wake of the revolution there were plenty of these needs around.

Even before the Revolution had run its course — as early as 1796 — several of the older congregations had started to rebuild, and new communities to pop up here and there. Already by 1800 they had started recruiting, and over the following years, with Napoleon's blessing, they made serious headway. Later governments sometimes encouraged them, sometimes treated them with disdain. It made no difference; nothing seemed to slow them down. With the census of 1861 the country woke up to the fact that it was home to a lot of nuns — some 90,000 of them, in fact. The fields of social service and nursing, primary schooling and, above all, secondary female education were dominated by them. Their numbers continued to grow; by

1880 they made up a large segment of the entire teaching, nursing, and professional caregiving corps of France. Only then, under the Third Republic, did the authorities move to cut into their monopoly, with the establishment of training schools for lay schoolmistresses.

Why did the female congregations enjoy such success?

They were fortunate in two respects: the welcome they received from society and the willingness of women to join them. As to the first: local administrations were in desperate straits after the chaos of the revolutionary years. At the very time when their social systems were stressed as never before, they had to operate without the charitable supports of the *ancien régime,* the almsgiving of the clergy, and the de rigueur benevolences of the elites. But here and now they had well-intentioned women, ready to do the necessary work at a low cost. The sisters' piety must have been grating to some of the more progressive officials, but it was a small price to pay for the services they rendered. What was more, no one seemed to think religious women held the political threat that the men did, and for that reason they needed little watching. Thus their perceived insignificance worked to their advantage in the early days. Only later did governments become anxious about them, and look for ways to reduce their influence.

From the point of view of the women who became nuns, the fact was that in an age of limited opportunities, the congregations promised substantial advantages. The careers they offered in teaching or nursing were as close to professionalism as anything that women in the nineteenth century could hope for. Better still: for the more capable among them, the running of hospitals, schools, and convents allowed for the practice of real managerial skills. Of course, there was a quid pro quo: celibacy and obedience to superiors. But since, in keeping with long-standing custom, a high proportion (as high as 12 percent) of French women remained celibate anyway, the commitment would not have seemed as grave as it would today. There were compensations, too: the pride that their families took in them, and the respect that society gave them. Doctors and educationists might groan at their outmoded ways, but the sisters paid no attention; they had their public solidly behind them. It would be some time before they felt the need to modernize themselves.

These were the practical reasons for the extraordinary success of the female congregations in nineteenth-century France. But there was a deeper, stronger reason that cannot be ignored: the attachment that women felt for their religion. Somewhere between the later years of the *ancien régime* and the beginning of the Napoleonic years, the "weaker sex" became the anchor of the faith. Indications that men were drifting away from the Church had begun to appear in the mid–eighteenth century, and during the Revolution the drift turned into a stampede. Women, on the other hand, entered the revolution devout and came out of it militant. Throughout the nineteenth century they filled the church pews, followed all the public devotions — novenas, retreats, processions, and so on — and worked in charitable organizations. It is hardly surprising, then, that many of them took their commitment a step further and entered the religious life. The result was that from 1860 onward, there were more female "regulars" than male in France. And this was the way the rest of the Church would go in years to come.

Republican partisans became increasingly uncomfortable with feminine religiosity. They saw it as a sign that women were still under the domination of priests (Jesuits especially); they feared that through the confessional those priests would be able to undermine the natural authority of husbands over their wives. In his 1845 works *Des jésuites* and *Du prêtre, de la femme, de la famille,* Jules Michelet described in lurid terms the hidden ways in which confessors could take possession of women's souls. And then, "Whoever has the women is sure to have the men in the end." The only way to scotch this threat was to strike at the source of the women's weakness, their education. "Our wives and daughters are raised, governed by our enemies. Enemies of the modern spirit of liberty and of the future" — in other words, the nuns. Those unassuming ladies had become a danger to the nation.

In due course public opinion began to turn against the congregations. Perhaps the nuns were not as harmless as one had thought. And if truth be told, they were not. Like everyone else in nineteenth-century France, they saw education as the key to the future. But because they were members of the church militant, the future they were aiming toward was one in which the country was again Catholic. That was exactly what the secular parties suspected, and why the secular parties became alarmed. As long as the girls' schools, primary and secondary, belonged to the nuns, there was, in their opinion, a fifth column within the country.

And so, after a long period of grace, the women's congregations joined the men's, as a danger to the public good.

In 1901 the republican government began a series of moves to disempower the Church, by removing the supports that Napoleon had mandated in the concordat and by placing all congregations under supervision and weeding out those that were not authorized. Then in 1904 came an even more draconian law. Henceforth *all* congregations, male and female, even those that had always operated within the law, were banned from teaching and their property was confiscated. Where the government had the authority — as in its own military and prison hospitals — it discharged the nursing sisters. Only a few communities, either because they were unimportant or because they were in charge of unattractive institutions (such as institutions for the deaf or, in the colonies, leprosaria), were spared. Further legislation, the Law of Separation (1905), made it final: France was to be not only a republic, but a resolutely secular republic. It remains so to this day.

This left the regulars, both men and women, with few choices. As members of associations they had no future in France. If as private individuals they could find a place to teach in the public schools, they were forbidden to teach religion. Religious by the tens of thousands took the road to exile, as their predecessors had done at moments of crisis throughout the century. From then on, whole communities began to appear in other countries across the world. Wherever they ended up, they continued, by and large, to grow and prosper.

America, 1790-1900

One of the congregations' greatest strengths lay in their flexibility, their readiness to change direction, to go anywhere at short notice, to adapt their ministry to different conditions. Nowhere was this flexibility more tested than in America.

In 1790 the Catholic population of the United States stood at about 35,000. In 1850 it stood at 1,606,000; in 1865, at 3,500,000. A population explosion, in other words, and much of it from the Catholic countries of Europe, along with French Canada and Mexico.

Without a doubt, it was immigration that built the Catholic church of America. Once little more than an enclave largely confined to Maryland and Pennsylvania, at midcentury it burst from its cocoon with stunning suddenness. In four years the original lone ecclesiastical province of Baltimore was divided into six by the creation of New York, Cincinnati, New Orleans, Saint Louis, and Oregon City. Within the provinces, twenty-six bishoprics were created. It was an impressive expansion, even if only on paper. But the American church was still dismally undermanned, underfunded, and overextended, while its flock, growing by the day, was crying out for its services in a babel of different tongues.

It is a sort of reverse hyperbole to speak of "a shortage of priests." In the beginning there were virtually no priests at all. In 1785 John Carroll, the newly minted bishop of Baltimore, had reported to Rome that "there are 19 priests in Maryland and five in Pennsylvania. Of these, two are more than seventy years old, and three others very near that age." These would have been ex-Jesuits, the inheritors of a 150-year-old mission in Maryland, whose institution had been crippled by the dissolution of the Society in 1773. There was as yet in America no means of replacing them when they died. For the most part the men Carroll would have at his disposal were a motley crew wandering in from different corners of Europe, often without authorization or testimonial, or even much respect for authority. He tried to watch them carefully, on the principle that no priests would be better than bad priests. He had to balance his concern for the Church's good name against the fact that in much of America, Catholics were living and dying without the sacraments. Only later, after his time, did the congregations of Europe come in force. However, he did manage to take one major step forward.

It was Carroll's good fortune to be in London in 1790, at the very time that the Revolution was making life difficult for the religious congregations of France. While there he met with a representative of Monsieur Emery, the superior general of the French Society of Saint-Sulpice. The Sulpicians, founded in Paris in 1642, were priests who lived in community but took no religious vows. They were specialists in the training of priests. Emery was looking for an opportunity to place a part of his society beyond the reach of the Revolution, and the United States seemed the perfect solution. In 1791 five Sulpician priests and five students arrived in Maryland to set up a seminary. They were the first of nearly a hundred French priests to serve in America during John Carroll's time.

It was some years, however, before a seminary was up and running. There were as yet few American men able or willing to enter the Catholic priesthood. In the 1790s the United States was Protestant to its very core; it had been built from the start on anti-Catholic principles; its lately declared independence had served to emphasize its difference from the monarchical, hierarchical Catholic states of Europe. Most of the colonies had enacted antipapist laws, and in some cases these remained on the books. Of the thirteen new states, only Pennsylvania had a tradition of toleration, while Maryland's Catholics were a special case, in that, having been around for 150 years, they were grandfathered into the new republic. The religion now coming from Europe was alien to the American way of thinking, and therefore unlikely to stir young American hearts. As a result, the church would have to import its priests for the foreseeable future. So after ten years the Sulpicians switched direction; they turned their seminary into a men's college and took to parish ministry, from Maine to the Mississippi.

Other priests, driven from their homes in Europe or drawn by the promise of America's open society, came trickling in. Two Augustinian friars, John Rosseter and Matthew Carr, arrived in 1794 and 1796, the lonely harbingers of the flood of priests that would later arrive from Ireland. Two groups of French Trappist monks arrived separately in the early years of the new century, to travel far and wide in search of a home before returning to France in 1814. During the few years that they were in America, they broke out of their customary monastic routine to set up parish services for their Catholic neighbors. But with their departure these services were left to an uncertain future. For the rest, we see mention of a Dominican here, a Lazarist or a Franciscan there, but always alone or near so, wanderers amidst the flotsam and jetsam of escapees from the revolutionary storm.

Much as they were needed in their new country, their language, or lack of it, remained a thorny issue. Many of the incoming priests never learned to communicate well in English. John Carroll and his successors made the best of it, assigning them as far as possible to the care of their own countrymen. But their broken or nonexistent English only contributed to the foreignness of their religion. In a society already suspicious of their intentions, that was unfortunate. Because, in fact, the differences in language signaled a much more serious division in mind-set. The incoming Catholicism was culturally European. Insofar as the American church became, and remained for a long time, a church run by immigrants for immigrants, it remained "different," and separated in significant ways from the mainstream.

*   *   *

The Society of Jesus returned officially in 1808, after the American ex-Jesuits of Maryland decided to affiliate with the nucleus of the Society still subsisting in Russia, an alliance hardly likely to enhance their image among democratic Americans. The first to arrive was Anthony Kohlmann, an Alsatian by birth and a member of the Company of Fathers of the Sacred Heart, the proto-Jesuit society that had once been the Fathers of Faith. He came to New York in 1808 to take over what was then the only Catholic church in the city. He and the five young Jesuit scholastics who joined him were able to preach in English, French, and German, which made their masses popular events for the patchwork Catholic population of New York City.

The Jesuits brought discipline, dedication, and talent to the American mission. But they also brought their negative reputation. In 1816 John Adams, in a letter to Thomas Jefferson, wrote: "I do not like the late resurrection of the Jesuits. They have a General, now in Russia, in correspondence with the Jesuits in the U.S. . . . Shall we not have swarms of them here?" He envisaged them in their various disguises, covertly wreaking their damage upon the young democracy. But he added that in spite of the danger they posed, "Our system however of Religious Liberty must afford them an Asylum." And Jefferson looked at the bright side of things: "We are destined to be a barrier against the returns of ignorance and barbarism. Old Europe will have to lean on our shoulders, and to hobble along at our side, under the monkish trammels of priests and kings, as she can."

As time passed and the Catholic (therefore foreign) presence became more intrusive, the old fears took wing. The Jesuits, it was widely proclaimed by people supposedly in the know, were up to their old tricks, stirring up trouble and building up political influence. They had their fingers in every pie. Particularly sinister was the freedom with which they were ranging across the West, filling the minds of Indians and frontiersmen with their un-American teachings.

There was some substance to the naysayers' angst. Jesuits were indeed following in the steps of the frontier as it moved west. They did so in traditional Jesuit fashion, by establishing colleges farther and farther west in leapfrog fashion, starting from the Georgetown college that Carroll had founded in 1789 and closing out the next century in Seattle in 1891. Each college became the springboard for further religious services to the surrounding people: parish churches, grammar schools, charitable societies, and so on. The strategy had been effective in sixteenth-century Germany, and it was effective now.

Of all these colleges established in the nineteenth century, only two were opened by American-born rectors. The Jesuits' dependence on foreigners persisted for a long time. So long, in fact, that when Italian Jesuits took over the Rocky Mountain mission later in the century, some of them learned and mastered Indian dialects but never succeeded in speaking English.

Blackrobe

The colleges, established as they were in the up-and-coming towns of white America, lent themselves to one kind of ministry. The Indian missions required another. Where the one was familiar, the other was not. The nomadic lifestyle of the western tribes, complicated by the ever-shifting policies of the federal government and already wounded by the relentless forward movement of the settlers, made success uncertain. In 1823, when the Jesuits were invited by a bishop to take over this difficult task, they accepted with who knows what misgivings. The job was handed to a small group — two priests, three brothers, and seven seminarians — freshly arrived from Belgium. In fifty days the men walked, rode, and riverboated their way to Florissant, near Saint Louis, where they settled down to schooling the Indians in the neighborhood. But within seven years the enterprise began to falter. The Belgian Jesuits experienced what others would also experience: the dwindling away of the Indian mission before the force of oncoming white settlement. The mission lost much of its dynamism.

Then in 1840 came a breakthrough from an unexpected quarter. A band of Iroquois had migrated from the Montreal region to the land of the Flatheads in Montana, and now they wanted a priest — a "Blackrobe" — badly enough to come east looking for one. The priest they found was Pierre-Jean De Smet, one of the men who had made the arduous journey to Florissant seventeen years before. He now undertook another trek to northwestern Montana, where he was welcomed by the Flatheads, and spent several happy months in their company. When he returned he brought with him an ambitious plan to create for the Indians of the Rocky Mountains the same sort of "reductions" that had been successful in Paraguay over a century before.

That was the plan. It was estimable in the eyes of Rome, because it had solid Jesuit tradition behind it. As in Paraguay, the Jesuits would create and run their own colonies, free from the contamination of the outside world. The general of the Society gave him twenty-three assistants, and over time he recruited others, as well as five sisters of Notre-Dame de Namur from Belgium. But the mission languished and, after six years, failed. The Flatheads and the Coeur d'Alenes were not, like the Guarani, a sedentary people; the government in Washington was not, like the eighteenth-century government in Madrid, distant and vaguely beneficent. And there was no possibility of isolation. The world was pressing in, in the form of traders and settlers and alcohol.

In 1851 De Smet changed course. The superintendent for Indian Affairs, based in Saint Louis, was planning a conference with the Rocky Mountain tribes to secure conditions for the safe passage of settlers through their territory. Knowing of the Jesuit's expertise and good relations with the Indians, he invited him along as adviser and interlocutor. After a three months' journey by riverboat and on foot, the delegation arrived at Fort Laramie in Wyoming, to meet with the thousands of Sioux and Cheyenne gathered there. The treaty that resulted set up a corridor for people traveling west, in return for a large annual indemnity for fifty years and the promise that Washington would respect the traditional Sioux lands. De Smet was filled with optimism; this was the beginning, he thought, of an era of peace for both Indians and whites. In fact, it was nothing of the sort. Ten years later the Senate reduced the duration of the indemnity to fifteen years, and created two new territories out of the land that had been ceded to the Sioux. Steadily, irreversibly, the hunting grounds on which the tribes depended were being whittled away, while the compensation that they had been promised was being reduced through bad faith and outright embezzlement. The consequence was an Indian rampage into Minnesota in 1861, and a punitive campaign by the army in 1862. In 1864 the commissioner of the Indian Department asked De Smet to act as a peacemaker, and again the Jesuit traveled into Indian country. The esteem in which the Indians held him was enormous, and he returned it with unwavering affection. But he was more and more oppressed by the ambiguity of his mission. Was he speaking (to use his own words) for the "Great Father" or for "the Big Chief of the Long Knives"? Was he being used to secure peace, or pacification?

More peacemaking expeditions followed. The last was in 1868, when, despite his age and ill health, he traveled without military escort into the Sioux camp near Yellowstone. There Sitting Bull, together with other chiefs, sat with him and spoke of the injustices and cruelties that their people had suffered. The priest could only agree with them, but he continued to argue for peace, which he saw as the only hope for the Indians' survival. Two weeks later a peace treaty was signed at Fort Rice. De Smet reported it with his usual optimism. Eight years later came the battle at Little Big Horn. Fortunately, De Smet did not live to see it.

Pierre-Jean De Smet was not a typical Jesuit. The men who worked with him, the soldiers and civil agents who knew the West, treated him with esteem, and the many Indian tribes with whom he made common cause trusted him implicitly. But his fellow Jesuits and his superiors regarded him with ambivalence. In their Society, committed as it was to a certain way of proceeding, his mission was eccentric. But was it any more eccentric than Francis Xavier's? De Smet's hopes and dreams ended in failure. But so did those of the Jesuits of Paraguay. And so, for that matter, did those of the great sixteenth-century champion of the Indians, Bartholomé de Las Casas.

Some of the Church's grandest moments are to be found in its failures.

"For the Sake of the Indians"

The Missouri Territory to which the Belgian missionaries came in 1823 was no longer Indian country in any real sense. For some time white settlers had been pouring in, either by riverboat from the south or by land from the east. Saint Louis, the capital of the territory, had already grown from a frontier trading post into a small city. It was, at the time of the Jesuits' arrival, the headquarters of the U.S. army in the West. It was the seat of the new Catholic diocese of Louisiana, and it boasted a men's college, Saint Mary's, already in Jesuit hands. It also had, close by, what was on the frontier a unique facility: a convent of nuns. The Ladies of the Sacred Heart, members of a society only recently founded in France, were already teaching school at Florissant, the village on the Missouri River to which the Belgians were headed.

For these five women, and those behind their mission, it had been an extraordinary leap of faith. When, in January 1817, the bishop of Louisiana, the Sulpician William DuBourg, came to Europe begging for help, their little society was barely out of its formation stage. It had been born in Paris in 1800, when Joseph Varin, one of the underground Fathers of Faith whom Fouché so rightly distrusted, persuaded the young sister of a fellow priest to take up the teaching of girls, not as a career but as a sacred ministry. Under his coaching Madeleine Sophie Barat and three companions became nuns, and within a year they were running a boarding school in Amiens. They were soon joined by other women. In their early days they went under the title of Ladies of Christian Instruction, because the name they desired, and would later adopt, was still a red flag to the authorities. Under that innocuous title their society was approved by Napoleon in 1807, only months before he ordered the suppression of the Fathers of Faith. Their femininity, which was deemed to make them nonpolitical, gave them an entry that was forbidden to their masculine mentors. The fact that they were Jesuit-inspired did not seem to matter, not in those early years.

By this time Madeleine Sophie had recruited a most remarkable woman, Philippine Duchesne, into the society. A Visitandine novice before the Revolution, sent packing when all the convents were suppressed, she was ready, in her thirties, to start again on a religious life that would open her to all the rigors of the American frontier. It was she who, literally, opened the door to Bishop DuBourg, and she who, almost on the spot, begged to be allowed to follow him back. In her departure a year later, two of the characteristics that made congregations like hers so strong were evident. First, even though she and the nuns chosen to go with her were given only a few days to pack and leave, they were able to do so successfully. Second, her society, young as it was, was capable of finding the wherewithal to finance the mission and to keep financing, provisioning, and staffing it for years, until it was able to stand on its own feet. Logistics must always have been a challenge in the early nineteenth century, but the congregations were probably better able to handle them than most. In addition, Christians were beginning to feel an extraordinary zeal for the missions, a zeal that would grow more intense as the century progressed.

Years later Madeleine Sophie would write that "it was for the sake [of] the Indians that she [Philippine Duchesne] felt inspired to establish the order in America." But whatever Philippine imagined when she started out, it would be twenty years before her original hopes were fulfilled. Like the Jesuits, the nuns found that Indian students were few and far between in Florissant, and there was nothing to do but settle down to teaching the children of the white residents. Over the following years they established several schools up and down the Mississippi Valley. Then in 1841 both Jesuits and Ladies got the opportunity they had been looking for.

Among the Indian tribes forced by the government to move westward were the Potawatomi. When their lands in Indiana were taken from them by treaty in 1835, they migrated to territory on the Osage River in Kansas. With them came their priest, an old Breton, Benjamin-Marie Petit. He brought with him a written promise from the government to build a church and rectory on the new reservation; this he bequeathed, along with his Indian parishioners, to the Jesuits of Saint Louis. After visiting the Potawatomi, they accepted the legacy.

As soon as the Sacred Heart nuns learned of this, they began to plead to be included. Among the pleaders was Philippine Duchesne, now in her seventies. "If I did not know you well, I would say it is too much for you," wrote her bishop. But he knew her well, so she got to go. And so it was that she and three other nuns set off up the Missouri River into Kansas. Within a month they were living in borrowed quarters on the Indian reservation, and teaching school. Mother Duchesne, whose strength and energy had served the American mission well for twenty-three years, was soon too infirm to contribute much to the daily work. But she became, in the words of the Indians, "the woman who always prays," the spiritual center of the enterprise. After a year her own personal mission came to an end, and she had to retire to Florissant. But the work was well enough established to go on without her.

For the Ladies, raised in very different circumstances, life on the reservation must have been a shock. In France the society had adopted a cloistered form of life, enclosed within well-built walls and far from the rough-and-tumble of life; most of their day-to-day contact was with the daughters and families of the better-off. Here their living quarters were open not only to the winds that blew, but also to the constant visits of friendly men and women who brought gifts from the hunt, and in return were glad to share the nuns' food and sit for a while. There was real poverty. The convent, when finally built, was made of rough-hewn logs lined on the inside by canvas sheets that would billow inward on bad days; the benches that the students sat on during the day were taken over at night by chickens; prairie dogs felt free to come and go as they pleased. The winter cold was unlike anything to be experienced in France. Yet the nuns adapted, as many other missionary women and settlers' wives would adapt through the years. There was an unusual twist to their lives, however. Any one of them might be lifted out at a moment's notice and placed in one of the society's other schools, where life was orderly once more, and where young ladies sat at their desks or played in the gardens, and possibly, where slaves labored in the fields.

After ten good years the enterprise began to falter. The Potawatomi were, again, being pushed farther west. In 1846 they were given a new territory in western Kansas, guaranteed "as their land and home forever." The mission moved, complete with nuns, Jesuits, and everything they could carry. The new mission of Saint Mary's, with buildings financed by the government, took time and effort to establish. But it succeeded, and in 1851 was elevated into a vicariate with its own Jesuit bishop. By the late 1850s glowing reports about the progress of the nuns' Indian school were coming in from the Indian agents. But in the 1860s the same sad story was repeated once again. The Potawatomi were eased out, and settlers took their place. In 1868 the Sacred Heart nuns bowed to the inevitable and reestablished their school as an academy for white girls. From then on, they would be the teachers of the daughters of white America.

*   *   *

The Ladies of the Sacred Heart were the first nuns to cross the Mississippi, but they were not the first nuns in North America. That honor must, of course, go to the cloistered religious who appeared in Mexico in the sixteenth century, to the four teaching and nursing religious congregations who came to Canada in the seventeenth, and to the Ursulines who had been in New Orleans since 1727 and had therefore been French then Spanish subjects before becoming Americans. But the first female community to establish in the United States was Carmelite. Three members of a prominent Baltimore family had gone to Belgium to enter a Carmelite convent. In 1790, with one war finished in America and another threatening in Europe, they evacuated back to Maryland and managed to build themselves a community not far from Baltimore. Though Archbishop Carroll welcomed them, he made no bones about the fact that he would have preferred teaching nuns. Schools of any sort were in short supply in America, and as far as girls were concerned, schools that did exist were small and privately run. Illiteracy rates were high, even among the affluent.

In keeping with the practical needs of American society, the communities that appeared after the Carmelites were all in the work of education. The first was the Visitation. It was built in a somewhat random fashion. A group of Poor Clares, refugees from the French Revolution, had established a convent in Georgetown and tried their hand at teaching school. But language difficulties and their lack of training for such work brought them close to ruin. In 1799 a priest at Georgetown college saved the situation by bringing in three Irish-born women to replace them. The Poor Clares departed, and the three women, soon publicly known as "the Pious Ladies," adopted both the school and a conventual lifestyle. But therein lay a difficulty: they could not be real nuns without a rule, and neither they nor anyone around them knew enough to create one. So they picked one that they had heard of: the rule written two centuries before by Saint Francis de Sales. By 1817, with papal approval, the three, together with seventeen followers, were Visitandine nuns. Within a few more years they were running a highly regarded academy for young ladies and a school for poor girls that they financed with fees from the academy.

The carmel was European in character; the Visitation, because of the unusual way it was founded, less so. The teaching congregations that appeared in the following years were American with European underpinnings. For the most part their rules were of European inspiration, but most of their members were American and therefore accustomed to a freer, less deferential way of thinking. Many of the strictures and demands of old-world religious life were difficult for them to accept. But they were Catholics, with a Catholic reverence for tradition. Besides, the French priests who were their mentors had clear ideas of what a "real" religious life entailed, and did their best to press these ideas upon them. Thus enforced by both tradition and authority, the European way of doing things was hard to put aside, even when it threatened to impede the sisters' teaching vocation. For this reason the foundation years were not free of tension. This can be seen in the early history of the third and, in terms of expansion, most successful women's order to be founded in the United States, the Sisters of Charity.

The society came into being in Baltimore in 1809, and its foundress was a widow and a convert to Catholicism. Elizabeth Bayley was born into a prominent New York family and married in 1794 to William Seton, member of a flourishing trading firm with connections to Italy. During the following eight years they lived the happy life as members of New York society. But the early promise of their marriage collapsed when William found himself both bankrupt and sick with the tuberculosis that was to kill him. They sailed to Italy, hoping that the voyage would reestablish his health — in vain, as it turned out. In 1803 he died, and a few months later Elizabeth returned to New York, a widow with five children to support, and woefully poor.

Even though difficult, her situation did not seem altogether desperate. Elizabeth had friends and relatives in New York who might have been ready to support her and her family. But while in Italy she had fallen in love with Catholicism, and in 1805, to the horror of her social circle, she left the Episcopalian faith in which she had been raised and became a Catholic. The penalty that society levied upon her was severe. The support she had hoped for fell away. Worse still: when, to earn her own living, she tried to open a school, parents withheld their children for fear that her religious views might contaminate them. Her financial situation became desperate. At this point the Sulpicians stepped in, suggesting that she might be more successful in Maryland. And so in 1808 Elizabeth Bayley Seton migrated to Baltimore and opened a Catholic boarding school. Given her own strong devotion and the natural bent of her Sulpician advisers, the next step was not long in coming. A friendly priest coming back from France brought her a copy of Saint Vincent's rule. In 1809 she took vows as a Sister of Charity and received the first members into her community. A short time later the little group were given a property in Emmitsburg, a village in rural Maryland. Here they established themselves in a small house close by the new Sulpician college of Mount Saint Mary's. In 1810 they opened both a day school and a boarding school.

Considering the minority situation of Catholicism in early-nineteenth-century America, the growth of the congregation was remarkable. Before Mother Seton died in 1821, 140 women, both native- and foreign-born, had entered the community, and colonies had been sent out to Philadelphia and New York. By 1850, several hundred Sisters of Charity were running schools, hospitals, and orphanages in thirty-five towns and cities across the country, from north to south, from New England to the Mississippi. With phenomenal growth, however, came problems. In these early days American sisters did not enjoy government grants or bequests from prominent families. Their most important patrons were the local bishops, who provided funding and protection and, often, a place to live. But did the bishops' support mean that they were also in charge? The bishops thought so; Emmitsburg thought not. In 1846 a clash developed between the society's ecclesiastical superior, Father Deluol, and the bishop of New York, John Hughes. Since coming to New York the sisters had had charge of an orphanage in the city, in which they cared for both boys and girls. Deluol, respecting the very firm French prejudice against coeducation, ordered that they withdraw from the care of boys. The bishop objected; a war of wills followed; and in the end thirty-three New York sisters split away from the motherhouse, to form a separate community with the bishop as their canonical superior. This was the first time in America that a bishop's plans for "his" sisters conflicted with those of an order's central direction. It was not the last. Bishop Hughes set a precedent that other bishops would soon follow. The old European rivalry between bishops and regulars came to life again in America.

Another secession followed in 1851. Deluol was growing old, and he feared that with his departure the society would lose its central direction and break into a collection of diocesan congregations. The solution, he decided, was to join it to its French counterpart, the Daughters of Charity of Saint Vincent de Paul; to place it under the direction of the Lazarists and to adjust its rule to fit the French model. Whatever the advantages of such a move, it met with resistance from a sizable community of sisters in Cincinnati, who regarded it as a betrayal of their foundress. Their many substantive reservations crystallized in their objection to the proposed change in dress: the replacement of Mother Seton's black widow's bonnet by the high-flying white *cornette* that had meant something to the peasant women of seventeenth-century France but looked strange in nineteenth-century America. They broke away from Emmitsburg. From midcentury onward the two societies dressed differently, followed different versions of the Vincentian rule, and obeyed different superiors. And once started, the splintering continued. Other communities appeared, looking not to Emmitsburg but to their own bishops for their legitimacy. Yet they were all still members of the same tradition; they were all still Sisters, or Daughters, of Charity. Even as other women's orders appeared and grew, they remained the most visible of religious women, serving in the schools and hospitals and parishes of the American church.

*   *   *

So the sisters faced challenges in fashioning forms of community life that matched their life experience and their profession. They also had to cope with the prejudice and hostility of outsiders. One of the most serious problems these pioneering nuns faced was that they did not fit into the ethos of Protestant America. Not only did they belong to a religion much despised, but they also were vowed virgins, strange unnatural creatures in the eyes of a society that prized domesticity and held marriage and motherhood to be a woman's highest calling. So they were doubly reprehensible. When in the 1830s the antiforeign, antipapist forces of nativism became rampant among great sections of the American public, the nuns were fodder for their indignation, and sometimes easy targets for their violence. A community of Ursulines had set up a successful academy for girls in Charlestown, Massachusetts; in 1834 a mob burned their house to the ground, forcing them to leave. In 1844 the fires raged in Philadelphia, and two Catholic churches and a convent, as well as many Catholic homes, were destroyed. For other nuns in other cities the threat of similar attacks remained alive for some time. Only later, when the possibility of war came to consume the public mind, did the nativist furor subside.

Though the young republic had enshrined the principle of pluralism, it was the sort of pluralism that only worked because of social separation, in this case the separation of largely foreign Catholicism from homegrown Protestantism, enforced by strong barriers of mutual prejudice. Many Protestant Americans, like John Adams, tolerated papists but hated popery. Many other Protestant Americans, as the riots proved, hated both. Many Catholics returned the favor, though until they achieved the numbers to put up a good fight they were more likely to keep their feelings to themselves. The marked preference of everyone was to stick, whenever possible, to their own kind. This had consequences. The particular problem for the nuns was that, more than anyone else, they appeared to stand apart from the

mainstream, and the image they presented to the world — eccentric clothing, "unnatural" lifestyle, a self-imposed seclusion that gave the impression
of something to hide — allowed for every misapprehension that hostile
minds could invent. "Maria Monk" and other scurrilous representations of
convent life made good reading in the popular press.

As if to add fuel to the fire, some nuns went even further: they aspired
to be "persons of color and religious at the same time." In 1828, in Baltimore, three black women came together "to consecrate themselves to God,
and to the Christian education of young girls of color." With that, the first
black sisterhood was born.

Among the refugees who had come to America in the 1790s and early
1800s was a sizable population from the French Caribbean island of Saint
Domingue. Hundreds of black and mulatto members of the landowning
classes of the colony who had been driven out by the slave revolution came
to settle in Baltimore. In 1796 they began to receive religious services from
the Sulpicians, French-speakers like themselves. When James Hector
Joubert, a Sulpician who was also an émigré from the islands, conceived the
idea of a school for their daughters with religious schoolmistresses to run it,
he had allies close to hand: two women who had already made their mark as
teachers. Together with one other companion, Elizabeth Lange and Marie
Magdeleine Balas formed the nucleus of a new religious community, the
Oblate Sisters of Providence.

Their progress was slow and laborious. It was not that the black citizens
of Baltimore were unused to sending their children to school; the city was already provided with black Protestant churches and their affiliated schools.
But that there should be such a thing as a black religious community — that
took some getting used to. Could black women lead a *real* religious life? Fortunately, the sisters had a strong champion in Joubert, and he was able to use
his connections to secure authorization from the archbishop and approval
from Rome. They also enjoyed support from the black community, not, of
course, the level of support that the Carmelites enjoyed from their affluent
white patrons, but support that was enough to keep them afloat.

Another factor that worked in the Oblates' favor was their own self-
effacement, and the inclination of the Catholic establishment to pay as little
attention to them as possible. Unlike the Ursuline academy in Charleston
that catered to "society," their activities were unthreatening. They confined
their ministry to their own people; this made them more or less invisible to
white society, and much safer than they might otherwise have been. But the
condescending remarks of their "betters" make painful reading, and the si-

lences are even worse. The sisters built an irreproachably observant community; they attained good standards in their teaching; they remained solvent under difficult conditions; they showed their mettle by volunteering to nurse the sick during the 1832 cholera epidemic. For all this they received scant recognition. White Baltimore tolerated them, but it did not much admire them. This attitude, unfortunately, extended to some of the hierarchy. After Joubert's death in 1843 the nuns were subjected to several years of neglect. "It was unfortunately the wish of high Ecclesiastical authority that the Sisters should dissolve and disband," wrote the man who eventually came to their rescue. In 1847 Thaddeus Anwander, a young Bavarian Redemptorist, actually had to kneel before the archbishop and plead to be made their spiritual director before the archbishop consented.

During these years the situation of blacks, whether slave or free, was steadily worsening in Maryland. In the 1850s nativism reared its ugly head again. In 1857, the year of the Dred Scott decision, the sisters' new school for boys was attacked and vandalized, and they found themselves threatened. But they were strong enough to outlast the hostility of outsiders, now that support from within was strong. The dynamism of their director and the arrival in 1851 of a friendly archbishop, together with their own fortitude and dedication, opened an era of prosperity for the community. Gradually, very gradually, they gained in numbers and in public recognition. They stood the test of time.

The anomalous situation of the first generation of Oblate Sisters of Providence tells us something about the way contemporary American Catholics regarded blacks. Of the two disadvantaged races with which they were faced, blacks and Indians, Indians had (in theory at least) the better part. Since first meeting them in the New World, Europeans had had them on their conscience. They invested them with a mythical nobility and they admired their freedom of spirit, even as they longed to convert them to a more "civilized" life. No matter how harshly the people on the ground treated them, the people back home romanticized them. Their human rights became established doctrine within the Catholic Church. Blacks, on the other hand, had from time immemorial been associated in the European mind with slavery, and slavery, since it appeared in the Bible, was seen as consistent with humanity. So Catholics could own slaves, though they were expected to treat them kindly. In any case, whatever individual Catholics felt about the issue, as far as the church in America was concerned, it was loath, given its minority status, to challenge the racism of the mainstream. It was left to the Protestant churches to raise the cry for emancipation.

If it was not ingrained prejudice, then it was sheer timidity that made the American church ambivalent about free blacks. In 1853, when a young African American was about to be ordained in Rome, the archbishop of Baltimore asked the Vatican not to send him back to the United States, at the same time regretting "that these inveterate prejudices be found among us with nothing able to be done to overcome them." For the American hierarchy, the elevation of a black man to the priesthood was a red flag that they did not wish to wave. It was 1886 before a black priest was allowed to serve in the United States. Black sisters, on the other hand, were nothing like the same problem; they could be tolerated — only just — because they were women, because they were harmless. Their situation can be compared to that of the nuns of France during the same era. The threats were different — in one case racism, in the other anticlericalism — but the strategy was the same. They kept safe by staying out of the way.

"Sisters of All Mankind" (General Benjamin Butler)

In a time of deep tragedy for the nation, the nuns of America came face-to-face with the outside world. In the course of the Civil War, more than six hundred Catholic sisters — one-fifth of all the nuns then in the country — nursed thousands and thousands of soldiers, both Union and Confederate. With their skill and devotion they gained the respect of administrators, doctors, and patients. For their own part, they found themselves touched in spirit by the sometimes distrustful, sometimes appreciative men with whose care they were entrusted. For all concerned, it was an eye-opener.

The country entered the war dismally unprepared for what was about to happen. In the battles that followed, 110,000 Union soldiers would die, either at once or in the immediate aftermath; 250,000 more would die from disease; 130,000 more would survive with severe physical damage. The South would suffer a similar toll of death, disease, and injury. At the beginning, however, the North had only one military hospital and the South had none. While there were some competent doctors, there were no nursing corps and no system in place to transport the sick and wounded. The public mobilized at once to supply what needs it could. Women, in particular, rushed forward to prepare clothing and bandages, to make food parcels, and to volunteer as nurses. But everything was swamped by the magnitude of the catastrophe.

The main problem was the deficiency of prewar health care. This was an age before antiseptics, before anesthetics; an age, too, that saw a frightening succession of epidemics: plague, smallpox, measles in a virulent form, cholera, malaria, yellow fever, as well as typhoid, typhus, and the ever-present tuberculosis. American society, however, still clung to the principle that the sick should be cared for at home. Such hospitals as there were existed for the indigent or the contagious. Such nurses as there were, were poorly trained and held in low regard. People looked across the ocean and admired what Florence Nightingale and her corps of nursing sisters had done in the Crimean War, but they made no effort to imitate them. Women of good family had never nursed professionally, and it was difficult for them to start doing so now. All the good will in the world could not make up for lack of experience. Four years of war were not enough to create a nursing profession.

Before long doctors and administrators were turning to the sisters. Not that they were all experienced hospital nurses; far from it. Some Sisters of Mercy, freshly arrived from Ireland, did have a solid nursing background, as did some French Sisters of Charity. But for the American-born orders, nursing had always been peripheral to their central activity of school teaching. Indeed, Archbishop Carroll had assured Mother Seton in 1811 that education would be the sisters' principal employment for a long time to come; that "a century at least will pass before the exigencies and habits of this country will . . . admit of the charitable exercises towards the sick." Fate had decreed otherwise. The vicious epidemics that raged through the immigrant populations created a need for hospitals and, at the same time, left behind an extraordinary number of orphans in need of institutional care. Even before the war broke out, several of the existing orders had perforce taken up nursing. In the centuries-old European tradition, most of them resisted specialization; the sisters moved from hospital to school and back again, nursing, teaching, or caring for orphans as they were directed. Thus most of them came to the war with a general training that was still short of professional standards. What they did bring, however, was the competence that their communities had built into them, a familiarity with hardship, and, above all, a powerful sense of mission. This was the Lord's work (so they insisted, over and over again); they were serving neither North nor South, but only the poor afflicted children of God.

Sometimes they went straight into the army hospitals and fell to work scrubbing, washing, cooking, and nursing. Sometimes they opened up their own hospitals and schools, filling every available space with the sick and injured men. Sometimes they went out onto the battlefields to collect the wounded, bringing them back to field hospitals in jolting carts along rutted roads. Wherever they went, they demonstrated the adaptability that was one of their strengths. We can see this, for instance, in the four Holy Cross sisters from South Bend, Indiana, members of a strictly teaching order, who found themselves serving onboard a hospital transport boat, thus becoming the officially recognized forerunners of the U.S. Navy Nurse Corps. Good order, cleanliness, dedication to the patients: these were the building blocks of good nursing, and for the most part, the sisters provided them.

Their reception was not always positive. In places the religious issue still lingered. After all, many of the men had grown up thinking of Catholics as the spawn of the devil, and their prejudices were not easily overcome. On their side, the nuns occasionally pushed their zeal for souls beyond comfortable limits, seeking to proselytize as well as to heal. There were also, sometimes, significant power struggles between the sisters and the other nurses. But overall, the praise that flowed in, from government officials and generals down to the common soldiers whom the sisters tended, is evidence of an important battle won in the war for the hearts and minds of Americans. In 1866 the Catholic bishops acknowledged this, praising the "devotedness and spirit of self-sacrifice [that] have, more perhaps than any other cause, contributed to effect a favorable change in the minds of thousands estranged from our faith." And the work of the sisters had a second beneficial effect. Thinking women asked themselves, "If they can do it, why can't we?" The elevation of nursing to a respected profession would take some time, but it did happen, and the sister-nurses of the Civil War must be given some of the credit.

*   *   *

Through these years, and the years to come, the United States continued to grow, in size, in wealth, and in population. And the Catholic population grew with it. From 35,000 in 1820 to close to a million in 1840 to more than a million and a half in 1850, their numbers were bolstered by 1900 by over three million immigrants, not so much now from Ireland as from eastern and southern Europe. The foreignness of their language and culture presented a huge challenge both to them and to their host country.

Amidst the strangeness, one institution was familiar to them: the Catholic Church. Its liturgical language and rituals and teachings all spoke to them of home. Where there were heavy concentrations of newcomers, ethnic churches and schools were set up, staffed by priests, brothers, and sisters who spoke the newcomers' language and understood their difficulties. In many instances these priests, brothers, and sisters actually came from the same countries as the immigrants. From the beginning of the nineteenth century to the end, Catholic Europe supplied the United States with personnel, largely by way of the religious orders. In 1832 the Redemptorists from Germany, in 1836 the Sisters of Saint Joseph from France, in 1840 the Sisters of Notre-Dame de Namur from Belgium, in 1846 the Irish Sisters of Mercy, in 1847 the French Oblates of Mary Immaculate — the list could go on indefinitely. They brought with them their own traditions about how the faith should be lived and taught, and in the early years they encouraged their countrymen to keep a certain distance from the mainstream. But more or less swiftly, along with the laity they had come to lead, these orders became Americanized. Without forgetting the land of their forebears, they took on the characteristics of their adopted country. Together with Catholic citizens of long standing, they built communities that were prosperous and independent and distinctively American. In some cases they even came to overshadow their founding bodies back in Europe.

The Congregation of Holy Cross is one striking example. It was French in its origins, and founded specifically to deal with a French problem, the shortage of Catholic educators in the postrevolutionary years. It came into being incrementally. First, in 1820, a community of teaching brothers was established in Le Mans, to which, in 1835, was added a small group of "auxiliary priests," spiritual guides, if you will, and mentors for the brothers, but not, to begin with, teachers themselves. Within a few years, however, under the hand of the founder, Basil Moreau, this fairly humble project expanded into something more ambitious. The priests entered the field of higher education, and the community took the vows of poverty, chastity, and obedience, thus officially proclaiming its desire to become a religious congregation. In the same year (1840), a small group of sisters was incorporated, largely to take care of the housekeeping.

The new congregation grew, but did not exactly thrive, in its homeland. There were too many crosscurrents to negotiate, too many prejudices and professional jealousies to overcome. Its greatest growth would be elsewhere. In 1841, on the invitation of the bishop, a contingent of six brothers and one priest made their way to Indiana. A year later, in the dead of winter, they accepted an Indian mission some 250 miles north of Vincennes, near the settlement of South Bend. The center of the mission, a small log house standing beside a lake then frozen over, bore the name Notre-Dame du Lac. This was the beginning of the University of Notre Dame.

The priest was Edward Frederick Sorin, then aged twenty-six and ordained only three years earlier; he can fairly be named the founder of Holy Cross in America. His enormous dynamism, freed from the usual constraints by the vastness of his "domain" and the convenient distance from all authority, made for instant success. Within four years of its arrival at South Bend, the community was running nine mission stations and five schools, and the nucleus of a university. What was more, two groups of sisters had arrived from France, and they, together with several local entrants, had opened two schools, one for the children of settlers, the other for Indians. Impressive as this may be, it was only the beginning of a remarkable growth. By 1856 the province of Notre Dame boasted eighteen houses and 238 religious — priests, brothers, and sisters — and was educating three thousand youths and children. And it was moving toward virtual autonomy vis-à-vis the French congregation. The generalate in Le Mans found it more and more impossible to control its buoyant offspring, especially since that offspring was led by the brilliant, headstrong Edward Sorin. To add to its difficulties, the French component was shrinking, battered by anticlericalism and undermined by its own financial problems. The legislation of 1901 and 1904 temporarily wiped it out. The generalate then moved to Notre Dame, remaining there until, years later, it moved to Rome.

Unlike many other missionaries, Father Sorin did not yearn for the old country. From the moment he landed, he was entranced by America and thrilled by its possibilities. He argued forcibly that the church would have a great future here if only it could free itself from the shackles of Europe. By the time he died in 1893, his hopes were being fulfilled. A decade into the twentieth century, the church in the United States ceased to be a mission church and took its place as a major power in the Catholic world.

"Onward, Christian Soldiers": The Canadian Northwest, 1841-1900

As you approach Ottawa, the capital of Canada, you will be struck by the fact that, until the very last moments of your flight, the landscape below is an almost unbroken vista of trees, lakes, and rivers. The city itself seems little more than an island of habitation surrounded by miles of fields and forest. And if you fly down the Saint Lawrence from Montreal to Quebec, looking northward you will see, beyond the narrow stretch of cultivated land, a not-too-distant range of forested mountains looming down toward the river. That is what much of the country is like. Canada covers close to four million square miles of landmass stretching from ocean to ocean and northward to the pole, with a thin ribbon of population lining its southern border.

If the ratio of population to space is small today, how much smaller was it in the early nineteenth century! "Canada" was, as yet, for the most part a scattering of farms and small towns, with only a few cities worthy of the name. White settlement was confined to the east: the Maritimes, Upper Canada (what is today Ontario), and, of course, Lower Canada, or Quebec. In what is now Manitoba there lived several thousand Métis, people of French-Indian blood. Everything beyond that — the prairies, the Rockies, the Pacific coast, the North — belonged to the Amerindians and the Inuit. From Red River to Vancouver Island, virtually the only white men to be found anywhere were the employees of the fur-trading companies, the largest of which was the Hudson's Bay Company.

In this Canada of the early nineteenth century, Catholicism was perilously weak. The English-speaking colonists were as robustly antipapist here as were their neighbors in the United States — from which, incidentally, many of them had moved at the time of the Revolution. The great Irish immigration that would change the demographic balance lay still in the future. As for Quebec, though the British government maintained a policy of tolerance toward its French-speaking subjects, it did little to sustain their religion. Left to themselves, and deprived of much of their clergy, the *Canadiens* struggled on against heavy odds. After fifty years of compromise and neglect, their church was in poor shape. Its revival began in the 1840s, thanks in large part to the leadership of its bishops and the influx of religious orders, both male and female, from France.

Among these religious orders was the congregation of the Oblates of Mary Immaculate. It was a brand-new company, founded in 1816 by Eugène de Mazenod, for re-Christianizing an extremely unchristian postrevolutionary society in France. Distressed at what he saw — the decay of the churches, the shortage of priests, the religious ignorance of ordinary people — Mazenod resolved to establish a society of mission preachers along the lines of the congregation that Vincent de Paul had inaugurated almost two centuries before. His initial theater of operations was Provence, and it was only by chance that he turned his face outward toward Canada. In 1841 Bishop Bourget of Montreal, on one of those recruiting drives through Europe that many North American bishops were taking around this time, stopped off in Marseilles and, while there, learned of the young congregation and immediately asked for its help. It had not been doing particularly well, for when Bourget arrived, its total membership stood at a mere fifty-five. The idea of overseas mission, however, acted like a spark on tinder. In 1841, when Mazenod signed over four priests and two brothers to the bishop, a new frontier opened for the Oblates. Before the end of the century they would become the largest and most widespread order of men in Canada.

They established themselves first in parishes close to Montreal, then moved into the city itself. Once their base was secured and new forces had arrived, they branched out to Ottawa and the Ottawa Valley. Before long they were journeying farther and farther afield, preaching missions wherever there were enough people to listen to them. Then, as though their territory was not already vast enough, they decided to go even farther. In 1844 they undertook to send priests to Red River, the tiny colony that would one day become Saint Boniface, just across the river from today's Winnipeg. The following year, after a sixty-day journey in Hudson's Bay Company canoes, two of them, along with some Sisters of Charity from Montreal, arrived there to set up a beachhead for their missions. By 1846 they were ranging far and wide into the northwest, and before the end of the 1850s they had reached the Pacific slope. By this time almost every priest working in western Canada was an Oblate.

The Oblates' takeover of the Catholic missions in the west has been compared to a successful military campaign. Indeed, there were many similarities, both in their personal way of thinking and in their methods. They were soldiers for the faith as, three centuries before, the Jesuits had been soldiers. Their commander in chief was the pope, and their cause, ultramontane Catholicism. For them, victory would only come with the conquest of the country for Christ. There were no two ways about it: salvation lay within the Church, and the way to gain it was through obedience to the Church. Their message to the native peoples, therefore, was an uncompromising one: if you seek conversion, surrender to our direction and adopt our discipline. What is more, if you wish to be truly Christian, you must exchange your primitive ways for those of the white man. This would take time, and the application of social control. The word that many of the missionaries themselves used was "molding"; we might call it behavior modification. Christianization would be perfected by assimilation.

This missionary approach is now generally discredited. But to be fair, this has been a latter-day conversion. Not so long ago, governments, whether in Canada, the United States, Australia, or New Zealand, and churches of every stripe considered assimilation to be the optimum "solution" for the aboriginal people. Only time has shown us what was lost, in culture and in a people's spirit. But the fact is that the concept of assimilation worked well in the minds and consciences of the people of the nineteenth century. Was it not an act of charity to offer these men and women the values of the dominant civilization? The missionaries, whether Catholic or Protestant, were only putting into action what the rest of the white world believed.

The Oblates were not alone in northwest Canada. There were Anglican, evangelical, and Methodist missionaries already on the ground when the priests arrived. Theirs was a mission at cross-purposes with that of the Catholics: they were out to win the west for church and country — *their* church and *their* country. This, of course, did not please the Oblates, who had no good reason to love either Protestantism or Great Britain. And since there was nothing in the missionary lexicon of virtues that promoted compromise, both sides geared up for battle. The centuries-old confessional struggle that had torn Europe apart was reignited in Canada, in a race for influence and for physical control of the strategic points where Indians lived or congregated.

In this race each side had some advantages. The preachers of "the English religion," as the native people called it, had generous funding from the Church Missionary Society in London. The priests of "the French religion" had less money but greater endurance. They had no families, for one thing, which meant they were able to live on less — a fact that appealed not only to the Indians who understood the hard life, but also to the agents of the Hudson's Bay Company who were tasked with supplying the missions' needs. They expected to learn the native languages, which few of the English missionaries did. The religion they preached, with its rituals and physical symbolism, appealed more to the Indians than did the bare, austere religion of the Word. In the end, of course, what mattered was the authenticity of the missionaries' witness, and here, according to at least one contemporary, the Oblates had the edge. In 1854 Superintendent John Ryerson of the Canadian Methodist Conference complained that "the Roman Catholic missionaries throughout these extensive regions, in zeal, in labor, self-denial, and in success in their work, are very, very much before us, and unless we bestir ourselves . . . this whole country will be overspread and hedged in with the briars, thorns, and hedges of Popery." The "conquest" that the Oblates sought seemed almost within their grasp.

The northwest was a harsh environment, bitter cold in winter and lonely year-round. It was physically challenging. The successful missionary had not only to know the language and understand the ways of the people, he had to be able to swing an axe and travel long distances with dog team and canoe; he had to be prepared to live rough, with few companions or none at all. Some of the men seemed made for the work, because they were adventurers at heart or rugged individualists. Others were less successful. Some broke under the strain; a few actually went mad. Most were somewhere in between, being faithful to their calling for the greater or lesser time that they were directed to stay. Between 1845, when they first arrived in the northwest, and 1900, 237 Oblates, almost all either French- or Canadian-born, worked in the mission, many of them for their entire adult lives. We must acknowledge their dedication and try to enter their way of thinking if we wish to do justice to the great missionary élan that was such a feature of the nineteenth century.

"To the Ends of the Earth"

From the Americas to Africa to the Orient, from the age of revolutions to the age of steam and high explosives, the story of the European missionary endeavor is a story of growth but also of deformation, of high idealism but also of misconception and sorry compromise.

To start with: growth. In 1786, so the story goes, a young English Baptist, William Carey, proposed to his local group that it form a foreign missionary society; to which the chairman of the group replied, "Sit down, young man, when it pleases God to convert the Heathen, He'll do it without your help or mine." Some forty years later the same advice was offered, though perhaps with a little more sensitivity, by Pope Pius VII to an ardent young Catholic priest who sought to revive the China mission: "Without a doubt your project is good, but it is more important to help the people that surround us, especially our brothers in the faith." Europe did not yet feel an overwhelming urge to export its religion to foreign lands. However, within a few years everything changed.

The missionary impulse ballooned in the mid–nineteenth century, partly because men and women both Protestant and Catholic began taking the dictates of their religion more seriously, but partly also because of the changing environment. Europeans, believers and unbelievers alike, were caught up by a newfound fascination with the wider world. The Middle East, the Orient, Africa, Oceania, the Americas: everywhere people looked, adventure beckoned. With every passing year scores of scientific reports and travelogues appeared, to challenge minds and titillate imaginations with descriptions of exotic places. And the difficulties involved in getting to those places were shrinking perceptibly, as faster travel and improved communications brought the faraway closer to home. By the middle years of the century, Europeans had decided that the world was there for the taking, whether that taking was for settlement, or trade, or conversion, or empire. It is not surprising that for many fervent Christians of every religious persuasion, this general mood of expansionism put wings under the command that their Lord had given them, to preach the gospel to all nations.

But the front-runners in this movement were often spectacularly ill-prepared for the work in hand. They knew little of the world they planned to conquer; they blundered into the unknown with nothing but the certainty of their faith to guide them.

Take the Marists as an example. Theirs was a brand-new religious order created in 1836 and immediately assigned a vicariate covering a vast stretch of the western Pacific. In early 1845 seven priests and six brothers set out for Melanesia, knowing little more about their destination than what they learned from whalers and explorers. Their ignorance of the environment into which they were inserting themselves did not trouble them; they trusted that the Word of God would by itself be sufficient to overcome all heathen resistance. In any case, their first concern seems to have been to enhance their own personal holiness. They saw their missionary vocation as a sure path to sanctity — a sanctity that, God willing, might be sealed by martyrdom. The culture shock that they suffered when they actually met with the Melanesians was devastating. The gulf between their way of life and that of the bushmen, made deeper by their inability to speak the language, led them from crisis to crisis. To make things worse, the deadly diseases that so often accompanied Europeans struck the natives hard; their obvious conclusion was that the alien god, Jehovah, must be driven away together with his messengers. After ten fruitless years and the deaths of eight of their brothers, the Marists withdrew from Melanesia. They would return in 1898 to a scene much changed by European colonial activity. And by this time they, too, had changed. Like many other missionary orders, the Marists had learned on the job, so successfully in fact that they were now running missions in the Americas and China.

Other missionaries also learned on the job. In North Africa the White Fathers, members of a congregation specifically created for work in that region, undertook early on to adapt their living arrangements to those of the native people. Only by shedding their European character, insisted their founder, Bishop (later Cardinal) Lavigerie, would they be able to make the Christian message palatable to the Africans. Their dress (the white robes from which they took their name), their eating habits, their approach to daily life must become African. He himself tried various experimental approaches to evangelization, and was ready to discard those that did not work. North Africa was, perhaps, one of the most unreceptive environments in the world for missionary work, given the already strong religious traditions of these Muslim regions. But the White Fathers survived and prospered.

*   *   *

Passing mention has been made of the Sisters of Notre-Dame de Namur who left Belgium to follow Father De Smet into the Great Plains; of the Sisters of Charity of Montreal who traveled west with the Oblates. This is rather typical of the way mission history, until recently, has been written: the missionary sisters have usually been treated as the "also-rans," the dependable but unremarkable chorus that fills in behind the main actors on the stage. One fact has never been denied, though: in sheer numbers they outperformed the men. Forty-four thousand Catholic nuns went out to the missions during the course of the nineteenth century. Wherever in the world there were priests and brothers, the sisters, too, could be found. As for the value of the work they did, we can quote the tribute of Lavigerie, founder not only of the White Fathers but also of the White Sisters of Africa. The sisters' apostolate, he wrote, was even more vital than that of his priests, because only they could form bonds with the women, and thereby plant religion in the hearts of families where it could grow and mature.

Wherever they went, much of the maintenance of what we might call the infrastructure of Christianity was the responsibility of the sisters. With a few exceptions, theirs were the traditional roles: the schooling, the nursing, the home visiting, the care of orphans and abandoned children. Whereas the priests, tasked as often as not with the care of numerous mission stations, tended to be always on the move, the sisters usually remained in one place, within one set of buildings, thus providing a continuous presence in the nascent Christian communities. On the whole it was a muted presence: they did not take part in the unseemly wars of words that sometimes broke out between missionaries, nor did they get down and dirty in the political arena. This was to their advantage. Speaking of the impression they made on the local populations, Lavigerie waxed lyrical. "They think them superior to human nature. They compare them to the angels of God." One might surmise that their good reputation would keep them safe. This was not always so, as the nuns found out in China during the Boxer Rebellion.

China had always been a dangerous place for missionaries, but never more so than at the end of the nineteenth century. Xenophobia, fed by a series of humiliating treaties forced upon it by alien powers, was building in the empire. Westerners living in the country, whether in groups or by themselves, were obvious targets for native anger. Traders, diplomats, missionaries — they were all hateful, they all deserved death. This was the general mood when, in 1900, the rebellion broke out.

In the Peitang, a Christian compound within the Imperial City of Peking, a community of sisters ran an orphanage for some 500 Chinese children. When it was learned that the Boxers were advancing on the city, the sisters with their children, along with several thousand local converts, crowded into the cathedral, a fortress-like building at the center of the compound. Here, through a steaming Peking summer, 43 French and Italian marines and a small contingent of able-bodied converts held out against wave after wave of attackers. Inside the cathedral, bullets and mines played havoc among the besieged, and starvation became a looming threat (and it should be noted that, unlike the people in the foreign legations, the Europeans here resolved to share what food there was equally with the Chinese). It was a terrifying time. Bishop Favier, who remained in the cathedral throughout the siege, would never forget the sound of 300 crying children. "I felt as though I were listening to the bleating of a flock of little lambs destined for sacrifice," he later wrote. Finally on August 16 an international force, sent to relieve the siege of the legations in another part of the city, arrived also at the Peitang; the Boxers disappeared. By then over 400 people in the cathedral had died, including 166 children and babies. Favier looked out across the ruined compound and the scores of shallow graves, and wrote: "the work of forty years is nearly annihilated; the courage of the missionaries, nevertheless, is not on the wane; we shall begin over again."

The sisters had expected to die, and they certainly would have if the Peitang had been overrun. After all, no matter how gentle and caring they were, they were the feminine wing of the "foreign devils" so deeply loathed by many Chinese. Thirty years earlier a mob had broken into an orphanage run by the Sisters of Charity in Tientsin and had raped, mutilated, and murdered the sixteen nuns they found there. And even now, in the year 1900, missionaries were everywhere being hunted down, two hundred in all of every denomination and both sexes. And yet they were ready to begin again.

Missionary work was not for the faint of heart. But women continued to flock to it. The age that we call "Victorian" may have been steeped in notions of feminine frailty, but here and there women stepped over the customary boundaries into a world of risk. And among these women were the missionary nuns.

It had been a long, slow evolution in the Church's way of thinking. Consecrated virgins, those fragile creatures for whose preservation so many cloisters had been built, had now broken out of their protective shells and proven themselves ready to shoulder all the hardships and dangers of the apostolate. From then until now, many of them have died at their posts, and some of them have suffered indignity and murder. But they have not retreated.

*   *   *

The nineteenth-century foreign missions were grassroots ventures. For every man or woman who went overseas, hundreds, perhaps thousands, of people back home gave support. A large segment of European society was now politically aware. The campaign for the abolition of the slave trade had demonstrated the power of mass action. The masses were still there, and so were the means to mobilize them: newspapers, periodicals, public lectures, demonstrations — and to raise funds. In 1821, when news reached Lyons of a cholera epidemic raging in Tonkin, a young woman named Pauline Jaricot hit upon the idea of enlisting a large circle of donors to give a coin once a week to a relief fund. Within months the pledges numbered over a thousand. It was the beginning of an extraordinary success story. By midcentury the organization that was her brainchild, the Association for the Propagation of the Faith, was collecting over 3.5 million francs per year from some 400 dioceses in Europe and America, enough to finance numerous missionary ventures. Another fund of similar inspiration, the Holy Childhood, which was set up specifically for the care of orphans in the missions (even appealing to children to contribute their pennies for the sake of other children), enjoyed similar success, pulling in 1.5 million francs annually by the 1860s. A similar movement had begun even earlier in the Protestant communions. In England, the evangelical Church Missionary Society was by midcentury drawing 80 percent of its income from small donations. Other societies were springing up with the same objective. All told, by the early years of the twentieth century, over 250 charities had been set up to support the Christian missions, with contributions from the faithful mounting into the hundreds of millions. The various missionary organizations kept the fire alive by turning out periodicals — "news from the missions" — in such numbers that they became, in late Victorian times, the most widely circulated literature of their kind. Across all the national and religious divides that scarred the Continent, people were on fire for this great, godly adventure.

No wonder, then, that thousands of young men and women felt inspired to join the foreign missions. Their idealism should never be doubted: they volunteered, and continued to volunteer, for postings that offered, at best, a life of hardship, and at worst, an early death through disease or violence. The West African missions are a case in point: many groups were wiped out almost as soon as they landed, by microbes against which Europeans and Americans had no natural immunity. And still they came. As for the deaths that conferred the crown of martyrdom (of which there were many), every such occasion reported back home inspired a new surge of vocations. Even in this world with all its modernity, the words that Tertullian had spoken seventeen centuries before still rang true: "we increase in numbers whenever we are mown down . . . the blood of Christians is seed."

But all is not sweetness and light in the history of the missions. The European missionaries are often accused of having been the running dogs for their respective countries, as ready to promote their nations' colonial agendas as they were to spread the faith. Obviously the local powers thought so at the time; it was one of the reasons they gave for banishing or persecuting them. It had not started that way: in the early days the foreign missions had functioned more or less at arm's length from their mother countries, a not surprising fact, considering the home governments' ambivalence about, even hostility to, religious activism. As the century went on, however, the cross tended, more and more ostentatiously, to be wrapped in the flag. As the competition for colonies heated up among European nations, governments and missions entered into a marriage of convenience. The governments protected the missionaries, the missionaries inculcated patriotism along with Christianity. For the governments the advantage was the same as it had ever been: missionaries offered essential services that few other people were willing to undertake, and they offered them at low cost. As for the missionaries, they gained security and authority from the deal. If a hostile movement by the natives could be nipped in the bud by the appearance of a gunboat offshore, or if the difficulties created by local officials could be smoothed over at once by the sight of a foreign passport — well, why not? The Lord's workers could use that kind of help.

No matter how practical the deal was, however, it put the apostolate at a serious disadvantage. Rome recognized this: How could the Church be truly universal if it was carved up into national segments? It was unseemly enough that Catholics and Protestants were at loggerheads; how did it look when missionaries of the same faith divided along national lines? "The Christian religion . . . unites all men in the bonds of brotherhood with no distinction of country or race," wrote Pope Leo XIII to the Chinese emperor in 1885. But even as he wrote, King Leopold II of Belgium was seeking to remove the French White Fathers from his territories, because they were "not generally well disposed towards Belgian influence in the Congo." And his suspicion was justified. "The only standard apostles serve under is the Cross," wrote Lavigerie; "the only flag a Frenchman can place alongside the Cross is the flag of his fatherland." The two men were reading from the same playbook: missionaries were expected to further the interests of their homelands. During the years of scramble for empire, "Christian brotherhood" was subject to serious qualifications.

Damaging as this misplaced patriotism was to the Christian mission, another characteristic of Europeans abroad was more damaging still. This was the inbred sense of superiority that white men carried with them wherever they went, and which missionaries, unfortunately, shared. Few among them were able to see the native peoples as their equals. Later in the century the spread of social Darwinism only strengthened the general prejudice. "Lesser breeds without the law," the British imperialist Rudyard Kipling would later call the non-Western peoples: lesser in innate ability and intelligence, lesser in the culture and laws that guided their lives. Too many well-meaning missionaries acted on these assumptions; indeed, they made use of them. Much too often their periodicals described the local populations as primitive, ignorant, debased, all for promoting the importance of their own work. Not only must they Christianize their catechumens, they were saying; they must also civilize them — which meant, in effect, Europeanizing them. The understanding was that the locals were rarely to be trusted to manage their own lives.

The first rethinking of these assumptions came in Germany in the 1860s, and the first rethinkers were Protestant theologians. But it would be many years before missionaries at the grass roots, spread out as they were across the world and deeply invested in the works they had created, surrendered their biases. For Catholics, it would take the firm leadership of twentieth-century popes to reorient the missions and to hand ownership of the apostolate over to the indigenous peoples to whom it rightly belonged.

The story of the nineteenth-century missions is distressing and inspiring at the same time. On the distressing side, it cannot be denied that their presence in the field helped to legitimize the European scramble for empire. And beyond that, the missionaries did damage on their own account. No matter how noble their motivation, they disrupted long-established patterns of life and behavior. Indeed, some historians maintain that of all the predators who preyed on and exploited the native populations, the missionaries were the most invidious, because they wormed their way into the very soul of other people's cultures. But surely this is going too far. It has been pointed out that, with or without the missionaries, the juggernaut was coming; that no matter how primitive, how remote the society, the expanding "first world" was making ready to break down its door. Modernization was going to happen. By introducing practical advancements, by encouraging literacy, and by educating a corps of elites, the missionaries were preparing the indigenous people to handle that modernization.

While this was a significant achievement, it was not what the missionaries came to do. Their first objective was to spread the gospel. How well did they succeed?

Certainly there are many more Christians in the world, and in different parts of the world, than there would have been if all those missionaries had stayed home. In sub-Saharan Africa, the religion that was born on the banks of the Jordan and nurtured through the centuries in more northern climes now took root, and prospered dramatically. Elsewhere, while the increase may not have been so spectacular, vibrant Christian communities stood, and still stand, by their faith through good times and bad. What is not so commonly seen anymore is the white man in the Roman collar, or the white woman in her traditional European habit. The missionaries have largely ceded their place to indigenous Christians. The local churches have come into their own — so successfully, in fact, that they now send members of their clergy back to serve in the priest-starved churches of Europe and America.

*   *   *

This had been a century like no other. From Waterloo to Sarajevo — from the close of one great war to the opening shot of another — the Western world lived through ninety-nine years of rapid material progress and social turmoil. What did this mean for Catholicism?

"It was the best of times, it was the worst of times." For the upper echelons of the church, there were, from the very start of the century, impoverishment and derogation. The bishops had once walked the halls of power, but no longer: though not the servants of the state, they were very clearly its subjects. A centuries-long power struggle had definitively turned against them. As for the papacy, the crushing loss of its temporal possessions and its forced confinement to a small enclave within the city of Rome seemed to threaten it with extinction. Though it exercised moral power over its followers, in terms of realpolitik it counted for very little. And out in the world, godlessness appeared to be on the march. The urbanizing masses, having lost touch with the old religion, saw no reason to bother with the new.

Yet in spite of — and perhaps because of — the general religious decadence, the industrial age saw the growth of a dynamic form of Catholicism, fiercely militant and highly exclusionary. Central to this growth were the religious orders, both the newly born and the born-again. For them, it was without a doubt "the best of times," as the weight of their influence in the church and the huge increase in their numbers clearly show. In the army of Christ, they were the shock troops, the elite forces. At the century's end there seemed no limit to where they could go, and what they could achieve. They had every reason to believe that the future belonged to them and to their cause.

And this was true — for the time being. But not for very long.

Suggested Reading for Chapter 6

As before, *The Christian Centuries* is a good place to start. Since the history of the religious orders in the nineteenth century is closely connected to that of the papacy, the works by E. E. Y. Hales, *Pio Nono* (1954) and *Revolution and Papacy* (1966), and also Owen Chadwick's *The Popes and European Revolution* (1981), provide useful background. For a look at the larger scene, see Ralph Gibson's *A Social History of Catholicism, 1789-1914* (1989).

Europe was, of course, the cockpit in which the great ideological battles were fought. Chapter 7 of Jonathon Wright's work, *God's Soldiers* (2004), places the Church's elite force, the Jesuits, right in the center of the battle, where they certainly belonged. G. Cubitt's *The Jesuit Myth* (1993) deals with the huge impact, both positive and negative, that they had on the mind of their times. But lest we conclude that the times were totally given over to doing battle, we should also look at the other side of Catholicism. *Don Bosco, Life and Works,* by Pietro Stella (1985), is one of many books worth reading on the great man.

Another great man, for American readers in particular, is the Jesuit Pierre-Jean De Smet. *"Come, Blackrobe,"* by J. Killoren (1994), gives an excellent picture of the man, and the American frontier in which he spent his adult years. For a broader view of his society, there is R. Schroth, *The American Jesuits: A History* (2007).

One of the most dramatic chapters in the history of nineteenth-century American nuns concerns their service during the Civil War. For this, read Sister Mary Denis Maher, *To Bind Up the Wounds: Catholic Sister Nurses in the U.S. Civil War* (1989). For the sisterhoods' beginnings in the United States, there is *"Highly Respectable and Accomplished Ladies,"* by Barbara Misner (1988). For the various feminine congregations of America, a number of excellent works are worth reading, but I would like to signal one: *Persons of Color and Religious at the Same Time,* by Diane Batts Morrow (2002).

As a Canadian, I regret that I have given so little attention to the history of the religious orders in my country. The book I mention here is only one of many; it is, however, a great book, and it gives insights not only into the Canadian missions, but also into the general missionary ethos of the nineteenth century. It is *The Oblate Assault on Canada's Northwest,* by Robert Choquette (1995).

For the missions, there is — as always — *The Christian Centuries.* See also J. P. Daughton, *An Empire Divided* (2006).

Epilogue

In 1950 Pope Pius XII summoned the heads of the major congregations to Rome for an exercise in self-examination. He ordered them to consider how they could renew the spirit of their institutions, and at the same time bring themselves into harmony with the changing times.

Outside observers might have wondered why he needed to make the effort. To all appearances, the religious orders were doing well. Throughout the past fifty years, in spite of two world wars, a depression, and the ravages of communism and Nazism, they had held their own. Between 1900 and 1950 the number of regulars (men in religious orders) had more than doubled to 300,000; the number of nuns had passed a million. They were now more international in composition, too; they were, increasingly, North American and Australian as well as European, while a small but growing percentage of them were African and Asian. Their reach extended to the farthest corners of the world. Everywhere they went, they put down their markers: universities, colleges, academies, hospitals, orphanages, hospices, huge basilicas and modest churches. Their major houses were monuments to past success: mammoth piles of stone, built to accommodate communities that sometimes ran into the many hundreds. Their convents — lesser in size, and resembling branch plants in their purpose — were everywhere, sandwiched between the parish churches that they helped to keep up and the parish schools that they staffed and ran. Large and international or small and local, the congregations of religious men and women were still the strong right arm of the Catholic Church.

But something was amiss. The great expansion of the last hundred years had come to an end, and the first signs of shrinkage had appeared. Within the congregations there was more and more questioning of the traditional way of doing things, more and more criticism of rules and regulations that seemed to modern minds to be irrelevant. Outsiders looking in may have regarded the religious life with a sort of sentimental respect, but they privately thought it anachronistic. Most Catholics loved the sight of the sisters in veil and flowing habit, but fewer and fewer of them encouraged their daughters to wear that veil and flowing habit.

Some fifteen years later the malaise had become a crisis. The Second Vatican Council delivered to the religious orders a tough challenge: not only must they work to rekindle their original fervor, they must adapt themselves to the ethos of the modern world. Even more difficult, they must strip themselves of all sense of exclusivity; they must accept that the religious life is not a state set apart and above, but simply one of several ways to love and serve God, as are also the many different lay states. It was a kind of psychological diminishment that many were unable to accept. For after all, if all the sacrifice and self-deprivation of life in community did not amount to something "better" than run-of-the-mill Christianity, why undertake it? There were plenty of worthy careers to be had in the world. Morale dropped. The religious orders began to thin out. Members departed in large numbers, and few people came to replace them. For those who stayed, it was the beginning of a difficult time.

We give one example. In December 2008, 159 elderly Sisters of Charity prepared to leave their motherhouse in Montreal. This motherhouse had once held more than a thousand women at a time, but now, being far too large for the needs of the congregation, it had been sold to one of the city's universities. The sisters were allowed to take their foundress's body with them, but had to leave those of their other predecessors behind for health reasons. The work that those earlier generations did among the typhus and smallpox victims of the nineteenth century turned their bodies into a threat that has lasted to this day.

One can only hope that the memory of their service has lasted just as long.

The same story can be told over and over again, always with a touch of nostalgia and regret. But the fact is that much of the work that the religious of the past — those sisters of Montreal and thousands of other men and women — once did, is now being done just as competently by people who do not take the vows of poverty, chastity, and obedience. The world has changed. Families are smaller; the choices that the children of these families enjoy are much more varied. They can join the professions without also joining communities. Whether they live alone, or with partners, or with children, they can still pursue their careers. Those few of them who are so inspired can walk away from the comfortable life and become the first world's missionaries, caring for disadvantaged people at home or abroad. And increasingly, if they have the calling, they can deepen their commitment to their religion in the many secular institutes that have been appearing since mid–twentieth century. Where in past history can we find a greater dedication to Christian principles than in Jean Vanier and his communities of L'Arche, where handicapped and nonhandicapped care for each other and young volunteers are always welcome? The Catholic laity, that sturdy multitude of souls who for so many years were content only to "pray, pay, and obey," have now become fully active participants in the work of the gospel.

But if we have reached this point of maturity, it is partly because of the orders. From the early days of our Western civilization they were its pioneers and its mentors. Go back to the beginnings and there they were, the monks: mystics who first pulled heaven down close to earth for the people of a darkened continent; who stamped that continent with their own enduring spirituality. Later, when Europe grew out of its swaddling clothes, they became its evangelizers, its thinkers, its writers, its learned professors, its ambassadors, its explorers, its writers, its schoolteachers, its hospitallers, its welfare workers. When Christendom went to war, either with the outsider or against itself, they were in the front lines of the battle. Everything they did — even fighting — they claimed to do better than anyone else. Most importantly of all, they conserved the fundamental documents of the Christian faith.

During the turbulent centuries that we know as the Dark Ages, when the wandering tribes from the east were making Europe their own, the only secure repositories of the faith were its monasteries. There the ancient words of life, or what survived of them, were kept safe from further physical destruction. The people of the monasteries were the guardians of a precious deposit. They intoned it, they transcribed it, they adorned it. But most importantly, they guarded it.

The day came, after several centuries had passed, when they were able to preach it. The world was growing more civilized, more thoughtful; it was ready for an active sharing in the work of the Lord. Everywhere that preachers appeared — hermits, canons, and later, friars — their preaching fell upon fertile ground. Crowds in their hundreds, even thousands, responded to the challenge. Ordinary folk gave away their possessions, adopted austere and self-denying lives, went to war, learned how to pray, all because of the preachers.

Then came the Reformation, and civilization's huge leap forward. It should not be forgotten that many of its early leaders had begun their journey in faith as friars or monks. That was where they received their formation. More significant, however, was the response of the men and women in the street, people hungry for a Word that the preachers had promised but not delivered. One of the most momentous developments of the sixteenth century was the religious maturing of the laity, a maturing in which the orders had over the past centuries played a significant part. For neither the first nor the last time in history, the teachers found themselves outpaced by their students.

Protestantism rejected monasticism; Catholicism embraced and rejuvenated it. At a time when Rome was still stumbling and uncertain, new societies were already coming into being, dedicated to reforming the world from the ground up. Then, with the Council of Trent, a new militant Catholicism was born, and a war plan was put in place. Trent initially set little store by the religious orders, but it became clear before long that they would be its most effective protagonists.

It was a new age, and it demanded a new spirit, a spirit of mission. From then on, though the contemplative tradition remained strong within Catholicism, the momentum was with the active orders. This led to other developments. The religious life became more socially inclusive, more broadly based. Where once the monasteries had been the preserve of the aristocracy, and the mendicants' priories the power bases of the urban elites, the new orders reached further and further down into society, enabling many lesser men to rise to positions of influence. At the same time, another source of talent opened up. Steadily, after living for centuries in the shadows, and despite the best efforts of the fathers of Trent to keep them there, women began their movement into the work of the apostolate. And they did so largely within the framework of the religious life.

In the seventeenth and eighteenth centuries this army of men and women became indispensable to Catholic society. Seminaries, colleges, schools of every kind, hospitals, workhouses, asylums, orphanages: virtually everything that made up the social infrastructure of Catholic Europe fell under its control. Few others desired, or were able, to compete with it. Governments in the later eighteenth century scattered the army but were unable to replace it; with the end of the Napoleonic Wars it started to regroup.

Only in the later nineteenth century would a more secular-minded society manage to break the mold and create serious alternatives in the fields of education and social service. But even then, spreading out to other continents, the religious orders continued to exercise their traditional roles. In fact, in the late 1800s and early 1900s, despite the grinding hostility of many European governments and the general growth of secularism, they stood at the pinnacle of success. There were few parts of the world where their footprint was not visible.

And then, quite rapidly in historical terms, they dropped out of sight. Or at least, out of our sight. The presence of the orders in first-world Catholicism has diminished so as to be almost invisible. But the real news is that they are flourishing in other parts of the world, above all in Africa and in Asia. The best-known religious order of the twentieth century was founded in Calcutta, and its members wear the sari. They continue to attract members to their side.

"Monks, like oak trees, are eternal." So said a great French Dominican in the nineteenth century. Whether or not he is right remains to be seen. Like oak trees, religious orders draw their sustenance from the soil in which they are planted, and that soil seems in many parts of the world to have become dry and infertile. But whatever may be their future, their past remains beyond dispute. The influence they had on the making of Christianity is immeasurable, as too is the part they played in the making of European civilization, and in the projecting of that civilization to other parts of the world.

Like it or not, they are a part of our cultural and spiritual ancestry. Their DNA is planted within us. We may ignore it, but we cannot get rid of it.

Glossary

ancien régime A term created in the aftermath of the French Revolution to describe the governmental and social systems that had existed before 1789.

cahiers de doléances According to old French law, when the king called the Estates General together for consultation, the people also had the right to express their grievances *(doléances)*. In 1788, when Louis XVI convoked the Estates General, an extensive consultation took place across the country and the collected remarks and complaints were printed in booklets *(cahiers)* and forwarded to Paris.

canon law The law as it pertains to church matters. It made its debut during the eleventh century. A relatively new discipline, heavily influenced by Roman law, it was going to become increasingly influential within the Church as generations of canon lawyers tidied up and retouched what had hitherto been a disorderly collection of canons and decretals. The Gregorian reform was, to a great degree, a reorganization of church law. And its thrust was always toward the greater centralization of power in the office of the pope.

catechism A question-and-answer system designed to teach the basics of a faith. Simple in its initial design, it became more sophisticated in its technique as uniform texts became available and teaching methods improved.

cenobitism From the Greek word *koinobion* — "common life." Cenobites were monks or nuns who lived in community.

chapter The guiding council of a religious community, composed of senior members and led by the superior. *See also* General chapter

church triumphant In ancient Catholic tradition, the faithful are divided into three bodies: the church militant (those still alive), the church suffering (those in purgatory), and the church triumphant (those in heaven). Clearly, the saints and martyrs belong to the last group.

clausura The obligation, imposed at the time that solemn vows were taken, to live the rest of one's life inside the cloister. Originally intended for both monks and nuns, it came in time to be applied to nuns only.

commenda The practice of appointing outsiders to high positions in the church (bishoprics or abbeys) as patronage rewards.

commendatory abbot A person enjoying a position in the church as a reward for patronage, and the revenues that flowed from it.

concordat An agreement between the papacy and an individual ruler, defining and regulating their respective powers.

confraternity An ancient form of lay sociability, confraternities were "clubs" of like-minded people, formed for religious and charitable purposes, as well as for mutual assistance. Confraternities decorated and maintained side chapels in churches, usually dedicated to their patron saint whose feast day they celebrated in grand style. They assisted the poor. They also took care of distressed and dying members and supported their bereaved families. Occasionally they served other purposes, for example, the confraternities of flagellants in the fourteenth century.

eremitism From the Greek word *eremos,* "solitary." An eremite (hermit) withdrew from society to live an ascetic life of prayer.

excommunication A solemn act banning a person from the church community, and therefore sentencing him to live and die without the sacraments.

Gallicanism A position held by French thinkers in the *ancien régime* that gave the church in France quasi independence from Rome.

general chapter When true religious orders developed, this served as guiding council for the collective, by bringing representatives from each community together to advise on the running of the order. *See also* Chapter

Huguenot A nickname given to the Calvinists in France; derived from the Swiss word *eidgenoss,* or "comrade."

indulgence The forgiveness of some of the "debt" that the sinner owed to God for the wrongs he had committed.

Jacobin The extreme, and for a time the dominant, party in the French Revolution. So called because the party met in an old "Jacobin" (Dominican) monastery in Paris.

Jansenism A rigorous form of Catholicism, stressing man's depravity and advocating a severe morality. Condemned by Rome as heretical in 1713.

mendicant From the Latin *mendicus,* "beggar." A member of one of the orders that lived by begging.

Opus Dei Divine office (matins, lauds, terce, sext, nones, vespers, compline). The sevenfold set of prayers and canticles that monastic communities were required to intone together every day. Divine office was regarded as the heart of monastic life.

papal bull A solemn edict, so called because bearing the papal seal, or *bulla.* Among others, the following papal bulls are referred to in the text:

> ***Periculoso*** (1298) — ordering all religious women to observe *clausura* or disband.

> ***Unigenitus*** (1713) — condemning Jansenism.

parlement A sovereign court, with the right to consult with the Crown and to register its laws. *Parlements* were active in the provinces, but the *parlement* that exercised the greatest political influence was that of Paris. In the early modern period it was frequently at odds with the Crown.

Pilgrimage of Grace A major uprising in 1536 in the north of England, in defense of the monasteries that were about to be closed. In the end the movement was dispersed, the leaders executed, and the monasteries suppressed.

pluralism The possession of more than one benefice at a time, a practice condemned by the Church but prevalent in the early modern period.

prebends Stipends created out of an institution's revenues and granted on a lifetime basis to members of that institution.

purgatory Neither heaven nor hell, but a place of atonement for those who die without having made full amends for their sins.

regular Sometimes a noun, sometimes an adjective, "regular" in either instance denotes a person living under a religious rule. Thus "canons regular" had the same function as secular canons (originally, though not exclusively, in service of the bishop), but also took the vows of poverty, chastity, and obedience and promised to live under a rule; "clerks regular" were simply priests who did the same. Occasionally the term "regular" simply means "person in a religious order."

regular clergy Men living under a rule: monks, canons, friars, clerks.

rule The foundational document of a religious order. To those men and women who pledged themselves to an order by taking the vows of poverty, chastity, and obedience, the rule became guide and ultimate authority, which they had henceforth to obey or be in serious sin.

tertiary Member of a Third Order. Every mendicant order was in fact three orders in one: the First Order was that of friars, the Second Order was that of nuns, and the Third Order was that of laymen and laywomen, who lived under a modified rule and enjoyed certain privileges but retained their secular status.

tonsure The shaving of the dome of the skull, leaving only a fringe of hair. The first mark of a man's commitment to become a priest.

ultramontanism Literally, something "beyond the mountains," that is, on the other side of the Alps: Rome as the central authority in the Church.

vita apostolica The last charge that Jesus gave his apostles was to "go out to the whole world; proclaim the good news to all creation." After centuries during which *contemptus mundi* (contempt for, and withdrawal from, the world) had been held to be the only road to perfection, religious activists — hermits and friars — began to argue that the outgoing "apostolic" life, with its engagement in the world, was equally, or more, worthy in the eyes of God. They met with considerable resistance.

Index